Also edited by Mary Helen Washington:

Invented Lives: Narratives of Black Women
1860–1960

Black-Eyed Susans/Midnight Birds: Stories By and
About Black Women

Memory

of

Kin

○   ○   ○

*Edited, with an Introduction
and Commentary, by*

Mary Helen Washington

D O U B L E D A Y

New York   London   Toronto   Sydney   Auckland

Memory

of

Kin

· · ·

Stories About Family
by Black Writers

PUBLISHED BY DOUBLEDAY

a division of Bantam Doubleday Dell Publishing Group, Inc.
666 Fifth Avenue, New York, New York 10103

D O U B L E D A Y and the portrayal of an anchor with a dolphin
are trademarks of Doubleday,
a division of Bantam Doubleday Dell Publishing Group, Inc.
Memory of Kin is published simultaneously in paperback
by Anchor Books,
a division of Bantam Doubleday Dell Publishing Group, Inc.

DESIGNED BY CHRIS WELCH

Library of Congress Cataloging-in-Publication Data
Memory of kin : stories about family by black writers / edited,
with an introduction and commentary, by Mary Helen
Washington.—1st ed.
p. cm.
1. Family—Literary collections. 2. Afro-Americans—Families—
Literary collections. 3. American literature—Afro-American
authors. I. Washington, Mary Helen.
PS509.F27M46 1991
810.8'035204—dc20 90-42487
CIP

ISBN 0-385-24782-6
ISBN 0-385-24783-4 (pbk.)

January 1991

1 3 5 7 9 10 8 6 4 2

FIRST EDITION

FOR MY SISTERS AND BROTHERS

Beverly Washington Wilson
Myrna Washington
David Washington
Byron Washington
Tommy Washington
Betty Ann Washington
Bernadette Washington

ACKNOWLEDGMENTS

This book began in a discussion group at St. Francis de Sales Church in Roxbury, Massachusetts, in the fall of 1987. For four weeks we read, analyzed, discussed and argued over the meanings of the stories that black writers told about family and what those stories helped to reveal to us about our own families and our place within them. We began with four stories—Richard Wright's "Big Boy Leaves Home," Paule Marshall's *Brown Girl, Brownstones*, James Baldwin's "Sonny's Blues," and Ernest J. Gaines' "The Sky Is Gray." By the end of the fourth week, I think we all felt that the understanding we gained about families helped us to feel better about our own kin—or at least better able to put up with them. That group made me realize that black literature continues to be available to students in high schools and colleges, but not to a general black reading public, one that is hungry for these stories and has much to add to the critical discourse about them. Those of us who are committed to reconstructing literary canons, to revising notions of how literature should be defined, ought to be equally concerned about what readers as well as what texts are excluded by our scholarly practices. My hope is that *Memory of Kin* will reach an audience like my church community at St. Francis de Sales, whose lives and experiences are reflected in these stories. My deepest thanks to all of the people who read diligently, prepared for class faithfully and offered a wealth of insight about the stories that have become *Memory of Kin*: Genevieve Diggs, Shirley Daway, Barbara and Stacie Tyler, Sr. Carolyn Caveny, Harriet Hayes, Sr. Dolores Harrall, Denise Washington, John Cort, Rev. Jim Hickey, Jacqui Townes, Maria Suarez, Reynold Verret, Joanne King, Ruth Andrews, Mary Manseau, Lois Salty, Barbara Hemenway, Sr. Mary Hart, Phyllis Holliday, Gail Holliday, Sr. Mary Gowern.

Thanks also to all my friends for the many stories about families they have shared with me which have helped form my sense of the variety and complexity of family.

To my sisters, Myrna, Betty Ann and Bernadette, who read some of these stories and told me what *not* to do.

To Ponchita Argieard, my editorial advisor on this project, who read these stories from the viewpoint of social worker, psychologist and community worker, and showed me how much richer literary criticism can be with the aid of these perspectives.

To Maryann Dupes for all the research on the writers.

Contents

Fathers and Daughters

Mothers and Sons

Fathers and Sons

Sisters

Introduction

I once told a friend that families were like minefields, that we walk and dance through them never knowing where or when something or someone is going to explode. Though I haven't lived in the same city as my mother for over twenty years, I can still go home to Cleveland, walk in her front door, and within hours begin to feel like the fourteen-year-old I once was, rebelling against my mother's control. Next to the image of the minefield, I have, as a result of reading and editing these stories and poems about family, added another: family as a living mystery, constantly changing, constantly providing us clues about who we are, and demanding that we recognize the new and challenging shapes it often takes. We are, of course, central players in that mystery. I did not grow up only as Mary Helen but as a Washington, daughter of Mary Catherine Dalton and David Washington; sister of Beverly, Myrna, David, Byron, Tommy, Betty Ann and Bernadette; niece of twenty-eight aunts and uncles; granddaughter of Malissa and Frank Dalton, Carrie and Green Washington. As Salvador Minuchin says in his book on families, "We live our lives like chips in a kaleidoscope, always part of patterns that are larger than ourselves and somehow more than the sum of their parts."[1] Or, as Mikhail Bakhtin would put it, we are inheritors of a multiplicity of voices and can only think of ourselves as a mixture of, an amalgam of voices, voices that were first shaped in the context of family. While we are encouraged by American culture to think of ourselves as highly singular, we actually experience ourselves in important ways as "essentially affiliated, joined to others and more like them than different from them."[2] In fact, family becomes so much a part of our essential self that we carry it around inside of us. We say, I have my father's feet, my mother's hair, my grandmother's determination. Sisters and brothers often look and sound alike. Once I was in the airport in Atlanta, and someone I did not know, who had grown up with my brothers, walked up to me and said, "You must be a Washington. I'd know your family anywhere." While I am still resistant to the claims of family, I find myself, after reading these stories and poems, more open to that mysterious process called family, more aware of how it enriches and enlarges my sense of self and less inclined to see myself merely as a survivor, carefully stepping around mines.

Memory of Kin opens with a chapter called "The Extended Family" and with Ernest J. Gaines' story "Just Like a Tree." The central character in that story, Aunt Fe, belongs to a network of "kinfolks," only one of whom is related to her by blood. Family, in Gaines' world, is a created construct, nourished and sustained by a thousand daily acts of support and love. Leola, one of the narrators in "Just Like a Tree," says that if you counted the days in the year, that number would be close to the number of times she has washed, ironed and cooked for the elderly Aunt Fe. Opening with this story establishes one of the main aims of this collection. I wanted to make it difficult for myself as well as other readers to fall back on conventional notions of family, especially of the black family. I wanted readers to question and to discard sentimental clichés about the family as a unit of supreme unselfishness and total support, a rock and a shelter on which we can always depend in hard times. I wanted stories that would shatter notions of an ideal family or myths that deny the complexities of family life, inhibiting our ability to see those complexities. I wanted the mystery of family to be enacted in the number and variety of stories in this collection. In nineteen stories and twelve poems, no two families are alike. The idea of family is constantly shifting, so varied in its many shapes that the narrative of family is as unpredictable as families themselves.

All of these stories question our traditional assumptions about family. William Melvin Kelley's "The Poker Party" deals with the subtle forms of violence in the family, suggesting that the structure of the nuclear family permits that violence. Jamaica Kincaid's "The Circling Hand" explores sexual tension as one of the dynamics of conflict between mother and daughter. Ernest J. Gaines' "A Long Day in November" shows a family made vulnerable by the father's need for the symbols of male power. In one of the most experimental stories in this collection, Alexis De Veaux's "Adventures of the Dread Sisters," a self-created family of women stands in opposition to the traditional family, suggesting that female growth and independence depend on a rejection of patriarchal family patterns. And the apparently powerless slave couple in Charles Chesnutt's "Po' Sandy," united in their resistance to the slave system, present the most compelling picture of an egalitarian marriage in American literature.

The poems that serve as introductions to each section are particularly forceful in helping us to reimagine the family in new ways. Audre Lorde's poem "Black Mother Woman" deals with maternal anger and the sense of self-division that anger has caused between mother and daughter. Recalling her mother's secrecy and denial of intimacy, the daughter thinks of how she has put on her own disguises: "my eyes conceal/a squadron of conflicting rebellions." The grandmother in Toi Derricotte's poem "The Weakness" is no stereotypical grandmother, all-wise and all-giving, and churchgoing, but a status-hungry woman religiously determined to make her granddaughter worthy to be accepted in the temple of Saks Fifth Avenue. The narrator of June Jordan's "The Wedding" does not see marriage through the haze of romance but reminds us that the couple—Tyrone and Dizzella—are young, black, poor, and that without the support of the larger society, these newlyweds are essentially vulnerable: "brave enough/but only two."

While the poems introduce each section, they are thematically separate and autonomous, making their own statements about family which do not necessarily correspond with the stories in that section. Lucille Clifton's "forgiving my father" is about the narrator's inability to forgive her father's deceit, even though she understands that he too was "the son of a needy father" who disappointed him. The story "New African" by Andrea Lee, which follows the Clifton poem, is about a generous and loving father who denies his own need in order to sanction his daughter's search for a separate self. I like having these two pieces together because of that juxtaposition of opposites.

When I began selecting stories for this collection, I was determined that this book present men and women writers equally. There are seven male writers and eight female writers, with ten stories by men and nine by women. No matter how hard I tried to create this egalitarian model, this collection resisted the gender symmetry I was imposing. In many ways this is a woman-centered book, and that is because the family has been the central concern of women. Women have been the caretakers in families, and that caretaking extends even to the stories of family history. Women characters pass down family stories—even in the fiction written by men: the narrator's mother in "Sonny's Blues" is the one who tells him the story of his father and uncle which enables him to change; the sister Geraldine is the family storyteller in John Edgar Wideman's "Little Brother." In Ernest Gaines' three stories, kinship networks are sustained by women. In seventeen of the nineteen stories, women are major characters, central to these family stories just as they are to the rituals of family life.

As this project got underway, I began to be more and more uneasy about constructing a text around the theme of family even though women are so prominently and powerfully represented in these stories. I know how the idea of family has been used to oppress women, especially black women. Fundamentalists can conjure up so-called "family values" whenever they want to assert male domination and canonize female subordination. Almost every effort on the part of women to achieve equality in this society has been associated with the loss of these so-called "family values." So a book that takes family as its major subject needs to be aware of the ideological traps that underlie the construction of family. Alice Walker's "Roselily" is one of the few stories that directly confronts the issue of women's inferior role in the family. The bride Roselily thinks on her wedding day of ropes, chains, handcuffs, as she is married to a Muslim, whose religion insists on male dominance. Other stories deal with this issue indirectly. The threat of male power and male violence undermines the boy's sense of security in "The Poker Party"; and the macho behavior of Eddie Sr. in Ernest Gaines' "A Long Day in November" leaves Eddie Jr. vulnerable and afraid and almost destroys his family. In stories of female adolescence, daughters, experiencing the dominance of the father in the family and the mother's dependency and powerlessness, resist the mother's fate. For Paulette White's young narrator in "Getting the Facts of Life," the idea of womanhood seems like "a suffocating rose." Annie, in Jamaica Kincaid's "The Circling Hand," also rejects the mother's domestic life for the larger world of culture and learning which the father represents. Over and over again, we see in these stories that the healthiest families are the ones in which there is a blurring of the distinctions between men's and women's roles, or in which there is an extended family, not a patriarchal one. I think especially of the example of Gaines' story "Just Like a Tree," in which family is a communal effort and where the knitting together of the family, like the telling of the stories, is a shared project. Or of the self-created family of women in Alexis De Veaux's "Adventures of the Dread Sisters" in which women are given the imaginative freedom to invent all sorts of possibilities for themselves.

In each of the essays that follow the stories, I have tried to suggest readings that do not assume a one-to-one correspondence with "real life" as though these stories were merely transparencies for us to look through and see "real-life families" on the other side. Like any art form, the narrative presents a series of signs that have to be interpreted so that we can judge the formal characteristics of that work of art. For example, "The Sky Is Gray" is a first-person narrative told from the point of view of eight-year-old James as he accompanies his mother on a trip to the dentist. While James seems to be trying to understand his mother's taciturnity and emotional muteness, a close reading of James' narrative strategies shows that he has structured his narrative in opposition to her, his outpouring of words and feelings actually becoming his defiant stand against her silence. In Charles Chesnutt's story "Po' Sandy," the frame story, which is told from the point of view of the white Northerner, John, can be read in opposition to the inner story told by the ex-slave Julius McAdoo, and since the "inner" story is set in slavery, that story becomes a critique of the outer or frame story. The egalitarian marriage of the two slaves, Tenie and Sandy, thus becomes a critique of the more conventional marriage of the white couple, John and Annie. We might contrast the idealized grandmother in Rudolph Fisher's 1933 story "Miss Cynthie" to the less sentimentalized depictions of grandmothers in Paule Marshall's "To Da-duh, In Memoriam" and in Toi Derricotte's poem "The Weakness."

In all of these stories race is the text within the text, another story which also must be read and deciphered. The narrator of "Sonny's Blues" cannot understand the troubles his brother Sonny is experiencing until his mother tells him the story of his father's rage and grief over the father's brother killed by whites in the South. One cannot read "Po' Sandy" simply as a story about a husband and wife or as a frame story contrasting and competing with an inner story. Sandy and his wife Tenie are slaves, bought and sold, and, in Sandy's case, given as a wedding present from a slave owner to his heirs. In Chesnutt's "The Wife of His Youth," slavery also separates husband and wife, but even their reunion after twenty-five years tragically disrupts their lives. The mother in Gaines' "The Sky Is Gray" is silent and unaffectionate, but when she pretends to examine axe handles in the white hardware store so that her son can spend a few minutes by the heater getting warm, as she guides him through the viciously segregated world of Louisiana in the 1950s, using her own body to keep him unharmed, we understand that her motherhood, complicated and threatened by racism, is a special kind of motherhood.

What makes Gaines' story different from the Chesnutt stories is that he is able to portray *both* the anger and the tremendous respect James has for his mother, a duality that opens the way for black writers to take greater risks in their representations of the family. In "Aunt Carrie," Rita Dove explores incest between brother and sister and its devastating effect on family relationships. In "New African," Andrea Lee inverts the black family story by making the daughter's freedom contingent upon her father's willingness to allow her to reject black cultural traditions. In Jamaica Kincaid's "The Circling Hand," the mother begins to distance herself from her daughter, Annie, when she senses from the hair and strange smell under the girl's arms her daughter's emergent sexuality, suggesting that the adolescent's anger and rebelliousness may be triggered as much by maternal rejection as by her own drive for independence. Paule Marshall's "To Daduh, In Memoriam" is also about loss, in this case the loss of a black cultural heritage which the granddaughter can only hope to recapture through her art.

The story of family has inspired some of the very best writing by black writers, and surely that is because the family is integral to black traditions. But, as many of these stories imply, much of what we call family is constructed through memory—what we remember and pass on becomes an essential part of family. In a sense all of these stories about family are also about loss and about the effort to retrieve something through art. Sometimes written from the viewpoint of the writer who has moved away from home and family, they are the writer's way to erase that distance and diminish loss. I am thinking specifically of James Baldwin writing from France about his family in Harlem or Ernest Gaines writing about rural Louisiana from an apartment in San Francisco, or Alice Walker writing from the California mountains about rural Georgia. I think of my own family at our last gathering, sitting around a table with a plastic-lined bushel basket in which we keep hundreds of old photographs, some from as far back as the 1880s, and saying as we pick up each picture, "Remember this." We look at these photographs of ourselves as children in the various rituals of growing up and being grown and we try to re-create the meaning(s) inscribed in those pictures. Like the twenty-four storytellers in this collection, we too become artists, re-creating our family in an imaginative act, retrieving what is lost by reconstructing our own "memory of kin."

1. Salvador Minuchin, *Family Kaleidoscope* (Cambridge: Harvard University Press, 1984), p. 3.
2. Wayne C. Booth, *The Company We Keep: An Ethics of Fiction* (Berkeley: University of California Press, 1988), p. 240.

The
Extended
Family

○ ○ ○

The Idea of Ancestry

ETHERIDGE KNIGHT

1

Taped to the wall of my cell are 47 pictures: 47 black
faces: my father, mother, grandmothers (1 dead), grandfathers (both dead), brothers, sisters, uncles, aunts,
cousins (1st & 2nd), nieces, and nephews. They stare
across the space at me sprawling on my bunk. I know
their dark eyes, they know mine. I know their style,
they know mine. I am all of them, they are all of me;
they are farmers, I am a thief, I am me, they are thee.

I have at one time or another been in love with my mother,
1 grandmother, 2 sisters, 2 aunts (1 went to the asylum),
and 5 cousins. I am now in love with a 7 yr old niece
(she sends me letters written in large block print, and
her picture is the only one that smiles at me).

I have the same name as 1 grandfather, 3 cousins, 3 nephews,
and 1 uncle. The uncle disappeared when he was 15, just took
off and caught a freight (they say). He's discussed each year
when the family has a reunion, he causes uneasiness in
the clan, he is an empty space. My father's mother, who is 93
and who keeps the Family Bible with everybody's birth dates
(and death dates) in it, always mentions him. There is no
place in her Bible for "whereabouts unknown."

*Each fall the graves of my grandfathers call me, the brown
hills and red gullies of mississippi send out their electric
messages, galvanizing my genes. Last yr / like a salmon quitting
the cold ocean-leaping and bucking up his birthstream / I
hitchhiked my way from L.A. with 16 caps in my pocket and a
monkey on my back. And I almost kicked it with the kinfolks.
I walked barefooted in my grandmother's backyard / I smelled the old
land and the woods / I sipped cornwhiskey from fruit jars with the
  men /
I flirted with the women / I had a ball till the caps ran out
and my habit came down. That night I looked at my grandmother
and split / my guts were screaming for junk / but I was almost
contented / I had almost caught up with me.
(The next day in Memphis I cracked a croaker's crib for a fix).*

*This yr there is a gray stone wall damming my stream, and when
the falling leaves stir my genes, I pace my cell or flop on my bunk
and stare at 47 black faces across the space. I am all of them,
they are all of me, I am me, they are thee, and I have no children
to float in the space between.*

Just Like a Tree

ERNEST J. GAINES

*I shall not;
    I shall not be moved.
I shall not;
    I shall not be moved.
Just like a tree that's
planted 'side the water.
    Oh, I shall not be moved.*

I made my home in glory;
 I shall not be moved.
Made my home in glory;
 I shall not be moved.
Just like a tree that's
planted 'side the water.
 Oh, I shall not be moved.

(from an old Negro spiritual)

CHUCKKIE

Pa hit him on the back and he jeck in them chains like he pulling, but ever'body in the wagon know he ain't, and Pa hit him on the back again. He jeck again like he pulling, but even Big Red know he ain't doing a thing.

"That's why I'm go'n get a horse," Pa say. "He'll kill that other mule. Get up there, Mr. Bascom."

"Oh, let him alone," Gran'mon say. "How would you like it if you was pulling a wagon in all that mud?"

Pa don't answer Gran'mon; he just hit Mr. Bascom on the back again.

"That's right, kill him," Gran'mon say. "See where you get mo' money to buy another one."

"Get up there, Mr. Bascom," Pa say.

"You hear me talking to you, Emile?" Gran'mon say. "You want me hit you with something?"

"Ma, he ain't pulling," Pa say.

"Leave him alone," Gran'mon say.

Pa shake the lines little bit, but Mr. Bascom don't even feel it, and you can see he letting Big Red do all the pulling again. Pa say something kind o' low to hisself, and I can't make out what it is.

I low' my head little bit, 'cause that wind and fine rain was hitting me in the face, and I can feel Mama pressing close to me to keep me warm. She sitting on one side o' me and Pa sitting on the other side o' me, and Gran'mon in the back o' me in her setting chair. Pa didn't want bring the setting chair, telling Gran'mon there was two boards in that wagon already and she could sit on one of 'em all by herself if she wanted to, but Gran'mon say she was taking her setting chair with her if Pa liked it or not. She say she didn't ride in no wagon on nobody board, and if Pa liked it or not, that setting chair was going.

"Let her take her setting chair," Mama say. "What's wrong with taking her setting chair."

"Ehhh, Lord," Pa say, and picked up the setting chair and took it out to the wagon. "I guess I'll have to bring it back in the house, too, when we come back from there."

Gran'mon went and clambed in the wagon and moved her setting chair back little bit and sat down and folded her arms, waiting for us to get in, too. I got in and knelt down 'side her, but Mama told me to come up there and sit on the board 'side her and Pa so I could stay warm. Soon 's I sat down, Pa hit Mr. Bascom on the back, saying what a trifling thing Mr. Bascom was, and soon 's he got some mo' money he was getting rid o' Mr. Bascom and getting him a horse.

I raise my head to look see how far we is.

"That's it, yonder," I say.

"Stop pointing," Mama say, "and keep your hand in your pocket."

"Where?" Gran'mon say, back there in her setting chair.

"'Cross the ditch, yonder," I say.

"Can't see a thing for this rain," Gran'mon say.

"Can't hardly see it," I say. "But you can see the light little bit. That chinaball tree standing in the way."

"Poor soul," Gran'mon say. "Poor soul."

I know Gran'mon was go'n say "poor soul, poor soul," 'cause she had been saying "poor soul, poor soul," ever since she heard Aunt Fe was go'n leave from back there.

EMILE

Darn cane crop to finish getting in and only a mule and a half to do it. If I had my way I'd take that shotgun and a load o' buckshots and—but what's the use.

"Get up, Mr. Bascom—please," I say to that little dried-up, long-eared, tobacco-color thing. "Please, come up. Do your share for God sake—if you don't mind. I know it's hard pulling in all that mud, but if you don't do your share, then Big Red'll have to do his and yours, too. So, please, if it ain't asking you too much to—"

"Oh, Emile, shut up," Leola say.

"I can't hit him," I say, "or Mama back there'll hit me. So I have to talk to him. Please, Mr. Bascom, if you don't mind it. For my sake. No, not for mine; for God sake. No, not even for His'n; for Big Red sake. A fellow mule just like yourself is. Please, come up."

"Now, you hear that boy blaspheming God right in front o' me there," Mama say. "Ehhh, Lord—just keep it up. All this bad weather there like this whole world coming apart—a clap o' thunder come there and knock the fool out you. Just keep it up."

Maybe she right, and I stop. I look at Mr. Bascom there doing nothing, and I just give up. That mule know long 's Mama's alive he go'n do just what he want to do. He know when Papa was dying he told Mama to look after him, and he know no matter what he do, no matter what he don't do, Mama ain't go'n never let me do him anything. Sometimes I even feel Mama care mo' for Mr. Bascom 'an she care for me her own son.

We come up to the gate and I pull back on the lines.

"Whoa up, Big Red," I say. "You don't have to stop, Mr. Bascom. You never started."

I can feel Mama looking at me back there in that setting chair, but she don't say nothing.

"Here," I say to Chuckkie.

He take the lines and I jump down on the ground to open the old beat-up gate. I see Etienne's horse in the yard, and I see Chris new red tractor 'side the house, shining in the rain. When Mama die, I say to myself, Mr. Bascom, you going. Ever'body getting tractors and horses and I'm still stuck with you. You going, brother.

"Can you make it through?" I ask Chuckkie. "That gate ain't too wide."

"I can do it," he say.

"Be sure to make Mr. Bascom pull," I say.

"Emile, you better get back up here and drive 'em through," Leola say. "Chuckkie might break up that wagon."

"No, let him stay down there and give orders," Mama say, back there in that setting chair.

"He can do it," I say. "Come on, Chuckkie boy."

"Come up, here, mule," Chuckkie say.

And soon 's he say that, Big Red make a lunge for the yard, and Mr. Bascom don't even move, and 'fore I can bat my eyes I hear *pow-wow; sagg-sagg; pow-wow*. But above all that noise, Leola up there screaming her head off. And Mama—not a word; just sitting in that chair, looking at me with her arms still folded.

"Pull Big Red," I say. "Pull Big Red, Chuckkie."

Poor little Chuckkie up there pulling so hard till one of his little arms straight out in back; and Big Red throwing his shoulders and ever'thing else in it, and Mr. Bascom just walking there just 's loose and free, like he's suppose to be there just for his good looks. I move out the way just in time to let the wagon go by me, pulling half o' the fence in the yard behind it. I glance up again, and there's Leola still hollering and trying to jump out, but Mama not saying a word—just sitting there in that setting chair with her arms still folded.

"Whoa," I hear little Chuckkie saying. "Whoa up, now."

Somebody open the door and a bunch o' people come out on the gallery.

"What the world—?" Etienne say. "Thought the whole place was coming to pieces there."

"Chuckkie had a little trouble coming in the yard," I say.

"Goodness," Etienne say. "Anybody hurt?"

Mama just sit there about ten seconds, then she say something to herself and start clambing out the wagon.

"Let me help you there, Aunt Lou," Etienne say, coming down the steps.

"I can make it," Mama say. When she get on the ground she look up at Chuckkie. "Hand me my chair there, boy."

Poor little Chuckkie, up there with the lines in one hand, get the chair and hold it to the side, and Etienne catch it just 'fore it hit the ground. Mama start looking at me again, and it look like for at least a' hour she stand there looking at nobody but me. Then she say, "Ehhh, Lord," like that again, and go inside with Leola and the rest o' the people.

I look back at half o' the fence laying there in the yard, and I jump back on the wagon and guide the mules to the side o' the house. After unhitching 'em and tying 'em to the wheels, I look at Chris pretty red tractor again, and me and Chuckkie go inside: I make sure he kick all that mud off his shoes 'fore he go in the house.

LEOLA

Sitting over there by that fireplace, trying to look joyful when ever'body there know she ain't. But she trying, you know; smiling and bowing when people say something to her. How can she be joyful, I ask you; how can she be? Poor thing, she been here all her life—or the most of it, let's say. 'Fore they moved in this house, they lived in one back in the woods 'bout a mile from here. But for the past twenty-five or thirty years, she been right in this one house. I know ever since I been big enough to know people I been seeing her right here.

Aunt Fe, Aunt Fe, Aunt Fe, Aunt Fe; the name's been 'mongst us just like us own family name. Just like the name o' God. Like the name of town—the city. Aunt Fe, Aunt Fe, Aunt Fe, Aunt Fe.

Poor old thing; how many times I done come here and washed clothes for her when she couldn't do it herself. How many times I done hoed in that garden, ironed her clothes, wrung a chicken neck for her. You count the days in the year and you'll be pretty close. And I didn't mind it a bit. No, I didn't mind it a bit. She there trying to pay me. Proud—Lord, talking 'bout pride. "Here." "No, Aunt Fe; no." "Here, here; you got a child there, you can use it." "No, Aunt Fe. No. No. What would Mama think if she knowed I took money from you? Aunt Fe, Mama would never forgive me. No. I love doing these thing for you. I just wish I could do more."

And there, now, trying to make 'tend she don't mind leaving. Ehhh, Lord.

I hear a bunch o' rattling round in the kitchen and I go back there. I see Louise stirring this big pot o' eggnog.

"Louise," I say.

"Leola," she say.

We look at each other and she stir the eggnog again. She know what I'm go'n say next, and she can't even look in my face.

"Louise, I wish there was some other way."

"There's no other way," she say.

"Louise, moving her from here's like moving a tree you been used to in your front yard all your life."

"What else can I do?"

"Oh, Louise, Louise."

"Nothing else but that."

"Louise, what people go'n do without her here?"

She stir the eggnog and don't answer.

"Louise, us'll take her in with us."

"You all no kin to Auntie. She go with me."

"And us'll never see her again."

She stir the eggnog. Her husband come back in the kitchen and kiss her on the back o' the neck and then look at me and grin. Right from the start I can see I ain't go'n like that nigger.

"Almost ready, honey?" he say.

"Almost."

He go to the safe and get one o' them bottles of whiskey he got in there and come back to the stove.

"No," Louise say. "Everybody don't like whiskey in it. Add the whiskey after you've poured it up."

"Okay, hon."

He kiss her on the back o' the neck again. Still don't like that nigger. Something 'bout him ain't right.

"You one o' the family?" he say.

"Same as one," I say. "And you?"

He don't like the way I say it, and I don't care if he like it or not. He look at me there a second, and then he kiss her on the ear.

"Un-unnn," she say, stirring the pot.

"I love your ear, baby," he say.

"Go in the front room and talk with the people," she say.

He kiss her on the other ear. A nigger do all that front o' public got something to hide. He leave the kitchen. I look at Louise.

"Ain't nothing else I can do," she say.

"You sure, Louise? You positive?"

"I'm positive," she say.

The front door open and Emile and Chuckkie come in. A minute later Washington and Adrieu come in, too. Adrieu come back in the kitchen, and I can see she been crying. Aunt Fe is her godmother, you know.

"How you feel, Adrieu?"

"That weather out there," she say.

"Y'all walked?"

"Yes."

"Us here in the wagon. Y'all can go back with us."

"Y'all the one tore the fence down?" she ask.

"Yes, I guess so. That brother-in-law o' yours in there letting Chuckkie drive that wagon."

"Well, I don't guess it'll matter too much. Nobody go'n be here, anyhow."

And she start crying again. I take her in my arms and pat her on the shoulder, and I look at Louise stirring the eggnog.

"What I'm go'n do and my nan-nane gone? I love her so much."

"Ever'body love her."

"Since my mama died, she been like my mama."

"Shhh," I say. "Don't let her hear you. Make her grieve. You don't want her grieving, now, do you?"

She sniffs there 'gainst my dress few times.

"Oh, Lord," she say. "Lord, have mercy."

"Shhh," I say. "Shhh. That's what life's 'bout."

"That ain't what life's 'bout," she say. "It ain't fair. This been her home all her life. These the people she know. She don't know them people she going to. It ain't fair."

"Shhh, Adrieu," I say. "Now, you saying things that ain't your business."

She cry there some mo'.

"Oh, Lord, Lord," she say.

Louise turn from the stove.

"About ready now," she say, going to the middle door. "James, tell everybody to come back and get some."

JAMES

Let me go on back here and show these country niggers how to have a good time. All they know is talk, talk, talk. Talk so much they make me buggy round here. Damn this weather—wind, rain. Must be a million cracks in this old house.

I go to that old beat-up safe in that corner and get that fifth of Mr. Harper (in the South now; got to say Mister), give the seal one swipe, the stopper one jerk, and head back to that old wood stove. (Man, like, these cats are primitive—goodness. You know what I mean? I mean like wood stoves. Don't mention

TV, man, these cats here never heard of that.) I start to dump Mr. Harper in the pot and Baby catches my hand again and say not all of them like it. You ever heard of anything like that? I mean a stud's going to drink eggnog, and he's not going to put whiskey in it. I mean he's going to drink it straight. I mean, you ever heard anything like that? Well, I wasn't pressing none of them on Mr. Harper. I mean, me and Mr. Harper get along too well together for me to go around there pressing.

I hold my cup there and let Baby put a few drops of this egg stuff in it; then I jerk my cup back and let Mr. Harper run a while. Couple of these cats come over (some of them aren't so lame) and set their cups, and I let Mr. Harper run for them. Then this cat says he's got 'nough. I let Mr. Harper run for this other stud, and pretty soon he says, "Hold it. Good." Country cat, you know. "Hold it. Good." Real country cat. So I raise the cup to see what Mr. Harper's doing. He's just right. I raise the cup again. Just right, Mr. Harper; just right.

I go to the door with Mr. Harper under my arm and the cup in my hand and I look into the front room where they all are. I mean, there's about ninety-nine of them in there. Old ones, young ones, little ones, big ones, yellow ones, black ones, brown ones—you name them, brother, and they were there. And what for? Brother, I'll tell you what for. Just because me and Baby are taking this old chick out of these sticks. Well, I'll tell you where I'd be at this moment if I was one of them. With that weather out there like it is, I'd be under about five blankets with some little warm belly pressing against mine. Brother, you can bet your hat I wouldn't be here. Man, listen to that thing out there. You can hear that rain beating on that old house like grains of rice; and that wind coming through them cracks like it does in those old Charlie Chaplin movies. Man, like you know—like *whooo-ee; whooo-ee.* Man, you talking about some weird cats.

I can feel Mr. Harper starting to massage my wig and I bat my eyes twice and look at the old girl over there. She's still sitting in that funny-looking little old rocking chair, and not saying a word to anybody. Just sitting there looking into the fireplace at them two pieces of wood that aren't giving out enough heat to warm a baby, let alone ninety-nine grown people. I mean, you know, like that sleet's falling out there like all get-up-and-go, and them two pieces of wood are lying there just as dead as the rest of these way-out cats.

One of the old cats—I don't know which one he is—Mose, Sam, or something like that—leans over and pokes in the fire a minute; then a little blaze shoots up, and he raises up, too, looking as satisfied as if he'd just sent a rocket into orbit. I mean, these cats are like that. They do these little bitty things, and they feel like they've really done something. Well, back in these sticks, I guess there just isn't nothing big to do.

I feel Mr. Harper touching my skull now—and I notice this little chick passing by me with these two cups of eggnog. She goes over to the fireplace and gives one to each of these old chicks. The one sitting in that setting chair she brought with her from God knows where, and the other cup to the old chick that Baby and I are going to haul from here sometime tomorrow morning. Wait, man, I mean like, you ever heard of anybody going to somebody else's house with a chair? I mean, wouldn't you call that an insult at the basest point? I mean, now, like tell me what you think of that? I mean—dig—here I am at my pad, and in you come with your own stool. I mean, now, like man, you know. I mean that's an insult at the basest point. I mean, you know . . . you know, like way out. . . .

Mr. Harper, what you trying to do, boy?—I mean, *sir.* (Got to watch myself, I'm in the South. Got to keep watching myself.)

This stud touches me on the shoulder and raise his cup and say, "How 'bout a taste?" I know what the stud's talking about, so I let Mr. Harper run for him. But soon 's I let a drop get in, the stud say, " 'Nough." I mean I let about two drops get in, and already the stud's got enough. Man, I mean, like you know. I mean these studs are 'way out. I mean like 'way back there.

This stud takes a swig of his eggnog and say, "Ahhh." I mean this real down-home way of saying "Ahhhh." I mean, man, like these studs—I notice this little chick passing by me again, and this time she's crying. I mean weeping, you know. And just because this old ninety-nine-year-old chick's packing up and leaving. I mean, you ever heard of anything like that? I mean, here she is pretty as the day is long and crying because Baby and I are hauling this old chick away. Well, I'd like to make her cry. And I can assure you, brother, it wouldn't be from leaving her.

I turn and look at Baby over there by the stove, pouring eggnog in all these cups. I mean, there're about twenty of these cats lined up there. And I bet you not half of them will take Mr. Harper along. Some way-out cats, man. Some way-out cats.

I go up to Baby and kiss her on the back of the neck and give her a little pat where she likes for me to pat her when we're in the bed. She say, "Uh-uh," but I know she likes it anyhow.

BEN O

I back under the bed and touch the slop jar, and I pull back my leg and back somewhere else, and then I get me a good sight on it. I spin my aggie couple times and sight again and then I shoot. I hit it right square in the middle and it go flying over the fireplace. I crawl over there to get it and I see 'em all over there drinking they eggnog and they didn't even offer me and Chuckkie none. I find my marble on the bricks, and I go back and tell Chuckkie they over there drinking eggnog.

"You want some?" I say.

"I want shoot marble," Chuckkie say. "Yo' shot. Shoot up."

"I want some eggnog," I say.

"Shoot up, Ben O," he say. "I'm getting cold staying in one place so long. You feel that draft?"

"Coming from that crack under that bed," I say.

"Where?" Chuckkie say, looking for the crack.

"Over by that bedpost over there," I say.

"This sure's a beat-up old house," Chuckkie say.

"I want me some eggnog," I say.

"Well, you ain't getting none," Gran'mon say, from the fireplace. "It ain't good for you."

"I can drink eggnog," I say. "How come it ain't good for me? It ain't nothing but eggs and milk. I eat chicken, don't I? I eat beef, don't I?"

Gran'mon don't say nothing.

"I want me some eggnog," I say.

Gran'mon still don't say no more. Nobody else don't say nothing, neither.

"I want me some eggnog," I say.

"You go'n get a eggnog," Gran'mon say. "Just keep that noise up."

"I want me some eggnog," I say; "and I 'tend to get me some eggnog tonight."

Next thing I know, Gran'mon done picked up a chip out o' that corner and done sailed it back there where me and Chuckkie is. I duck just in time, and the chip catch old Chuckkie side the head.

"Hey, who that hitting me?" Chuckkie say.

"Move, and you won't get hit," Gran'mon say.

I laugh at old Chuckkie over there holding his head, and next thing I know here's Chuckkie done haul back there and hit me in my side. I jump up from there and give him two just to show him how it feel, and he jump up and hit me again. Then we grab each other and start tussling on the floor.

"You, Ben O," I hear Gran'mon saying. "You, Ben O, cut that out. Y'all cut that out."

But we don't stop, 'cause neither one o' us want be first. Then I feel somebody pulling us apart.

"What I ought to do is whip both o' you," Mrs. Leola say. "Is that what y'all want?"

"No'm," I say.

"Then shake hand."

Me and Chuckkie shake hand.

"Kiss," Mrs. Leola say.

"No, ma'am," I say. "I ain't kissing no boy. I ain't that crazy."

"Kiss him, Chuckkie," she say.

Old Chuckkie kiss me on the jaw.

"Now, kiss him, Ben O."

"I ain't kissing no Chuckkie," I say. "No'm. Uh-uh. You kiss girls."

And the next thing I know, Mama done tipped up back o' me and done whop me on the leg with Daddy belt.

"Kiss Chuckkie," she say.

Chuckkie turn his jaw to me and I kiss him. I almost wipe my mouth. I even feel like spitting.

"Now, come back here and get you some eggnog," Mama say.

"That's right, spoil 'em," Gran'mon say. "Next thing you know, they be drinking from bottles."

"Little eggnog won't hurt 'em, Mama," Mama say.

"That's right, never listen," Gran'mon say. "It's you go'n suffer for it. I be dead and gone, me."

AUNT CLO

Be just like wrapping a chain round a tree and jecking and jecking, and then shifting the chain little bit and jecking and jecking some in that direction, and then shifting it some mo' and jecking and jecking in that direction. Jecking and jecking till you get it loose, and then pulling with all your might. Still it might not be loose enough and you have to back the tractor up some and fix the chain round the tree again and start jecking all over. Jeck, jeck, jeck. Then you hear the roots crying, and then you keep on jecking, and then it give, and you jeck some mo', and then it falls. And not till then that you see what you done done. Not till then you see the big hole in the ground and piece of the taproot still way down in it—a piece you won't never get out no matter if you dig till doomsday. Yes, you got the tree—least got it down on the ground, but did you get the taproot? No. No, sir, you didn't get the taproot. You stand there and look down in this hole at it and you grab yo' axe and jump

down in it and start chopping at the taproot, but do you get
the taproot? No. You don't get the taproot, sir. You never get
the taproot. But, sir, I tell you what you do get. You get a big
hole in the ground, sir; and you get another big hole in the air
where the lovely branches been all these years. Yes, sir, that's
what you get. The holes, sir, the holes. Two holes, sir, you can't
never fill no matter how hard you try.

So you wrap yo' chain round yo' tree again, sir, and you start
dragging it. But the dragging ain't so easy, sir, 'cause she's a
heavy old tree—been there a long time, you know—heavy. And
you make yo' tractor strain, sir, and the elements work 'gainst
you, too, sir, 'cause the elements, they on her side, too, 'cause
she part o' the elements, and the elements, they part o' her. So
the elements, they do they little share to discourage you—yes,
sir, they does. But you will not let the elements stop you. No,
sir, you show the elements that they just elements, and man is
stronger than elements, and you jeck and jeck on the chain, and
soon she start to moving with you, sir, but if you look over yo'
shoulder one second you see her leaving a trail—a trail, sir, that
can be seen from miles and miles away. You see her trying to
hook her little fine branches in different little cracks, in between
pickets, round hills o' grass, round anything they might brush
'gainst. But you is a determined man, sir, and you jeck and you
jeck, and she keep on grabbing and trying to hold, but you
stronger, sir—course you the strongest—and you finally get her
out on the pave road. But what you don't notice, sir, is just 'fore
she get on the pave road she leave couple her little branches to
remind the people that it ain't her that want leave, but you, sir,
that think she ought to. So you just drag her and drag her, sir,
and the folks that live in the houses 'side the pave road, they
come out on they gallery and look at her go by, and then they
go back in they house and sit by the fire and forget her. So you
just go on, sir, and you just go and you go—and for how many
days? I don't know. I don't have the least idea. The North to
me, sir, is like the elements. It mystify me. But never mind, you
finally get there, and then you try to find a place to set her.

You look in this corner and you look in that corner, but no corner is good. She kind o' stand in the way no matter where you set her. So finally, sir, you say, "I just stand her up here a little while and see, and if it don't work out, if she keep getting in the way, I guess we'll just have to take her to the dump."

CHRIS

Just like him, though, standing up there telling them lies when everybody else feeling sad. I don't know what you do without people like him. And, yet, you see him there, he sad just like the rest. But he just got to be funny. Crying on the inside, but still got to be funny.

He didn't steal it, though; didn't steal it a bit. His grandpa was just like him. Mat? Mat Jefferson? Just like that. Mat could make you die laughing. 'Member once at a wake. Who was dead? Yes—Robert Lewis. Robert Lewis laying up in his coffin dead as a door nail. Everybody sad and droopy. Mat look at that and start his lying. Soon, half o' the place laughing. Funniest wake I ever went to, and yet—

Just like now. Look at 'em. Look at 'em laughing. Ten minutes ago you would 'a' thought you was at a funeral. But look at 'em now. Look at her there in that little old chair. How long she had it? Fifty years—a hundred? It ain't a chair no mo', it's little bit o' her. Just like her arm, just like her leg.

You know, I couldn't believe it. I couldn't. Emile passed the house there the other day, right after the bombing, and I was in my yard digging a water drain to let the water run out in the ditch. Emile, he stopped the wagon there 'fore the door. Little Chuckkie, he in there with him with that little rain cap buckled up over his head. I go out to the gate and I say, "Emile, it's the truth?"

"The truth," he say. And just like that he say it. "The truth."

I look at him there, and he looking up the road to keep from looking back at me. You know, they been pretty close to Aunt

Fe ever since they was children coming up. His own mon, Aunt Lou, and Aunt Fe, they been like sisters, there, together.

Me and him, we talk there little while 'bout the cane cutting, then he say he got to get on to the back. He shake the lines and drive on.

Inside me, my heart feel like it done swole up ten times the size it ought to be. Water come in my eyes, and I got to 'mit I cried right there. Yes sir, I cried right there by that front gate.

Louise come in the room and whisper something to Leola, and they go back in the kitchen. I can hear 'em moving things round back there, still getting things together they go'n be taking along. If they offer me anything, I'd like that big iron pot out there in the back yard. Good for boiling water when you killing hog, you know.

You can feel the sadness in the room again. Louise brought it in when she come in and whispered to Leola. Only, she didn't take it out when her and Leola left. Every pan they move, every pot they unhook keep telling you she leaving, she leaving.

Etienne turn over one o' them logs to make the fire pick up some, and I see that boy, Lionel, spreading out his hands over the fire. Watch out, I think to myself, here come another lie. People, he just getting started.

ANNE-MARIE DUVALL

"You're not going?"

"I'm not going," he says, turning over the log with the poker. "And if you were in your right mind, you wouldn't go, either."

"You just don't understand, do you?"

"Oh, I understand. She cooked for your daddy. She nursed you when your mama died."

"And I'm trying to pay her back with a seventy-nine-cents scarf. Is that too much?"

He is silent, leaning against the mantel, looking down at the fire. The fire throws strange shadows across the big, old room.

Father looks down at me from against the wall. His eyes do not say go nor stay. But I know what he would do.

"Please go with me, Edward."

"You're wasting your breath."

I look at him a long time, then I get the small package from the coffee table.

"You're still going?"

"I am going."

"Don't call for me if you get bogged down anywhere back there."

I look at him and go out to the garage. The sky is black. The clouds are moving fast and low. A fine drizzle is falling, and the wind coming from the swamps blows in my face. I cannot recall a worse night in all my life.

I hurry into the car and drive out of the yard. The house stands big and black in back of me. Am I angry with Edward? No, I'm not angry with Edward. He's right. I should not go out into this kind of weather. But what he does not understand is I must. Father definitely would have gone if he were alive. Grandfather definitely would have gone, also. And, therefore, I must. Why? I cannot answer why. Only, I must go.

As soon as I turn down that old muddy road, I begin to pray. Don't let me go into that ditch, I pray. Don't let me go into that ditch. Please, don't let me go into that ditch.

The lights play on the big old trees along the road. Here and there the lights hit a sagging picket fence. But I know I haven't even started yet. She lives far back into the fields. Why? God, why does she have to live so far back? Why couldn't she have lived closer to the front? But the answer to that is as hard for me as is the answer to everything else. It was ordained before I—before Father—was born—that she should live back there. So why should I try to understand it now?

The car slides towards the ditch, and I stop it dead and turn the wheel, and then come back into the road again. Thanks, Father. I know you're with me. Because it was you who said that I must look after her, didn't you? No, you did not say it directly,

Father. You said it only with a glance. As Grandfather must have said it to you, and as his father must have said it to him.

But now that she's gone, Father, now what? I know. I know. Aunt Lou, Aunt Clo, and the rest.

The lights shine on the dead, wet grass along the road. There's an old pecan tree, looking dead and all alone. I wish I was a little nigger gal so I could pick pecans and eat them under the big old dead tree.

The car hits a rut, but bounces right out of it. I am frightened for a moment, but then I feel better. The windshield wipers are working well, slapping the water away as fast as it hits the glass. If I make the next half mile all right, the rest of the way will be good. It's not much over a mile now.

That was too bad about that bombing—killing that woman and her two children. That poor woman; poor children. What is the answer? What will happen? What do they want? Do they know what they want? Do they really know what they want? Are they positively sure? Have they any idea? Money to buy a car, is that it? If that is all, I pity them. Oh, how I pity them.

Not much farther. Just around that bend and—there's a water hole. Now what?

I stop the car and just stare out at the water a minute; then I get out to see how deep it is. The cold wind shoots through my body like needles. Lightning comes from towards the swamps and lights up the place. For a split second the night is as bright as day. The next second it is blacker than it has ever been.

I look at the water, and I can see that it's too deep for the car to pass through. I must turn back or I must walk the rest of the way. I stand there a while wondering what to do. Is it worth it all? Can't I simply send the gift by someone tomorrow morning? But will there be someone tomorrow morning? Suppose she leaves without getting it, then what? What then? Father would never forgive me. Neither would Grandfather or Great-grandfather, either. No, they wouldn't.

The lightning flashes again and I look across the field, and I can see the tree in the yard a quarter of a mile away. I have but one choice: I must walk. I get the package out of the car and stuff it in my coat and start out.

I don't make any progress at first, but then I become a little warmer and I find I like walking. The lightning flashes just in time to show up a puddle of water, and I go around it. But there's no light to show up the second puddle, and I fall flat on my face. For a moment I'm completely blind, then I get slowly to my feet and check the package. It's dry, not harmed. I wash the mud off my raincoat, wash my hands, and I start out again.

The house appears in front of me, and as I come into the yard, I can hear the people laughing and talking. Sometimes I think niggers can laugh and joke even if they see somebody beaten to death. I go up on the porch and knock and an old one opens the door for me. I swear, when he sees me he looks as if he's seen a ghost. His mouth drops open, his eyes bulge— I swear.

I go into the old crowded and smelly room, and every one of them looks at me the same way the first one did. All the joking and laughing has ceased. You would think I was the devil in person.

"Done, Lord," I hear her saying over by the fireplace. They move to the side and I can see her sitting in that little rocking chair I bet you she's had since the beginning of time. "Done, Master," she says. "Child, what you doing in weather like this? Y'all move; let her get to that fire. Y'all move. Move, now. Let her warm herself."

They start scattering everywhere.

"I'm not cold, Aunt Fe," I say. "I just brought you something— something small—because you're leaving us. I'm going right back."

"Done, Master," she says. Fussing over me just like she's done all her life. "Done, Master. Child, you ain't got no business in a place like this. Get close to this fire. Get here. Done, Master."

I move closer, and the fire does feel warm and good.

"Done, Lord," she says.

I take out the package and pass it to her. The other niggers gather around with all kinds of smiles on their faces. Just think of it—a white lady coming through all of this for one old darky. It is all right for them to come from all over the plantation, from all over the area, in all kinds of weather: this is to be expected of them. But a white lady, a white lady. They must think we white people don't have their kind of feelings.

She unwraps the package, her bony little fingers working slowly and deliberately. When she sees the scarf—the seventy-nine-cents scarf—she brings it to her mouth and kisses it.

"Y'all look," she says. "Y'all look. Ain't it the prettiest little scarf y'all ever did see? Y'all look."

They move around her and look at the scarf. Some of them touch it.

"I go'n put it on right now," she says. "I go'n put it on right now, my lady."

She unfolds it and ties it round her head and looks up at everybody and smiles.

"Thank you, my lady," she says. "Thank you, ma'am, from the bottom of my heart."

"Oh, Aunt Fe," I say, kneeling down beside her. "Oh, Aunt Fe."

But I think about the other niggers there looking down at me, and I get up. But I look into that wrinkled old face again, and I must go back down again. And I lay my head in that bony old lap, and I cry and I cry—I don't know how long. And I feel those old fingers, like death itself, passing over my hair and my neck. I don't know how long I kneel there crying, and when I stop, I get out of there as fast as I can.

ETIENNE

The boy come in, and soon, right off, they get quiet, blaming the boy. If people could look little farther than the tip of they nose—No, they blame the boy. Not that they ain't behind the boy, what he doing, but they blame him for what she must do.

What they don't know is that the boy didn't start it, and the people that bombed the house didn't start it, neither. It started a million years ago. It started when one man envied another man for having a penny mo' 'an he had, and then the man married a woman to help him work the field so he could get much 's the other man, but when the other man saw the man had married a woman to get much 's him, he, himself, he married a woman, too, so he could still have mo'. Then they start having children— not from love; but so the children could help 'em work so they could have mo'. But even with the children one man still had a penny mo' 'an the other, so the other man went and bought him a ox, and the other man did the same—to keep ahead of the other man. And soon the other man had bought him a slave to work the ox so he could get ahead of the other man. But the other man went out and bought him two slaves so he could stay ahead of the other man, and the other man went out and bought him three slaves. And soon they had a thousand slaves apiece, but they still wasn't satisfied. And one day the slaves all rose and kill the masters, but the masters (knowing slaves was men just like they was, and kind o' expected they might do this) organized theyself a good police force, and the police force, they come out and killed the two thousand slaves.

So it's not this boy you see standing here 'fore you, 'cause it happened a million years ago. And this boy here's just doing something the slaves done a million years ago. Just that this boy here ain't doing it they way. 'Stead of raising arms 'gainst the masters, he bow his head.

No, I say; don't blame the boy 'cause she must go. 'Cause when she's dead, and that won't be long after they get her up there, this boy's work will still be going on. She's not the only one that's go'n die from this boy's work. Many mo' of 'em go'n die 'fore it's over with. The whole place—everything. A big wind is rising, and when a big wind rise, the sea stirs, and the drop o' water you see laying on top the sea this day won't be there tomorrow. 'Cause that's what wind do, and that's what life is. She ain't nothing but one little drop o' water laying on top the sea, and what this boy's doing is called the wind . . . and she must be moved. No, don't blame the boy. Go out and blame the wind. No, don't blame him, 'cause tomorrow, what he's doing today, somebody go'n say he ain't done a thing. 'Cause tomorrow will be his time to be turned over just like it's hers today. And after that, be somebody else time to turn over. And it keep going like that till it ain't nothing left to turn—and nobody left to turn it.

"Sure, they bombed the house," he say; "because they want us to stop. But if we stopped today, then what good would we have done? What good? Those who have already died for the cause would have just died in vain."

"Maybe if they had bombed your house you wouldn't be so set on keeping this up."

"If they had killed my mother and my brothers and sisters, I'd press just that much harder. I can see you all point. I can see it very well. But I can't agree with you. You blame me for their being bombed. You blame me for Aunt Fe's leaving. They died for you and for your children. And I love Aunt Fe as much as anybody in here does. Nobody in here loves her more than I do. Not one of you." He looks at her. "Don't you believe me, Aunt Fe?"

She nods—that little white scarf still tied round her head.

"How many times have I eaten in your kitchen, Aunt Fe? A thousand times? How many times have I eaten tea cakes and drank milk on the back steps, Aunt Fe? A thousand times? How many times have I sat at this same fireplace with you, just the two of us, Aunt Fe? Another thousand times—two thousand times? How many times have I chopped wood for you, chopped grass for you, ran to the store for you? Five thousand times? How many times have we walked to church together, Aunt Fe? Gone fishing at the river together—how many times? I've spent as much time in this house as I've spent in my own. I know every crack in the wall. I know every corner. With my eyes shut, I can go anywhere in here without bumping into anything. How many of you can do that? Not many of you." He looks at her. "Aunt Fe?"

She looks at him.

"Do you think I love you, Aunt Fe?"

She nods.

"I love you, Aunt Fe, much as I do my own parents. I'm going to miss you much as I'd miss my own mother if she were to leave me now. I'm going to miss you, Aunt Fe, but I'm not going to stop what I've started. You told me a story once, Aunt Fe, about my great-grandpa. Remember? Remember how he died?"

She looks in the fire and nods.

"Remember how they lynched him—chopped him into pieces?"

She nods.

"Just the two of us were sitting here beside the fire when you told me that. I was so angry I felt like killing. But it was you who told me get killing out of my mind. It was you who told me I would only bring harm to myself and sadness to the others if I killed. Do you remember that, Aunt Fe?"

She nods, still looking in the fire.

"You were right. We cannot raise our arms. Because it would mean death for ourselves, as well as for the others. But we will do something else—and that's what we will do." He looks at the people standing round him. "And if they were to bomb my own mother's house tomorrow, I would still go on."

"I'm not saying for you not to go on," Louise says. "That's up to you. I'm just taking Auntie from here before hers is the next house they bomb."

The boy look at Louise, and then at Aunt Fe. He go up to the chair where she sitting.

"Good-bye, Aunt Fe," he say, picking up her hand. The hand done shriveled up to almost nothing. Look like nothing but loose skin's covering the bones. "I'll miss you," he say.

"Good-bye, Emmanuel," she say. She look at him a long time. "God be with you."

He stand there holding the hand a while longer, then he nods his head, and leaves the house. The people stir round little bit, but nobody say anything.

AUNT LOU

They tell her good-bye, and half of 'em leave the house crying, or want cry, but she just sit there 'side the fireplace like she don't mind going at all. When Leola ask me if I'm ready to go, I tell her I'm staying right there till Fe leave that house. I tell her I ain't moving one step till she go out that door. I been knowing her for the past fifty some years now, and I ain't 'bout to leave her on her last night here.

That boy, Chuckkie, want stay with me, but I make him go. He follow his mon and paw out the house and soon I hear that wagon turning round. I hear Emile saying something to Mr. Bascom even 'fore that wagon get out the yard. I tell myself, well, Mr. Bascom, you sure go'n catch it, and me not there to take up for you—and I get up from my chair and go to the door.

"Emile?" I call.

"Whoa," he say.

"You leave that mule 'lone, you hear me?"

"I ain't done Mr. Bascom a thing, Mama," he say.

"Well, you just mind you don't," I say. "I'll sure find out."

"Yes'm," he say. "Come up here, Mr. Bascom."

"Now, you hear that boy. Emile?" I say.

"I'm sorry, Mama," he say. "I didn't mean no harm."

They go out in the road, and I go back to the fireplace and sit down again. Louise stir round in the kitchen a few minutes, then she come in the front where we at. Everybody else gone. That husband o' hers, there, got drunk long 'fore midnight, and Emile and them had to put him to bed in the other room.

She come there and stand by the fire.

"I'm dead on my feet," she say.

"Why don't you go to bed," I say. "I'm go'n be here."

"You all won't need anything?"

"They got wood in that corner?"

"Plenty."

"Then we won't need a thing."

She stand there and warm, and then she say good night and go round the other side.

"Well, Fe?" I say.

"I ain't leaving here tomorrow, Lou," she say.

" 'Course you is," I say. "Up there ain't that bad."

She shake her head. "No, I ain't going nowhere."

I look at her over in her chair, but I don't say nothing. The fire pops in the fireplace, and I look at the fire again. It's a good little fire—not too big, not too little. Just 'nough there to keep the place warm.

"You want sing, Lou?" she say, after a while. "I feel like singing my 'termination song."

"Sure," I say.

She start singing in that little light voice she got there, and I join with her. We sing two choruses, and then she stop.

"My 'termination for Heaven," she say. "Now—now—"

"What's the matter, Fe?" I say.

"Nothing," she say. "I want get in my bed. My gown hanging over there."

I get the gown for her and bring it back to the fireplace. She get out of her dress slowly, like she don't even have 'nough strength to do it. I help her on with her gown, and she kneel down there 'side the bed and say her prayers. I sit in my chair and look at the fire again.

She pray there a long time—half out loud, half to herself. I look at her kneeling down there, little like a little old girl. I see her making some kind o' jecking motion there, but I feel she crying 'cause this her last night here, and 'cause she got to go and leave ever'thing behind. I look at the fire.

She pray there ever so long, and then she start to get up. But she can't make it by herself. I go to help her, and when I put my hand on her shoulder, she say, "Lou? Lou?"

I say, "What's the matter, Fe?"

"Lou?" she say. "Lou?"

I feel her shaking in my hand with all her might. Shaking, shaking, shaking—like a person with the chill. Then I hear her take a long breath, longest I ever heard anybody take before. Then she ease back on the bed—calm, calm, calm.

"Sleep on, Fe," I tell her. "When you get up there, tell 'em all I ain't far behind."

COMMENTARY ON ERNEST J. GAINES

Just Like a Tree / The Sky Is Gray / A Long Day in November

Ernest J. Gaines was born in 1933 on a sugar plantation in a rural section of Louisiana just northwest of Baton Rouge. The oldest of eight brothers and three sisters, Gaines was picking cotton and digging potatoes by age nine, for fifty cents a day. He lived for the first fourteen years of his life on this Louisiana plantation, then migrated with his mother and stepfather to California. But that cane and cotton country, where people live on plantations, working the land as farmers and sharecroppers, has remained the fictional world that Gaines portrays in his novels and short stories. From his earliest novel, *Catherine Carmier* (1964), to his most well-known work, *The Autobiography of Miss Jane Pittman* (1971), Gaines has explored the lives of these simple folk, who often live near each other for a lifetime, whose daily acts of caring for one another, though deceptively simple, sometimes reflect extraordinary courage and determination. Gaines' own Aunt Augusteen Jefferson, who is the model for Gaines' Miss Jane Pittman, was one of these folk. While Gaines' mother worked in the fields, his aunt, so crippled from birth that she could only crawl, took care of everything at home:

She completely ignored the wheelchair that welfare gave her (we kids played with it). She'd crawl over the floor like an infant, down the steps and into the garden to weed and hoe, then to the backyard to collect pecans and back into the house. When we misbehaved she made us cut the switch that would punish us. If it wasn't the right size, she sent us back for another one . . . My aunt never felt sorry for herself . . . She had a great moral strength.

(*Essence* Interview with Tom Carter, May 1975)

Though Gaines was brought to prominence by the 1974 television adaptation of his novel *The Autobiography of Miss Jane Pittman*, that television production in some ways misrepresents the ethic that informs Gaines' fiction. The TV Miss Jane, though she is like Gaines' Aunt Augusteen, is a highly individualistic character, marching defiantly but alone up to the segregated water fountain. Gaines' stories are more often about communal bonds, about the ways in which a community creates and sustains the courage of its individual members.

The structure of "Just Like a Tree," which is taken from Gaines' short-story collection, *Bloodline* (1968), suggests these tight communal bonds. The story is told by ten different characters, beginning with the youngest member of the community, Chuckkie, and ending with one of the oldest, Aunt Lou. They are young and old, black and white, male and female, and together they constitute Aunt Fe's extended family. As we listen to their collective story we begin to be aware of the relationships among these characters; in fact the only way we can understand their stories is through these relationships. A reflection of the way they live, their kinship networks, like nothing else in their lives, are dependable, lasting, and necessary for their survival.

In this story, family transcends blood kin. While the final effect of "Just Like a Tree" is of a large extended family, Aunt Fe is related by blood only to Louise. She has no children of her own, no brothers or sisters, no husband. She is "like" a mother to Anne-Marie Duvall and to Leola and Emile; she is a godmother to Adrieu; she is "like" a sister to Aunt Lou. Leola and Emile are so close to Aunt Fe they have to be reminded that they are not blood kin.

What constitutes family in Gaines' view is not necessarily blood kinship. These familial relationships are nourished and sustained by the accumulation of thousands of daily acts of support and care. Count the days in the year, Leola says, and that number would be close to the number of times she has washed, ironed and cooked for Aunt Fe. Aunt Fe and Emmanuel have eaten together, fished together, walked to church together. And the stories Aunt Fe has passed on to Emmanuel about his great-grandpa become the fuel for the fire of his political passion.

"A Long Day in November," also set in rural Louisiana where Gaines grew up, depicts the strong influence of family and community on the younger generation. Eddie Jr. (called Sonny) urinates on himself in class and is unable to learn his lessons because of the conflict between his mother (Amy) and his father (Eddie Sr.). In this story, community constantly interacts with the family—from the men who offer Eddie Sr. their definitions of manhood to the minister and the conjure woman whom Eddie consults for advice. While the traditionally conservative suggestions of the minister, who does not challenge the community to change, are ineffectual in Eddie's present situation, the conjure woman, whose profession "lacks social responsibility and official institutional affiliation,"[1] offers advice that is psychologically astute as well as effective. The fact that Madame Toussaint makes Eddie burn his car, that traditional symbol of masculinity, in front of the entire community again demonstrates that family exists always as part of a communal network, what Salvador Minuchin calls the kaleidoscopic nature of our lives: the self, he says, is like a chip in a kaleidoscope, always part of patterns that are larger than ourselves and somehow more than the sum of their parts.[2]

Because James and his mother, Octavia, in "The Sky Is Gray" are so much more isolated from community, the struggles of the eight-year-old James to understand himself and his mother seem more desperate. James is threatened not just by poverty and racism but by the stultifying effect of his mother's stern and emotionless silence. That he is ambivalent toward his mother is reflected in his desperation to understand and accept her. That ambivalence is also enacted in the structure of his first-person narrative. His story is literally an outpouring of words to counteract his mother's silence and her distance. The two figures James identifies with are his brother Ty and the student in the dentist's office, both of whom are associated with words, Ty as a teller of stories and jokes, and the student as one who is immersed in studying texts: "When I grow up," James thinks, "I want be just like him. I want clothes like that and I want keep a book with me, too." Even when he tries to convey that he understands the reasons for his mother's strictness, James is merely mouthing what he has heard older people say: "Suppose she had to go away like Daddy went away? Then who was go'n look after us? They had to be somebody left to carry on." James can repeat these words given to him by adults, but we know that he does not believe them because he is fully capable of giving verbal expression to his own thoughts.

Unlike the younger and more protected Sonny, whose story takes place entirely within the rural black community, James' story includes the bus ride where blacks are forced to sit in the back of the bus, the segregated stores and cafés of Bayonne, a courthouse on which a Confederate flag is waving. Moreover, James' daddy is absent, drafted for the Army (perhaps the Korean War), leaving his mother as sole support of the family. James knows how desperate a situation they are in when three dollars has to cover the bus trip, dental fees and dinner. There is tremendous respect for and pride in Octavia's ability to negotiate a world in which she is poor, black, female—and a single parent. Surely her mute sternness reflects her own anger over her vulnerability. But in spite of his pride in and respect for his mother, James structures his narrative in opposition to her, ending it with the story of the white couple whose affection and generosity are accompanied by a constant stream of words between them as, together, they try to figure a way to rescue the boy and his mother. As is typical in much of Gaines' work, the final scene of the couple sharing their home and food with mother and son is a communal one, as though James' repertoire of words has triumphed over the isolation imposed by his mother.

Gaines represents the family as a series of concentric circles, a network of kin that includes neighbors and friends as well as relatives. That network also connects the generations. As Aunt Fe symbolically blesses Emmanuel, nodding her head in assent to his story and his political work; as Eddie and Amy "carry" Eddie Jr. over his school lessons; as Octavia makes James pull down his collar so he will not look like a bum—they are all enacting that crucial sign of kinship, passing on to the next generation the signs and symbols that enable their continued growth.

1. John W. Roberts, "The Individual and the Community in Two Short Stories by Ernest J. Gaines," *Black American Literature Forum* (Fall 1984); 111.

2. Salvador Minuchin, *Family Kaleidoscope* (Cambridge: Harvard University Press, 1984), p. 3.

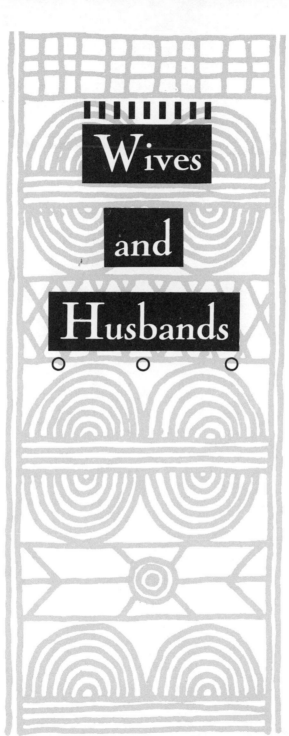

Wives and Husbands

The Wedding

JUNE JORDAN

Tyrone married her this afternoon
not smiling as he took the aisle
and her slightly rough hand.
Dizzella listened to the minister
staring at his wrist and twice
forgetting her name:
Do you promise to obey?
Will you honor humility and love
as poor as you are?
Tyrone stood small but next
to her person
trembling. Tyrone stood
straight and bony
black alone with one key
in his pocket.
By marrying today
they made themselves a man
and woman
answered friends or unknown
curious about the Cadillacs
displayed in front of Beaulah Baptist.
Beaulah Baptist
life in general
indifferent
barely known

nor caring to consider
the earlywed Tyrone
and his Dizzella
brave enough
but only two.

The Poker Party

WILLIAM MELVIN KELLEY

As I remember them, late-summer Saturdays were always hot, dry, and colored a deep green. I know now some Saturdays must have been gray; rain must have made water princesses dance in gutter puddles, as my grandmother assured me they did, each time a drop plunked down. But I will never really believe it rained on Saturdays, for I can remember only the sun playing with bits of broken glass in the vacant lot next to my house and myself running all day up and down the block like a heathen.

I never watched the sun when it was overhead dragging the day after it. I saw it twice each day: in the morning outside the kitchen window, up the hill and behind the elevated subway, so close to the pillars they seemed crisp and flimsy like burnt match sticks, and later when it had hopped to the other side of the sky, and, as big as a saucer and the color of orange sherbet, it slid behind the stiff old monuments in Woodlawn Cemetery. I should have watched it glide overhead, for surely that was the way Indians told time, and I was an Indian most Saturdays. But then I was not concerned with time, for time was the ticking of watches and clocks and had nothing to do with the length of a day.

When the sun was gone and car windshields reflected the sky and became pale blue, it would be dinner time. I would run to my house, prance up the porch steps, press the black button below the small window of thick glass through which I could see my father's name—*Thomas Carey*—and soon would come the buzz, somehow sweet, of my mother's answer on the second floor.

My mother always came to meet me. She knew it was I, for no one else pushed the bell so hard—grownups were usually not so urgent, would thumb once lightly, stand and wait, tumbling hats in their hands. I would climb the stairs, and even before I had gained half of them, she would appear at the landing. She would wait, and as I hopped level with her, would touch my cheek or run her hand over my forehead, and if she found sweat, would march me to the bathroom and swab my face with a clean-smelling washcloth.

Some Saturday nights, the Poker Party was at my house. I would not be awake (bedtime was much earlier than the beginning of the party), but I would know it was at my house, because my mother would boil and cut potatoes for salad and buy olives, and my father would come home those nights with five new decks of cards in cellophane as smooth as ice. I did not like the Poker Parties. They lasted very late, almost until I woke on Sunday morning, and my father would sleep all day and would not take me to the park like other fathers.

My father was a tall, very thin Negro man. The bald skin on his head seemed also thin, for it was stretched until it shone brightly. He wore a white shirt to wherever he went in the daytime, and it was clean when he came home at night, except for the collar where oil from his neck gathered dust. His nose was round with tiny pockmarks in it; his eyes were red, shallow, and sad. He had once been even darker than I (I had seen pictures of him in a floppy bow tie and baggy knickerbockers), the color of chocolate drink, but working indoors had diluted his skin until it was the same shade as my own, perhaps even as light as my mother's. She was small and very Cuban, being half that race, and her hair was black, straight, and soft as smoke. Her nose was sharp, her lips thin, her eyes deep-set and brown. At dinner she sat on my left, my father on my right.

"Is everything ready?" he asked after he had swallowed.

"Yes." She did not look up.

"I told the fellows to come at ten—after he was asleep." He was speaking of me. "Will you have everything ready by then?" He seemed very excited and anxious.

My mother looked at him squarely, then glanced quickly at me. "I told you I had everything ready." We finished eating in silence, even me, although I liked to talk a great deal.

When dinner was over, I squatted on a small stool beside the radio. It was far bigger than I, bigger even than it had to be. It was mostly speaker in an ornate cabinet as large as a refrigerator. I listened until night pressed gently against the windows. Then it was time for me to go to bed. I crawled between sheets which had been warm that morning, but were now cold and unfamiliar. My mother sat with me and helped me say the prayers I could hardly understand, the words being too long, and the black outline of my father watched us from the doorway. They both kissed me, and I nestled down with my head under the covers. I pretended I was in the cockpit of a plane carrying bombs to Burma, fighting the Japanese, who, being nearly the same color as I, seemed, no matter how I tried, as much my friends as my enemies. And there, flying somewhere over Burma, I raced my plane straight to its destination, to unload my bombs, but never reached that destination, for sleep always rushed toward me faster than I, dawdling at my games, sped to my target, and swept me into a tailspin where my games ended and my dreams began.

I blinked and was awake. The soft street lamp printed dark shadows on the walls of my room. I lay in bed, sleep stinging the corners of my eyes, and then came the low grumblings of joking men.

I had not heard the men come, had not heard them press the bell—much the same as I would have, without searching for the button, knowing where it was as well as I—had not heard them climb the stairs in shining heavy shoes, or the loud friendly greetings, or my father say, as I am sure he had, "Quiet, the boy's asleep," or the men tiptoe past my door to the back of the house and the kitchen. But now I was awake, the darkness soft and as close around me as my one soft blanket. I was afraid; each shape was a man in a long coat coming with a silver knife to slice my neck.

Faintly above the rumble of their talk, I heard the sound of the chips my father never let me touch (they were plaster and easily broken) thudding on the kitchen table. I climbed from between my sheets and opened the door.

The long narrow hall was dark, the walls straight on either side of me, moving up into a blackness so thick I was not certain there was a ceiling to stop them. I shuffled toward the kitchen, the hard wood floor warm beneath my bare feet. Ahead was the doorway, a tall rectangle of smoky yellow light. I could hear the men's words now but did not know what they meant. As I crept closer, I smelled something burning, not as if my mother had left food on the stove too long, not the rich smoke of fish or bacon, but more like the musty and ancient odor of dust in a cellar.

I stood in the doorway and watched them play a long while before they noticed me. My eyes smarted from the smoke, but still I recognized everyone at the table; I knew them all. My father sat with his back to me, his shoulders slightly hunched. Even from behind I knew that his eyes would be narrow, that he was annoyed. On his left was my mother's brother, whose last name was Cortés, and was therefore named Hernando after the *conquistador*. He was half Cuban like my mother, but not as dark as most Cubans. His face was kind and handsome; his hair was black and shiny. And then came Mister Bixby, small, as bald as my father, his remaining hair plastered to his scalp. A cigar blacker even than himself poked out between yellow teeth and parted pink lips. Heavy steel spectacles weighed on his nose and bent his ears forward. Next was my Aunt Petunia, Uncle Hernando's wife, who was West Indian and did not believe in combing her hair or in false teeth. I did not like her very much, because when she came to our house in the daytime, she always said, "Why don't you run along, child."

My mother sat next to her, clutching her cards almost des-

perately to her chest, looking very sleepy and as though she
was not enjoying herself. Between her and my father was the
table which I used on rainy days to cut pictures from magazines,
filled now with liquor bottles.

Tossing her cards on the table, my mother looked up and
saw me, and turned to my father. "We have a visitor." He had
just slid two chips onto the table. He half turned, holding his
cards close to him just below his chin, and looked at me, as did
everybody else.

They all seemed surprised, even fugitive, as if they had been
caught at something they were not supposed to be doing. My
mother threw open her arms. "Come here." I ran to her, and she
hoisted me into her lap, my back to her chest. "I'll put him to
bed, Carey." My mother, and everyone else, called my father
by his surname.

"You can't go until the hand's played out. And besides, he's
up and probably hungry and might as well stay and watch. What
say, son, you want to watch?"

I nodded, Yes. I had seen older boys playing cards in the
corner of the schoolyard, had heard the ringing of their money
on the pavement, but now, as I looked at the table covered with
green felt softer even than my blanket, I was certain of two
things: the chips were more valuable than money, and that I
wanted to stay.

My mother did not dispute my father, although I am sure she
did not want me up. She wrapped her arms around me tightly
and asked if I was cold. I shook my head, not knowing whether
I was cold or not, too interested in watching the chips that were
being thrown by my father, Mister Bixby, and by my uncle, who
had more chips stacked in front of him than did anyone else.

My father clicked his tongue and spread out his cards. Mister
Bixby, smiling so broadly his cigar jounced ashes down the front
of his white shirt, scooped the chips from the middle of the
table with one dark hand as my mother might have gathered
red beans into her apron.

"Say hello to everyone," my mother ordered quietly. Everyone smiled at me, and Aunt Petunia moved her lips and said something which I did not hear, for I was still watching Mister Bixby smile as he arranged his chips so high in front of him it seemed he might disappear behind them.

"How the child doing, Pablina?" my aunt fairly shouted. She would have known had she not always shooed me along when she visited.

"He's been doing fine. Haven't you?" My mother tickled my stomach so I was forced to giggle a reply.

My father, who had hardly any chips, was irritated as if I had done something bad, and without looking at me asked, "Who's dealing this hand?"

"Me." Uncle Hernando took the cards into his hands.

"I'm out. I might as well let Carey lose for both of us." My mother squeezed me and kissed my ear warmly. The others laughed except my father; Mister Bixby laughed the loudest.

My father waited for them to stop. "*That* is not very funny, Pablina."

Uncle Hernando winked at me and shuffled the cards, then began to throw them in front of everyone except my mother.

"Misdeal." My father clenched his fists. "You didn't cut them."

They all looked at my father acidly and threw the cards back to Uncle Hernando, who took them up and burred them again, then planted them in front of my father as forcefully as he might have squashed a scampering bug. My father cut them; the deck looked the same to me. Uncle Hernando dealt them, some face down, others face up, and I saw the red and black figures, the numbers, and the beautiful pictures. I watched him closely, watched the cards sliding and popping from his fingers as if they were being made within his fingers themselves. He seemed to love the cards even more than the pile of chips in front of him (he never counted the chips) and enjoyed even more than the cards the gasps and sighs each card forced from the players.

Once the cards had been dealt, no one spoke. All I heard was the men blowing smoke heavily from beneath their business

shirts, Aunt Petunia whistling through the gaps in her teeth, and
the thud of the chips on the blanketed table. My father's face
was motionless, as if he had been photographed when bored.

Uncle Hernando began to snap the cards once more and spin
them across the table. Soon he and Mister Bixby turned theirs
over and sat back in their chairs. Only Aunt Petunia and my
father were playing. I hoped very much he would win and stared
at him, seeing small jewels of sweat slowly appearing on his
forehead and running over his brows until he pulled a handkerchief from his back pocket and wiped them away.

"You ready to stop, Carey? I know I got you beat." My aunt
spoke with such certainty I thought she must be telling the truth,
and fully expected my father to admit defeat, but instead, a
slight smile crossed his face.

"I'll just call you, madam." He tossed two more chips onto
the table.

One by one, tantalizingly, she flipped over her cards: a red
three, two jacks, and two queens, one red, one black.

My father grinned broadly and turned his cards over so we
could see his three tens, a two, and a five. The men around the
table gasped, then chuckled, drawing smoke deep into their
lungs. My father laughed triumphantly, scraped in his chips,
spread his arms wide, and bent slightly toward me. I took the
two steps between us and hopped into his lap. "You brought me
luck, offspring." The way he said it made me believe I really
had.

He looked over my head at my mother. "Since you're not
doing anything but heckling, why don't you get us some food."

She stood, nodded slightly, went to the refrigerator, and
pulled out potato salad and cold cuts on huge frosted platters.

"Want to keep playing?" Mister Bixby had gathered the cards
and was shuffling them loudly. His voice sounded like small-
grained sandpaper on hard wood.

My father nodded, as did the rest, and Mister Bixby began
to deal.

"Mis*deal!*" My father leaned over me impatiently. I had expected him to say this, and I looked at Mister Bixby and wondered how silly he must be to forget the ritual of the game.

"Man!" Uncle Hernando shook his head. "Let's play and forget it this time. We ain't on no river boat."

"Sure. Come on. Let's play." Mister Bixby continued to deal.

My father said nothing, but I could feel his body becoming stiff behind me. He had always told me to follow the rules. I knew he must have been disappointed with his friends.

Mister Bixby kept flipping cards onto the table. I counted four to each player. Then he turned over a card in the center. "This game, my friends, is 'Spit in the Ocean.'"

My father reached around me and gathered his cards, pulled them just to my eye level, and made a small fan of them. His hands in front of me seemed my own; his arms seemed attached to my shoulders. I could see the cards very plainly. He had two queens. The card on the table was a queen too, and I turned slightly on his lap and pointed at it. "Look."

He put his hand over my mouth and bent to me. "Now be quiet. You want me to lose?"

I was silent, thinking perhaps I had already made him lose, and looked around the table. Mister Bixby was grinning at me. I knew then I had made a mistake and that my father *would lose*. I wished I would never be able to talk again.

I squirmed and looked over my father's shoulder. My mother was by the sink spooning potato salad onto plates. She smiled at me warmly, as if to forgive me, as if she knew I meant no harm, and then turned back to her work.

Now chips almost buried the card on the table. Aunt Petunia was no longer playing. And then Uncle Hernando spun his cards down and stared at them. "Too rich for my blood."

"All right, Bix, I'll raise you." My father's voice rumbled and shook me.

"You wants to drop out now, Carey?" Mister Bixby was talking to my father, but smiling at me—as if we were great friends! "Well then, I'll just call you." He tossed three chips onto the middle of the table. My father spread out his hand, as did Mister

Bixby, whose cards all had the same kind of markings and were in order, an eight, a nine, a ten, and a jack. I watched him rake in all the chips and snort a laugh. Then he looked at me. "Thanks, little man."

I turned away.

"Now I know why you didn't want to redeal." I could feel my father's body stiffen again; a warm fear shot over me.

Everybody stopped and looked at my father, and it seemed they were looking at me too. Their faces were alike, as humorless as if they were relatives at a funeral, and as accusing as my father's must have been.

"Come on, Carey," nagged my Uncle Hernando good-naturedly.

"That ain't funny at all," scolded Aunt Petunia, who had been collecting the cards.

My father grew even more rigid and grabbed my shoulders so tightly they hurt. "I simply said it was a misdeal. We all lost. Figure it out."

I twisted to face him. "But it was my fault. I made you lose," I blurted foolishly.

For an instant I did not know if he had heard me, and then I was certain he had, for he pushed me off his lap and turned to my mother. "Put him to bed where he belongs!" His voice was louder than it had to be.

He shoved me away from him and I stumbled backwards, always facing the table, and finally my mother was behind me, her hands light on my shoulders. "Shhhh, don't cry. It wasn't your fault." It was then I realized I was tasting salt.

I paid no attention to that, watched my father with his back to me, his neck red above his stiff collar. "It was a misdeal. We should have stopped." *But it was my fault*, I yelled to myself, too afraid to utter it aloud.

"Maaaan, you saying I cheated." Mister Bixby seemed almost to be pleading. "That ain't right."

My father breathed deeply. "I did not say you cheated. I just said we should have stopped after the misdeal."

Uncle Hernando leaned over and touched my father's arm. "Why don't you just forget it, Carey?" Before he had finished, my father pulled away.

"You may be rich enough to forget about nine dollars." His voice cracked and rose higher than normal. "But I can't."

"You want your money back?" chided Mister Bixby.

"No!" my father shouted. "I'm no poor sport. I just said it was a misdeal."

"Well then, don't yell."

"This is my house and I'll yell if I want to."

"Okay, but you know damn well I didn't cheat."

"I don't know anything of the kind. And *watch* your language in front of the boy."

Both men stood slowly, as if by the same unheard signal, and glared at each other across the table. Uncle Hernando stood too. "Come on, you guys. Sit down and forget it."

"You stay out of this," snapped my father; my aunt too began very slowly to get up, her empty mouth open.

"You've seen enough." My mother's hands tightened on my shoulders and navigated me in a circle so we both headed down the hall to my room. "Now don't you act like a child too. Don't you cry." But I was not thinking of tears, was not crying now because I felt I had made my father lose the game or the nine dollars, but because for the first time in my life I was afraid of grownups. I had never *seen* them argue; perhaps I had heard my father's voice raised to my mother, or hers to him, their voices seeping through my door at night, but I had never seen it, or the anger in their eyes, or their bodies bent and stiff like dogs fighting and snarling in the street. And even as my mother lifted me into bed and I felt the sheets cold against my feet, and her hands through the mattress tucking me tightly, I heard my father arguing with Mister Bixby.

She sat with me until I stopped crying. Then she kissed me and went out, closing the door behind her.

I listened intently as the guests gathered their coats from my parents' bed, then filed down the hall, one by one, without speaking, heard my mother undress, cross the tile in the bath-room, and the water travel explosively through the walls, and in the bedroom again, my mother climb into bed. After that the house was silent and dark, except for the light in the kitchen which crept up the hall and under my door. I knew then my father was still sitting, alone now, at the kitchen table.

COMMENTARY ON
WILLIAM MELVIN KELLEY
The Poker Party

Born in 1937, William Melvin Kelley grew up in New York, in an Italian-American neighborhood in the Bronx where his family were the only blacks. He attended an exclusive private school in New York, the Fieldston School, and went from there to Harvard University where he spent three and a half years, failing in all his courses except his fiction course. At Harvard he studied prose fiction first with John Hawkes and then with Archibald MacLeish, and gave up his plans to become a lawyer in order to devote full time to writing. He won Harvard's Dana Reed Literary Prize, which helped him to complete his first novel. He graduated from Harvard in 1959.

Kelley began publishing his fiction in the late 1950s. His first novel, *A Different Drummer*, published by Doubleday in 1962 and reissued in 1990, is the story of a sudden mass exodus of blacks from a small southern town and the disastrous effects their leav-ing has on the whites and blacks who remain behind. There is a strong sense of racial anger and racial awareness in *A Different Drummer*, as Tucker Caliban, the hero of the novel, destroys his own farm and livestock, which represent decades of drudgery for himself and his ancestors. Tucker's act of self-emancipation forces the whites in that town to come to terms with the eco-nomic hardships of losing a vast pool of black labor.

In comparison to *A Different Drummer*, which was published

after "The Poker Party," race seems almost incidental to this story, with the only direct racial references being the boy's descriptions of his relatives. He describes his father as a "tall, very thin Negro," his mother as "small and very Cuban, being half that race," his uncle as "half Cuban like my mother, but not as dark as most Cubans," and his aunt as West Indian. In his introduction to *Dancers on the Shore* (1964), the collection of stories from which "The Poker Party" is taken, critic Mel Watkins says Kelley's "non-racial" stories are part of the period of idealism before the rebellious resistance of the late sixties and seventies, a period when 'the American Dream' of assimilation, the 'melting pot' syndrome, still had high priority for the majority of American blacks." Unlike the stories of childhood by black writers that precede Kelley's—Richard Wright's "Big Boy Leaves Home" (1936) and *Black Boy* (1945) or James Baldwin's *Go Tell It on the Mountain* (1953)—the threat to childhood innocence in this story is neither poverty nor racism. The ornate, oversized radio, the warm hardwood floors, the sense of an abundance of food, the considerable attention lavished on the young protagonist suggest comfortable economic circumstances that John Grimes and Richard Wright could never have known. Kelley's story, appearing just two years after Paule Marshall's *Brown Girl, Brownstones* (1959) is much closer in emotional tone to that novel, to its young protagonist, Selina Boyce, whose experience of family conflict is the result of the clash of wills between her mother and father rather than economic hardship.

The focus of "The Poker Party" is the awakening of the young boy's sensibility as he becomes aware of a threatening adult world. Images of threat begin to intrude into the story almost from the very beginning. Bits of broken glass and gray gutter puddles mar the idyllic summer Saturdays of the narrator's youth. His dreams of unloading bombs on people who are "as much my friends as my enemies," his fears of "a man in a long coat coming with a silver knife to slice my neck," and "the black outline of my father" watching him and his mother from the doorway convey a sense of violence and threat.

Kelley's story quite clearly identifies the source of that violence as male power. Even though there are women present at the poker party, it is men who predominate. The boy is aware that "the men" have entered the house, of "the men's words," which he cannot understand, of "the men blowing smoke heavily from beneath their business shirts," of the anger of the three men with its potential to explode into physical violence. Even the father's refusal to call his son by name is a form of distance and coldness that contributes to the boy's fears. We might also trace the threat of violence back to a sign that seems insignificant at first—the father's name on the door of their house, suggesting ownership and domination over everything and everyone within his domain.

Roselily

A L I C E   W A L K E R

Dearly Beloved,

She dreams; dragging herself across the world. A small girl in her mother's white robe and veil, knee raised waist high through a bowl of quicksand soup. The man who stands beside her is against this standing on the front porch of her house, being married to the sound of cars whizzing by on highway 61.

we are gathered here

Like cotton to be weighed. Her fingers at the last minute busily removing dry leaves and twigs. Aware it is a superficial sweep. She knows he blames Mississippi for the respectful way the men turn their heads up in the yard, the women stand waiting and knowledgeable, their children held from mischief by teachings from the wrong God. He glares beyond them to the occupants of the cars, white faces glued to promises beyond a country wedding, noses thrust forward like dogs on a track. For him they usurp the wedding.

in the sight of God

Yes, open house. That is what country black folks like. She dreams she does not already have three children. A squeeze around the flowers in her hands chokes off three and four and five years of breath. Instantly she is ashamed and frightened in her superstition. She looks for the first time at the preacher, forces humility into her eyes, as if she believes he is, in fact, a man of God. She can imagine God, a small black boy, timidly pulling the preacher's coattail.

to join this man and this woman

She thinks of ropes, chains, handcuffs, his religion. His place of worship. Where she will be required to sit apart with covered head. In Chicago, a word she hears when thinking of smoke, from his description of what a cinder was, which they never had in Panther Burn. She sees hovering over the heads of the clean neighbors in her front yard black specks falling, clinging, from the sky. But in Chicago. Respect, a chance to build. Her children at last from underneath the detrimental wheel. A chance to be on top. What a relief, she thinks. What a vision, a view, from up so high.

in holy matrimony.

Her fourth child she gave away to the child's father who had some money. Certainly a good job. Had gone to Harvard. Was a good man but weak because good language meant so much to him he could not live with Roselily. Could not abide TV in the living room, five beds in three rooms, no Bach except from four to six on Sunday afternoons. No chess at all. She does not forget to worry about her son among his father's people. She wonders if the New England climate will agree with him. If he will ever come down to Mississippi, as his father did, to try to right the country's wrongs. She wonders if he will be stronger than his father. His father cried off and on throughout her pregnancy. Went to skin and bones. Suffered nightmares, retching and falling out of bed. Tried to kill himself. Later told his wife he found the right baby through friends. Vouched for the sterling qualities that would make up his character.

It is not her nature to blame. Still, she is not entirely thankful. She supposes New England, the North, to be quite different from what she knows. It seems right somehow to her that people who move there to live return home completely changed. She thinks of the air, the smoke, the cinders. Imagines cinders big as hailstones; heavy, weighing on the people. Wonders how this pressure finds its way into the veins, roping the springs of laughter.

if there's anybody here that knows a reason why

But of course they know no reason why beyond what they daily have come to know. She thinks of the man who will be her husband, feels shut away from him because of the stiff severity of his plain black suit. His religion. A lifetime of black and white. Of veils. Covered head. It is as if her children are already gone from her. Not dead, but exalted on a pedestal, a stalk that has no roots. She wonders how to make new roots. It is beyond her. She wonders what one does with memories in a brand-new life. This had seemed easy, until she thought of it. "The reasons why . . . the people who" . . . she thinks, and does not wonder where the thought is from.

these two should not be joined

She thinks of her mother, who is dead. Dead, but still her mother. Joined. This is confusing. Of her father. A gray old man who sold wild mink, rabbit, fox skins to Sears, Roebuck. He stands in the yard, like a man waiting for a train. Her young sisters stand behind her in smooth green dresses, with flowers in their hands and hair. They giggle, she feels, at the absurdity of the wedding. They are ready for something new. She thinks the man beside her should marry one of them. She feels old. Yoked. An arm seems to reach out from behind her and snatch her backward. She thinks of cemeteries and the long sleep of grandparents mingling in the dirt. She believes that she believes in ghosts. In the soil giving back what it takes.

together,

In the city. He sees her in a new way. This she knows, and is grateful. But is it new enough? She cannot always be a bride and virgin, wearing robes and veil. Even now her body itches to be free of satin and voile, organdy and lily of the valley. Memories crash against her. Memories of being bare to the sun. She wonders what it will be like. Not to have to go to a job. Not to work in a sewing plant. Not to worry about learning to sew straight seams in workingmen's overalls, jeans, and dress pants. Her place will be in the home, he has said, repeatedly, promising her rest she had prayed for. But now she wonders. When she is rested, what will she do? They will make babies— she thinks practically about her fine brown body, his strong black one. They will be inevitable. Her hands will be full. Full of what? Babies. She is not comforted.

let him speak

She wishes she had asked him to explain more of what he meant. But she was impatient. Impatient to be done with sewing. With doing everything for three children, alone. Impatient to leave the girls she had known since childhood, their children growing up, their husbands hanging around her, already old, seedy. Nothing about them that she wanted, or needed. The fathers of her children driving by, waving, not waving; reminders of times she would just as soon forget. Impatient to see the South Side, where they would live and build and be respectable and respected and free. Her husband would free her. A romantic hush. Proposal. Promises. A new life! Respectable, reclaimed, renewed. Free! In robe and veil.

or forever hold

She does not even know if she loves him. She loves his sobriety. His refusal to sing just because he knows the tune. She loves his pride. His blackness and his gray car. She loves his under-standing of her *condition*. She thinks she loves the effort he will make to redo her into what he truly wants. His love of her makes her completely conscious of how unloved she was before. This is something; though it makes her unbearably sad. Melancholy. She blinks her eyes. Remembers she is finally being married, like other girls. Like other girls, women? Something strains upward behind her eyes. She thinks of the something as a rat trapped, cornered, scurrying to and fro in her head, peering through the windows of her eyes. She wants to live for once. But doesn't know quite what that means. Wonders if she has ever done it. If she ever will. The preacher is odious to her. She wants to strike him out of the way, out of her light, with the back of her hand. It seems to her he has always been standing in front of her, barring her way.

his peace.

The rest she does not hear. She feels a kiss, passionate, rousing, within the general pandemonium. Cars drive up blowing their horns. Firecrackers go off. Dogs come from under the house and begin to yelp and bark. Her husband's hand is like the clasp of an iron gate. People congratulate. Her children press against her. They look with awe and distaste mixed with hope at their new father. He stands curiously apart, in spite of the people crowding about to grasp his free hand. He smiles at them all but his eyes are as if turned inward. He knows they cannot understand that he is not a Christian. He will not explain himself. He feels different, he looks it. The old women thought he was like one of their sons except that he had somehow got away from them. Still a son, not a son. Changed.

She thinks how it will be later in the night in the silvery gray car. How they will spin through the darkness of Mississippi and in the morning be in Chicago, Illinois. She thinks of Lincoln, the president. That is all she knows about the place. She feels ignorant, *wrong*, backward. She presses her worried fingers into his palm. He is standing in front of her. In the crush of well-wishing people, he does not look back.

COMMENTARY ON ALICE WALKER

Roselily

Alice Walker was born in Eatonton, Georgia, in 1944, the last of eight children of southern sharecroppers Minnie Lou and Willie Lee Walker. With the help of scholarships, she attended Spelman College in Atlanta and graduated in 1965 from Sarah Lawrence College in New York.

Besides being a prolific writer of fiction and poetry, Walker is also a teacher. She taught courses on black women writers at Wellesley College, at the University of Massachusetts at Boston and at Brandeis University. In her role as teacher and scholar, Walker has written many powerful essays on black literary figures, among them Jean Toomer, Langston Hughes, Rebecca Jackson, Phillis Wheatley and Zora Neale Hurston. She was one of the earliest scholars of Wheatley to insist on a personal and intimate look at that poetry, to consider how remarkable it was that this sickly and frail, highly gifted girl child, whose body was owned by others and whose psyche was constrained by "contrary instincts," should even attempt to write poetry.

Such personal and intimate attention to black women—both known and unknown—is characteristic of almost all of Walker's writing. In her most famous essay, "In Search of Our Mothers' Gardens," Walker imagines nineteenth- and early twentieth-century black women as both Saints and Artists, "frail whirlwinds," toiling in an age that could only acknowledge them as mules of the world. With extraordinary empathy for these much-ignored women, Walker imagines that many of them were driven to a kind of madness because of this total denial of their talent and creativity:

> Did you have a genius of a great-great grandmother who died under some ignorant and depraved white overseer's lash? Or was she required to bake biscuits for a lazy backwater tramp, when she cried out in her soul to paint watercolors of sunsets, or the rain falling on the green and peaceful pasturelands? Or was her body broken and forced to bear children (who were more often than not sold away from her)—eight, ten, fifteen, twenty children—when her one joy was the thought of modeling heroic figures of rebellion, in stone or clay?[1]

In her first collection of short stories, *In Love and Trouble* (1974), from which the story "Roselily" is taken, Walker is also dealing with the violence done to women, particularly to poor southern black women. Like her later novel, *The Color Purple* (1982), these stories are set in the menacing world of the Jim Crow South, but, unlike *The Color Purple*, the stories in this collection do not have happy endings. From the young mother in "Strong Horse Tea" who cannot get medical attention for her dying child, to the daughter in "The Child Who Favored Daughter" whose father mutilates her for having an affair with a white man, black women in *In Love and Trouble* experience terrible psychological and physical violence, and Walker makes no attempt to soften the effect of that violence.

The subject of "Roselily" is the more subtle kind of violence fostered by political movements that perpetuate a tradition of women's subordination to men. Walker is particularly angry over the hypocrisy of so-called militant movements of the 1960s that preached revolutionary change but insisted on female subservience:

> I used to know men who would tell me "Oh Baby, be an African woman." Then I started to study and find out what they really wanted me to be, and it's great if they mean, be yourself by being an African woman, but if they mean be what the traditional African woman has been, they can have it. Read the novels and see what the traditional African woman's place has been. "My master this, my master that, my master can I do this?"—and she isn't talking about the white man. The same thing is true, as far as I'm concerned, with the Muslims; and that's why "Roselily" is one of my favorite stories. I'm very interested in all their economic programs because I believe firmly that in a place like America unless we own something, we'll never make it. But the minute they start telling me that I have to cover my hair or that women's place is in the home and all that other archaic nonsense, they can really have it. You know I find the arrogance of it incredible.[2]

"Roselily" challenges some of our most cherished myths about family. The ceremony that knits together husband and wife is represented as threatening and stifling. The words "to join this man and this woman" make Roselily think of "ropes, chains, handcuffs." According to her husband's religion, she will be required to cover her head, to go to her husband's world, to take his name, to produce children. She is not comforted by the thought of her hands full of babies nor by his promise of a restful life that will confine her to the home. Though "Roselily" does not have the idyllic ending of *The Color Purple*, it anticipates the novel in several ways. Like Celie, Roselily begins at "the absolute rock-bottom of a woman's economic and sexual enslavement."[3] But in the narrative structure of both stories Walker provides a sense of transformation for both characters. However exploited and humiliated Roselily is, she is aligned with a highly literate narrator who transforms Roselily's thoughts into an explicit critique of the ideologies which oppress her—here, the traditional marriage ceremony. Just as *The Color Purple* is indebted to the nineteenth-century writings of black women, "Roselily" invokes Margaret Walker's 1942 poem, "For My People," which reaffirms the importance of ordinary people like Roselily.[4] The alliance of Roselily, the narrator and the tradition of black women's writing counters Roselily's sealed fate, asserting at least the possibility of overcoming domination.

1. Alice Walker, *In Search of Our Mothers' Gardens: Womanist Prose* (New York: Harcourt Brace Jovanovich, 1983), p. 233.

2. Interview with Mary Helen Washington, June 1972. Jackson, Mississippi.

3. Susan Willis, "Alice Walker's Women" in *Specifying: Black Women Writing the American Experience* (Madison, Wisconsin: University of Wisconsin Press, 1987), p. 118.

4. The lines "The reasons why . . . the people who," which Roselily remembers vaguely but cannot place, are from the fourth stanza of "For My People":

> For the cramped bewildered years we went to school to learn
> to know the reasons why and the answers to and the
> people who and the places where and the days when,
> in memory of the bitter hours when we discovered we
> were black and poor and small and different and
> nobody cared and nobody wondered and nobody
> understood;

The Wife of His Youth

CHARLES CHESNUTT

I

Mr. Ryder was going to give a ball. There were several reasons why this was an opportune time for such an event.

Mr. Ryder might aptly be called the dean of the Blue Veins. The original Blue Veins were a little society of colored persons organized in a certain Northern city shortly after the war. Its purpose was to establish and maintain correct social standards among a people whose social condition presented almost unlimited room for improvement. By accident, combined perhaps with some natural affinity, the society consisted of individuals who were, generally speaking, more white than black. Some envious outsider made the suggestion that no one was eligible for membership who was not white enough to show blue veins. The suggestion was readily adopted by those who were not of the favored few, and since that time the society, though possessing a longer and more pretentious name, had been known far and wide as the "Blue Vein Society," and its members as the "Blue Veins."

The Blue Veins did not allow that any such requirement existed for admission to their circle, but, on the contrary, declared that character and culture were the only things considered; and that if most of their members were light-colored, it was because such persons, as a rule, had had better opportunities to qualify themselves for membership. Opinions differed, too, as to the usefulness of the society. There were those who had been known to assail it violently as a glaring example of the very prejudice from which the colored race had suffered most;

and later, when such critics had succeeded in getting on the
inside, they had been heard to maintain with zeal and earnestness
that the society was a lifeboat, an anchor, a bulwark and a
shield—a pillar of cloud by day and of fire by night, to guide
their people through the social wilderness. Another alleged pre-
requisite for Blue Vein membership was that of free birth; and
while there was really no such requirement, it is doubtless true
that very few of the members would have been unable to meet
it if there had been. If there were one or two of the older
members who had come up from the South and from slavery,
their history presented enough romantic circumstances to rob
their servile origin of its grosser aspects.

While there were no such tests of eligibility, it is true that the
Blue Veins had their notions on these subjects, and that not all of
them were equally liberal in regard to the things they collectively
disclaimed. Mr. Ryder was one of the most conservative. Though
he had not been among the founders of the society, but had come
in some years later, his genius for social leadership was such that
he had speedily become its recognized adviser and head, the cus-
todian of its standards, and the preserver of its traditions. He
shaped its social policy, was active in providing for its entertainment, and when the interest fell off, as it sometimes did, he
fanned the embers until they burst again into a cheerful flame.

There were still other reasons for his popularity. While he
was not as white as some of the Blue Veins, his appearance was
such as to confer distinction upon them. His features were of a
refined type, his hair was almost straight; he was always neatly
dressed; his manners were irreproachable, and his morals above
suspicion. He had come to Groveland a young man, and ob-
taining employment in the office of a railroad company as mes-
senger had in time worked himself up to the position of
stationery clerk, having charge of the distribution of the office
supplies for the whole company. Although the lack of early
training had hindered the orderly development of a naturally
fine mind, it had not prevented him from doing a great deal of
reading or from forming decidedly literary tastes. Poetry was

his passion. He could repeat whole pages of the great English poets; and if his pronunciation was sometimes faulty, his eye, his voice, his gestures, would respond to the changing sentiment with a precision that revealed a poetic soul and disarmed criticism. He was economical, and had saved money; he owned and occupied a very comfortable house on a respectable street. His residence was handsomely furnished, containing among other things a good library, especially rich in poetry, a piano, and some choice engravings. He generally shared his house with some young couple, who looked after his wants and were company for him; for Mr. Ryder was a single man. In the early days of his connection with the Blue Veins he had been regarded as quite a catch, and young ladies and their mothers had maneuvered with much ingenuity to capture him. Not, however, until Mrs. Molly Dixon visited Groveland had any woman ever made him wish to change his condition to that of a married man.

Mrs. Dixon had come to Groveland from Washington in the spring, and before the summer was over she had won Mr. Ryder's heart. She possessed many attractive qualities. She was much younger than he; in fact, he was old enough to have been her father, though no one knew exactly how old he was. She was whiter than he, and better educated. She had moved in the best colored society of the country, at Washington, and had taught in the schools of that city. Such a superior person had been eagerly welcomed to the Blue Vein Society, and had taken a leading part in its activities. Mr. Ryder had at first been attracted by her charms of person, for she was very good-looking and not over twenty-five; then by her refined manners and the vivacity of her wit. Her husband had been a government clerk, and at his death had left a considerable life insurance. She was visiting friends in Groveland, and, finding the town and the people to her liking, had prolonged her stay indefinitely. She had not seemed displeased at Mr. Ryder's attentions, but on the contrary had given him every proper encouragement; indeed, a younger and less cautious man would long since have spoken. But he had made up his mind, and had only to determine the time when he would ask her to be his wife. He decided to give a ball in her honor, and at some time during the evening of the ball to offer her his heart and hand. He had no special fears about the outcome, but, with a little touch of romance, he wanted the surroundings to be in harmony with his own feelings when he should have received the answer he expected.

Mr. Ryder resolved that this ball should mark an epoch in the social history of Groveland. He knew, of course—no one could know better—the entertainments that had taken place in past years, and what must be done to surpass them. His ball must be worthy of the lady in whose honor it was to be given, and must, by the quality of its guests, set an example for the future. He had observed of late a growing liberality, almost a laxity, in social matters, even among members of his own set, and had several times been forced to meet in a social way persons whose complexions and callings in life were hardly up to the standard which he considered proper for the society to maintain. He had a theory of his own.

"I have no race prejudice," he would say, "but we people of mixed blood are ground between the upper and the nether millstone. Our fate lies between absorption by the white race and extinction in the black. The one doesn't want us yet, but may take us in time. The other would welcome us, but it would be for us a backward step. 'With malice towards none, with charity for all,' we must do the best we can for ourselves and those who are to follow us. Self-preservation is the first law of nature."

His ball would serve by its exclusiveness to counteract leveling tendencies, and his marriage with Mrs. Dixon would help to further the upward process of absorption he had been wishing and waiting for.

II

The ball was to take place on Friday night. The house had been put in order, the carpets covered with canvas, the halls and stairs decorated with palms and potted plants; and in the afternoon

Mr. Ryder sat on his front porch, which the shade of a vine running up over a wire netting made a cool and pleasant lounging place. He expected to respond to the toast "The Ladies" at the supper, and from a volume of Tennyson—his favorite poet— was fortifying himself with apt quotations. The volume was open at "A Dream of Fair Women." His eyes fell on these lines, and he read them aloud to judge better of their effect:

> "At length I saw a lady within call,
> Stiller than chisell'd marble, standing there;
> A daughter of the gods, divinely tall,
> And most divinely fair."

He marked the verse, and turning the page read the stanza beginning

> "O sweet pale Margaret,
> O rare pale Margaret."

He weighed the passage a moment, and decided that it would not do. Mrs. Dixon was the palest lady he expected at the ball, and she was of a rather ruddy complexion, and of lively disposition and buxom build. So he ran over the leaves until his eye rested on the description of Queen Guinevere:

> "She seem'd a part of joyous Spring:
> A gown of grass-green silk she wore,
> Buckled with golden clasps before;
> A light-green tuft of plumes she bore
> Closed in a golden ring.
> .   .   .   .   .   .
> "She look'd so lovely, as she sway'd
> The rein with dainty finger-tips,
> A man had given all other bliss,
> And all his worldly worth for this,

> *To waste his whole heart in one kiss*
> *Upon her perfect lips."*

As Mr. Ryder murmured these words audibly, with an appreciative thrill, he heard the latch of his gate click, and a light footfall sounding on the steps. He turned his head, and saw a woman standing before his door.

She was a little woman, not five feet tall, and proportioned to her height. Although she stood erect, and looked around her with very bright and restless eyes, she seemed quite old; for her face was crossed and recrossed with a hundred wrinkles, and around the edges of her bonnet could be seen protruding here and there a tuft of short gray wool. She wore a blue calico gown of ancient cut, a little red shawl fastened around her shoulders with an old-fashioned brass brooch, and a large bonnet profusely ornamented with faded red and yellow artificial flowers. And she was very black—so black that her toothless gums, revealed when she opened her mouth to speak, were not red, but blue. She looked like a bit of the old plantation life, summoned up from the past by the wave of a magician's wand, as the poet's fancy had called into being the gracious shapes of which Mr. Ryder had just been reading.

He rose from his chair and came over to where she stood.

"Good afternoon, madam," he said.

"Good evenin', suh," she answered, ducking suddenly with a quaint curtsy. Her voice was shrill and piping, but softened somewhat by age. "Is dis yere whar Mistuh Ryduh lib, suh?" she asked, looking around her doubtfully, and glancing into the open windows, through which some of the preparations for the evening were visible.

"Yes," he replied, with an air of kindly patronage, unconsciously flattered by her manner, "I am Mr. Ryder. Did you want to see me?"

"Yas, suh, ef I ain't 'sturbin' of you too much."

"Not at all. Have a seat over here behind the vine, where it is cool. What can I do for you?"

" 'Scuse me, suh," she continued, when she had sat down on

the edge of a chair, " 'scuse me, suh, I's lookin' for my husban'. I heerd you wuz a big man an' had libbed heah a long time, an' I 'lowed you wouldn't min' ef I'd come roun' an' ax you ef you'd ever heerd of a merlatter man by de name er Sam Taylor 'quirin' roun' in de chu'ches ermongs' de people fer his wife 'Liza Jane?"

Mr. Ryder seemed to think for a moment.

"There used to be many such cases right after the war," he said, "but it has been so long that I have forgotten them. There are very few now. But tell me your story, and it may refresh my memory."

She sat back farther in her chair so as to be more comfortable, and folded her withered hands in her lap.

"My name's 'Liza," she began, " 'Liza Jane. W'en I wuz young I us'ter b'long ter Marse Bob Smif, down in ole Missoura. I wuz bawn down dere. W'en I wuz a gal I wuz married ter a man named Jim. But Jim died, an' after dat I married a merlatter man named Sam Taylor. Sam wuz freebawn, but his mammy and daddy died, an' de w'ite folks 'prenticed him ter my marster fer ter work fer 'im 'tel he wuz growed up. Sam worked in de fiel', an' I wuz de cook. One day Ma'y Ann, ole miss's maid, came rushin' out ter de kitchen, an' says she, ' 'Liza Jane, ole marse gwine sell yo' Sam down de ribber.'

" 'Go way f'm yere,' says I; 'my husban' 's free!'

" 'Don' make no diff'ence. I heerd ole marse tell ole miss he wuz gwine take yo' Sam 'way wid 'im ter-morrow, fer he needed money, an' he knowed whar he could git a t'ousan' dollars fer Sam an' no questions axed.'

"W'en Sam come home f'm de fiel' dat night, I tole him 'bout ole marse gwine steal 'im, an' Sam run erway. His time wuz mos' up, an' he swo' dat w'en he wuz twenty-one he would come back an' he'p me run erway, er else save up de money ter buy my freedom. An' I know he'd 'a' done it, fer he thought a heap er me, Sam did. But w'en he come back he didn' fin' me, fer I wuzn' dere. Ole marse had heerd dat I warned Sam, so he had me whip' an' sol' down de ribber.

"Den de wah broke out, an' w'en it wuz ober de cullud folks

wuz scattered. I went back ter de ole home; but Sam wuzn' dere, an' I couldn' l'arn nuffin' 'bout 'im. But I knowed he'd be'n dere to look fer me an' hadn' foun' me, an' had gone erway ter hunt fer me.

"I's be'n lookin' fer 'im eber sence," she added simply, as though twenty-five years were but a couple of weeks, "an' I knows he's be'n lookin' fer me. Fer he sot a heap er sto' by me, Sam did, an' I know he's be'n huntin' fer me all dese years—'less'n he's be'n sick er sump'n, so he couldn' work, er out'n his head, so he couldn' 'member his promise. I went back down de ribber, fer I 'lowed he'd gone down dere lookin' fer me. I's be'n ter Noo Orleens, an' Atlanty, an' Charleston, an' Richmon'; an' w'en I'd be'n all ober de Souf I come ter de Norf. Fer I knows I'll fin' 'im some er dese days," she added softly, "er he'll fin' me, an' den we'll bofe be as happy in freedom as we wuz in de ole days befo' de wah." A smile stole over her withered countenance as she paused a moment, and her bright eyes softened into a faraway look.

This was the substance of the old woman's story. She had wandered a little here and there. Mr. Ryder was looking at her curiously when she finished.

"How have you lived all these years?" he asked.

"Cookin', suh. I's a good cook. Does you know anybody w'at needs a good cook, suh? I's stoppin' wid a cullud fam'ly roun' de corner yonder 'tel I kin git a place."

"Do you really expect to find your husband? He may be dead long ago."

She shook her head emphatically. "Oh no, he ain' dead. De signs an' de tokens tells me. I dremp three nights runnin' on'y dis las' week dat I foun' him."

"He may have married another woman. Your slave marriage would not have prevented him, for you never lived with him after the war, and without that your marriage doesn't count."

"Wouldn' make no diff'ence wid Sam. He wouldn' marry no yuther 'ooman 'tel he foun' out 'bout me. I knows it," she added. "Sump'n 's be'n tellin' me all dese years dat I's gwine fin' Sam 'fo' I dies."

"Perhaps he's outgrown you, and climbed up in the world where he wouldn't care to have you find him."

"No, indeed, suh," she replied, "Sam ain' dat kin' er man. He wuz good ter me, Sam wuz, but he wuzn' much good ter nobody e'se, fer he wuz one er de triflin'es' han's on de plantation. I 'spec's ter haf ter suppo't 'im w'en I fin' 'im, fer he nebber would work 'less'n he had ter. But den he wuz free, an' he didn' git no pay fer his work, an' I don' blame 'im much. Mebbe he's done better sence he run erway, but I ain' 'spectin' much."

"You may have passed him on the street a hundred times during the twenty-five years, and not have known him; time works great changes."

She smiled incredulously. "I'd know 'im 'mongs' a hund'ed men. Fer dey wuzn' no yuther merlatter man like my man Sam, an' I couldn' be mistook. I's toted his picture roun' wid me twenty-five years."

"May I see it?" asked Mr. Ryder. "It might help me to remember whether I have seen the original."

As she drew a small parcel from her bosom he saw that it was fastened to a string that went around her neck. Removing several wrappers, she brought to light an old-fashioned daguerreotype in a black case. He looked long and intently at the portrait. It was faded with time, but the features were still distinct, and it was easy to see what manner of man it had represented.

He closed the case, and with a slow movement handed it back to her.

"I don't know of any man in town who goes by that name," he said, "nor have I heard of anyone making such inquiries. But if you will leave me your address, I will give the matter some attention, and if I find out anything I will let you know."

She gave him the number of a house in the neighborhood, and went away, after thanking him warmly.

He wrote the address on the flyleaf of the volume of Tennyson, and, when she had gone, rose to his feet and stood looking after her curiously. As she walked down the street with mincing step, he saw several persons whom she passed turn and look back at her with a smile of kindly amusement. When she had turned the corner, he went upstairs to his bedroom, and stood for a long time before the mirror of his dressing case, gazing thoughtfully at the reflection of his own face.

III

At eight o'clock the ballroom was a blaze of light and the guests had begun to assemble; for there was a literary programme and some routine business of the society to be gone through with before the dancing. A black servant in evening dress waited at the door and directed the guests to the dressing rooms.

The occasion was long memorable among the colored people of the city; not alone for the dress and display, but for the high average of intelligence and culture that distinguished the gathering as a whole. There were a number of schoolteachers, several young doctors, three or four lawyers, some professional singers, an editor, a lieutenant in the United States army spending his furlough in the city, and others in various polite callings; these were colored, though most of them would not have attracted even a casual glance because of any marked difference from white people. Most of the ladies were in evening costume, and dress coats and dancing pumps were the rule among the men. A band of string music, stationed in an alcove behind a row of palms, played popular airs while the guests were gathering.

The dancing began at half past nine. At eleven o'clock supper was served. Mr. Ryder had left the ballroom some little time before the intermission, but reappeared at the supper table. The spread was worthy of the occasion, and the guests did full justice to it. When the coffee had been served, the toastmaster, Mr. Solomon Sadler, rapped for order. He made a brief introductory speech, complimenting host and guests, and then presented in their order the toasts of the evening. They were responded to with a very fair display of after-dinner wit.

"The last toast," said the toastmaster, when he reached the end of the list, "is one which must appeal to us all. There is no one of us of the sterner sex who is not at some time dependent upon woman—in infancy for protection, in manhood for companionship, in old age for care and comforting. Our good host has been trying to live alone, but the fair faces I see around me tonight prove that he too is largely dependent upon the gentler sex for most that makes life worth living—the society and love of friends—and rumor is at fault if he does not soon yield entire subjection to one of them. Mr. Ryder will now respond to the toast—The Ladies."

There was a pensive look in Mr. Ryder's eyes as he took the floor and adjusted his eyeglasses. He began by speaking of woman as the gift of Heaven to man, and after some general observations on the relations of the sexes he said: "But perhaps the quality which most distinguishes woman is her fidelity and devotion to those she loves. History is full of examples, but has recorded none more striking than one which only today came under my notice."

He then related, simply but effectively, the story told by his visitor of the afternoon. He gave it in the same soft dialect, which came readily to his lips, while the company listened attentively and sympathetically. For the story had awakened a responsive thrill in many hearts. There were some present who had seen, and others who had heard their fathers and grandfathers tell, the wrongs and sufferings of this past generation, and all of them still felt, in their darker moments, the shadow hanging over them. Mr. Ryder went on:

"Such devotion and confidence are rare even among women. There are many who would have searched a year, some who would have waited five years, a few who might have hoped ten years; but for twenty-five years this woman has retained her affection for and her faith in a man she has not seen or heard of in all that time.

"She came to me today in the hope that I might be able to help her find this long-lost husband. And when she was gone I gave my fancy rein, and imagined a case I will put to you.

"Suppose that this husband, soon after his escape, had learned that his wife had been sold away, and that such inquiries as he could make brought no information of her whereabouts. Suppose that he was young, and she much older than he; that he was light, and she was black; that their marriage was a slave marriage, and legally binding only if they chose to make it so after the war. Suppose, too, that he made his way to the North, as some of us have done, and there, where he had larger opportunities, had improved them, and had in the course of all these years grown to be as different from the ignorant boy who ran away from fear of slavery as the day is from the night. Suppose, even, that he had qualified himself, by industry, by thrift, and by study, to win the friendship and be considered worthy the society of such people as these I see around me tonight, gracing my board and filling my heart with gladness; for I am old enough to remember the day when such a gathering would not have been possible in this land. Suppose, too, that, as the years went by, this man's memory of the past grew more and more indistinct, until at last it was rarely, except in his dreams, that any image of this bygone period rose before his mind. And then suppose that accident should bring to his knowledge the fact that the wife of his youth, the wife he had left behind him—not one who had walked by his side and kept pace with him in his upward struggle, but one upon whom advancing years and a laborious life had set their mark—was alive and seeking him, but that he was absolutely safe from recognition or discovery, unless he chose to reveal himself. My friends, what would the man do? I will presume that he was one who loved honor, and tried to deal justly with all men. I will even carry the case further, and suppose that perhaps he had set his heart upon another, whom he had hoped to call his own. What would he do, or rather what ought he to do, in such a crisis of a life-time?

"It seemed to me that he might hesitate, and I imagined that I was an old friend, a near friend, and that he had come to me for advice; and I argued the case with him. I tried to discuss it impartially. After we had looked upon the matter from every point of view, I said to him, in words that we all know:

> *'This above all: to thine own self be true,*
> *And it must follow, as the night the day,*
> *Thou canst not then be false to any man.'*

Then, finally, I put the question to him, 'Shall you acknowledge her?'

"And now, ladies and gentlemen, friends and companions, I ask you, what should he have done?"

There was something in Mr. Ryder's voice that stirred the hearts of those who sat around him. It suggested more than mere sympathy with an imaginary situation; it seemed rather in the nature of a personal appeal. It was observed, too, that his look rested more especially upon Mrs. Dixon, with a mingled expression of renunciation and inquiry.

She had listened, with parted lips and streaming eyes. She was the first to speak: "He should have acknowledged her."

"Yes," they all echoed, "he should have acknowledged her."

"My friends and companions," responded Mr. Ryder, "I thank you, one and all. It is the answer I expected, for I knew your hearts."

He turned and walked toward the closed door of an adjoining room, while every eye followed him in wondering curiosity. He came back in a moment, leading by the hand his visitor of the afternoon, who stood startled and trembling at the sudden plunge into this scene of brilliant gaiety. She was neatly dressed in gray, and wore the white cap of an elderly woman.

"Ladies and gentlemen," he said, "this is the woman, and I am the man, whose story I have told you. Permit me to introduce to you the wife of my youth."

Po' Sandy

CHARLES CHESNUTT

On the northeast corner of my vineyard in central North Carolina, and fronting on the Lumberton plank road, there stood a small frame house, of the simplest construction. It was built of pine lumber, and contained but one room, to which one window gave light and one door admission. Its weather-beaten sides revealed a virgin innocence of paint. Against one end of the house, and occupying half its width, there stood a huge brick chimney: the crumbling mortar had left large cracks between the bricks; the bricks themselves had begun to scale off in large flakes, leaving the chimney sprinkled with unsightly blotches. These evidences of decay were but partially concealed by a creeping vine, which extended its slender branches hither and thither in an ambitious but futile attempt to cover the whole chimney. The wooden shutter, which had once protected the unglazed window, had fallen from its hinges, and lay rotting in the rank grass and jimsonweeds beneath. This building, I learned when I bought the place, had been used as a schoolhouse for several years prior to the breaking out of the war, since which time it had remained unoccupied, save when some stray cow or vagrant hog had sought shelter within its walls from the chill rains and nipping winds of winter.

One day my wife requested me to build her a new kitchen. The house erected by us, when we first came to live upon the vineyard, contained a very conveniently arranged kitchen; but for some occult reason my wife wanted a kitchen in the back yard, apart from the dwelling house, after the usual Southern fashion. Of course I had to build it.

To save expense, I decided to tear down the old schoolhouse, and use the lumber, which was in a good state of preservation, in the construction of the new kitchen. Before demolishing the old house, however, I made an estimate of the amount of material contained in it, and found that I would have to buy several hundred feet of lumber additional, in order to build the new kitchen according to my wife's plan.

One morning old Julius McAdoo, our colored coachman, harnessed the gray mare to the rockaway, and drove my wife and me over to the sawmill from which I meant to order the new lumber. We drove down the long lane which led from our house to the plank road; following the plank road for about a mile, we turned into a road running through the forest and across the swamp to the sawmill beyond. Our carriage jolted over the half-rotted corduroy road which traversed the swamp, and then climbed the long hill leading to the sawmill. When we reached the mill, the foreman had gone over to a neighboring farmhouse, probably to smoke or gossip, and we were compelled to await his return before we could transact our business. We remained seated in the carriage, a few rods from the mill, and watched the leisurely movements of the mill hands. We had not waited long before a huge pine log was placed in position, the machinery of the mill was set in motion, and the circular saw began to eat its way through the log, with a loud whir which resounded throughout the vicinity of the mill. The sound rose and fell in a sort of rhythmic cadence, which, heard from where we sat, was not unpleasing, and not loud enough to prevent conversation. When the saw started on its second journey through the log, Julius observed, in a lugubrious tone, and with a perceptible shudder:

"Ugh! but dat des do cuddle my blood!"

"What's the matter, Uncle Julius?" inquired my wife, who is of a very sympathetic turn of mind. "Does the noise affect your nerves?"

"No, Mis' Annie," replied the old man, with emotion, "I ain' narvous; but dat saw, a-cuttin' en grindin' thoo dat stick er timber,

en moanin', en groanin,' en sweekin', kyars my 'memb'ance back
ter ole times, en 'min's me er po' Sandy." The pathetic intonation
with which he lengthened out the "po' Sandy" touched a responsive chord in our own hearts.

"And who was poor Sandy?" asked my wife, who takes a deep
interest in the stories of plantation life which she hears from
the lips of the older colored people. Some of these stories are
quaintly humorous; others wildly extravagant, revealing the Oriental cast of the negro's imagination; while others, poured freely
into the sympathetic ear of a Northern-bred woman, disclose
many a tragic incident of the darker side of slavery.

"Sandy," said Julius, in reply to my wife's question, "was a
nigger w'at useter b'long ter ole Mars Marrabo McSwayne. Mars
Marrabo's place wuz on de yuther side'n de swamp, right nex'
ter yo' place. Sandy wuz a monst'us good nigger, en could do
so many things erbout a plantation, en alluz 'ten' ter his wuk so
well, dat w'en Mars Marrabo's chilluns growed up en married
off, dey all un 'em wanted dey daddy fer ter gin 'em Sandy fer
a weddin' present. But Mars Marrabo knowed de res' wouldn' be
satisfied ef he gin Sandy ter a'er one un 'em; so w'en dey wuz
all done married, he fix it by 'lowin' one er his chilluns ter take
Sandy fer a mont' er so, en den ernudder for a mont' er so, en
so on dat erway tel dey had all had 'im de same lenk er time;
en den dey would all take him roun' ag'in, 'cep'n' oncet in a w'ile
w'en Mars Marrabo would len' 'im ter some er his yuther kinfolks
'roun' de country, w'en dey wuz short er han's; tel bimeby it go
so Sandy didn' hardly knowed whar he wuz gwine ter stay fum
one week's een' ter de yuther.

"One time w'en Sandy wuz lent out ez yushal, a spekilater
come erlong wid a lot er niggers, en Mars Marrabo swap' Sandy's
wife off fer a noo 'oman. W'en Sandy come back, Mars Marrabo
gin 'im a dollar, en 'lowed he wuz monst'us sorry fer ter break
up de fambly, but de spekilater had gin 'im big boot, en times
wuz hard en money skase, en so he wuz bleedst ter make de
trade. Sandy tuk on some 'bout losin' his wife, but he soon seed
dey want no use cryin' ober spilt merlasses; en bein' ez he lacked

de looks er de noo 'oman, he tuk up wid her atter she'd be'n on de plantation a mont' er so.

"Sandy en his noo wife got on mighty well tergedder, en de niggers all 'mence' ter talk about how lovin' dey wuz. W'en Tenie wuz tuk sick oncet, Sandy useter set up all night wid 'er, en den go ter wuk in de mawnin' des lack he had his reg'lar sleep; en Tenie would 'a' done anythin' in de worl' for her Sandy.

"Sandy en Tenie hadn' be'n libbin' tergedder fer mo' d'n two mont's befo' Mars Marrabo's old uncle, w'at libbed down in Robeson County, sent up ter fin' out ef Mars Marrabo couldn' len' 'im er hire 'im a good han' fer a mont' er so. Sandy's marster wuz one er dese yer easy-gwine folks w'at wanter please eve'y-body, en he says yas, he could len' 'im Sandy. En Mars Marrabo tol' Sandy fer ter git ready ter go down ter Robeson nex' day, fer ter stay a mont' er so.

"It wuz monst'us hard on Sandy fer ter take 'im 'way fum Tenie. It wuz so fur down ter Robeson dat he didn' hab no chance er comin' back ter see her tel de time wuz up; he wouldn' 'a' mine comin' ten er fifteen mile at night ter see Tenie, but Mars Marrabo's uncle's plantation wuz mo' d'n forty mile off. Sandy wuz mighty sad en cas' down atter w'at Mars Marrabo tol' 'im, en he says ter Tenie, sezee:

" 'I'm gittin' monst'us ti'ed er dish yer gwine roun' so much. Here I is lent ter Mars Jeems dis mont', en I got ter do so-en-so; en ter Mars Archie de nex' mont', en I got ter do so-en-so; den I got ter go ter Miss Jinnie's: en hit 's Sandy dis en Sandy dat, en Sandy yer en Sandy dere, tel it 'pears ter me I ain' got no home, ner no marster, ner no mistiss, ner no nuffin. I can't eben keep a wife: my yuther ole 'oman wuz sol' away widout my gittin' a chance fer ter tell her good-bye; en now I got ter go off en leab you, Tenie, en I dunno whe'r I'm eber gwine ter see you ag'in er no. I wisht I wuz a tree, er a stump, er a rock, er sump'n w'at could stay on de plantation fer a w'ile.'

"Atter Sandy got thoo talkin', Tenie didn' say naer word, but des sot dere by de fier, studyin' en studyin'. Bimeby she up'n' says:

" 'Sandy, is I eber tol' you I wuz a cunjuh 'oman?'

"Co'se Sandy hadn' nebber dremp' er nuffin lack dat, en he made a great 'miration w'en he hear w'at Tenie say. Bimeby Tenie went on:

" 'I ain' goophered nobody, ner done no cunjuh wuk, fer fifteen year er mo'; en w'en I got religion I made up my mine I wouldn' wuk no mo' goopher. But dey is some things I doan b'lieve it's no sin fer ter do; en ef you doan wanter be sent roun' fum pillar ter pos', en ef you doan wanter go down ter Robeson, I kin fix things so you won't haf ter. Ef you'll des say de word, I kin turn you ter w'ateber you wanter be, en you kin stay right whar you wanter, ez long ez you mineter.'

"Sandy say he doan keer; he's willin' fer ter do anythin' fer ter stay close ter Tenie. Den Tenie ax 'im ef he doan wanter be turnt inter a rabbit.

"Sandy say, 'No, de dogs mought git atter me.'

" 'Shill I turn you ter a wolf?' sez Tenie.

" 'No, eve'ybody's skeered er a wolf, en I doan want nobody ter be skeered er me.'

" 'Shill I turn you ter a mawkin'bird?'

" 'No, a hawk mought ketch me. I wanter be turnt inter sump'n w'at'll stay in one place.'

" 'I kin turn you ter a tree,' sez Tenie. 'You won't hab no mouf ner years, but I kin turn you back oncet in a w'ile, so you kin git sump'n ter eat, en hear w'at 's gwine on.'

"Well, Sandy say dat'll do. En so Tenie tuk 'im down by de aidge er de swamp, not fur fum de quarters, en turnt 'im inter a big pine tree, en sot 'im out 'mongs' some yuther trees. En de nex' mawnin', ez some er de fiel' han's wuz gwine long dere, dey seed a tree w'at dey didn' 'member er habbin' seed befo'; it wuz monst'us quare, en dey wuz bleedst ter 'low dat dey hadn' 'membered right, er e'se one er de saplin's had be'n growin' monst'us fas'.

"W'en Mars Marrabo 'skiver' dat Sandy wuz gone, he 'lowed Sandy had runned away. He got de dogs out, but de las' place dey could track Sandy ter wuz de foot er dat pine tree. En dere

de dogs stood en barked, en bayed, en pawed at de tree, en
tried ter climb up on it; en w'en dey wuz tuk roun' thoo de
swamp ter look fer de scent, dey broke loose en made fer dat
tree ag'in. It wuz de beatenis' thing de w'ite folks eber hearn of,
en Mars Marrabo 'lowed dat Sandy must 'a' clim' up on de tree
en jump' off on a mule er sump'n, en rid fur ernuff fer ter spile
de scent. Mars Marrabo wanted ter 'cuse some er de yuther
niggers er heppin' Sandy off, but dey all 'nied it ter de las'; en
eve'ybody knowed Tenie sot too much sto' by Sandy fer ter he'p
'im run away whar she couldn' nebber see 'im no mo'.

"W'en Sandy had be'n gone long ernuff fer folks ter think he
done got clean away, Tenie useter go down ter de woods at
night en turn 'im back, en den dey'd slip up ter de cabin en set
by de fire en talk. But dey ha' ter be monst'us keerful, er e'se
somebody would 'a' seed 'em, en dat would 'a' spile' de whole
thing; so Tenie alluz turnt Sandy back in de mawnin' early, befo'
anybody wuz a-stirrin'.

"But Sandy didn' git erlong widout his trials en tribberlations.
One day a woodpecker come erlong en 'mence' ter peck at de
tree; en de nex' time Sandy wuz turnt back he had a little roun'
hole in his arm, des lack a sharp stick be'n stuck in it. Atter dat
Tenie sot a sparrer-hawk fer ter watch de tree; en w'en de
woodpecker come erlong nex' mawnin' fer ter finish his nes', he
got gobble' up mos' 'fo' he stuck his bill in de bark.

"Nudder time, Mars Marrabo sent a nigger out in de woods
fer ter chop tuppentime boxes. De man chop a box in dish yer
tree, en hack' de bark up two er th'ee feet, fer ter let de tuppentime run. De nex' time Sandy wuz turnt back he had a big
skyar on his lef' leg, des lack it be'n skunt; en it tuk Tenie nigh
'bout all night fer ter fix a mixtry ter kyo it up. Atter dat, Tenie
sot a hawnet fer ter watch de tree; en w'en de nigger come back
ag'in fer ter cut ernudder box on de yuther side'n de tree, de
hawnet stung 'im so hard dat de ax slip en cut his foot nigh
'bout off.

"W'en Tenie see so many things happenin' ter de tree, she
'cluded she'd ha' ter turn Sandy ter sump'n e'se; en atter studyin'

de matter ober, en talkin' wid Sandy one ebenin', she made up
her mine fer ter fix up a goopher mixtry w'at would turn herse'f
en Sandy ter foxes, er sump'n, so dey could run away en go
some'rs whar dey could be free en lib lack w'ite folks.

"But dey ain' no tellin' w'at's gwine ter happen in dis worl'.
Tenie had got de night sot fer her en Sandy ter run away, w'en
dat ve'y day one er Mars Marrabo's sons rid up ter de big house
in his buggy, en say his wife wuz monst'us sick, en he want his
mammy ter len' 'im a 'oman fer ter nuss his wife. Tenie's mistiss
say sen' Tenie; she wuz a good nuss. Young mars wuz in a
tarrible hurry fer ter git back home. Tenie wuz washin' at de
big house dat day, en her mistiss say she should go right 'long
wid her young marster. Tenie tried ter make some 'scuse fer ter
git away en hide 'tel night, w'en she would have eve'ything fix'
up fer her en Sandy; she say she wanter go ter her cabin fer ter
git her bonnet. Her mistiss say it doan matter 'bout de bonnet;
her head-hankcher wuz good ernuff. Den Tenie say she wanter
git her bes' frock; her mistiss say no, she doan need no mo'
frock, en w'en dat one got dirty she could git a clean one whar
she wuz gwine. So Tenie had ter git in de buggy en go 'long
wid young Mars Dunkin ter his plantation, w'ich wuz mo' d'n
twenty mile away; en dey wa'n't no chance er her seein' Sandy
no mo' 'tel she come back home. De po' gal felt monst'us bad
'bout de way things wuz gwine on, en she knowed Sandy mus'
be a wond'rin' why she didn' come en turn 'im back no mo'.

"W'iles Tenie wuz away nussin' young Mars Dunkin's wife,
Mars Marrabo tuk a notion fer ter buil' 'im a noo kitchen; en
bein' ez he had lots er timber on his place, he begun ter look
'roun' fer a tree ter hab de lumber sawed out'n. En I dunno how
it come to be so, but he happen fer ter hit on de ve'y tree w'at
Sandy wuz turnt inter. Tenie wuz gone, en dey wa'n't nobody
ner nuffin fer ter watch de tree.

"De two men w'at cut de tree down say dey nebber had sech
a time wid a tree befo': dey axes would glansh off, en didn' 'pear
ter make no progress thoo de wood; en of all de creakin', en
shakin', en wobblin' you eber see, dat tree done it w'en it commence' ter fall. It wuz de beatenis' thing!

"W'en dey got de tree all trim' up, dey chain it up ter a timber waggin, en start fer de sawmill. But dey had a hard time gittin' de log dere: fus' dey got stuck in de mud w'en dey wuz gwine crosst de swamp, en it wuz two er th'ee hours befo' dey could git out. W'en dey start' on ag'in, de chain kep' a-comin' loose, en dey had ter keep a-stoppin' en a-stoppin' fer ter hitch de log up ag'in. W'en dey commence' ter climb de hill ter de sawmill, de log broke loose, en roll down de hill en in 'mongs' de trees, en hit tuk nigh 'bout half a day mo' ter git it haul' up ter de sawmill.

"De nex' mawnin' atter de day de tree wuz haul' ter de sawmill, Tenie come home. W'en she got back ter her cabin, de fus' thing she done wuz ter run down ter de woods en see how Sandy wuz gittin' on. W'en she seed de stump standin' dere, wid de sap runnin' out'n it, en de limbs layin' scattered roun', she nigh 'bout went out'n her min'. She run ter her cabin, en got her goopher mixtry, en den follered de track er de timber waggin ter de sawmill. She knowed Sandy could n' lib mo' d'n a minute er so ef she turnt him back, fer he wuz all chop' up so he'd 'a' be'n bleedst ter die. But she wanted ter turn 'im back long ernuff fer ter 'splain ter 'im dat she hadn' went off a-purpose, en lef' 'im ter be chop' down en sawed up. She didn' want Sandy ter die wid no hard feelin's to'ds her.

"De han's at de sawmill had des got de big log on de kerridge, en wuz startin' up de saw, w'en dey seed a 'oman runnin' up de hill, all out er bref, cryin' en gwine on des lack she wuz plumb 'stracted It wuz Tenie; she come right inter de mill, en th'owed herse'f on de log, right in front er de saw, a-hollerin' en cryin' ter her Sandy ter fergib her, en not ter think hard er her, fer it wa'n't no fault er hern. Den Tenie 'membered de tree didn' hab no years, en she wuz gittin' ready fer ter wuk her goopher mixtry so ez ter turn Sandy back, w'en de mill hands kotch holt er her en tied her arms wid a rope, en fasten' her to one er de posts in de sawmill; en den dey started de saw up ag'in, en cut de log up inter bo'ds en scantlin's right befo' her eyes. But it wuz mighty hard wuk; fer of all de sweekin', en moanin', en groanin', dat log done it w'iles de saw wuz a-cuttin' thoo it. De saw wuz one er dese yer ole-timey, up-en-down saws, en hit tuk longer dem days ter saw a log 'en it do now. Dey greased de saw, but dat did n' stop de fuss; hit kep' right on, tel fin'ly dey got de log all sawed up.

"W'en de oberseah w'at run de sawmill come fum breakfas', de han's up en tell him 'bout de crazy 'oman—ez dey s'posed she wuz—w'at had come runnin' in de sawmill, a-hollerin' en gwine on, en tried ter th'ow herse'f befo' de saw. En de oberseah sent two er th'ee er de han's fer ter take Tenie back ter her marster's plantation.

"Tenie 'peared ter be out'n her min' fer a long time, en her marster ha' ter lock her up in de smoke'ouse 'tel she got ober her spells. Mars Marrabo wuz monst'us mad, en hit would 'a' made yo' flesh crawl fer ter hear him cuss, 'caze he say de spekilater w'at he got Tenie fum had fooled 'im by wukkin' a crazy 'oman off on him. W'iles Tenie wuz lock up in de smoke'ouse, Mars Marrabo tuk 'n' haul de lumber fum de sawmill, en put up his noo kitchen.

"W'en Tenie got quiet' down, so she could be 'lowed ter go 'roun' de plantation, she up 'n' tole her marster all erbout Sandy en de pine tree; en w'en Mars Marrabo hearn it, he 'lowed she wuz de wuss 'stracted nigger he eber hearn of. He didn' know w'at ter do wid Tenie: fus' he thought he'd put her in de po'house; but fin'ly, seein' ez she didn' do no harm ter nobody ner nuffin, but des went 'roun' moanin', en groanin', en shakin' her head, he 'cluded ter let her stay on de plantation en nuss de little nigger chilluns w'en dey mammies wuz ter wuk in de cotton fiel'.

"De noo kitchen Mars Marrabo buil' wuz n' much use, fer it had n' be'n put up long befo' de niggers 'mence' ter notice quare things erbout it. Dey could hear sump'n moanin' en groanin' 'bout de kitchen in de nighttime, en w'en de win' would blow dey could hear sump'n a-hollerin' en sweekin' lack it wuz in great pain en sufferin'. En it got so atter a w'ile dat it wuz all Mars Marrabo's wife could do ter git a 'oman ter stay in de kitchen in de daytime long ernuff ter do de cookin'; en dey wa'n't naer nigger on de plantation w'at wouldn' rudder take forty dan ter go 'bout dat kitchen atter dark—dat is, 'cep'n' Tenie; she didn' 'pear ter min' de ha'nts. She useter slip 'roun' at night, en set on de kitchen steps, en lean up agin de do'-jamb, en run on ter herse'f wid some kine er foolishness w'at nobody couldn' make out; fer Mars Marrabo had th'eaten' ter sen' her off'n de plantation ef she say anything ter any er de yuther niggers 'bout de pine tree. But somehow er 'nudder de niggers foun' out all erbout it, en dey all knowed de kitchen wuz ha'nted by Sandy's sperrit. En bimeby hit got so Mars Marrabo's wife herse'f wuz skeered ter go out in de yard atter dark.

"W'en it come ter dat, Mars Marrabo tuk en to' de kitchen down, en use' de lumber fer ter buil' dat ole school'ouse w'at you er talkin' 'bout pullin' down. De school'ouse wuzn' use' 'cep'n' in de daytime, en on dark nights folks gwine 'long de road would hear quare soun's en see quare things. Po' ole Tenie useter go down dere at night, en wander 'roun' de school'ouse; en de niggers all 'lowed she went fer ter talk wid Sandy's sperrit. En one winter mawnin', w'en one er de boys went ter school early fer ter start de fire, w'at should he fin' but po' ole Tenie, layin' on de flo', stiff, en col', en dead. Dere didn' 'pear ter be nuffin pertickler de matter wid her—she had des grieve' herse'f ter def fer her Sandy. Mars Marrabo didn' shed no tears. He thought Tenie wuz crazy, en dey wa'n't no tellin' w'at she mought do nex'; en dey ain' much room in dis worl' fer crazy w'ite folks, let 'lone a crazy nigger.

"Hit wa'n't long atter dat befo' Mars Marrabo sol' a piece er his track er lan' ter Mars Dugal' McAdoo—*my* ole marster—en dat's how de ole school'ouse happen to be on yo' place. W'en de wah broke out, de school stop', en de ole school'ouse be'n stannin' empty ever sence—dat is, 'cep'n' fer de ha'nts. En folks sez dat de ole school'ouse, er any yuther house w'at got any er dat lumber in it w'at wuz sawed out'n de tree w'at Sandy wuz turnt inter, is gwine ter be ha'nted tel de las' piece er plank is rotted en crumble' inter dus'."

Annie had listened to this gruesome narrative with strained attention.

"What a system it was," she exclaimed, when Julius had finished, "under which such things were possible!"

"What things?" I asked, in amazement. "Are you seriously considering the possibility of a man's being turned into a tree?"

"Oh, no," she replied quickly, "not that"; and then she murmured absently, and with a dim look in her fine eyes, "Poor Tenie!"

We ordered the lumber, and returned home. That night, after we had gone to bed, and my wife had to all appearances been sound asleep for half an hour, she startled me out of an incipient doze by exclaiming suddenly,

"John, I don't believe I want my new kitchen built out of the lumber in that old schoolhouse."

"You wouldn't for a moment allow yourself," I replied, with some asperity, "to be influenced by that absurdly impossible yarn which Julius was spinning today?"

"I know the story is absurd," she replied dreamily, "and I am not so silly as to believe it. But I don't think I should ever be able to take any pleasure in that kitchen if it were built out of that lumber. Besides, I think the kitchen would look better and last longer if the lumber were all new."

Of course she had her way. I bought the new lumber, though not without grumbling. A week or two later I was called away from home on business. On my return, after an absence of several days, my wife remarked to me,

"John, there has been a split in the Sandy Run Colored Baptist Church, on the temperance question. About half the members have come out from the main body, and set up for themselves. Uncle Julius is one of the seceders, and he came to me yesterday and asked if they might not hold their meetings in the old schoolhouse for the present."

"I hope you didn't let the old rascal have it," I returned, with some warmth. I had just received a bill for the new lumber I had bought.

"Well," she replied, "I couldn't refuse him the use of the house for so good a purpose."

"And I'll venture to say," I continued, "that you subscribed something toward the support of the new church?"

She did not attempt to deny it.

"What are they going to do about the ghost?" I asked, somewhat curious to know how Julius would get around this obstacle.

"Oh," replied Annie, "Uncle Julius says that ghosts never disturb religious worship, but that if Sandy's spirit *should* happen to stray into meeting by mistake, no doubt the preaching would do it good."

COMMENTARY ON CHARLES CHESNUTT

The Wife of His Youth / Po' Sandy

Though Charles Chesnutt was born in Cleveland, Ohio, in 1858, he spent many of his formative years—from age eight to age twenty-five—in Fayetteville, North Carolina. His family, who were originally from North Carolina, moved back there after the Civil War, hoping that Reconstruction would make the South a more hospitable place for blacks. But as a young man of twenty-five with ambitions to become a writer, Chesnutt returned to Cleveland where he spent nearly all of his adult years, working as a legal stenographer, as a lawyer and later as a writer. Chesnutt's preoccupation with characters of mixed racial ancestry is a reflection of his own background. Light enough to pass for white, he was deeply aware of the prejudice against light-skinned blacks, and he was also very much aware of the dramatic appeal in exploring the psychological, social and racial marginality of a class of people he knew well.

For a while, Chesnutt devoted himself full time to writing, producing two volumes of short stories (*The Wife of His Youth* and *The Conjure Woman*, both published in 1899) and three novels, *The House Behind the Cedars* (1900), *The Marrow of Tradition* (1901) and *The Colonel's Dream* (1905). *The Marrow of Tradition*, which deals forthrightly with issues of racism and violence toward blacks, caused whites a great deal of discomfort, and they rejected it with harsh criticism and low sales. Chesnutt realized that white America at the turn of the century would not accept a strong and honest portrayal of race relations in this country, and after 1905 he ceased to function as a full-time writer.

Published in 1899, "The Wife of His Youth" (from the collection with the same title) is one of the color-line stories. Much about this story seems autobiographical. It is set in Groveland, Chesnutt's pseudonym for Cleveland. Like Mr. Ryder, Chesnutt worked for a time with the railroad company, and he was a member of a social and cultural gathering for better-educated people of color, the Cleveland Social Club. He had also moved away from his black southern past in North Carolina and felt some ambivalence about his own privileged status. Is Chesnutt being ironic in his portrayal of Mr. Ryder and the Blue Vein Society with its elitist values? Or does he, as a middle-class intellectual who was never at home among ordinary black people, share Mr. Ryder's desire for the "upward process of absorption"? Even though Chesnutt is clearly satirizing a group whose "high standards" include maintaining the proper complexion, he also admires (and perhaps identified with) the man who steps forward to acknowledge voluntarily the wife of his youth. The choice for Mr. Ryder is a moral one; perhaps for Chesnutt it was also a literary one; for, like most turn-of-the-century black writers, Chesnutt had to decide on his relationship to the black past—to slavery, to black traditions, to black culture, to black dialect. Though he chose to write about slavery in his conjure stories, Chesnutt always maintained a certain distance from his black heritage. Like Mr. Ryder, he makes the choice to accept that heritage, but the choice is a troubling one, for his heart lies elsewhere.

In spite of Chesnutt's ambiguous relationship to black culture, Liza Jane's twenty-five-year search for her lost husband and her telling of that tale are the powerful center of "The Wife of His Youth." Recent historical studies of slavery have documented that the desperate measures which Liza undertakes to find Sam are part of the history of many black families in this country. In *The Black Family in Slavery and Freedom*, Herbert Gutman examines the extraordinary lengths black men and women went to in order to protect familial bonds. After the Civil War, according to official registration records, they went by the tens of thousands to register their slave marriages and, as one Union soldier observed, "they had an almost universal anxiety . . . to abide by first connections."[1]

The determined and resolute Liza Jane is a sharp contrast to the kind of wife Mr. Ryder has planned for his middle years. Liza is strong, active, articulate, mobile, and she expects to have to support Sam when she finds him. Molly Dixon, by comparison, is depicted almost as a sex object: good-looking, whiter and younger than Ryder, vivacious, charming (to men), and well supported by her late husband's life insurance. Such rigid gender distinctions which insist on women as the weaker sex, as the fair and beautiful sex, as the sex supported by men and upon whom men depend for care and comfort grant women an elevated personal status at the expense of any real social power. It is interesting to see how much more fully dimensional Chesnutt makes his non-elite, usually dialect-speaking women characters. Not only does Liza Jane initiate the encounter with Mr. Ryder, she tells her own tale, she revises the original portrait of Mr. Ryder, and ultimately she revises his story. Molly Dixon is merely the marriage prop in a conventional sentimental romance; Liza Jane gives the story its power.

"Po' Sandy" is taken from Chesnutt's 1899 collection of stories called *The Conjure Woman*, which is set in the mythical city of Patesville, modeled after Chesnutt's boyhood home of Fayetteville, North Carolina. There are two narrators in the conjure stories: the narrator of the frame story is John, a white Northerner come South because of his wife Annie's poor health. The second and more important narrator is Julius McAdoo, who was for many years a slave on the plantation John and Annie now own. Unlike Joel Chandler Harris' Uncle Remus stories, Chesnutt's conjure stories are not mere entertainment for white folks; they are allegories about the brutality and injustice of slavery.

Sandy's separation from his beloved Tenie and her subsequent

efforts to protect him against being "loaned" from one white to
another is no fabrication; it reflects the separations between
husbands and wives and children that were a fact of slave life
and the heroic efforts slaves made to resist being torn apart.
The fact that slavery was a system of abuse and destruction acted
out upon the bodies of men and women makes Sandy's death
as a tree chopped down and carved up to be used as lumber for
his master's kitchen all the more real.

Annie is so disturbed by the implications of this tale that she
cannot use the lumber from the old kitchen. John, on the other
hand, is too rational and superior to consider the deeper, more
emotional and spiritual meanings of the tale, dismissing it as an
"absurdly impossible yarn" and, in effect, aligning himself with
the slaveowners who refuse to acknowledge their own inhu-
manity and their own complicity in maintaining that system.
Sandy and Tenie's egalitarian relationship thus becomes an im-
plicit criticism of John and Annie's marriage. Whereas John sees
himself as superior to the more emotional Annie and separates
himself from her by refusing to be affected by the inherent
power of Julius' tale, Sandy and Tenie who "ain got no home,
ner no master, ner no mistiss, 'ner no nuffin" are portrayed as
equals in every way. Once, when Tenie was sick, Julius explains
that "Sandy useter set up all night wid 'er, en den go ter wuk
in de mawnin' des lack he had his reg'lar sleep; en Tenie would
'a' don anythin' in de worl' for her Sandy." Annie's illness is
something John for all his wealth cannot cure, and, except for
his efforts to provide her with material comforts, he seems totally
disconnected from her suffering. Both "The Wife of His Youth"
and "Po' Sandy" revise our conventional notions of power, as
the apparently powerless characters like Julius, Liza Jane, Tenie
and Sandy reveal personal dignity and courage in the midst of
the most inhumane violations of the human spirit.

1. Herbert Gutman, *The Black Family in Slavery and Freedom, 1750–1925* (New
York: Vintage Books, 1976), p. 21.

Mothers
and
Daughters

Momma

PAULETTE CHILDRESS WHITE

Momma
pale as the Southern secrets
in her blood
was princess of morning.

She rose alone
to apocalyptic silence,
set the sun in our windows
and daily mended the world

through years of never-enough,
hiding her dreams
in a typewriter
rusting beneath the kitchen sink.

In weary dresses
that would not survive the Fifties
she gifted us with memory
and created home.

Black Mother Woman

AUDRE LORDE

I cannot recall you gentle.
Through your heavy love
I have become
an image of your once delicate flesh
split with deceitful longings.
When strangers come and compliment me
your aged spirit takes a bow
jingling with pride
but once you hid that secret
in the center of furies
hanging me
with deep breasts and wiry hair
with your own split flesh and long suffering eyes
buried in myths of no worth.

But I have peeled away your anger
down to its core of love
and look mother
I am
a dark temple where your true spirit rises
beautiful and tough as a chestnut
stanchion against your nightmares of weakness
and if my eyes conceal
a squadron of conflicting rebellions
I learned from you
to define myself
through your denials.

Mother

ANDREA LEE

In the summer my mother got up just after sunrise, so that when she called Matthew and me for breakfast, the house was filled with sounds and smells of her industrious mornings. Odors of frying scrapple or codfish cakes drifted up the back stairs, mingling sometimes with the sharp scent of mustard greens she was cooking for dinner that night. Up the laundry chute from the cellar floated whiffs of steamy air and the churning sound of the washing machine. From the dining room, where she liked to sit ironing and chatting on the telephone, came the fragrance of hot clean clothes and the sound of her voice: cheerful, resonant, reverberating a little weirdly through the high-ceilinged rooms, as if she were sitting happily at the bottom of a well.

My father left early in the morning to visit parishioners or to attend church board meetings. Once the door had closed behind him, the house entered what I thought of as its natural state—that of the place on earth that most purely reflected my mother. It was a big suburban house, handsomer than most, built of fieldstone in a common, vaguely Georgian design; it was set among really magnificent azaleas in a garden whose too-small size gave the house a faintly incongruous look, like a dowager in a short skirt. The house seemed little different from any other in my neighborhood, but to me, in my early-acquired role as a detective, a spy, a snooper into dark corners, there were about it undeniable hints of mystery. The many closets had crooked shapes that suggested secret passages; in the basement, the walls of the wine cellar—its racks filled by our teetotaling family with old galoshes and rusty roller skates—gave a suspicious hollow sound when rapped, and on the front doorbell, almost obliterated by the pressure of many fingers, was printed a small crescent moon.

The house stayed cool on breathless summer days when tar oozed in the streets outside, the heat excluded by thick walls and drawn shades, and the dim rooms animated by a spirit of order and abundance. When I came dawdling down to breakfast, long after Matthew had eaten and gone plunging off on his balloon-tired Schwinn, I usually found my mother busy in the kitchen, perhaps shelling peas, or stringing beans, or peeling a basket of peaches for preserves. She would fix me with her lively, sarcastic dark eyes and say, "Here comes Miss Sarah, the cow's tail. What, pray tell, were you doing all that time upstairs?"

"Getting dressed."

What I'd been doing, in fact—what I did every summer morning—was reading. Lounging voluptuously in my underpants on the cool bare expanse of my bed, while flies banged against the screen and greenish sunlight glowed through the shades, I would read with the kind of ferocious appetite that belongs only to garden shrews, bookish children, and other small creatures who need double their weight in nourishment daily. With impartial gluttony I plunged into fairy tales, adult novels, murder mysteries, poetry, and magazines while my mother moved about downstairs. The sense of her presence, of, even, a sort of tacit complicity, was always a background at these chaotic feasts of the imagination.

"You were reading," Mama would say calmly when I stood before her in the kitchen. "You must learn not to tell obvious lies. Did you make up your bed?"

"I forgot."

"Well, you're not going outside until you've done something to that room of yours. It looks like a hooraw's nest. Your place is set at the table, and the cantaloupe is over there—we've had such delicious cantaloupe this week! Scrape out the seeds and cut yourself a slice. No—wait a minute, come here. I want to show you how to cut up a chicken."

Each time she did this I would wail with disgust, but I had

to watch. The chicken was a pimply yellow-white, with purplish shadows and a cavernous front opening; my mother would set her big knife to it, baring her teeth in an ogress's grin that made fun of my squeamishness. "You saw along the backbone like this—watch carefully; it takes a strong arm—and then you *crack* the whole thing open!"

In her hands the cave would burst apart, exposing its secrets to the light of day, and with another few strokes of the knife would be transformed into ordinary meat, our uncooked dinner.

It was easy for me to think of my mother in connection with caves, with anything in the world, in fact, that was dimly lit and fantastic. Sometimes she would rivet Matthew and me with a tale from her childhood: how, at nine years old, walking home through the cobblestone streets of Philadelphia with a package of ice cream from the drugstore, she had slipped and fallen down a storm drain accidentally left uncovered by workmen. No one was around to help her; she dropped the ice cream she was carrying (something that made a deep impression on my brother and me) and managed to cling to the edge and hoist herself out of the hole. The image of the little girl—who was to become my mother—hanging in perilous darkness was one that haunted me; sometimes it showed up in my dreams.

Perhaps her near-fatal tumble underground was responsible for my mother's lasting attraction to the bizarre side of life. Beneath a sometimes prudish exterior, she quivered with excitement in the same way her children did over newspaper accounts of trunk murders, foreign earthquakes, Siamese twins, Mafia graves in the New Jersey pine barrens. When she commented on these subjects, she attempted a firm neutrality of tone but gave herself away in the heightened pitch of her voice and in a little breathy catch that broke the rhythm of each sentence she spoke. This was the voice she used to whisper shattering bits of gossip over the phone. "When Mr. Tillet died," I heard her say once, with that telltale intake of breath, "the funeral parlor did such a poor job that his daughter had to *wire her own father together!*"

My mother, Grace Renfrew Phillips, had been brought up

with all the fussy little airs and graces of middle-class colored girls born around the time of World War I. There was about her an endearing air of a provincial maiden striving for sophistication, a sweet affectation of culture that reminded me, when I was older, of Emma Bovary. She and her cluster of pretty, light-skinned sisters grew up in a red-brick house with marble steps in South Philadelphia. They all played the piano, knew a bit of French and yards of Wordsworth, and expected to become social workers, elementary-school teachers, or simply good wives to suitable young men from their own background—sober young doctors, clergymen, and postal administrators, not too dark of complexion. Gracie Renfrew fit the pattern, but at the same time dismayed her family by attending Communist Party meetings, joining a theater group, and going off to a Quaker work camp.

When she married my father, the prescribed young minister, my mother had become, inevitably, a schoolteacher—a beautiful one. She was full-faced, full-bodied, with an indestructible olive skin and an extraordinary forehead—high, with two handsome hollows over the temples. She had a bright, perverse gaze, accentuated by a slight squint in her left eye, and a quite unusual physical strength. She swam miles every summer at the swim club, and at the small Quaker school where I was a student and she taught sixth grade, it was common to see her jumping rope with the girls, her large bosom bobbing and a triumphant, rather disdainful smile on her face. Her pupils adored her, probably because her nature held a touch of the barbarism that all children admire: she would quell misbehavior, for instance, by threatening in a soft, convincing voice to pull off the erring student's ears and fry them for supper.

At home Mama was a housekeeper in the grand old style that disdains convenience, worships thrift, and condones extravagance only in the form of massive Sunday dinners, which, like acts of God, leave family members stunned and reeling. Her kitchen, a long, dark, inconvenient room joined to a crooked pantry, was entirely unlike the cheerful kitchens I saw on television, where mothers who looked like June Cleaver unwrapped food done up in cellophane. This kitchen had more the feeling of a workshop, a laboratory in which the imperfect riches of nature were investigated and finally transformed into something near sublimity. The sink and stove were cluttered with works in progress: hot plum jelly dripping into a bowl through cheesecloth; chocolate syrup bubbling in a saucepan; string beans and ham bones hissing in the pressure cooker; cooling rice puddings flavored with almond and vanilla; cooked apples waiting to be forced through a sieve to make applesauce; in a vat, a brownish, aromatic mix for root beer.

The instruments my mother used were a motley assemblage of blackened cast-iron pots, rusty-handled beaters, graters, strainers, and an array of mixing bowls that included the cheapest plastic variety as well as tall, archaic-looking stoneware tubs inherited from my grandmother, who had herself been a legendary cook. Mama guarded these ugly tools with jealous solicitude, suspicious of any new introductions, and she moved in her kitchen with the modest agility of a master craftsman.

Like any genuine passion, her love of food embraced every aspect of the subject. She read cookbooks like novels, and made a businesslike note in her appointment book of the date that Wanamaker's received its yearly shipment of chocolate-covered strawberries. Matthew and I learned from her a sort of culinary history of her side of the family: our grandfather, for instance, always asked for calf brains scrambled with his eggs on weekend mornings before he went out hunting. Grandma Renfrew, a sharp-tongued beauty from North Carolina, loved to drink clabbered milk, and was so insistent about the purity of food that once when Aunt Lily had served her margarine instead of butter, she had refused to eat at Lily's table again for a year. My mother's sole memory of her mother's mother, a Meherrin Indian called Molly, was of the withered dark-faced woman scraping an apple in the corner of the kitchen, and sucking the pulp between her toothless jaws.

Mama took most pleasure in the raw materials that became

meals. She enjoyed the symmetry, the unalterable rules, and also the freaks and vagaries that nature brought to her kitchen. She showed me with equal pleasure the handsome shape of a fish backbone; the little green gallbladder in the middle of a chicken liver; and the double-yolked eggs, the triple cherries, the peculiar worm in a cob of corn. As she enjoyed most the follies, the bizarre twists of human nature and experience, so also she had a particular fondness for the odd organs and connective tissues that others disdained. "Gristle is delectable," she would exclaim as Matthew and I groaned. "The best part of the cow!"

I was a rather lazy and dunderheaded apprentice to my mother. She could be snappish and tyrannical, but I hung around the kitchen anyway, in quest of scrapings of batter, and because I liked to listen to her. She loved words, not, as my father the minister did, for their ceremonial qualities, but with an off-handed playfulness that resulted in a combination of wit and nonsense. In her mischievous brain, the broad country imagery of her Virginia-bred mother mingled with the remains of a la-dylike education that had classical pretensions. When she was annoyed at Matthew and me, we were "pestilential Pestalozzis"; we were also, from time to time, as deaf as adders, as dumb as oysters, as woolly as sheep's backs; we occasionally thrashed around like horses with the colic. At odd moments she addressed recitations to the family cat, whom she disliked; her favorite selections were versions of "O Captain! My Captain!" ("O Cat! my Cat! our fearful trip is done . . .") and Cicero's address to Catiline ("How long, Cat, will you abuse our patience? . . .").

On summer evenings, after the dinner dishes had been washed and as the remains of the iced tea stood growing tepid in the pitcher, my mother, dreamy and disheveled, finally would emerge from the kitchen. "Look at me," she'd murmur, wandering into the living room and patting her hair in the mirror over the piano. "I look like a Wild Man of Borneo."

She would change into a pair of oxfords and take a walk with me, or with a neighbor. At that time of day June bugs hurled themselves against the screens of the house, and my father, covered with mosquito repellent and smoking cigarette after cigarette, sat reading under the maple tree. In the diffuse light after sunset, the shadows around the perfectly ordinary houses up and down the street made the unambitious details of their designs—turrets, round Victorian towers, vague half-timbering—seem for once dramatic. All the backyards of the town seemed to have melted into one darkening common where packs of kids yelled faintly and fought their last battles before bedtime. Cars pulled out of driveways and headed for movie theaters or the shopping centers along the Pike, and the air smelled like honeysuckle and onion grass. When Mama and I walked together, we would wander up and down the long blocks until the streetlights came on.

One evening during the summer that I was six years old, we stopped to visit a neighboring family in which something sad and shocking had happened the previous winter. The father, a district judge named Roland Barber, had driven one gray afternoon to the marshland outside the airport and there had shot himself. Judge Barber, a short, grave, brown-skinned man with a curiously muted voice, had been a member of my father's congregation and had served with him on the board of the NAACP. His suicide, with hints of further-reaching scandal, sent a tremendous shock through the staid circles of my parents' friends, a shock that reached down even into the deep waters that normally insulated Matthew and me from adult life. For a few weeks after the suicide we held long grisly discussions on arcane, even acrobatic ways to do away with oneself.

The house in which Mrs. Barber continued to live with her teenage daughter was little different from our house, or any other in our neighborhood: a brick Colonial with myrtle and ivy planted around it instead of grass, and a long backyard that sloped down to a vegetable garden. I knew the Barbers' yard well, because there was an oak tree near the vegetable garden, with a swing in it that neighborhood kids were allowed to use. On the evening my mother and I came to visit, the daylight was fading, and the windows of the house were dark. It seemed that no one was home, but in the summers in our town, people often waited a long time in the evening before turning on lamps. It occurred to me as we walked up the driveway that the house itself seemed to be in mourning, with its melancholy row of blue spruces by the fence; I gave way, with a feeling that was almost like ecstasy, to a sudden shudder. Mama rubbed my goosepimply arms. "We'll just stay a minute," she said.

My mother was carrying a recipe for peach cobbler. It was intended for Mrs. Barber, a bony woman who had fascinated me even before her husband's death, because she wore a very thick pair of elasticized stockings. However, after we'd knocked and waited for a while, the front door was finally opened by Phyllis, the Barbers' sixteen-year-old daughter. Mama, who had taught Phyllis, sometimes referred to her as "the fair and brainless"; I had seen her plenty of times at the swim club, pretty and somewhat fat-faced, drawing the stares of the men to her plump legs in Bermuda shorts. That night, though it was only about eight o'clock, she opened the door in a light summer bathrobe and peered out at us without turning on the porch lights.

"Hello, Mrs. Phillips. Hi, Sarah," she said in a low, hesitant voice. She came out onto the dark steps as she spoke, and let the screen door bang behind her. She explained that her mother wasn't there, and that she had been taking a shower when the bell rang; she radiated a fresh scent of soap and shampoo. When my mother asked her how she was feeling, she answered in the same hesitant tone, "All right."

I looked at her with a kind of awe. It was the first time I had seen her since I had heard the news about Judge Barber, and the first time I had ever stood right in front of anyone associated with an event that had caused such a convulsion in the adult world. In the light-colored robe, with her wet hair—which normally she wore flipped up at the ends and pulled back with a band, like other high-school girls in the neighborhood— combed back from her forehead, she had a mysterious, imposing look that I never would have suspected of her. I immediately ascribed it—as I was ascribing the ordinary shadow of the summer twilight around the doorway—to the extraordinary thing that had happened to her. Her face seemed indefinably swollen, whether with tears or temper, and she kept her top lip tightly clenched as she talked to my mother. She looked beautiful to me, like a dream or an illustration from a book, and as I stared at her, I felt intensely interested and agitated.

In a few minutes Phyllis went back inside. My mother and I, as we had done many times before, walked quietly up the Barbers' driveway and through the backyard to the swing in the oak tree. Mama stopped to pick a few tomatoes from the overloaded plants in the Barbers' vegetable garden, and I helped her, though my second tomato was a rotten one that squashed in my fingers.

It was completely dark by then. Lightning bugs flashed their cold green semaphores across the backyards of the neighborhood, and a near-tropical din of rasping, creaking, buzzing night insects had broken out in the trees around us. I walked over and sat down in the oak-tree swing, and Mama, pausing occasionally to slap at mosquitoes, gave me a few good pushes, so that I flew high out of the leaves, toward the night sky.

I couldn't see her, but I felt her hands against my back; that was enough. There are moments when the sympathy between mother and child becomes again almost what it was at the very first. At that instant I could discern in my mother, as clearly as if she had told me of it, the same almost romantic agitation that I felt. It was an excitement rooted in her fascination with grotesque anecdotes, but it went beyond that. While my mother pushed me in the swing, it seemed as if we were conducting, without words, a troubling yet oddly exhilarating dialogue about pain and loss.

In a few minutes I dragged my sneakered feet in a patch of dust to stop the swing. The light of a television had gone on inside the Barber house, and I imagined fat, pretty Phyllis Barber carefully rolling her hair on curlers, alone in front of the screen. I grabbed my mother's hand and said, "It's very sad, isn't it?"

"It certainly is," said Mama.

We took a shortcut home, and by the time we got there, it was time for me to scrub my grimy arms and legs and go to bed. Mama went immediately to the refrigerator and got out an uncooked roast of pork, which she stood contemplating as if it were the clue to something. She smelled of sage and dried mustard when she came upstairs to kiss Matthew and me goodnight.

COMMENTARY ON
ANDREA LEE
Mother / New African

Andrea Lee's autobiographical first novel, *Sarah Phillips*, first appeared as a series of short stories in *The New Yorker* in 1983 and 1984. The young protagonist, Sarah Phillips, grows up in a Philadelphia suburb where the neat, tree-lined streets and rambling houses of the elite black families who live there represent the culmination of the dreams of the doctors, ministers and teachers whose own childhoods were more narrowly defined by the row houses of Philadelphia's inner city. Born in 1953, Sarah is the daughter of a Baptist minister and a schoolteacher. By any standards, her childhood is a privileged one. She attends private schools, shops at Saks Fifth Avenue, graduates from Harvard and spends the year after graduation studying French literature in France. So highly protected is her childhood world that the parents of her community build a neighborhood swimming pool so that their children will not have to experience the humiliation of being barred from the whites-only pools.

In spite of her parents' valiant attempts to smooth the paths of her childhood, the issue of racism constantly intrudes, disrupting the polished exterior of Sarah's life: Gypsies come into her neighborhood and make racist remarks; at the fancy prep school where she is enrolled, she accidentally comes across the

bleak and cramped quarters where the black servants are forced
to live; at the summer camp she attends some inner city children
threaten Sarah and her friends. And though she constantly distances herself from black historical events ("the civil rights movement had been unrolling like a dim frieze behind the small
pleasures and defeats of my childhood"), her entire girlhood is
counterpointed by the events of that momentous era between
1957 and 1974: school integrations, bombings and murders in
the South, the northern riots, the 1963 march on Washington.
While her father, a prominent Baptist minister, is active in civil
rights, Sarah is secretly embarrassed to know that he was jailed
in the South for his activities. Lee, herself a product of the upper
middle class, knows well the paradoxes of privilege: that a generation who struggled gallantly for civil rights could produce a
generation of children who would disdain the very rituals that
guaranteed their privileged status.

Like William Melvin Kelley's "The Poker Party," the sense of
abundance in Sarah's world is conveyed through the child's keen
awareness of the richly sensual details of her childhood: the
alluring smell of morning breakfast, the fragrance of hot clean
clothes, the cheerful sound of her mother's voice, the cicadas
singing in the summer night, the smell of smoke from burning
autumn leaves, slippery patent leather shoes and starched eyelet
dresses—all mark the childhood of privilege as well as the development of the imagination of the child whose destiny (as the
author) is to write.

In "Mother" we see Sarah's mother giving her permission to
indulge in these "chaotic feasts of the imagination," and, through
her own example, confirming the daughter's right to an imaginative and artistic life. Sarah's attraction to her mother's love of
words and her pleasure in the bizarre aspects of life remind me
very much of the young Selina Boyce and her relationship to
her mother, Silla, in Paule Marshall's *Brown Girl, Brownstones*
(1959). Selina also is drawn to her mother's kitchen—for its
smells of Barbadian delicacies: "the intestines of the pigs stuffed
with grated sweet potato, beets, animal blood and spices. . . ."

Selina's mother makes her think of words as living things "bestriding the air and charging the room with strong colors." In both these stories it is the mother who provides the daughter the model of a powerful female figure, allowing the daughter to take up the subversive pen. Adrienne Rich says that women writers must find such a maternal figure in order to write, and she says this figure is rarely their mothers. But there are many such mothers in black women's literature. Sarah's mother is a tamer version of the passionate and vengeful Silla Boyce, but she too has had her subversive moments—as a politically progressive young woman drawn to the Communist Party and to the Quakers, and as a kind of artist herself with her fascination for the grotesque and for the perilous edges of life. Her willingness to engage her daughter in the "troubling yet oddly exhilarating dialogue about pain and loss" makes me realize how often the writer-daughter describes herself as her mother's peer, acting as an adult long before she is one. When Silla is angry with Selina (Marshall's *Brown Girl, Brownstones*), she sees in her daughter's face her own rebelliousness and resistance, and she knows her daughter is equal to her own anger. In her memoir, *Generations* (1976) Lucille Clifton tells the story of being sent downtown by her mother to return a ring her mother couldn't pay for because her mother was afraid to go. In some way these womanlike girl children are describing the process by which they become equal to or superior to the mother, preparing to write themselves and their version of their mothers into existence.[1]

In "New African," a second selection from *Sarah Phillips*, the parent again gives the child permission to rebel. By denying his own cultural gifts, Reverend Phillips gives Sarah a "peculiar gift of freedom," which allows her not to be baptized into New African Baptist Church—a choice with larger implications, for it is a sign of her disconnection from the cultural and historical legacy of the black church. No longer linked to the traditions of her parents, Sarah is truly the "new African" of this story. Her voice and perspective belong to a new generation of black writers whose privileges of class may create an entirely new relationship to the black cultural past.

1. Marianne Hirsch argues in *The Mother-Daughter Plot: Narrative, Psychoanalysis, Feminism* (Bloomington: Indiana University Press, 1989) that most mother-daughter stories are told from the point of view of the daughter, that the mother in many novels by women is absent, silent, devalued or repressed. While I think black women writers differ from white writers in their treatment of mother-daughter stories, they still tend to be daughters writing about mothers, and, in speaking for their mothers, they do, to some extent, silence them.

The Circling Hand

JAMAICA KINCAID

During my holidays from school, I was allowed to stay in bed until long after my father had gone to work. He left our house every weekday at the stroke of seven by the Anglican church bell. I would lie in bed awake, and I could hear all the sounds my parents made as they prepared for the day ahead. As my mother made my father his breakfast, my father would shave, using his shaving brush that had an ivory handle and a razor that matched; then he would step outside to the little shed he had built for us as a bathroom, to quickly bathe in water that he had instructed my mother to leave outside overnight in the dew. That way, the water would be very cold, and he believed that cold water strengthened his back. If I had been a boy, I would have gotten the same treatment, but since I was a girl, and on top of that went to school only with other girls, my mother would always add some hot water to my bathwater to take off the chill. On Sunday afternoons, while I was in Sunday

school, my father took a hot bath; the tub was half filled with
plain water, and then my mother would add a large caldronful
of water in which she had just boiled some bark and leaves from
a bay-leaf tree. The bark and leaves were there for no reason
other than that he liked the smell. He would then spend hours
lying in this bath, studying his pool coupons or drawing examples of pieces of furniture he planned to make. When I came
home from Sunday school, we would sit down to our Sunday
dinner.

My mother and I often took a bath together. Sometimes it
was just a plain bath, which didn't take very long. Other times,
it was a special bath in which the barks and flowers of many
different trees, together with all sorts of oils, were boiled in the
same large caldron. We would then sit in this bath in a darkened
room with a strange-smelling candle burning away. As we sat
in this bath, my mother would bathe different parts of my body;
then she would do the same to herself. We took these baths
after my mother had consulted with her obeah woman, and with
her mother and a trusted friend, and all three of them had
confirmed that from the look of things around our house—the
way a small scratch on my instep had turned into a small sore,
then a large sore, and how long it had taken to heal; the way
a dog she knew, and a friendly dog at that, suddenly turned and
bit her; how a porcelain bowl she had carried from one eternity
and hoped to carry into the next suddenly slipped out of her
capable hands and broke into pieces the size of grains of sand;
how words she spoke in jest to a friend had been completely
misunderstood—one of the many women my father had loved,
had never married, but with whom he had had children was
trying to harm my mother and me by setting bad spirits on us.

When I got up, I placed my bedclothes and my nightie in
the sun to air out, brushed my teeth, and washed and dressed
myself. My mother would then give me my breakfast, but since,
during my holidays, I was not going to school, I wasn't forced
to eat an enormous breakfast of porridge, eggs, an orange or
half a grapefruit, bread and butter, and cheese. I could get away

with just some bread and butter and cheese and porridge and cocoa. I spent the day following my mother around and observing the way she did everything. When we went to the grocer's, she would point out to me the reason she bought each thing. I was shown a loaf of bread or a pound of butter from at least ten different angles. When we went to market, if that day she wanted to buy some crabs she would inquire from the person selling them if they came from near Parham, and if the person said yes my mother did not buy the crabs. In Parham was the leper colony, and my mother was convinced that the crabs ate nothing but the food from the lepers' own plates. If we were then to eat the crabs, it wouldn't be long before we were lepers ourselves and living unhappily in the leper colony.

How important I felt to be with my mother. For many people, their wares and provisions laid out in front of them, would brighten up when they saw her coming and would try hard to get her attention. They would dive underneath their stalls and bring out goods even better than what they had on display. They were disappointed when she held something up in the air, looked at it, turning it this way and that, and then, screwing up her face, said, "I don't think so," and turned and walked away— off to another stall to see if someone who only last week had sold her some delicious christophine had something that was just as good. They would call out after her turned back that next week they expected to have eddoes or dasheen or whatever, and my mother would say, "We'll see," in a very disbelieving tone of voice. If then we went to Mr. Kenneth, it would be only for a few minutes, for he knew exactly what my mother wanted and always had it ready for her. Mr. Kenneth had known me since I was a small child, and he would always remind me of little things I had done then as he fed me a piece of raw liver he had set aside for me. It was one of the few things I liked to eat, and, to boot, it pleased my mother to see me eat something that was so good for me, and she would tell me in great detail the effect the raw liver would have on my red blood corpuscles.

We walked home in the hot midmorning sun mostly without

event. When I was much smaller, quite a few times while I was walking with my mother she would suddenly grab me and wrap me up in her skirt and drag me along with her as if in a great hurry. I would hear an angry voice saying angry things, and then, after we had passed the angry voice, my mother would release me. Neither my mother nor my father ever came straight out and told me anything, but I had put two and two together and I knew that it was one of the women that my father had loved and with whom he had had a child or children, and who never forgave him for marrying my mother and having me. It was one of those women who were always trying to harm my mother and me, and they must have loved my father very much, for not once did any of them ever try to hurt him, and whenever he passed them on the street it was as if he and these women had never met.

When we got home, my mother started to prepare our lunch (pumpkin soup with droppers, banana fritters with salt fish stewed in antroba and tomatoes, fungie with salt fish stewed in antroba and tomatoes, or pepper pot, all depending on what my mother had found at market that day). As my mother went about from pot to pot, stirring one, adding something to the other, I was ever in her wake. As she dipped into a pot of boiling something or other to taste for correct seasoning, she would give me a taste of it also, asking me what I thought. Not that she really wanted to know what I thought, for she had told me many times that my taste buds were not quite developed yet, but it was just to include me in everything. While she made our lunch, she would also keep an eye on her washing. If it was a Tuesday and the colored clothes had been starched, as she placed them on the line I would follow, carrying a basket of clothespins for her. While the starched colored clothes were being dried on the line, the white clothes were being whitened on the stone heap. It was a beautiful stone heap that my father had made for her: an enormous circle of stones, about six inches high, in the middle of our yard. On it the soapy white clothes were spread out; as the sun dried them, bleaching out all stains, they had to be made wet again by dousing them with buckets of water. On my holidays, I did this for my mother. As I watered the clothes, she would come up behind me, instructing me to get the clothes thoroughly wet, showing me a shirt that I should turn over so that the sleeves were exposed.

Over our lunch, my mother and father talked to each other about the houses my father had to build; how disgusted he had become with one of his apprentices, or with Mr. Oatie; what they thought of my schooling so far; what they thought of the noises Mr. Jarvis and his friends made for so many days when they locked themselves up inside Mr. Jarvis's house and drank rum and ate fish they had caught themselves and danced to the music of an accordion that they took turns playing. On and on they talked. As they talked, my head would move from side to side, looking at them. When my eyes rested on my father, I didn't think very much of the way he looked. But when my eyes rested on my mother, I found her beautiful. Her head looked as if it should be on a sixpence. What a beautiful long neck, and long plaited hair, which she pinned up around the crown of her head because when her hair hung down it made her too hot. Her nose was the shape of a flower on the brink of opening. Her mouth, moving up and down as she ate and talked at the same time, was such a beautiful mouth I could have looked at it forever if I had to and not mind. Her lips were wide and almost thin, and when she said certain words I could see small parts of big white teeth—so big, and pearly, like some nice buttons on one of my dresses. I didn't much care about what she said when she was in this mood with my father. She made him laugh so. She could hardly say a word before he would burst out laughing. We ate our food, I cleared the table, we said goodbye to my father as he went back to work, I helped my mother with the dishes, and then we settled into the afternoon.

When my mother, at sixteen, after quarreling with her father, left his house on Dominica and came to Antigua, she packed all her things in an enormous wooden trunk that she had bought

in Roseau for almost six shillings. She painted the trunk yellow
and green outside, and she lined the inside with wallpaper that
had a cream background with pink roses printed all over it. Two
days after she left her father's house, she boarded a boat and
sailed for Antigua. It was a small boat, and the trip would have
taken a day and a half ordinarily, but a hurricane blew up and
the boat was lost at sea for almost five days. By the time it got
to Antigua, the boat was practically in splinters, and though two
or three of the passengers were lost overboard, along with some
of the cargo, my mother and her trunk were safe. Now, twenty-
four years later, this trunk was kept under my bed, and in it
were things that had belonged to me, starting from just before
I was born. There was the chemise, made of white cotton, with
scallop edging around the sleeves, neck, and hem, and white
flowers embroidered on the front—the first garment I wore after
being born. My mother had made that herself, and once, when
we were passing by, I was even shown the tree under which she
sat as she made this garment. There were some of my diapers,
with their handkerchief hemstitch that she had also done herself;
there was a pair of white wool booties with matching jacket and
hat; there was a blanket in white wool and a blanket in white
flannel cotton; there was a plain white linen hat with lace trim-
ming; there was my christening outfit; there were two of my
baby bottles: one in the shape of a normal baby bottle, and the
other shaped like a boat, with a nipple on either end; there was
a thermos in which my mother had kept a tea that was supposed
to have a soothing effect on me; there was the dress I wore on
my first birthday: a yellow cotton with green smocking on the
front; there was the dress I wore on my second birthday: pink
cotton with green smocking on the front; there was also a photograph of me on my second birthday wearing my pink dress
and my first pair of earrings, a chain around my neck, and a pair
of bracelets, all specially made of gold from British Guiana; there
was the first pair of shoes I grew out of after I knew how to
walk; there was the dress I wore when I first went to school,
and the first notebook in which I wrote; there were the sheets

for my crib and the sheets for my first bed; there was my first straw hat, my first straw basket—decorated with flowers—my grandmother had sent me from Dominica; there were my report cards, my certificates of merit from school, and my certificates of merit from Sunday school.

From time to time, my mother would fix on a certain place in our house and give it a good cleaning. If I was at home when she happened to do this, I was at her side, as usual. When she did this with the trunk, it was a tremendous pleasure, for after she had removed all the things from the trunk, and aired them out, and changed the camphor balls, and then refolded the things and put them back in their places in the trunk, as she held each thing in her hand she would tell me a story about myself. Sometimes I knew the story first hand, for I could remember the incident quite well; sometimes what she told me had happened when I was too young to know anything; and sometimes it happened before I was even born. Whichever way, I knew exactly what she would say, for I had heard it so many times before, but I never got tired of it. For instance, the flowers on the chemise, the first garment I wore after being born, were not put on correctly, and that is because when my mother was embroidering them I kicked so much that her hand was unsteady. My mother said that usually when I kicked around in her stomach and she told me to stop I would, but on that day I paid no attention at all. When she told me this story, she would smile at me and say, "You see, even then you were hard to manage." It pleased me to think that, before she could see my face, my mother spoke to me in the same way she did now. On and on my mother would go. No small part of my life was so unimportant that she hadn't made a note of it, and now she would tell it to me over and over again. I would sit next to her and she would show me the very dress I wore on the day I bit another child my age with whom I was playing. "Your biting phase," she called it. Or the day she warned me not to play around the coal pot, because I liked to sing to myself and dance around the fire. Two seconds later, I

fell into the hot coals, burning my elbows. My mother cried
when she saw that it wasn't serious, and now, as she told me
about it, she would kiss the little black patches of scars on my
elbows.

As she told me the stories, I sometimes sat at her side, leaning
against her, or I would crouch on my knees behind her back
and lean over her shoulder. As I did this, I would occasionally
sniff at her neck, or behind her ears, or at her hair. She smelled
sometimes of lemons, sometimes of sage, sometimes of roses,
sometimes of bay leaf. At times I would no longer hear what it
was she was saying; I just liked to look at her mouth as it opened
and closed over words, or as she laughed. How terrible it must
be for all the people who had no one to love them so and no
one whom they loved so, I thought. My father, for instance.
When he was a little boy, his parents, after kissing him goodbye
and leaving him with his grandmother, boarded a boat and sailed
to South America. He never saw them again, though they wrote
to him and sent him presents—packages of clothes on his birthday and at Christmas. He then grew to love his grandmother,
and she loved him, for she took care of him and worked hard
at keeping him well fed and clothed. From the beginning, they
slept in the same bed, and as he became a young man they
continued to do so. When he was no longer in school and had
started working, every night, after he and his grandmother had
eaten their dinner, my father would go off to visit his friends.
He would then return home at around midnight and fall asleep
next to his grandmother. In the morning, his grandmother would
awake at half past five or so, a half hour before my father, and
prepare his bath and breakfast and make everything proper and
ready for him, so that at seven o'clock sharp he stepped out the
door off to work. One morning, though, he overslept, because
his grandmother didn't wake him up. When he awoke, she was
still lying next to him. When he tried to wake her, he couldn't.
She had died lying next to him sometime during the night. Even
though he was overcome with grief, he built her coffin and made
sure she had a nice funeral. He never slept in that bed again,

and shortly afterward he moved out of that house. He was eighteen years old then.

When my father first told me this story, I threw myself at him at the end of it, and we both started to cry—he just a little, I quite a lot. It was a Sunday afternoon; he and my mother and I had gone for a walk in the botanical gardens. My mother had wandered off to look at some strange kind of thistle, and we could see her as she bent over the bushes to get a closer look and reach out to touch the leaves of the plant. When she returned to us and saw that we had both been crying, she started to get quite worked up, but my father quickly told her what had happened and she laughed at us and called us her little fools. But then she took me in her arms and kissed me, and she said that I needn't worry about such a thing as her sailing off or dying and leaving me all alone in the world. But if ever after that I saw my father sitting alone with a faraway look on his face, I was filled with pity for him. He had been alone in the world all that time, what with his mother sailing off on a boat with his father and his never seeing her again, and then his grandmother dying while lying next to him in the middle of the night. It was more than anyone should have to bear. I loved him so and wished that I had a mother to give him, for, no matter how much my own mother loved him, it could never be the same.

When my mother got through with the trunk, and I had heard again and again just what I had been like and who had said what to me at what point in my life, I was given my tea—a cup of cocoa and a buttered bun. My father by then would return home from work, and he was given his tea. As my mother went around preparing our supper, picking up clothes from the stone heap, or taking clothes off the clothesline, I would sit in a corner of our yard and watch her. She never stood still. Her powerful legs carried her from one part of the yard to the other, and in and out of the house. Sometimes she might call out to me to go and get some thyme or basil or some other herb for her, for she grew all her herbs in little pots that she kept in a corner of our little garden. Sometimes when I gave her the herbs, she might stoop down and kiss me on my lips and then on my neck. It was in such a paradise that I lived.

The summer of the year I turned twelve, I could see that I had grown taller; most of my clothes no longer fit. When I could get a dress over my head, the waist then came up to just below my chest. My legs had become more spindlelike, the hair on my head even more unruly than usual, small tufts of hair had appeared under my arms, and when I perspired the smell was strange, as if I had turned into a strange animal. I didn't say anything about it, and my mother and father didn't seem to notice, for they didn't say anything, either. Up to then, my mother and I had many dresses made out of the same cloth, though hers had a different, more grownup style, a boat neck or a sweetheart neckline, and a pleated or gored skirt, while my dresses had high necks with collars, a deep hemline, and, of course, a sash that tied in the back. One day, my mother and I had gone to get some material for new dresses to celebrate her birthday (the usual gift from my father), when I came upon a piece of cloth—a yellow background, with figures of men, dressed in a long-ago fashion, seated at pianos that they were playing, and all around them musical notes flying off into the air. I immediately said how much I loved this piece of cloth and how nice I thought it would look on us both, but my mother replied, "Oh, no. You are getting too old for that. It's time you had your own clothes. You just cannot go around the rest of your life looking like a little me." To say that I felt the earth swept away from under me would not be going too far. It wasn't just what she said, it was the way she said it. No accompanying little laugh. No bending over and kissing my little wet forehead (for suddenly I turned hot, then cold, and all my pores must have opened up, for fluids just flowed out of me). In the end, I got my dress with the men playing their pianos, and my mother got a dress with red and yellow overgrown hibiscus, but I was never able to wear my own dress or see my mother in hers without feeling bitterness and hatred, directed not so much toward my mother as toward, I suppose, life in general.

As if that were not enough, my mother informed me that I was on the verge of becoming a young lady, so there were quite a few things I would have to do differently. She didn't say exactly just what it was that made me on the verge of becoming a young lady, and I was so glad of that, because I didn't want to know. Behind a closed door, I stood naked in front of a mirror and looked at myself from head to toe. I was so long and bony that I more than filled up the mirror, and my small ribs pressed out against my skin. I tried to push my unruly hair down against my head so that it would lie flat, but as soon as I let it go it bounced up again. I could see the small tufts of hair under my arms. And then I got a good look at my nose. It had suddenly spread across my face, almost blotting out my cheeks, taking up my whole face, so that if I didn't know I was me standing there I would have wondered about that strange girl—and to think that only so recently my nose had been a small thing, the size of a rosebud. But what could I do? I thought of begging my mother to ask my father if he could build for me a set of clamps into which I could screw myself at night before I went to sleep and which would surely cut back on my growing. I was about to ask her this when I remembered that a few days earlier I had asked in my most pleasing, winning way for a look through the trunk. A person I did not recognize answered in a voice I did not recognize, "Absolutely not! You and I don't have time for that anymore." Again, did the ground wash out from under me? Again, the answer would have to be yes, and I wouldn't be going too far.

Because of this young-lady business, instead of days spent in perfect harmony with my mother, I trailing in her footsteps, she showering down on me her kisses and affection and attention, I was now sent off to learn one thing and another. I was sent to someone who knew all about manners and how to meet and greet important people in the world. This woman soon asked me not to come again, since I could not resist making farting-like noises each time I had to practice a curtsy, it made the other girls laugh so. I was sent for piano lessons. The piano teacher, a shriveled-up old spinster from Lancashire, England, soon asked me not to come back, since I seemed unable to resist eating from the bowl of plums she had placed on the piano purely for decoration. In the first case, I told my mother a lie—I told her that the manners teacher had found that my manners needed no improvement, so I needn't come anymore. This made her very pleased. In the second case, there was no getting around it—she had to find out. When the piano teacher told her of my misdeed, she turned and walked away from me, and I wasn't sure that if she had been asked who I was she wouldn't have said, "I don't know," right then and there. What a new thing this was for me: my mother's back turned on me in disgust. It was true that I didn't spend all my days at my mother's side before this, that I spent most of my days at school, but before this young-lady business I could sit and think of my mother, see her doing one thing or another, and always her face bore a smile for me. Now I often saw her with the corners of her mouth turned down in disapproval of me. And why was my mother carrying my new state so far? She took to pointing out that one day I would have my own house and I might want it to be a different house from the one she kept. Once, when showing me a way to store linen, she patted the folded sheets in place and said, "Of course, in your own house you might choose another way." That the day might actually come when we would live apart I had never believed. My throat hurt from the tears I held bottled up tight inside. Sometimes we would both forget the new order of things and would slip into our old ways. But that didn't last very long.

In the middle of all these new things, I had forgotten that I was to enter a new school that September. I had then a set of things to do, preparing for school. I had to go to the seamstress to be measured for new uniforms, since my body now made a mockery of the old measurements. I had to get shoes, a new school hat, and lots of new books. In my new school, I needed a different exercise book for each subject, and in addition to the usual—English, arithmetic, and so on—I now had to take

Latin and French, and attend classes in a brand-new science building. I began to look forward to my new school. I hoped that everyone there would be new, that there would be no one I had ever met before. That way, I could put on a new set of airs; I could say I was something that I was not, and no one would ever know the difference.

On the Sunday before the Monday I started at my new school, my mother became cross over the way I had made my bed. In the center of my bedspread, my mother had embroidered a bowl overflowing with flowers and two lovebirds on either side of the bowl. I had placed the bedspread on my bed in a lopsided way so that the embroidery was not in the center of my bed, the way it should have been. My mother made a fuss about it, and I could see that she was right and I regretted very much not doing that one little thing that would have pleased her. I had lately become careless, she said, and I could only silently agree with her.

I came home from church, and my mother still seemed to hold the bedspread against me, so I kept out of her way. At half past two in the afternoon, I went off to Sunday school. At Sunday school, I was given a certificate for best student in my study-of-the-Bible group. It was a surprise that I would receive the certificate on that day, though we had known about the results of a test weeks before. I rushed home with my certificate in hand, feeling that with this prize I would reconquer my mother—a chance for her to smile on me again.

When I got to our house, I rushed into the yard and called out to her, but no answer came. I then walked into the house. At first, I didn't hear anything. Then I heard sounds coming from the direction of my parents' room. My mother must be in there, I thought. When I got to the door, I could see that my mother and father were lying in their bed. It didn't interest me what they were doing—only that my mother's hand was on the small of my father's back and that it was making a circular motion. But her hand! It was white and bony, as if it had long been dead and had been left out in the elements. It seemed not to be her hand, and yet it could only be her hand, so well did I know it. It went around and around in the same circular motion, and I looked at it as if I would never see anything else in my life again. If I were to forget everything else in the world, I could not forget her hand as it looked then. I could also make out that the sounds I had heard were her kissing my father's ears and his mouth and his face. I looked at them for I don't know how long.

When I next saw my mother, I was standing at the dinner table that I had just set, having made a tremendous commotion with knives and forks as I got them out of their drawer, letting my parents know that I was home. I had set the table and was now half standing near my chair, half draped over the table, staring at nothing in particular and trying to ignore my mother's presence. Though I couldn't remember our eyes having met, I was quite sure that she had seen me in the bedroom, and I didn't know what I would say if she mentioned it. Instead, she said in a voice that was sort of cross and sort of something else, "Are you going to just stand there doing nothing all day?" The something else was new; I had never heard it in her voice before. I couldn't say exactly what it was, but I know that it caused me to reply, "And what if I do?" and at the same time to stare at her directly in the eyes. It must have been a shock to her, the way I spoke. I had never talked back to her before. She looked at me, and then, instead of saying some squelching thing that would put me back in my place, she dropped her eyes and walked away. From the back, she looked small and funny. She carried her hands limp at her sides. I was sure I could never let those hands touch me again; I was sure I could never let her kiss me again. All that was finished.

I was amazed that I could eat my food, for all of it reminded me of things that had taken place between my mother and me. A long time ago, when I wouldn't eat my beef, complaining that it involved too much chewing, my mother would first chew up pieces of meat in her own mouth and then feed it to me. When I had hated carrots so much that even the sight of them would send me into a fit of tears, my mother would try to find all sorts of ways to make them palatable for me. All that was finished now. I didn't think that I would ever think of any of it again with fondness. I looked at my parents. My father was just the same, eating his food in the same old way, his two rows of false teeth clop-clopping like a horse being driven off to market. He was regaling us with another one of his stories about when he was a young man and played cricket on one island or the other. What he said now must have been funny, for my mother couldn't stop laughing. He didn't seem to notice that I was not entertained.

My father and I then went for our customary Sunday-afternoon walk. My mother did not come with us. I don't know what she stayed home to do. On our walk, my father tried to hold my hand, but I pulled myself away from him, doing it in such a way that he would think I felt too big for that now.

That Monday, I went to my new school. I was placed in a class with girls I had never seen before. Some of them had heard about me, though, for I was the youngest among them and was said to be very bright. I liked a girl named Albertine, and I liked a girl named Gweneth. At the end of the day, Gwen and I were in love, and so we walked home arm in arm together.

When I got home, my mother greeted me with the customary kiss and inquiries. I told her about my day, going out of my way to provide pleasing details, leaving out, of course, any mention at all of Gwen and my overpowering feelings for her.

COMMENTARY ON JAMAICA KINCAID
The Circling Hand

Annie John (1985), the autobiographical coming-of-age novel from which "The Circling Hand" is taken, is set in Jamaica Kincaid's homeland of Antigua, a tiny West Indian island, twelve miles long and nine miles wide, according to the description in her book *A Small Place* (1988). Kincaid describes Antigua as a place of almost unreal beauty, with pink and white sand surrounding navy blue waters, flowers of red, yellow, orange, blue and white growing profusely, lilies that bloom at night perfuming the air, and fruits and vegetables as bright as the colors people wear. For Kincaid it is a place of heightened intensity, as though its very uneventfulness makes every event an occasion for drama: "The small event is isolated, blown up, turned over and over and then absorbed into the everyday." Such passionate involvement in small, seemingly mundane events rendered in vibrant and unique detail by Kincaid's narrator, the young Annie John, make the traditional story of a girl coming of age seem new and unique.

The images of "The Circling Hand" evoke the Eden-like atmosphere that is the backdrop for the idyllic relationship between Annie and her mother. The early intimacy of mother and daughter is beautifully depicted as they bathe together in bath water scented with bay leaves, bark and oil in a candle-lit room, or as they shop together in the Antiguan marketplace. Her mother includes Annie in everything, making sure that they even wear dresses cut from the same cloth. Their shared life is symbolized by the trunk her mother has brought with her from Dominica when she left home at sixteen. In the trunk Annie's mother keeps all the mementos of Annie's growing up, each item associated with a story the mother tells Annie about her childhood: "No small part of my life was so unimportant that she hadn't made a note of it." The first suggestion that there could be a break in their close bond occurs when Annie recalls during the trunk stories the story of her father, who is abandoned by his parents and left with a grandmother who dies when he is still a young man. Annie's hysterical tears when she first hears this story suggests that it triggers her own fears of maternal abandonment. The end of the passionate mother-child attachment begins when her mother begins to talk sternly about "this young-lady business," visually enacting that separation by insisting that Annie's dresses must now be cut from a different pattern from hers.

Most of the literature on the developing adolescent has prepared us to expect that this intense and complex mother-daughter bond will eventually conflict with the daughter's need to establish a life independent of her mother. But in this story it is the mother who senses her daughter's emergent sexuality and moves away from their earlier closeness. As soon as the hair and strange smell under Annie's arms appear, her mother decides they cannot dress alike: "You just cannot go around the rest of your life looking like a little me." Resentful and fearful of her daughter's emerging sexuality, she cuts off signs of physical affection—"No bending over and kissing my little wet forehead." Her voice becomes stern along with the end of kisses and affection and, for the first time, she "allows" Annie to come home from school and find her in bed with the father.

Annie reacts to her mother's rejection by asserting her own power. She is rebellious in school and refuses to act like a young lady, taking up and excelling at the boys-only game of marbles (in a later chapter of the novel). The first time Annie talks back defiantly, her mother drops her eyes and walks away looking "small and funny." By the end of the novel, the girl has grown so tall that she notes, "I now towered over her," her physical growth signifying her independence from her mother as well as her increasing power. She has decided that, as her mother did at the same age, she will leave home for England where she plans to become a nurse. As the ship sails away from the dock, Annie looks at her mother, receding in the distance, until she becomes "just a dot . . . swallowed up in the big blue sea."

Of course there is deep-seated ambivalence in the daughter's assertion of power and independence. Annie really wishes "to reconquer" her mother's heart, but those efforts are thwarted by the father's position in the mother's life. At times she wishes to go away with her mother and live "somewhere quiet and beautiful with her alone." Other times she wants "to see her lying dead, all withered and in a coffin at my feet." Finally she decides on the perfect punishment for the mother's betrayal. She finds a new love, and the erotic bond she has experienced with the mother is replaced by one with her girlfriend Gwen.

I am wondering if the natural and inevitable urge toward separation from the mother serves another purpose. A culture that is dominated by men and devalues women has a profound effect on the mother-daughter bond and on the way the adolescent girl views her mother and her own development into womanhood. Is there something in the mother's role, in the "inferior" status of women that makes it necessary for the girl not only to leave the mother but to diminish her as well? At the beginning of "The Circling Hand," Annie has already experienced the lesser status of women—she is not allowed to bathe outside—like the father—because she is not a boy, and she understands that a girls-only school that she attends is a source of shame. At the end of *Annie John* the passionate maternal love has been displaced and what is left is a tremendous chasm, mother and daughter separated by an ocean and by the daughter's need to "add up" to more than the mother. There is no suggestion of how Annie can reestablish a relationship of mutuality with the mother, though, ironically, as she distances herself from her mother, she also imitates her, leaving home with a new trunk just as her mother did before her. At the end of *Sula*, Nel too has become like Helene—conventional and fearful and overly attached to her children. Of these three novels, only *Brown Girl* suggests a reconciliation with the mother. Selina acknowledges her strong identification with her mother, recognizing that her defiance and risk-taking are qualities that make her truly her mother's daughter.

In her study of mother-daughter stories, Marianne Hirsch has made clear that these stories are very much one-sided, heavily weighted in favor of the daughter since most are written from the daughter's point of view. The daughter's story leaves spaces and gaps which only the mother can fill. Hirsch insists that the story of female development in narrative must be written in the voice of the mother as well as the daughter; for such a narrative would allow the mother to be subject, not just the object of the daughter's quest and would finally "yield a multiple female consciousness, creating the possibility for the daughter to achieve both autonomy and a healthier relationship with the mother."[1]

1. Marianne Hirsch, *The Mother-Daughter Plot: Narrative, Psychoanalysis, Feminism* (Bloomington: Indiana University Press, 1989), p. 161.

Getting the Facts of Life

PAULETTE CHILDRESS WHITE

The August morning was ripening into a day that promised to be a burner. By the time we'd walked three blocks, dark patches were showing beneath Momma's arms, and inside tennis shoes thick with white polish, my feet were wet against the cushions. I was beginning to regret how quickly I'd volunteered to go.

"Dog. My feet are getting mushy," I complained.

"You should've wore socks," Momma said, without looking my way or slowing down.

I frowned. In 1961, nobody wore socks with tennis shoes. It was bare legs, Bermuda shorts and a sleeveless blouse. Period.

Momma was chubby but she could really walk. She walked the same way she washed clothes—up-and-down, up-and-down until she was done. She didn't believe in taking breaks.

This was my first time going to the welfare office with Momma. After breakfast, before we'd had time to scatter, she corralled everyone old enough to consider and announced in her serious-business voice that someone was going to the welfare office with her this morning. Cries went up.

Junior had his papers to do. Stella was going swimming at the high school. Dennis was already pulling the *Free Press* wagon across town every first Wednesday to get the surplus food—like that.

"You want clothes for school, don't you?" That landed. School opened in two weeks.

"I'll go," I said.

"Who's going to baby-sit if Minerva goes?" Momma asked.

Stella smiled and lifted her small golden nose. "I will," she said. "I'd rather baby-sit than do *that*."

That should have warned me. Anything that would make Stella offer to baby-sit had to be bad.

A small cheer probably went up among my younger brothers in the back rooms where I was not too secretly known as "The Witch" because of the criminal licks I'd learned to give on my rise to power. I was twelve, third oldest under Junior and Stella, but I had long established myself as first in command among the kids. I was chief baby-sitter, biscuit-maker and broom-wielder. Unlike Stella, who'd begun her development at ten, I still had my girl's body and wasn't anxious to have that changed. What would it mean but a loss of power? I liked things just the way they were. My interest in bras was even less than my interest in boys, and that was limited to keeping my brothers—who seemed destined for wildness—from taking over completely.

Even before we left, Stella had Little Stevie Wonder turned up on the radio in the living room, and suspicious jumping-bumping sounds were beginning in the back. They'll tear the house down, I thought, following Momma out the door.

We turned at Salliotte, the street that would take us straight up to Jefferson Avenue where the welfare office was. Momma's face was pinking in the heat, and I was huffing to keep up. From here, it was seven more blocks on the colored side, the railroad tracks, five blocks on the white side and there you were. We'd be cooked.

"Is the welfare office near the Harbor Show?" I asked. I knew the answer, I just wanted some talk.

"Across the street."

"Umm. Glad it's not way down Jefferson somewhere."

Nothing. Momma didn't talk much when she was outside. I knew that the reason she wanted one of us along when she had far to go was not for company but so she wouldn't have to walk by herself. I could understand that. To me, walking alone was like being naked or deformed—everyone seemed to look at you harder and longer. With Momma, the feeling was probably worse because you knew people were wondering if she were white, Indian maybe or really colored. Having one of us along, brown and clearly hers, probably helped define that. Still, it was like being a little parade, with Momma's pale skin and straight brown hair turning heads like the clang of cymbals. Especially on the colored side.

"Well," I said, "here we come to the bad part."

Momma gave a tiny laugh.

Most of Salliotte was a business street, with Old West–looking storefronts and some office places that never seemed to open. Ecorse, hinged onto southwest Detroit like a clothes closet, didn't seem to take itself seriously. There were lots of empty fields, some of which folks down the residential streets turned into vegetable gardens every summer. And there was this block where the Moonflower Hotel raised itself to three stories over the poolroom and Beaman's drugstore. Here, bad boys and drunks made their noise and did an occasional stabbing. Except for the cars that lined both sides of the block, only one side was busy—the other bordered a field of weeds. We walked on the safe side.

If you were a woman or a girl over twelve, walking this block—even on the safe side—could be painful. They usually hollered at you and never mind what they said. Today, because it was hot and early, we made it by with only one weak *Hey baby* from a drunk sitting in the poolroom door.

"Hey baby yourself," I said but not too loudly, pushing my flat chest out and stabbing my eyes in his direction.

"Minerva girl, you better watch your mouth with grown men like that," Momma said, her eyes catching me up in real warning though I could see that she was holding down a smile.

"Well, he can't do nothing to me when I'm with you, can he?" I asked, striving to match the rise and fall of her black pumps.

She said nothing. She just walked on, churning away under a sun that clearly meant to melt us. From here to the tracks it was mostly gardens. It felt like the Dixie Peach I'd used to help water-wave my hair was sliding down with the sweat on my face, and my throat was tight with thirst. Boy, did I want a pop. I looked at the last little store before we crossed the tracks without bothering to ask.

Across the tracks, there were no stores and no gardens. It was shady, and the grass was June green. Perfect-looking houses sat in unfenced spaces far back from the street. We walked these five blocks without a word. We just looked and hurried to get through it. I was beginning to worry about the welfare office in earnest. A fool could see that in this part of Ecorse, things got serious.

We had been on welfare for almost a year. I didn't have any strong feelings about it—my life went on pretty much the same. It just meant watching the mail for a check instead of Daddy getting paid, and occasional visits from a social worker that I'd always managed to miss. For Momma and whoever went with her, it meant this walk to the office and whatever went on there that made everyone hate to go. For Daddy, it seemed to bring the most change. For him, it meant staying away from home more than when he was working and a reason not to answer the phone.

At Jefferson, we turned left and there it was, halfway down the block. The Department of Social Services. I discovered some strong feelings. That fine name meant nothing. This was the welfare. The place for poor people. People who couldn't or wouldn't take care of themselves. Now I was going to face it, and suddenly I thought what I knew the others had thought, *What if I see someone I know?* I wanted to run back all those blocks to home.

I looked at Momma for comfort, but her face was closed and her mouth looked locked.

Inside, the place was gray. There were rows of long benches like church pews facing each other across a middle aisle that led to a central desk. Beyond the benches and the desk, four hallways led off to a maze of partitioned offices. In opposite corners, huge fans hung from the ceiling, humming from side to side, blowing the heavy air for a breeze.

Momma walked to the desk, answered some questions, was given a number and told to take a seat. I followed her through, trying not to see the waiting people—as though that would keep them from seeing me.

Gradually, as we waited, I took them all in. There was no one there that I knew, but somehow they all looked familiar. Or maybe I only thought they did, because when your eyes connected with someone's, they didn't quickly look away and they usually smiled. They were mostly women and children, and a few low-looking men. Some of them were white, which surprised me. I hadn't expected to see them in there.

Directly in front of the bench where we sat, a little girl with blond curls was trying to handle a bottle of Coke. Now and then, she'd manage to turn herself and the bottle around and watch me with big gray eyes that seemed to know quite well how badly I wanted a pop. I thought of asking Momma for fifteen cents so I could get one from the machine in the back but I was afraid she'd still say no so I just kept planning more and more convincing ways to ask. Besides, there was a water fountain near the door if I could make myself rise and walk to it.

We waited three hours. White ladies dressed like secretaries kept coming out to call numbers, and people on the benches would get up and follow down a hall. Then more people came in to replace them. I drank water from the fountain three times and was ready to put my feet up on the bench before us—the little girl with the Coke and her momma got called—by the time we heard Momma's number.

"You wait here," Momma said as I rose with her.

I sat down with a plop.

The lady with the number looked at me. Her face reminded me of the librarian's at Bunch school. Looked like she never cracked a smile. "Let her come," she said.

"She can wait here," Momma repeated, weakly.

"It's OK. She can come in. Come on," the lady insisted at me.

I hesitated, knowing that Momma's face was telling me to sit.

"Come on," the woman said.

Momma said nothing.

I got up and followed them into the maze. We came to a small room where there was a desk and three chairs. The woman sat behind the desk and we before it.

For a while, no one spoke. The woman studied a folder open before her, brows drawn together. On the wall behind her there was a calendar with one heavy black line drawn slantwise through each day of August, up to the twenty-first. That was today.

"Mrs. Blue, I have a notation here that Mr. Blue has not reported to the department on his efforts to obtain employment since the sixteenth of June. Before that, it was the tenth of April. You understand that department regulations require that he report monthly to this office, do you not?" Eyes brown as a wren's belly came up at Momma.

"Yes," Momma answered, sounding as small as I felt.

"Can you explain his failure to do so?"

Pause. "He's been looking. He says he's been looking."

"That may be. However, his failure to report those efforts here is my only concern."

Silence.

"We cannot continue with your case as it now stands if Mr. Blue refuses to comply with departmental regulations. He is still residing with the family, is he not?"

"Yes, he is. I've been reminding him to come in . . . he said he would."

"Well, he hasn't. Regulations are that any able-bodied man, head-of-household and receiving assistance who neglects to report to this office any effort to obtain work for a period of sixty days or more is to be cut off for a minimum of three months, at which time he may reapply. As of this date, Mr. Blue is over sixty days delinquent, and officially, I am obliged to close the case and direct you to other sources of aid."

"What is that?"

"Aid to Dependent Children would be the only source available to you. Then, of course, you would not be eligible unless it was verified that Mr. Blue was no longer residing with the family."

Another silence. I stared into the gray steel front of the desk, everything stopped but my heart.

"Well, can you keep the case open until Monday? If he comes in by Monday?"

"According to my records, Mr. Blue failed to come in May and such an agreement was made then. In all, we allowed him a period of seventy days. You must understand that what happens in such cases as this is not wholly my decision." She sighed and watched Momma with hopeless eyes, tapping the soft end of her pencil on the papers before her. "Mrs. Blue, I will speak to my superiors on your behalf. I can allow you until Monday next . . . that's the"—she swung around to the calendar—"twenty-sixth of August, to get him in here."

"Thank you. He'll be in," Momma breathed. "Will I be able to get the clothing order today?"

Hands and eyes searched in the folder for an answer before she cleared her throat and tilted her face at Momma. "We'll see what we can do," she said, finally.

My back touched the chair. Without turning my head, I moved my eyes down to Momma's dusty feet and wondered if she could still feel them; my own were numb. I felt bodyless—there was only my face, which wouldn't disappear, and behind it, one word pinging against another in a buzz that made no sense. At home, we'd have the house cleaned by now, and I'd be waiting for the daily appearance of my best friend, Bernadine, so we could comb each other's hair or talk about stuck-up Evelyn and Brenda. Maybe Bernadine was already there, and Stella was teaching her to dance the bop.

Then I heard our names and ages—all eight of them—being called off like items in a grocery list.

"Clifford, Junior, age fourteen." She waited.

"Yes."

"Born? Give me the month and year."

"October 1946," Momma answered, and I could hear in her voice that she'd been through these questions before.

"Stella, age thirteen."

"Yes."

"Born?"

"November 1947."

"Minerva, age twelve." She looked at me. "This is Minerva?"

"Yes."

No. I thought, no, this is not Minerva. You can write it down if you want to, but Minerva is not here.

"Born?"

"December 1948."

The woman went on down the list, sounding more and more like Momma should be sorry or ashamed, and Momma's answers grew fainter and fainter. So this was welfare. I wondered how many times Momma had had to do this. Once before? Three times? Every time?

More questions. How many in school? Six. Who needs shoes? Everybody.

"Everybody needs shoes? The youngest two?"

"Well, they don't go to school . . . but they walk."

My head came up to look at Momma and the woman. The woman's mouth was left open. Momma didn't blink.

The brown eyes went down. "Our allowances are based on the median costs for moderately priced clothing at Sears, Roebuck." She figured on paper as she spoke. "That will mean thirty-four dollars for children over ten . . . thirty dollars for children under ten. It comes to one hundred ninety-eight dollars. I can allow eight dollars for two additional pairs of shoes."

"Thank you."

"You will present your clothing order to a salesperson at the store, who will be happy to assist you in your selections. Please be practical as further clothing requests will not be considered for a period of six months. In cases of necessity, however, requests for winter outerwear will be considered beginning November first."

Momma said nothing.

The woman rose and left the room.

For the first time, I shifted in the chair. Momma was looking into the calendar as though she could see through the pages to November first. Everybody needed a coat.

I'm never coming here again, I thought. If I do, I'll stay out front. Not coming back in here. Ever again.

She came back and sat behind her desk. "Mrs. Blue, I must make it clear that, regardless of my feelings, I will be forced to close your case if your husband does not report to this office by Monday, the twenty-sixth. Do you understand?"

"Yes. Thank you. He'll come. I'll see to it."

"Very well." She held a paper out to Momma.

We stood. Momma reached over and took the slip of paper. I moved toward the door.

"Excuse me, Mrs. Blue, but are you pregnant?"

"What?"

"I asked if you were expecting another child."

"Oh. No, I'm not," Momma answered, biting down on her lips.

"Well, I'm sure you'll want to be careful about a thing like that in your present situation."

"Yes."

I looked quickly to Momma's loose white blouse. We'd never known when another baby was coming until it was almost there.

"I suppose that eight children are enough for anyone," the

woman said, and for the first time her face broke into a smile.

Momma didn't answer that. Somehow, we left the room and found our way out onto the street. We stood for a moment as though lost. My eyes followed Momma's up to where the sun was burning high. It was still there, blazing white against a cloudless blue. Slowly, Momma put the clothing order into her purse and snapped it shut. She looked around as if uncertain which way to go. I led the way to the corner. We turned. We walked the first five blocks.

I was thinking about how stupid I'd been a year ago, when Daddy lost his job. I'd been happy.

"You-all better be thinking about moving to Indianapolis," he announced one day after work, looking like he didn't think much of it himself. He was a welder with the railroad company. He'd worked there for eleven years. But now, "Company's moving to Indianapolis," he said. "Gonna be gone by November. If I want to keep my job, we've got to move with it."

We didn't. Nobody wanted to move to Indianapolis—not even Daddy. Here, we had uncles, aunts and cousins on both sides. Friends. Everybody and everything we knew. Daddy could get another job. First came unemployment compensation. Then came welfare. Thank goodness for welfare, we said, while we waited and waited for the job that hadn't yet come.

The problem was that Daddy couldn't take it. If something got repossessed or somebody took sick or something was broken or another kid was coming, he'd carry on terribly until things got better—by which time things were always worse. He'd always been that way. So when the railroad left, he began to do everything wrong. Stayed out all hours. Drank and drank some more. When he was home, he was so grouchy we were afraid to squeak. Now when we saw him coming, we got lost. Even our friends ran for cover.

At the railroad tracks, we sped up. The tracks were as far across as a block was long. Silently, I counted the rails by the heat of the steel bars through my thin soles. On the other side, I felt something heavy rise up in my chest and I knew that I wanted to cry. I wanted to cry or run or kiss the dusty ground. The little houses with their sun-scorched lawns and backyard gardens were mansions in my eyes. "Ohh, Ma . . . look at those collards!"

"Umm-humm," she agreed, and I knew that she saw it too.

"Wonder how they grew so big?"

"Cow dung, probably. Big Poppa used to put cow dung out to fertilize the vegetable plots, and everything just grew like crazy. We used to get tomatoes this big"—she circled with her hands—"and don't talk about squash or melons."

"I bet y'all ate like rich people. Bet y'all had everything you could want."

"We sure did," she said. "We never wanted for anything when it came to food. And when the cash crops were sold, we could get whatever else that was needed. We never wanted for a thing."

"What about the time you and cousin Emma threw out the supper peas?"

"Oh! Did I tell you about that?" she asked. Then she told it all over again. I didn't listen. I watched her face and guarded her smile with a smile of my own.

We walked together, step for step. The sun was still burning, but we forgot to mind it. We talked about an Alabama girlhood in a time and place I'd never know. We talked about the wringer washer and how it could be fixed, because washing every day on a scrub-board was something Alabama could keep. We talked about how to get Daddy to the Department of Social Services.

Then we talked about having babies. She began to tell me things I'd never known, and the idea of womanhood blossomed in my mind like some kind of suffocating rose.

"Momma," I said, "I don't think I can be a woman."

"You can," she laughed, "and if you live, you will be. You gotta be some kind of woman."

"But it's hard," I said, "sometimes it must be hard."

"Umm-humm," she said, "sometimes it is hard."

When we got to the bad block, we crossed to Beaman's drugstore for two orange crushes. Then we walked right through the groups of men standing in the shadows of the poolroom and the Moonflower Hotel. Not one of them said a word to us. I supposed they could see in the way we walked that we weren't afraid. We'd been to the welfare office and back again. And the facts of life, fixed in our minds like the sun in the sky, were no burning mysteries.

COMMENTARY ON PAULETTE CHILDRESS WHITE

Getting the Facts of Life

Like Minerva Blue, the twelve-year-old narrator of the autobiographical story "Getting the Facts of Life," Paulette Childress White was born in December 1948 and grew up in Ecorse, Michigan, a little suburb "hinged onto southwest Detroit like a clothes closet." Though it had a fairly even mix of working- and middle-class families, Ecorse was a strictly segregated town, divided racially by the railroad tracks. With their comfortable little brick homes and closely knit communities, the black families who had migrated there from rural Mississippi and Alabama must have felt like Ecorse was a little piece of the South transplanted.

In *The Bluest Eye* (1970), Toni Morrison's Breedlove family, like Minerva Blue's family, come to the industrial North from Alabama during the 1940s and 1950s, and like the Blue family, find themselves caught in the new poverty and dislocation of northern urban life. It is clear from the recollections of their Alabama past that both the Breedloves and the Blues experienced a sense of vibrancy and richness in the South that is lost among the cars, weeds and dilapidated storefronts of the city.

Few writers, in the books I've read, have described a welfare office; very few, I imagine, have ever had occasion to be in one. The effects of such a system on the family can be devastating.

Mrs. Blue becomes tight lipped and angry, forced to be both mother and father. Mr. Blue stays away from home, and the pressure on him to abandon the family is covertly applied when the worker suggests Mrs. Blue can receive ADC if she can verify that Mr. Blue no longer resides with them. Just as Morrison's Pecola makes little parts of her body disappear until nothing's left but her eyes, Minerva too feels as though she is bodyless, with only her face left to confirm that she has witnessed this humiliation.

The stories of poor families, says Salvador Minuchin, are often written by social institutions.

But the loss of power experienced by female characters in coming-of-age stories cuts across social and racial lines. Unlike *manhood*, which has such a variety of meanings—all active— *womanhood*, in our culture, signifies primarily sexuality, marriage-ability, maternity, passivity. Minerva, as chief baby-sitter, biscuit-maker, broom-wielder, has already begun to identify with her mother's domestic role, though she is still in conflict about what womanhood will mean. She says, "I still had my girl's body and wasn't anxious to have that changed"; as though she is fearful of discovering that an adult female body is only a trap.

In her essay describing how women come of age in fiction, Susan Rosowski draws clear distinctions between the male coming-of-age novel and the female counterpart, which she calls "the novel of awakening." The male protagonist seeking adulthood is expected to go out into the world and discover how to negotiate that world and then take his proper place in it. But there is a different pattern in novels about girls coming of age:

> [In the novel of awakening] movement is inward, toward greater self-knowledge that leads in turn to a revelation of the disparity between that self-knowledge and the nature of the world. The protagonist's growth results typically not with "an art of living" as for her male counterpart, but instead with a realization that for a woman such an art of living is difficult or impossible: it is an awakening to limitations.[1]

Since the only model presented for Minerva in this story is her mother, there is little hint that the daughter will be able to avoid the "limitations" of the mother's hard life. In fact, the adult wisdom Minerva achieves as a result of her trip to the welfare office is undercut when her mother links her growing sense of empowerment to sexuality and passivity, telling her about babies and the hard female fate that awaits her. The idea of womanhood seems to Minerva like a "suffocating rose." White's narrative does, however, suggest the possibility of change; for it is Minerva who tells this story, and her ending does not inscribe passivity nor defeat. She transforms the usual sexual meaning of the facts of life, making those "facts" refer now to her initiation into political realities. In the new shared equality between mother and daughter, Minerva enables her mother to become a storyteller, and, together, mother and daughter silence the men on the street whose verbal assaults are meant to sexualize them.

1. Susan J. Rosowski, "The Novel of Awakening," in *The Voyage In: Fictions of Female Development*, ed. Elizabeth Abel, Marianne Hirsch, Elizabeth Langland (Hanover: University Press of New England, 1983), p. 49.

Fathers
and
Daughters

forgiving my father

LUCILLE CLIFTON

it is friday. we have come
to the paying of the bills.
all week you have stood in my dreams
like a ghost, asking for more time
but today is payday, payday old man;
my mother's hand opens in her early grave
and i hold it out like a good daughter.

there is no more time for you. there will
never be time enough daddy daddy old lecher
old liar. i wish you were rich so i could take it all
and give the lady what she was due
but you were the son of a needy father,
the father of a needy son;
you gave her all you had
which was nothing. you have already given her
all you had.

you are the pocket that was going to open
and come up empty any friday.
you were each other's bad bargain, not mine.
daddy old pauper   old prisoner,   old dead man
what am i doing here collecting?
you lie side by side in debtors' boxes
and no accounting will open them up.

New African

ANDREA LEE

On a hot Sunday morning in the summer of 1963, I was sitting restlessly with my mother, my brother Matthew, and my aunts Lily, Emma, and May in a central pew of the New African Baptist Church. It was mid-August, and the hum of the big electric fans at the back of the church was almost enough to muffle my father's voice from the pulpit; behind me I could hear Mrs. Gordon, a stout, feeble old woman who always complained of dizziness, remark sharply to her daughter that at the rate the air-conditioning fund was growing, it might as well be for the next century. Facing the congregation, my father—who was Reverend Phillips to the rest of the world—seemed hot himself; he mopped his brow with a handkerchief and drank several glasses of ice water from the heavy pitcher on the table by the pulpit. I looked at him critically. He's still reading the text, I thought. Then he'll do the sermon, then the baptism, and it will be an hour, maybe two.

I rubbed my chin and then idly began to snap the elastic band that held my red straw hat in place. What I would really like to do, I decided, would be to go home, put on my shorts, and climb up into the tree house I had set up the day before with Matthew. We'd nailed an old bushel basket up in the branches of the big maple that stretched above the sidewalk in front of the house; it made a sort of crow's nest where you could sit comfortably, except for a few splinters, and read, or peer through the dusty leaves at the cars that passed down the quiet suburban road. There was shade and wind and a feeling of high adventure up in the treetop, where the air seemed to vibrate with the dry rhythms of the cicadas; it was as different as possible from church, where the packed congregation sat in a near-visible miasma of emotion and cologne, and trolleys passing in the city street outside set the stained-glass windows rattling.

I slouched between Mama and Aunt Lily and felt myself going limp with lassitude and boredom, as if the heat had melted my bones; the only thing about me with any character seemed to be my firmly starched eyelet dress. Below the scalloped hem, my legs were skinny and wiry, the legs of a ten-year-old amazon, scarred from violent adventures with bicycles and skates. A fingernail tapped my wrist; it was Aunt Emma, reaching across Aunt Lily to press a piece of butterscotch into my hand. When I slipped the candy into my mouth, it tasted faintly of Arpège; my mother and her three sisters were monumental women, ample of bust and slim of ankle, with a weakness for elegant footwear and French perfume. As they leaned back and forth to exchange discreet tidbits of gossip, they fanned themselves and me with fans from the Byron J. Wiggins Funeral Parlor. The fans, which were fluttering throughout the church, bore a depiction of the Good Shepherd: a hollow-eyed blond Christ holding three fat pink-cheeked children. This Christ resembled the Christ who stood among apostles on the stained-glass windows of the church. Deacon Wiggins, a thoughtful man, had also provided New African with a few dozen fans bearing the picture of a black child praying, but I rarely saw those in use.

There was little that was new or very African about the New African Baptist Church. The original congregation had been formed in 1813 by three young men from Philadelphia's large community of free blacks, and before many generations had passed, it had become spiritual home to a collection of prosperous, conservative, generally light-skinned parishioners. The church was a gray Gothic structure, set on the corner of a run-down street in South Philadelphia a dozen blocks below Rittenhouse Square and a few blocks west of the spare, clannish Italian neighborhoods that produced Frankie Avalon and Frank Rizzo. At the turn of the century, the neighborhood had been a tidy collection of brick houses with scrubbed marble steps—the homes of a group of solid citizens whom Booker T. Washington, in a centennial address to the church, described as "the ablest Negro businessmen of our generation." Here my father had grown up aspiring to preach to the congregation of New African—an ambition encouraged by my grandmother Phillips, a formidable churchwoman. Here, too, my mother and her sisters had walked with linked arms to Sunday services, exchanging affected little catchphrases of French and Latin they had learned at Girls' High.

In the 1950s many of the parishioners, seized by the national urge toward the suburbs, moved to newly integrated towns outside the city, leaving the streets around New African to fill with bottles and papers and loungers. The big church stood suddenly isolated. It had not been abandoned—on Sundays the front steps overflowed with members who had driven in—but there was a tentative feeling in the atmosphere of those Sunday mornings, as if through the muddle of social change, the future of New African had become unclear. Matthew and I, suburban children, felt a mixture of pride and animosity toward the church. On the one hand, it was a marvelous private domain, a richly decorated and infinitely suggestive playground where we were petted by a congregation that adored our father; on the other hand, it seemed a bit like a dreadful old relative in the city, one who forced us into tedious visits and who linked us to a past that came to seem embarrassingly primitive as we grew older.

I slid down in my seat, let my head roll back, and looked up at the blue arches of the church ceiling. Lower than these, in back of the altar, was an enormous gilded cross. Still lower, in a semicircle near the pulpit, sat the choir, flanked by two tall golden files of organ pipes, and below the choir was a somber crescent of dark-suited deacons. In front, at the center of everything, his bald head gleaming under the lights, was Daddy. On summer Sundays he wore white robes, and when he raised his arms, the heavy material fell in curving folds like the ridged petals of an Easter lily. Usually when I came through the crowd to kiss him after the service, his cheek against my lips felt wet and gravelly with sweat and a new growth of beard sprouted since morning. Today, however, was a baptismal Sunday, and I wouldn't have a chance to kiss him until he was freshly shaven and cool from the shower he took after the ceremony. The baptismal pool was in an alcove to the left of the altar; it had mirrored walls and red velvet curtains, and above it, swaying on a string, hung a stuffed white dove.

Daddy paused in the invocation and asked the congregation to pray. The choir began to sing softly:

> *Blessed assurance,*
> *Jesus is mine!*
> *Oh what a foretaste*
> *Of glory divine!*

In the middle of the hymn, I edged my head around my mother's cool, muscular arm (she swam every day of the summer) and peered at Matthew. He was sitting bolt upright holding a hymnal and a pencil, his long legs inside his navy-blue summer suit planted neatly in front of him, his freckled thirteen-year-old face that was so like my father's wearing not the demonic grin it bore when we played alone but a maddeningly composed, attentive expression. "Two hours!" I mouthed at him, and pulled back at a warning pressure from my mother. Then I joined in the singing, feeling disappointed: Matthew had returned me a glance of scorn. Just lately he had started acting very superior and tolerant about tedious Sunday mornings. A month before, he'd been baptized, marching up to the pool in a line of white-robed children as the congregation murmured happily about Reverend Phillips's son. Afterward Mrs. Pinkston, a tiny, yellow-skinned old woman with a blind left eye, had come up to me and given me a painful hug, whispering that she was praying night and day for the pastor's daughter to hear the call as well.

I bit my fingernails whenever I thought about baptism; the subject brought out a deep-rooted balkiness in me. Ever since I could remember, Matthew and I had made a game of dispelling the mysteries of worship with a gleeful secular eye: we knew how the bread and wine were prepared for Communion, and where Daddy bought his robes (Ekhardt Brothers, in North Philadelphia, makers also of robes for choirs, academicians, and judges). Yet there was an unassailable magic about an act as public and dramatic as baptism. I felt toward it the slightly exasperated awe a stagehand might feel on realizing that although he can identify with professional exactitude the minutest components of a show, there is still something indefinable in the power that makes it a cohesive whole. Though I could not have put it into words, I believed that the decision to make a frightening and embarrassing backward plunge into a pool of sanctified water meant that one had received a summons to Christianity as unmistakable as the blare of an automobile horn. I believed this with the same fervor with which, already, I believed in the power of romance, especially in the miraculous efficacy of a lover's first kiss. I had never been kissed by a lover, nor had I heard the call to baptism.

For a Baptist minister and his wife, my father and mother were unusually relaxed about religion; Matthew and I had never been required to read the Bible, and my father's sermons had been criticized by some older church members for omitting the word "sin." Mama and Daddy never tried to push me toward baptism, but a number of other people did. Often on holidays, when I had retreated from the noise of the family dinner table and sat trying to read in my favorite place (the window seat in Matthew's room, with the curtains drawn to form a tent), Aunt Lily would come and find me. Aunt Lily was the youngest of my mother's sisters, a kindergarten teacher with the fatally overdeveloped air of quaintness that is the infallible mark of an old maid. Aunt Lily hoped and hoped again with various suitors, but even I knew she would never find a husband. I respected her because she gave me wonderful books of fairy tales, inscribed in her neat, loopy hand; when she talked about religion, however, she assumed an anxious, flirtatious air that made me cringe.

"Well, Miss Sarah, what are you scared of?" she would ask, tugging gently on one of my braids and bringing her plump face so close to mine that I could see her powder, which was, in accordance with the custom of fashionable colored ladies, several shades lighter than her olive skin. "God isn't anyone to be afraid of!" she'd continue as I looked at her with my best deadpan expression. "He's someone nice, just as nice as your daddy"—I had always suspected Aunt Lily of having a crush on my father—"and he loves you, in the same way your daddy does!"

"You would make us all so happy!" I was told at different times by Aunt Lily, Aunt Emma, and Aunt May. The only people who said nothing at all were Mama and Daddy, but I sensed in them a thoughtful, suppressed wistfulness that maddened me.

After the hymn, Daddy read aloud a few verses from the third chapter of Luke, verses I recognized in the almost instinctive way in which I was familiar with all of the well-traveled parts of the Old and New Testaments. "Prepare the way of the Lord, make his paths straight," read my father in a mild voice. "Every valley shall be filled, and every mountain and hill shall be brought low, and the crooked shall be made straight, and the rough paths made smooth, and all flesh shall see the salvation of God."

He had a habit of pausing to fix his gaze on part of the congregation as he read, and that Sunday he seemed to be talking to a small group of strangers who sat in the front row. These visitors were young white men and women, students from Philadelphia colleges, who for the past year had been coming to hear him talk. It was hard to tell them apart: all the men seemed to have beards, and the women wore their hair long and straight. Their informal clothes stood out in that elaborate assembly, and church members whispered angrily that the young women didn't wear hats. I found the students appealing and rather romantic, with their earnest eyes and timid air of being perpetually sorry about something. It was clear that they had good intentions, and I couldn't understand why so many of the adults in the congregation seemed to dislike them so much. After services, they would hover around Daddy. "Never a more beautiful civil rights sermon!" they would say in low, fervent voices. Sometimes they seemed to have tears in their eyes.

I wasn't impressed by their praise of my father; it was only what everyone said. People called him a champion of civil rights; he gave speeches on the radio, and occasionally he appeared on television. (The first time I'd seen him on Channel 5, I'd been gravely disappointed by the way he looked: the bright lights exaggerated the furrows that ran between his nose and mouth, and his narrow eyes gave him a sinister air; he looked like an Oriental villain in a Saturday afternoon thriller.) During the past year he had organized a boycott that integrated the staff of a huge frozen-food plant in Philadelphia, and he'd been away several times to attend marches and meetings in the South. I was privately embarrassed to have a parent who freely admitted going to jail in Alabama, but the students who visited New African seemed to think it almost miraculous. Their conversations with my father were peppered with references to places I had never seen, towns I imagined as being swathed in a mist of darkness visible: Selma, Macon, Birmingham, Biloxi.

Matthew and I had long ago observed that what Daddy generally did in his sermons was to speak very softly and then surprise everyone with a shout. Of course, I knew that there was more to it than that; even in those days I recognized a genius of personality in my father. He loved crowds, handling them with the expert good humor of a man entirely in his element. At church banquets, at the vast annual picnic that was held beside a lake in New Jersey, or at any gathering in the backyards and living rooms of the town where we lived, the sound I heard most often was the booming of my father's voice followed by shouts of laughter from the people around him. He had a passion for oratory; at home, he infuriated Matthew and me by staging absurd debates at the dinner table, verbal melees that he won quite selfishly, with a loud crow of delight at his own virtuosity. "Is a fruit a vegetable?" he would demand. "Is a zipper a machine?" Matthew and I would plead with him to be quiet as we strained to get our own points across, but it was no use. When the last word had resounded and we sat looking at him in irritated silence, he would clear his throat, settle his collar, and resume eating, his face still glowing with an irrepressible glee.

When he preached, he showed the same private delight. A look of rapt pleasure seemed to broaden and brighten the contours of his angular face until it actually appeared to give off light as he spoke. He could preach in two very different ways. One was the delicate, sonorous idiom of formal oratory, with which he must have won the prizes he held from his seminary days. The second was a hectoring, insinuating, incantatory tone, full of the rhythms of the South he had never lived in, linking him to generations of thunderous Baptist preachers. When he used this tone, as he was doing now, affectionate laughter rippled through the pews.

"I know," he said, looking out over the congregation and blinking his eyes rapidly, "that there are certain people in this room—oh, I don't have to name names or point a finger—who have ignored that small true voice, the voice that is the voice of Jesus calling out in the shadowy depths of the soul. And while you all are looking around and wondering just who those 'certain people' are, I want to tell you all a secret: they are you and me, and your brother-in-law, and every man, woman, and child in this room this morning. All of us listen to our bellies when they tell us it is time to eat, we pay attention to our eyes when they grow heavy from wanting sleep, but when it comes to the sacred knowledge our hearts can offer, we are deaf, dumb, blind, and senseless. Throw away that blindness, that deafness, that sulky indifference. When all the world lies to you, Jesus will tell you what is right. Listen to him. Call on him. In these times of confusion, when there are a dozen different ways to turn, and Mama and Papa can't help you, trust Jesus to set you straight. Listen to him. The Son of God has the answers. Call on him. Call on him. Call on him."

The sermon was punctuated with an occasional loud "Amen!" from Miss Middleton, an excitable old lady whose eyes flashed

defiantly at the reproving faces of those around her. New African
was not the kind of Baptist church where shouting was a normal
part of the service; I occasionally heard my father mock the
staid congregation by calling it Saint African. Whenever Miss
Middleton loosed her tongue (sometimes she went off into fits
of rapturous shrieks and had to be helped out of the service by
the church nurse), my mother and aunts exchanged grimaces
and shrugged, as if confronted by incomprehensibly barbarous
behavior.

When Daddy had spoken the final words of the sermon, he
drank a glass of water and vanished through a set of red velvet
curtains to the right of the altar. At the same time, the choir
began to sing what was described in the church bulletin as a
"selection." These selections were always arenas for the running
dispute between the choirmaster and the choir. Jordan Grimes,
the choirmaster, was a Curtis graduate who was partial to Han-
del, but the choir preferred artistic spirituals performed in the
lush, heroic style of Paul Robeson. Grimes had triumphed that
Sunday. As the choir gave a spirited but unwilling rendition of
Agnus Dei, I watched old Deacon West smile in approval. A
Spanish-American War veteran, he admitted to being ninety-
four but was said to be older; his round yellowish face, otherwise
unwrinkled, bore three deep, deliberate-looking horizontal
creases on the brow, like carvings on a scarab. "That old man
is as flirtatious as a boy of twenty!" my mother often said, watching his stiff, courtly movements among the ladies of the church.
Sometimes he gave me a dry kiss and a piece of peppermint
candy after the service; I liked his crackling white collars and
smell of bay rum.

The selection ended; Jordan Grimes struck two deep chords
on the organ, and the lights in the church went low. A subtle
stir ran through the congregation, and I moved closer to my
mother. This was the moment that fascinated and disturbed me
more than anything else at church: the prelude to the ceremony
of baptism. Deacon West rose and drew open the draperies that
had been closed around the baptismal pool, and there stood my
father in water to his waist. The choir began to sing:

We're marching to Zion,
Beautiful, beautiful Zion,
We're marching upward to Zion,
The beautiful city of God!

Down the aisle, guided by two church mothers, came a procession of eight children and adolescents. They wore white robes, the girls with white ribbons in their hair, and they all had solemn expressions of terror on their faces. I knew each one of them. There was Billy Price, a big, slow-moving boy of thirteen, the son of Deacon Price. There were the Duckery twins. There was Caroline Piggee, whom I hated because of her long, soft black curls, her dimpled pink face, and her lisp that ravished grownups. There was Georgie Battis and Sue Anne Ivory, and Wendell and Mabel Cullen.

My mother gave me a nudge. "Run up to the side of the pool!" she whispered. It was the custom for unbaptized children to watch the ceremony from the front of the church. They sat on the knees of the deacons and church mothers, and it was not unusual for a child to volunteer then and there for next month's baptism. I made my way quickly down the dark aisle, feeling the carpet slip under the smooth soles of my patent-leather shoes.

When I reached the side of the pool, I sat down in the bony lap of Bessie Gray, an old woman who often took care of Matthew and me when our parents were away; we called her Aunt Bessie. She was a fanatically devout Christian whose strict ideas on child-rearing had evolved over decades of domestic service to a rich white family in Delaware. The link between us, a mixture of hostility and grudging affection, had been forged in hours of pitched battles over bedtimes and proper behavior. Her worshipful respect for my father, whom she called "the Rev," was exceeded only by her pride—the malice-tinged pride of an omniscient family servant—in her "white children," to whom she often unflatteringly compared Matthew and me. It was easy to see why my mother and her circle of fashionable matrons described Bessie Gray as "archaic"—one had only to look at her black straw hat attached with three enormous old-fashioned pins to her knot of frizzy white hair. Her lean, brown-skinned face was dominated by a hawk nose inherited from some Indian ancestor and punctuated by a big black mole; her eyes were small, shrewd, and baleful. She talked in ways that were already passing into history and parody, and she wore a thick orange face powder that smelled like dead leaves.

I leaned against her spare bosom and watched the other children clustered near the pool, their bonnets and hair ribbons and round heads outlined in the dim light. For a minute it was very still. Somewhere in the hot, darkened church a baby gave a fretful murmur; from outside came the sound of cars passing in the street. The candidates for baptism, looking stiff and self-conscious, stood lined up on the short stairway leading to the pool. Sue Anne Ivory fiddled with her sleeve and then put her fingers in her mouth.

Daddy spoke the opening phrases of the ceremony: "In the Baptist Church, we do not baptize infants, but believe that a person must choose salvation for himself."

I didn't listen to the words; what I noticed was the music of the whole—how the big voice darkened and lightened in tone, and how the grand architecture of the Biblical sentences ennobled the voice. The story, of course, was about Jesus and John the Baptist. One phrase struck me newly each time: "This is my beloved son, in whom I am well pleased!" Daddy sang out these words in a clear, triumphant tone, and the choir echoed him. Ever since I could understand it, this phrase had made me feel melancholy; it seemed to expose a hard knot of disobedience that had always lain inside me. When I heard it, I thought enviously of Matthew, for whom life seemed to be a sedate and ordered affair: he, not I, was a child in whom a father could be well pleased.

Daddy beckoned to Billy Price, the first baptismal candidate in line, and Billy, ungainly in his white robe, descended the steps into the pool. In soft, slow voices the choir began to sing:

Wade in the water,
Wade in the water, children,
Wade in the water,
God gonna trouble
The water.

In spite of Jordan Grimes's efforts, the choir swayed like a gospel chorus as it sang this spiritual; the result was to add an eerie jazz beat to the minor chords. The music gave me gooseflesh. Daddy had told me that this was the same song that the slaves had sung long ago in the South, when they gathered to be baptized in rivers and streams. Although I cared little about history, and found it hard to picture the slaves as being any ancestors of mine, I could clearly imagine them coming together beside a broad muddy river that wound away between trees drooping with strange vegetation. They walked silently in lines, their faces very black against their white clothes, leading their children. The whole scene was bathed in the heavy golden light that meant age and solemnity, the same light that seemed to weigh down the Israelites in illustrated volumes of Bible stories, and that shone now from the baptismal pool, giving the ceremony the air of a spectacle staged in a dream.

All attention in the darkened auditorium was now focused on the pool, where between the red curtains my father stood holding Billy Price by the shoulders. Daddy stared into Billy's face, and the boy stared back, his lips set and trembling. "And now, by the power invested in me," said Daddy, "I baptize you in the name of the Father, the Son, and the Holy Ghost." As he pronounced these words, he conveyed a tenderness as efficient and impersonal as a physician's professional manner; beneath it, however, I could see a strong private gladness, the same delight that transformed his face when he preached a sermon. He paused to flick a drop of water off his forehead, and then, with a single smooth, powerful motion of his arms, he laid Billy Price back into the water as if he were putting an infant to bed. I caught my breath as the boy went backward. When he came up, sputtering, two church mothers helped him out of the pool and through a doorway into a room where he would be dried and dressed. Daddy shook the water from his hands and gave a slight smile as another child entered the pool.

One by one, the baptismal candidates descended the steps. Sue Anne Ivory began to cry and had to be comforted. Caroline Piggee blushed and looked up at my father with such a coquettish air that I jealously wondered how he could stand it. After a few baptisms my attention wandered, and I began to gnaw the edge of my thumb and to peer at the pale faces of the visiting college students. Then I thought about Matthew, who had punched me in the arm that morning and had shouted, "No punchbacks!" I thought as well about a collection of horse chestnuts I meant to assemble in the fall, and about two books, one whose subject was adults and divorces, and another, by E. Nesbit, that continued the adventures of the Bastable children.

After Wendell Cullen had left the water (glancing uneasily back at the wet robe trailing behind him), Daddy stood alone among the curtains and the mirrors. The moving reflections from the pool made the stuffed dove hanging over him seem to flutter on its string. "Dear Lord," said Daddy, as Jordan Grimes struck a chord, "bless these children who have chosen to be baptized in accordance with your teaching, and who have been reborn to carry out your work. In each of them, surely, you are well pleased." He paused, staring out into the darkened auditorium. "And if there is anyone out there—man, woman, child—who wishes to be baptized next month, let him come forward now." He glanced around eagerly. "Oh, do come forward and give Christ your heart and give me your hand!"

Just then Aunt Bessie gave me a little shake and whispered sharply, "Go on up and accept Jesus!"

I stiffened and dug my bitten fingernails into my palms. The last clash of wills I had had with Aunt Bessie had been when she, crazily set in her old southern attitudes, had tried to make me wear an enormous straw hat, as her "white children" did, when I played outside in the sun. The old woman had driven me to madness, and I had ended up spanked and sullen, crouching moodily under the dining-room table. But this was different, outrageous, none of her business, I thought. I shook my head violently and she took advantage of the darkness in the church to seize both of my shoulders and jounce me with considerable roughness, whispering, "Now, listen, young lady! Your daddy up there is calling you to Christ. Your big brother has already offered his soul to the Lord. Now Daddy wants his little girl to step forward."

"No, he doesn't." I glanced at the baptismal pool, where my father was clasping the hand of a strange man who had come up to him. I hoped that this would distract Aunt Bessie, but she was tireless.

"Your mama and your aunt Lily and your aunt May all want you to answer the call. You're hurting them when you say no to Jesus."

"No, I'm not!" I spoke out loud and I saw the people nearby turn to look at me. At the sound of my voice, Daddy, who was a few yards away, faltered for a minute in what he was saying and glanced over in my direction.

Aunt Bessie seemed to lose her head. She stood up abruptly, pulling me with her, and, while I was still frozen in a dreadful paralysis, tried to drag me down the aisle toward my father. The two of us began a brief struggle that could not have lasted for more than a few seconds but that seemed an endless mortal conflict—my slippery patent-leather shoes braced against the floor, my straw hat sliding cockeyed and lodging against one ear, my right arm twisting and twisting in the iron circle of the old woman's grip, my nostrils full of the dead-leaf smell of her powder and black skirts. In an instant I had wrenched my arm free and darted up the aisle toward Mama, my aunts, and Matthew. As I slipped past the pews in the darkness, I imagined that I could feel eyes fixed on me and hear whispers. "What'd you do, dummy?" whispered Matthew, tugging on my sash as I reached our pew, but I pushed past him without answering. Although it was hot in the church, my teeth were chattering: it

was the first time I had won a battle with a grownup, and the
earth seemed to be about to cave in beneath me. I squeezed in
between Mama and Aunt Lily just as the lights came back on
in the church. In the baptismal pool, Daddy raised his arms for
the last time. "The Lord bless you and keep you," came his big
voice. "The Lord be gracious unto you, and give you peace."

What was curious was how uncannily subdued my parents
were when they heard of my skirmish with Aunt Bessie. Normally
they were swift to punish Matthew and me for misbehavior in
church and for breaches in politeness toward adults; this episode
combined the two, and smacked of sacrilege besides. Yet once
I had made an unwilling apology to the old woman (as I kissed
her she shot me such a vengeful glare that I realized that forever
after it was to be war to the death between the two of us), I
was permitted, once we had driven home, to climb up into the
green shade of the big maple tree I had dreamed of throughout
the service. In those days, more than now, I fell away into a
remote dimension whenever I opened a book; that afternoon,
as I sat with rings of sunlight and shadow moving over my arms
and legs, and winged yellow seeds plopping down on the pages
of *The Story of the Treasure Seekers*, I felt a vague uneasiness floating
in the back of my mind—a sense of having misplaced something,
of being myself misplaced. I was holding myself quite aloof from
considering what had happened, as I did with most serious
events, but through the adventures of the Bastables I kept remembering the way my father had looked when he'd heard what
had happened. He hadn't looked severe or angry, but merely
puzzled, and he had regarded me with the same puzzled expression, as if he'd just discovered that I existed and didn't know
what to do with me. "What happened, Sairy?" he asked, using
an old baby nickname, and I said, "I didn't want to go up there."
I hadn't cried at all, and that was another curious thing.

After that Sunday, through some adjustment in the adult
spheres beyond my perception, all pressure on me to accept
baptism ceased. I turned twelve, fifteen, then eighteen without
being baptized, a fact that scandalized some of the congregation;

however, my parents, who openly discussed everything else, never said a word to me. The issue, and the episode that had illuminated it, was surrounded by a clear ring of silence that, for our garrulous family, was something close to supernatural. I continued to go to New African—in fact, continued after Matthew, who dropped out abruptly during his freshman year in college; the ambiguousness in my relations with the old church gave me at times an inflated sense of privilege (I saw myself as a romantically isolated religious heroine, a sort of self-made Baptist martyr) and at other times a feeling of loss that I was too proud ever to acknowledge. I never went up to take my father's hand, and he never commented upon that fact to me. It was an odd pact, one that I could never consider in the light of day; I stored it in the subchambers of my heart and mind. It was only much later, after he died, and I left New African forever, that I began to examine the peculiar gift of freedom my father—whose entire soul was in the church, and in his exuberant, bewitching tongue—had granted me through his silence.

Mothers

and

Sons

Mother to Son

LANGSTON HUGHES

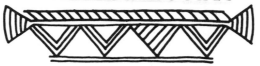

Well, son, I'll tell you:
Life for me ain't been no crystal stair.
It's had tacks in it,
And splinters,
And boards torn up,
And places with no carpet on the floor—
Bare.
But all the time
I'se been a-climbin' on,
And reachin' landin's,
And turnin' corners,
And sometimes goin' in the dark
Where there ain't been no light.
So boy, don't you turn back.
Don't you set down on the steps
'Cause you finds it's kinder hard.
Don't you fall now—
For I'se still goin', honey,
I'se still climbin',
And life for me ain't been no crystal stair.

The Sky Is Gray

ERNEST J. GAINES

1: Go'n be coming in a few minutes. Coming round that bend down there full speed. And I'm go'n get out my handkerchief and wave it down, and we go'n get on it and go.

I keep on looking for it, but Mama don't look that way no more. She's looking down the road where we just come from. It's a long old road, and far's you can see you don't see nothing but gravel. You got dry weeds on both sides, and you got trees on both sides, and fences on both sides, too. And you got cows in the pastures and they standing close together. And when we was coming out here to catch the bus I seen the smoke coming out of the cows's noses.

I look at my mama and I know what she's thinking. I been with Mama so much, just me and her, I know what she's thinking all the time. Right now it's home—Auntie and them. She's thinking if they got enough wood—if she left enough there to keep them warm till we get back. She's thinking if it go'n rain and if any of them go'n have to go out in the rain. She's thinking 'bout the hog—if he go'n get out, and if Ty and Val be able to get him back in. She always worry like that when she leaves the house. She don't worry too much if she leave me there with the smaller ones, 'cause she know I'm go'n look after them and look after Auntie and everything else. I'm the oldest and she say I'm the man.

I look at my mama and I love my mama. She's wearing that black coat and that black hat and she's looking sad. I love my mama and I want put my arm round her and tell her. But I'm not supposed to do that. She say that's weakness and that's crybaby stuff, and she don't want no crybaby round her. She don't want you to be scared, either. 'Cause Ty's scared of ghosts and she's always whipping him. I'm scared of the dark, too, but I make 'tend I ain't. I make 'tend I ain't 'cause I'm the oldest, and I got to set a good sample for the rest. I can't ever be scared and I can't ever cry. And that's why I never said nothing 'bout my teeth. It's been hurting me and hurting me close to a month now, but I never said it. I didn't say it 'cause I didn't want act like a crybaby, and 'cause I know we didn't have enough money to go have it pulled. But, Lord, it been hurting me. And look like it wouldn't start till at night when you was trying to get yourself little sleep. Then soon 's you shut your eyes-ummm-ummm, Lord, look like it go right down to your heartstring.

"Hurting, hanh?" Ty'd say.

I'd shake my head, but I wouldn't open my mouth for nothing. You open your mouth and let that wind in, and it almost kill you.

I'd just lay there and listen to them snore. Ty there, right 'side me, and Auntie and Val over by the fireplace. Val younger than me and Ty, and he sleeps with Auntie. Mama sleeps round the other side with Louis and Walker.

I'd just lay there and listen to them, and listen to that wind out there, and listen to that fire in the fireplace. Sometimes it'd stop long enough to let me get little rest. Sometimes it just hurt, hurt, hurt. Lord, have mercy.

2: Auntie knowed it was hurting me. I didn't tell nobody but Ty, 'cause we buddies and he ain't go'n tell nobody. But some kind of way Auntie found out. When she asked me, I told her no, nothing was wrong. But she knowed it all the time. She told me to mash up a piece of aspirin and wrap it in some cotton and jugg it down in that hole. I did it, but it didn't do no good. It stopped for a little while, and started right back again. Auntie wanted to tell Mama, but I told her, "Uh-uh." 'Cause I knowed we didn't have any money, and it just was go'n make her mad again. So Auntie told Monsieur Bayonne, and Monsieur Bayonne

came over to the house and told me to kneel down 'side him
on the fireplace. He put his finger in his mouth and made the
Sign of the Cross on my jaw. The tip of Monsieur Bayonne's
finger is some hard, 'cause he's always playing on that guitar. If
we sit outside at night we can always hear Monsieur Bayonne
playing on his guitar. Sometimes we leave him out there playing
on the guitar.

Monsieur Bayonne made the Sign of the Cross over and over
on my jaw, but that didn't do no good. Even when he prayed
and told me to pray some, too, that tooth still hurt me.

"How you feeling?" he say.

"Same," I say.

He kept on praying and making the Sign of the Cross and I
kept on praying, too.

"Still hurting?" he say.

"Yes, sir."

Monsieur Bayonne mashed harder and harder on my jaw. He
mashed so hard he almost pushed me over on Ty. But then he
stopped.

"What kind of prayers you praying, boy?" he say.

"Baptist," I say.

"Well, I'll be—no wonder that tooth still killing him. I'm going
one way and he pulling the other. Boy, don't you know any
Catholic prayers?"

"I know 'Hail Mary,' " I say.

"Then you better start saying it."

"Yes, sir."

He started mashing on my jaw again, and I could hear him
praying at the same time. And, sure enough, after while it
stopped hurting me.

Me and Ty went outside where Monsieur Bayonne's two
hounds was and we started playing with them. "Let's go hunting,"
Ty say. "All right," I say; and we went on back in the pasture.
Soon the hounds got on a trail, and me and Ty followed them
all 'cross the pasture and then back in the woods, too. And then
they cornered this little old rabbit and killed him, and me and

Ty made them get back, and we picked up the rabbit and started on back home. But my tooth had started hurting me again. It was hurting me plenty now, but I wouldn't tell Monsieur Bayonne. That night I didn't sleep a bit, and first thing in the morning Auntie told me to go back and let Monsieur Bayonne pray over me some more. Monsieur Bayonne was in his kitchen making coffee when I got there. Soon's he seen me he knowed what was wrong.

"All right, kneel down there 'side that stove," he say. "And this time make sure you pray Catholic. I don't know nothing 'bout that Baptist, and I don't want know nothing 'bout him."

3: Last night Mama say, "Tomorrow we going to town."

"It ain't hurting me no more," I say. "I can eat anything on it."

"Tomorrow we going to town," she say.

And after she finished eating, she got up and went to bed. She always go to bed early now. 'Fore Daddy went in the Army, she used to stay up late. All of us sitting out on the gallery or round the fire. But now, look like soon 's she finish eating she go to bed.

This morning when I woke up, her and Auntie was standing 'fore the fireplace. She say: "Enough to get there and get back. Dollar and a half to have it pulled. Twenty-five for me to go, twenty-five for him. Twenty-five for me to come back, twenty-five for him. Fifty cents left. Guess I get little piece of salt meat with that."

"Sure can use it," Auntie say. "White beans and no salt meat ain't white beans."

"I do the best I can," Mama say.

They was quiet after that, and I made 'tend I was still asleep.

"James, hit the floor," Auntie say.

I still made 'tend I was asleep. I didn't want them to know I was listening.

"All right," Auntie say, shaking me by the shoulder. "Come on. Today's the day."

I pushed the cover down to get out, and Ty grabbed it and pulled it back.

"You, too, Ty," Auntie say.

"I ain't getting no teef pulled," Ty say.

"Don't mean it ain't time to get up," Auntie say. "Hit it, Ty."

Ty got up grumbling.

"James, you hurry up and get in your clothes and eat your food," Auntie say. "What time y'all coming back?" she say to Mama.

"That 'leven o'clock bus," Mama say. "Got to get back in that field this evening."

"Get a move on you, James," Auntie say.

I went in the kitchen and washed my face, then I ate my breakfast. I was having bread and syrup. The bread was warm and hard and tasted good. And I tried to make it last a long time.

Ty came back there grumbling and mad at me.

"Got to get up," he say. "I ain't having no teefes pulled. What I got to be getting up for?"

Ty poured some syrup in his pan and got a piece of bread. He didn't wash his hands, neither his face, and I could see that white stuff in his eyes.

"You the one getting your teef pulled," he say. "What I got to get up for. I bet if I was getting a teef pulled, you wouldn't be getting up. Shucks; syrup again. I'm getting tired of this old syrup. Syrup, syrup, syrup. I'm go'n take with the sugar diabetes. I want me some bacon sometime."

"Go out in the field and work and you can have your bacon," Auntie say. She stood in the middle door looking at Ty. "You better be glad you got syrup. Some people ain't got that—hard 's time is."

"Shucks," Ty say. "How can I be strong."

"I don't know too much 'bout your strength," Auntie say; "but I know where you go'n be hot at, you keep that grumbling up. James, get a move on you; your mama's waiting."

I ate my last piece of bread and went in the front room. Mama was standing 'fore the fireplace warming her hands. I put on my coat and my cap, and we left the house.

4: I look down there again, but it still ain't coming. I almost say, "It ain't coming yet," but I keep my mouth shut. 'Cause that's something else she don't like. She don't like for you to say something just for nothing. She can see it ain't coming, I can see it ain't coming, so why say it ain't coming. I don't say it, I turn and look at the river that's back of us. It's so cold the smoke's just raising up from the water. I see a bunch of pool-doos not too far out—just on the other side the lilies. I'm wondering if you can eat pool-doos. I ain't too sure, 'cause I ain't never ate none. But I done ate owls and blackbirds, and I done ate redbirds, too. I didn't want kill the redbirds, but she made me kill them. They had two of them back there. One in my trap, one in Ty's trap. Me and Ty was go'n play with them and let them go, but she made me kill them 'cause we needed the food.

"I can't," I say. "I can't."

"Here," she say. "Take it."

"I can't," I say. "I can't. I can't kill him, Mama, please."

"Here," she say. "Take this fork, James."

"Please, Mama, I can't kill him," I say.

I could tell she was go'n hit me. I jerked back, but I didn't jerk back soon enough.

"Take it," she say.

I took it and reached in for him, but he kept on hopping to the back.

"I can't, Mama," I say. The water just kept on running down my face. "I can't," I say.

"Get him out of there," she say.

I reached in for him and he kept on hopping to the back. Then I reached in farther, and he pecked me on the hand.

"I can't, Mama," I say.

She slapped me again.

I reached in again, but he kept on hopping out my way. Then

he hopped to one side and I reached there. The fork got him on the leg and I heard his leg pop. I pulled my hand out 'cause I had hurt him.

"Give it here," she say, and jerked the fork out my hand.

She reached in and got the little bird right in the neck. I heard the fork go in his neck, and I heard it go in the ground. She brought him out and helt him right in front of me.

"That's one," she say. She shook him off and gived me the fork. "Get the other one."

"I can't, Mama," I say. "I'll do anything, but don't make me do that."

She went to the corner of the fence and broke the biggest switch over there she could find. I knelt 'side the trap, crying.

"Get him out of there," she say.

"I can't, Mama."

She started hitting me 'cross the back. I went down on the ground, crying.

"Get him," she say.

"Octavia?" Auntie say.

'Cause she had come out of the house and she was standing by the tree looking at us.

"Get him out of there," Mama say.

"Octavia," Auntie say, "explain to him. Explain to him. Just don't beat him. Explain to him."

But she hit me and hit me and hit me.

I'm still young—I ain't no more than eight; but I know now; I know why I had to do it. (They was so little, though. They was so little. I 'member how I picked the feathers off them and cleaned them and helt them over the fire. Then we all ate them. Ain't had but a little bitty piece each, but we all had a little bitty piece, and everybody just looked at me 'cause they was so proud.) Suppose she had to go away? That's why I had to do it. Suppose she had to go away like Daddy went away? Then who was go'n look after us? They had to be somebody left to carry on. I didn't know it then, but I know it now. Auntie and Monsieur Bayonne talked to me and made me see.

5: Time I see it I get out my handkerchief and start waving. It's still 'way down there, but I keep waving anyhow. Then it come up and stop and me and Mama get on. Mama tell me go sit in the back while she pay. I do like she say, and the people look at me. When I pass the little sign that say "White" and "Colored," I start looking for a seat. I just see one of them back there, but I don't take it, 'cause I want my mama to sit down herself. She comes in the back and sit down, and I lean on the seat. They got seats in the front, but I know I can't sit there, 'cause I have to sit back of the sign. Anyhow, I don't want sit there if my mama go'n sit back here.

They got a lady sitting 'side my mama and she looks at me and smiles little bit. I smile back, but I don't open my mouth, 'cause the wind'll get in and make that tooth ache. The lady take out a pack of gum and reach me a slice, but I shake my head. The lady just can't understand why a little boy'll turn down gum, and she reach me a slice again. This time I point to my jaw. The lady understands and smiles little bit, and I smile little bit, but I don't open my mouth, though.

They got a girl sitting 'cross from me. She got on a red overcoat and her hair's plaited in one big plait. First, I make 'tend I don't see her over there, but then I start looking at her little bit. She make 'tend she don't see me, either, but I catch her looking that way. She got a cold, and every now and then she h'ist that little handkerchief to her nose. She ought to blow it, but she don't. Must think she's too much a lady or something.

Every time she h'ist that little handkerchief, the lady 'side her say something in her ear. She shakes her head and lays her hands in her lap again. Then I catch her kind of looking where I'm at. I smile at her little bit. But think she'll smile back? Uh-uh. She just turn up her little old nose and turn her head. Well, I show her both of us can turn us head. I turn mine too and look out at the river.

The river is gray. The sky is gray. They have pool-doos on the water. The water is wavy, and the pool-doos go up and down. The bus go round a turn, and you got plenty trees hiding the river. Then the bus go round another turn, and I can see the river again.

I look toward the front where all the white people sitting. Then I look at that little old gal again. I don't look right at her, 'cause I don't want all them people to know I love her. I just look at her little bit, like I'm looking out that window over there. But she knows I'm looking that way, and she kind of look at me, too. The lady sitting 'side her catch her this time, and she leans over and says something in her ear.

"I don't love him nothing," that little old gal says out loud.

Everybody back there hear her mouth, and all of them look at us and laugh.

"I don't love you, either," I say. "So you don't have to turn up your nose, Miss."

"You the one looking," she say.

"I wasn't looking at you," I say. "I was looking out that window, there."

"Out that window, my foot," she say. "I seen you. Everytime I turned round you was looking at me."

"You must of been looking yourself if you seen me all them times," I say.

"Shucks," she say, "I got me all kind of boyfriends."

"I got girlfriends, too," I say.

"Well, I just don't want you getting your hopes up," she say.

I don't say no more to that little old gal 'cause I don't want have to bust her in the mouth. I lean on the seat where Mama sitting, and I don't even look that way no more. When we get to Bayonne, she jugg her little old tongue out at me. I make 'tend I'm go'n hit her, and she duck down 'side her mama. And all the people laugh at us again.

6: Me and Mama get off and start walking in town. Bayonne is a little bitty town. Baton Rouge is a hundred times bigger than Bayonne. I went to Baton Rouge once—me, Ty, Mama, and Daddy. But that was 'way back yonder, 'fore Daddy went in the Army. I wonder when we go'n see him again. I wonder when. Look like he ain't ever coming back home. . . . Even the pavement all cracked in Bayonne. Got grass shooting right out the sidewalk. Got weeds in the ditch, too; just like they got at home.

It's some cold in Bayonne. Look like it's colder than it is home. The wind blows in my face, and I feel that stuff running down my nose. I sniff. Mama says use that handkerchief. I blow my nose and put it back.

We pass a school and I see them white children playing in the yard. Big old red school, and them children just running and playing. Then we pass a café, and I see a bunch of people in there eating. I wish I was in there 'cause I'm cold. Mama tells me keep my eyes in front where they belong.

We pass stores that's got dummies, and we pass another café, and then we pass a shoe shop, and that bald-head man in there fixing on a shoe. I look at him and I butt into that white lady, and Mama jerks me in front and tells me stay there.

We come up to the courthouse, and I see the flag waving there. This flag ain't like the one we got at school. This one here ain't got but a handful of stars. One at school got a big pile of stars—one for every state. We pass it and we turn and there it is—the dentist office. Me and Mama go in, and they got people sitting everywhere you look. They even got a little boy in there younger than me.

Me and Mama sit on that bench, and a white lady come in there and ask me what my name is. Mama tells her and the white lady goes on back. Then I hear somebody hollering in there. Soon 's that little boy hear him hollering, he starts hollering, too. His mama pats him and pats him, trying to make him hush up, but he ain't thinking 'bout his mama.

The man that was hollering in there comes out holding his jaw. He is a big old man and he's wearing overalls and a jumper.

"Got it, hanh?" another man asks him.

The man shakes his head—don't want open his mouth.

"Man, I thought they was killing you in there," the other man says. "Hollering like a pig under a gate."

The man don't say nothing. He just heads for the door, and the other man follows him.

"John Lee," the white lady says. "John Lee Williams."

The little boy juggs his head down in his mama's lap and holler more now. His mama tells him go with the nurse, but he ain't thinking 'bout his mama. His mama tells him again, but he don't even hear her. His mama picks him up and takes him in there, and even when the white lady shuts the door I can still hear little old John Lee.

"I often wonder why the Lord let a child like that suffer," a lady says to my mama. The lady's sitting right in front of us on another bench. She's got on a white dress and a black sweater. She must be a nurse or something herself, I reckon.

"Not us to question," a man says.

"Sometimes I don't know if we shouldn't," the lady says.

"I know definitely we shouldn't," the man says. The man looks like a preacher. He's big and fat and he's got on a black suit. He's got a gold chain, too.

"Why?" the lady says.

"Why anything?" the preacher says.

"Yes," the lady says. "Why anything?"

"Not us to question," the preacher says.

The lady looks at the preacher a little while and looks at Mama again.

"And look like it's the poor who suffers the most," she says. "I don't understand it."

"Best not to even try," the preacher says. "He works in mysterious ways—wonders to perform."

Right then little John Lee bust out hollering, and everybody turn they head to listen.

"He's not a good dentist," the lady says. "Dr. Robillard is much better. But more expensive. That's why most of the colored people come here. The white people go to Dr. Robillard. Y'all from Bayonne?"

"Down the river," my mama says. And that's all she go'n say, 'cause she don't talk much. But the lady keeps on looking at her, and so she says, "Near Morgan."

"I see," the lady says.

7: "That's the trouble with the black people in this country today," somebody else says. This one here's sitting on the same side me and Mama's sitting, and he is kind of sitting in front of that preacher. He looks like a teacher or somebody that goes to college. He's got on a suit, and he's got a book that he's been reading. "We don't question is exactly our problem," he says. "We should question and question and question—question everything."

The preacher just looks at him a long time. He done put a toothpick or something in his mouth, and he just keeps on turning it and turning it. You can see he don't like that boy with that book.

"Maybe you can explain what you mean," he says.

"I said what I meant," the boy says. "Question everything. Every stripe, every star, every word spoken. Everything."

"It 'pears to me that this young lady and I was talking 'bout God, young man," the preacher says.

"Question Him, too," the boy says.

"Wait," the preacher says. "Wait now."

"You heard me right," the boy says. "His existence as well as everything else. Everything."

The preacher just looks across the room at the boy. You can see he's getting madder and madder. But mad or no mad, the boy ain't thinking 'bout him. He looks at that preacher just 's hard 's the preacher looks at him.

"Is this what they coming to?" the preacher says. "Is this what we educating them for?"

"You're not educating me," the boy says. "I wash dishes at night so that I can go to school in the day. So even the words you spoke need questioning."

The preacher just looks at him and shakes his head.

"When I come in this room and seen you there with your

book, I said to myself, 'There's an intelligent man.' How wrong a person can be."

"Show me one reason to believe in the existence of a God," the boy says.

"My heart tells me," the preacher says.

" 'My heart tells me,' " the boy says. " 'My heart tells me.' Sure, 'My heart tells me.' And as long as you listen to what your heart tells you, you will have only what the white man gives you and nothing more. Me, I don't listen to my heart. The purpose of the heart is to pump blood throughout the body, and nothing else."

"Who's your paw, boy?" the preacher says.

"Why?"

"Who is he?"

"He's dead."

"And your mon?"

"She's in Charity Hospital with pneumonia. Half killed herself, working for nothing."

"And 'cause he's dead and she's sick, you mad at the world?"

"I'm not mad at the world. I'm questioning the world. I'm questioning it with cold logic, sir. What do words like Freedom, Liberty, God, White, Colored mean? I want to know. That's why *you* are sending us to school, to read and to ask questions. And because we ask these questions, you call us mad. No sir, it is not us who are mad."

"You keep saying 'us'?"

" 'Us.' Yes—us. I'm not alone."

The preacher just shakes his head. Then he looks at everybody in the room—everybody. Some of the people look down at the floor, keep from looking at him. I kind of look 'way myself, but soon 's I know he done turn his head, I look that way again.

"I'm sorry for you," he says to the boy.

"Why?" the boy says. "Why not be sorry for yourself? Why are you so much better off than I am? Why aren't you sorry for these other people in here? Why not be sorry for the lady who had to drag her child into the dentist office? Why not be sorry for the lady sitting on that bench over there? Be sorry for them. Not for me. Some way or the other I'm going to make it."

"No, I'm sorry for you," the preacher says.

"Of course, of course," the boy says, nodding his head. "You're sorry for me because I rock that pillar you're leaning on."

"You can't ever rock the pillar I'm leaning on, young man. It's stronger than anything man can ever do."

"You believe in God because a man told you to believe in God," the boy says. "A white man told you to believe in God. And why? To keep you ignorant so he can keep his feet on your neck."

"So now we the ignorant?" the preacher says.

"Yes," the boy says. "Yes." And he opens his book again.

The preacher just looks at him sitting there. The boy done forgot all about him. Everybody else make 'tend they done forgot the squabble, too.

Then I see that preacher getting up real slow. Preacher's a great big old man and he got to brace himself to get up. He comes over where the boy is sitting. He just stands there a little while looking down at him, but the boy don't raise his head.

"Get up, boy," preacher says.

The boy looks up at him, then he shuts his book real slow and stands up. Preacher just hauls back and hit him in the face. The boy falls back 'gainst the wall, but he straightens himself up and looks right back at that preacher.

"You forgot the other cheek," he says.

The preacher hauls back and hit him again on the other side. But this time the boy braces himself and don't fall.

"That hasn't changed a thing," he says.

The preacher just looks at the boy. The preacher's breathing real hard like he just run up a big hill. The boy sits down and opens his book again.

"I feel sorry for you," the preacher says. "I never felt so sorry for a man before."

The boy makes 'tend he don't even hear that preacher. He

keeps on reading his book. The preacher goes back and gets his hat off the chair.

"Excuse me," he says to us. "I'll come back some other time. Y'all, please excuse me."

And he looks at the boy and goes out the room. The boy h'ist his hand up to his mouth one time to wipe 'way some blood. All the rest of the time he keeps on reading. And nobody else in there say a word.

8: Little John Lee and his mama come out the dentist office, and the nurse calls somebody else in. Then little bit later they come out, and the nurse calls another name. But fast 's she calls somebody in there, somebody else comes in the place where we sitting, and the room stays full.

The people coming in now, all of them wearing big coats. One of them says something 'bout sleeting, another one says he hope not. Another one says he think it ain't nothing but rain. 'Cause, he says, rain can get awful cold this time of year.

All round the room they talking. Some of them talking to people right by them, some of them talking to people clear 'cross the room, some of them talking to anybody'll listen. It's a a little bitty room, no bigger than us kitchen, and I can see everybody in there. The little old room's full of smoke, 'cause you got two old men smoking pipes over by that side door. I think I feel my tooth thumping me some, and I hold my breath and wait. I wait and wait, but it don't thump me no more. Thank God for that.

I feel like going to sleep, and I lean back 'gainst the wall. But I'm scared to go to sleep. Scared 'cause the nurse might call my name and I won't hear her. And Mama might go to sleep, too, and she'll be mad if neither one of us heard the nurse.

I look up at Mama. I love my mama. I love my mama. And when cotton come I'm go'n get her a new coat. And I ain't go'n get a black one, either. I think I'm go'n get her a red one.

"They got some books over there," I say. "Want read one of them?"

Mama looks at the books, but she don't answer me.

"You got yourself a little man there," the lady says.

Mama don't say nothing to the lady, but she must've smiled, 'cause I seen the lady smiling back. The lady looks at me a little while, like she's feeling sorry for me.

"You sure got that preacher out here in a hurry," she says to that boy.

The boy looks up at her and looks in his book again. When I grow up I want be just like him. I want clothes like that and I want keep a book with me, too.

"You really don't believe in God?" the lady says.

"No," he says.

"But why?" the lady says.

"Because the wind is pink," he says.

"What?" the lady says.

The boy don't answer her no more. He just reads in his book.

"Talking 'bout the wind is pink," that old lady says. She's sitting on the same bench with the boy and she's trying to look in his face. The boy makes 'tend the old lady ain't even there. He just keeps on reading. "Wind is pink," she says again. "Eh, Lord, what children go'n be saying next?"

The lady 'cross from us bust out laughing.

"That's a good one," she says. "The wind is pink. Yes sir, that's a good one."

"Don't you believe the wind is pink?" the boy says. He keeps his head down in the book.

"Course I believe it, honey," the lady says. "Course I do." She looks at us and winks her eye. "And what color is grass, honey?"

"Grass? Grass is black."

She bust out laughing again. The boy looks at her.

"Don't you believe grass is black?" he says.

The lady quits her laughing and looks at him. Everybody else looking at him, too. The place quiet, quiet.

"Grass is green, honey," the lady says. "It was green yesterday, it's green today, and it's go'n be green tomorrow."

"How do you know it's green?"

"I know because I know."

"You don't know it's green," the boy says. "You believe it's green because someone told you it was green. If someone had told you it was black you'd believe it was black."

"It's green," the lady says. "I know green when I see green."

"Prove it's green," the boy says.

"Sure, now," the lady says. "Don't tell me it's coming to that."

"It's coming to just that," the boy says. "Words mean nothing. One means no more than the other."

"That's what it all coming to?" that old lady says. That old lady got on a turban and she got on two sweaters. She got a green sweater under a black sweater. I can see the green sweater 'cause some of the buttons on the other sweater's missing.

"Yes ma'am," the boy says. "Words mean nothing. Action is the only thing. Doing. That's the only thing."

"Other words, you want the Lord to come down here and show Hisself to you?" she says.

"Exactly, ma'am," he says.

"You don't mean that, I'm sure?" she says.

"I do, ma'am," he says.

"Done, Jesus," the old lady says, shaking her head.

"I didn't go 'long with that preacher at first," the other lady says; "but now—I don't know. When a person say the grass is black, he's either a lunatic or something's wrong."

"Prove to me that it's green," the boy says.

"It's green because the people say it's green."

"Those same people say we're citizens of these United States," the boy says.

"I think I'm a citizen," the lady says.

"Citizens have certain rights," the boy says. "Name me one right that you have. One right, granted by the Constitution, that you can exercise in Bayonne."

The lady don't answer him. She just looks at him like she don't know what he's talking 'bout. I know I don't.

"Things changing," she says.

"Things are changing because some black men have begun to think with their brains and not their hearts," the boy says.

"You trying to say these people don't believe in God?"

"I'm sure some of them do. Maybe most of them do. But they don't believe that God is going to touch these white people's hearts and change things tomorrow. Things change through action. By no other way."

Everybody sit quiet and look at the boy. Nobody says a thing. Then the lady 'cross the room from me and Mama just shakes her head.

"Let's hope that not all your generation feel the same way you do," she says.

"Think what you please, it doesn't matter," the boy says. "But it will be men who listen to their heads and not their hearts who will see that your children have a better chance than you had."

"Let's hope they ain't all like you, though," the old lady says. "Done forgot the heart absolutely."

"Yes ma'am, I hope they aren't all like me," the boy says. "Unfortunately, I was born too late to believe in your God. Let's hope that the ones who come after will have your faith—if not in your God, then in something else, something definitely that they can lean on. I haven't anything. For me, the wind is pink, the grass is black."

9: The nurse comes in the room where we all sitting and waiting and says the doctor won't take no more patients till one o'clock this evening. My mama jumps up off the bench and goes up to the white lady.

"Nurse, I have to go back in the field this evening," she says.

"The doctor is treating his last patient now," the nurse says. "One o'clock this evening."

"Can I at least speak to the doctor?" my mama asks.

"I'm his nurse," the lady says.

"My little boy's sick," my mama says. "Right now his tooth almost killing him."

The nurse looks at me. She's trying to make up her mind if to let me come in. I look at her real pitiful. The tooth ain't hurting me at all, but Mama say it is, so I make 'tend for her sake.

"This evening," the nurse says, and goes on back in the office.

"Don't feel 'jected, honey," the lady says to Mama. "I been round them a long time—they take you when they want to. If you was white, that's something else; but we the wrong color."

Mama don't say nothing to the lady, and me and her go outside and stand 'gainst the wall. It's cold out there. I can feel that wind going through my coat. Some of the other people come out of the room and go up the street. Me and Mama stand there a little while and we start walking. I don't know where we going. When we come to the other street we just stand there.

"You don't have to make water, do you?" Mama says.

"No, ma'am," I say.

We go on up the street. Walking real slow. I can tell Mama don't know where she's going. When we come to a store we stand there and look at the dummies. I look at a little boy wearing a brown overcoat. He's got on brown shoes, too. I look at my old shoes and look at his'n again. You wait till summer, I say.

Me and Mama walk away. We come up to another store and we stop and look at them dummies, too. Then we go on again. We pass a café where the white people in there eating. Mama tells me keep my eyes in front where they belong, but I can't help from seeing them people eat. My stomach starts to growling 'cause I'm hungry. When I see people eating, I get hungry; when I see a coat, I get cold.

A man whistles at my mama when we go by a filling station. She makes 'tend she don't even see him. I look back and I feel like hitting him in the mouth. If I was bigger, I say; if I was bigger, you'd see.

We keep on going. I'm getting colder and colder, but I don't say nothing. I feel that stuff running down my nose and I sniff.

"That rag," Mama says.

I get it out and wipe my nose. I'm getting cold all over now— my face, my hands, my feet, everything. We pass another little café, but this'n for white people, too, and we can't go in there, either. So we just walk. I'm so cold now I'm 'bout ready to say it. If I knowed where we was going I wouldn't be so cold, but I don't know where we going. We go, we go, we go. We walk clean out of Bayonne. Then we cross the street and we come back. Same thing I seen when I got off the bus this morning. Same old trees, same old walk, same old weeds, same old cracked pave—same old everything.

I sniff again.

"That rag," Mama says.

I wipe my nose real fast and jugg that handkerchief back in my pocket 'fore my hand gets too cold. I raise my head and I can see David's hardware store. When we come up to it, we go in. I don't know why, but I'm glad.

It's warm in there. It's so warm in there you don't ever want to leave. I look for the heater, and I see it over by them barrels. Three white men standing round the heater talking in Creole. One of them comes over to see what my mama want.

"Got any axe handles?" she says.

Me, Mama, and the white man start to the back, but Mama stops me when we come up to the heater. She and the white man go on. I hold my hands over the heater and look at them. They go all the way to the back, and I see the white man pointing to the axe handles 'gainst the wall. Mama takes one of them and shakes it like she's trying to figure how much it weighs. Then she rubs her hand over it from one end to the other end. She turns it over and looks at the other side, then she shakes it again, and shakes her head and puts it back. She gets another one and she does it just like she did the first one, then she shakes her head. Then she gets a brown one and do it that, too. But she don't like this one, either. Then she gets another one, but 'fore she shakes it or anything, she looks at me. Look like she's trying to say something to me, but I don't know what it is. All I know is I done got warm now and I'm feeling right smart better. Mama shakes this axe handle just like she did the others, and shakes her head and says something to the white man. The white man just looks at his pile of axe handles, and when Mama pass him to come to the front, the white man just scratch his head and follows her. She tells me come on and we go on out and start walking again.

We walk and walk, and no time at all I'm cold again. Look like I'm colder now 'cause I can still remember how good it was back there. My stomach growls and I suck it in to keep Mama from hearing it. She's walking right 'side me, and it growls so loud you can hear it a mile. But Mama don't say a word.

10: When we come up to the courthouse, I look at the clock. It's got quarter to twelve. Mean we got another hour and a quarter to be out here in the cold. We go and stand 'side a building. Something hits my cap and I look up at the sky. Sleet's falling.

I look at Mama standing there. I want stand close 'side her, but she don't like that. She say that's crybaby stuff. She say you got to stand for yourself, by yourself.

"Let's go back to that office," she says.

We cross the street. When we get to the dentist office I try to open the door, but I can't. I twist and twist, but I can't. Mama pushes me to the side and she twist the knob, but she can't open the door, either. She turns 'way from the door. I look at her, but I don't move and I don't say nothing. I done seen her like this before and I'm scared of her.

"You hungry?" she says. She says it like she's mad at me, like I'm the cause of everything.

"No, ma'am," I say.

"You want eat and walk back, or you rather don't eat and ride?"

"I ain't hungry," I say.

I ain't just hungry, but I'm cold, too. I'm so hungry and cold I want to cry. And look like I'm getting colder and colder. My feet done got numb. I try to work my toes, but I don't even feel them. Look like I'm go'n die. Look like I'm go'n stand right here and freeze to death. I think 'bout home. I think 'bout Val and Auntie and Ty and Louis and Walker. It's 'bout twelve o'clock and I know they eating dinner now. I can hear Ty making jokes. He done forgot 'bout getting up early this morning and right now he's probably making jokes. Always trying to make somebody laugh. I wish I was right there listening to him. Give anything in the world if I was home round the fire.

"Come on," Mama says.

We start walking again. My feet so numb I can't hardly feel them. We turn the corner and go on back up the street. The clock on the courthouse starts hitting for twelve.

The sleet's coming down plenty now. They hit the pavement and bounce like rice. Oh, Lord, oh, Lord, I pray. Don't let me die, don't let me die, don't let me die, Lord.

11: Now I know where we going. We going back of town where the colored people eat. I don't care if I don't eat. I been hungry before. I can stand it. But I can't stand the cold.

I can see we go'n have a long walk. It's 'bout a mile down there. But I don't mind. I know when I get there I'm go'n warm myself. I think I can hold out. My hands numb in my pockets and my feet numb, too, but if I keep moving I can hold out. Just don't stop no more, that's all.

The sky's gray. The sleet keeps on falling. Falling like rain now—plenty, plenty. You can hear it hitting the pavement. You can see it bouncing. Sometimes it bounces two times 'fore it settles.

We keep on going. We don't say nothing. We just keep on going, keep on going.

I wonder what Mama's thinking. I hope she ain't mad at me. When summer come I'm go'n pick plenty cotton and get her a coat. I'm go'n get her a red one.

I hope they'd make it summer all the time. I'd be glad if it was summer all the time—but it ain't. We got to have winter, too. Lord, I hate the winter. I guess everybody hate the winter.

I don't sniff this time. I get out my handkerchief and wipe my nose. My hands 's so cold I can hardly hold the handkerchief.

I think we getting close, but we ain't there yet. I wonder

where everybody is. Can't see a soul but us. Look like we the only two people moving round today. Must be too cold for the rest of the people to move round in.

I can hear my teeth. I hope they don't knock together too hard and make that bad one hurt. Lord, that's all I need, for that bad one to start off.

I hear a church bell somewhere. But today ain't Sunday. They must be ringing for a funeral or something.

I wonder what they doing at home. They must be eating. Monsieur Bayonne might be there with his guitar. One day Ty played with Monsieur Bayonne's guitar and broke one of the strings. Monsieur Bayonne was some mad with Ty. He say Ty wasn't go'n ever 'mount to nothing. Ty can go just like Monsieur Bayonne when he ain't there. Ty can make everybody laugh when he starts to mocking Monsieur Bayonne.

I used to like to be with Mama and Daddy. We used to be happy. But they took him in the Army. Now, nobody happy no more. . . . I be glad when Daddy comes home.

Monsieur Bayonne say it wasn't fair for them to take Daddy and give Mama nothing and give us nothing. Auntie say, "Shhh, Etienne. Don't let them hear you talk like that." Monsieur Bayonne say, "It's God truth. What they giving his children? They have to walk three and a half miles to school hot or cold. That's anything to give for a paw? She's got to work in the field rain or shine just to make ends meet. That's anything to give for a husband?" Auntie say, "Shhh, Etienne, shhh." "Yes, you right," Monsieur Bayonne say. "Best don't say it in front of them now. But one day they go'n find out. One day." "Yes, I suppose so," Auntie say. "Then what, Rose Mary?" Monsieur Bayonne say. "I don't know, Etienne," Auntie say. "All we can do is us job, and leave everything else in His hand . . ."

We getting closer, now. We getting closer. I can even see the railroad tracks.

We cross the tracks, and now I see the café. Just to get in there, I say. Just to get in there. Already I'm starting to feel little better.

12: We go in. Ahh, it's good. I look for the heater; there 'gainst the wall. One of them little brown ones. I just stand there and hold my hands over it. I can't open my hands too wide 'cause they almost froze.

Mama's standing right 'side me. She done unbuttoned her coat. Smoke rises out of the coat, and the coat smells like a wet dog.

I move to the side so Mama can have more room. She opens out her hands and rubs them together. I rub mine together, too, 'cause this keep them from hurting. If you let them warm too fast, they hurt you sure. But if you let them warm just little bit at a time, and you keep rubbing them, they be all right every time.

They got just two more people in the café. A lady back of the counter, and a man on this side the counter. They been watching us ever since we come in.

Mama gets out the handkerchief and count up the money. Both of us know how much money she's got there. Three dollars. No, she ain't got three dollars, 'cause she had to pay us way up here. She ain't got but two dollars and a half left. Dollar and a half to get my tooth pulled, and fifty cents for us to go back on, and fifty cents worth of salt meat.

She stirs the money round with her finger. Most of the money is change 'cause I can hear it rubbing together. She stirs it and stirs it. Then she looks at the door. It's still sleeting. I can hear it hitting 'gainst the wall like rice.

"I ain't hungry, Mama," I say.

"Got to pay them something for they heat," she says.

She takes a quarter out the handkerchief and ties the handkerchief up again. She looks over her shoulder at the people, but she still don't move. I hope she don't spend the money. I don't want her spending it on me. I'm hungry, I'm almost starving I'm so hungry, but I don't want her spending the money on me.

She flips the quarter over like she's thinking. She's must be thinking 'bout us walking back home. Lord, I sure don't want

walk home. If I thought it'd do any good to say something, I'd
say it. But Mama makes up her own mind 'bout things.

She turns 'way from the heater right fast, like she better hurry
up and spend the quarter 'fore she change her mind. I watch
her go toward the counter. The man and the lady look at her,
too. She tells the lady something and the lady walks away. The
man keeps on looking at her. Her back's turned to the man, and
she don't even know he's standing there.

The lady puts some cakes and a glass of milk on the counter.
Then she pours up a cup of coffee and sets it 'side the other
stuff. Mama pays her for the things and comes on back where
I'm standing. She tells me sit down at the table 'gainst the wall.

The milk and the cakes 's for me; the coffee's for Mama. I
eat slow and I look at her. She's looking outside at the sleet.
She looking real sad. I say to myself, I'm go'n make all this up
one day. You see, one day, I'm go'n make all this up. I want say
it now; I want tell her how I feel right now; but Mama don't
like for us to talk like that.

"I can't eat all that," I say.

They ain't got but just three little old cakes there. I'm so
hungry right now, the Lord knows I can eat a hundred times
three, but I want my mama to have one.

Mama don't even look my way. She knows I'm hungry, she
knows I want it. I let it stay there a little while, then I get it
and eat it. I eat just on my front teeth, though, 'cause if cake
touch that back tooth I know what'll happen. Thank God it ain't
hurt me at all today.

After I finish eating I see the man go to the juke box. He
drops a nickel in it, then he just stand there a little while looking
at the record. Mama tells me keep my eyes in front where they
belong. I turn my head like she say, but then I hear the man
coming toward us.

"Dance, pretty?" he says.

Mama gets up to dance with him. But 'fore you know it, she
done grabbed the little man in the collar and done heaved him
'side the wall. He hit the wall so hard he stop the juke box from
playing.

"Some pimp," the lady back of the counter says. "Some pimp."

The little man jumps up off the floor and starts toward my mama. 'Fore you know it, Mama done sprung open her knife and she's waiting for him.

"Come on," she says. "Come on. I'll gut you from your neighbo to your throat. Come on."

I go up to the little man to hit him, but Mama makes me come and stand 'side her. The little man looks at me and Mama and goes on back to the counter.

"Some pimp," the lady back of the counter says. "Some pimp." She starts laughing and pointing at the little man. "Yes sir, you a pimp, all right. Yes sir-ree."

13: "Fasten that coat, let's go," Mama says.

"You don't have to leave," the lady says.

Mama don't answer the lady, and we right out in the cold again. I'm warm right now—my hands, my ears, my feet—but I know this ain't go'n last too long. It done sleet so much now you got ice everywhere you look.

We cross the railroad tracks, and soon 's we do, I get cold. That wind goes through this little old coat like it ain't even there. I got on a shirt and a sweater under the coat, but that wind don't pay them no mind. I look up and I can see we got a long way to go. I wonder if we go'n make it 'fore I get too cold.

We cross over to walk on the sidewalk. They got just one sidewalk back here, and it's over there.

After we go just a little piece, I smell bread cooking. I look, then I see a baker shop. When we get closer, I can smell it more better. I shut my eyes and make 'tend I'm eating. But I keep them shut too long and I butt up 'gainst a telephone post. Mama grabs me and see if I'm hurt. I ain't bleeding or nothing and she turns me loose.

I can feel I'm getting colder and colder, and I look up to see how far we still got to go. Uptown is 'way up yonder. A half mile more, I reckon. I try to think of something. They say think and you won't get cold. I think of that poem, "Annabel Lee." I ain't been to school in so long—this bad weather—I reckon they done passed "Annabel Lee" by now. But passed it or not, I'm sure Miss Walker go'n make me recite it when I get there. That woman don't never forget nothing. I ain't never seen nobody like that in my life.

I'm still getting cold. "Annabel Lee" or no "Annabel Lee," I'm still getting cold. But I can see we getting closer. We getting there gradually.

Soon 's we turn the corner, I see a little old white lady up in front of us. She's the only lady on the street. She's all in black and she's got a long black rag over her head.

"Stop," she says.

Me and Mama stop and look at her. She must be crazy to be out in all this bad weather. Ain't got but a few other people out there, and all of them's men.

"Y'all done ate?" she says.

"Just finish," Mama says.

"Y'all must be cold then?" she says.

"We headed for the dentist," Mama says. "We'll warm up when we get there."

"What dentist?" the old lady says. "Mr. Bassett?"

"Yes, ma'am," Mama says.

"Come on in," the old lady says. "I'll telephone him and tell him y'all coming."

Me and Mama follow the old lady in the store. It's a little bitty store, and it don't have much in there. The old lady takes off her head rag and folds it up.

"Helena?" somebody calls from the back.

"Yes, Alnest?" the old lady says.

"Did you see them?"

"They're here. Standing beside me."

"Good. Now you can stay inside."

The old lady looks at Mama. Mama's waiting to hear what she brought us in here for. I'm waiting for that, too.

"I saw y'all each time you went by," she says. "I came out to catch you, but you were gone."

"We went back of town," Mama says.

"Did you eat?"

"Yes, ma'am."

The old lady looks at Mama a long time, like she's thinking Mama might be just saying that. Mama looks right back at her. The old lady looks at me to see what I have to say. I don't say nothing. I sure ain't going 'gainst my mama.

"There's food in the kitchen," she says to Mama. "I've been keeping it warm."

Mama turns right around and starts for the door.

"Just a minute," the old lady says. Mama stops. "The boy'll have to work for it. It isn't free."

"We don't take no handout," Mama says.

"I'm not handing out anything," the old lady says. "I need my garbage moved to the front. Ernest has a bad cold and can't go out there."

"James'll move it for you," Mama says.

"Not unless you eat," the old lady says. "I'm old, but I have my pride, too, you know."

Mama can see she ain't go'n beat this old lady down, so she just shakes her head.

"All right," the old lady says. "Come into the kitchen."

She leads the way with that rag in her hand. The kitchen is a little bitty little old thing, too. The table and the stove just 'bout fill it up. They got a little room to the side. Somebody in there laying 'cross the bed—'cause I can see one of his feet. Must be the person she was talking to: Ernest or Alnest—something like that.

"Sit down," the old lady says to Mama. "Not you," she says to me. "You have to move the cans."

"Helena?" the man says in the other room.

"Yes, Alnest?" the old lady says.

"Are you going out there again?"

"I must show the boy where the garbage is, Alnest," the old lady says.

"Keep that shawl over your head," the old man says.

"You don't have to remind me, Alnest. Come, boy," the old
lady says.

We go out in the yard. Little old back yard ain't no bigger
than the store or the kitchen. But it can sleet here just like it
can sleet in any big back yard. And 'fore you know it, I'm
trembling.

"There," the old lady says, pointing to the cans. I pick up one
of the cans and set it right back down. The can's so light, I'm
go'n see what's inside of it.

"Here," the old lady says. "Leave that can alone."

I look back at her standing there in the door. She's got that
black rag wrapped round her shoulders, and she's pointing one
of her little old fingers at me.

"Pick it up and carry it to the front," she says. I go by her
with the can, and she's looking at me all the time. I'm sure the
can's empty. I'm sure she could've carried it herself—maybe both
of them at the same time. "Set it on the sidewalk by the door
and come back for the other one," she says.

I go and come back, and Mama looks at me when I pass her.
I get the other can and take it to the front. It don't feel a bit
heavier than that first one. I tell myself I ain't go'n be nobody's
fool, and I'm go'n look inside this can to see just what I been
hauling. First, I look up the street, then down the street. Nobody
coming. Then I look over my shoulder toward the door. That
little old lady done slipped up there quiet 's mouse, watching
me again. Look like she knowed what I was go'n do.

"Ehh, Lord," she says. "Children, children. Come in here, boy,
and go wash your hands."

I follow her in the kitchen. She points toward the bathroom,
and I go in there and wash up. Little bitty old bathroom, but
it's clean, clean. I don't use any of her towels; I wipe my hands
on my pants legs.

When I come back in the kitchen, the old lady done dished
up the food. Rice, gravy, meat—and she even got some lettuce
and tomato in a saucer. She even got a glass of milk and a piece
of cake there, too. It looks so good, I almost start eating 'fore I
say my blessing.

"Helena?" the old man says.

"Yes, Alnest?"

"Are they eating?"

"Yes," she says.

"Good," he says. "Now you'll stay inside."

The old lady goes in there where he is and I can hear them talking. I look at Mama. She's eating slow like she's thinking. I wonder what's the matter now. I reckon she's thinking 'bout home.

The old lady comes back in the kitchen.

"I talked to Dr. Bassett's nurse," she says. "Dr. Bassett will take you as soon as you get there."

"Thank you, ma'am," Mama says.

"Perfectly all right," the old lady says. "Which one is it?"

Mama nods toward me. The old lady looks at me real sad. I look sad, too.

"You're not afraid, are you?" she says.

"No, ma'am," I say.

"That's a good boy," the old lady says. "Nothing to be afraid of. Dr. Bassett will not hurt you."

When me and Mama get through eating, we thank the old lady again.

"Helena, are they leaving?" the old man says.

"Yes, Alnest."

"Tell them I say good-bye."

"They can hear you, Alnest."

"Good-bye both mother and son," the old man says. "And may God be with you."

Me and Mama tell the old man good-bye, and we follow the old lady in the front room. Mama opens the door to go out, but she stops and comes back in the store.

"You sell salt meat?" she says.

"Yes."

"Give me two bits worth."

"That isn't very much salt meat," the old lady says.

"That's all I have," Mama says.

The old lady goes back of the counter and cuts a big piece

off the chunk. Then she wraps it up and puts it in a paper bag.

"Two bits," she says.

"That looks like awful lot of meat for a quarter," Mama says.

"Two bits," the old lady says. "I've been selling salt meat behind this counter twenty-five years. I think I know what I'm doing."

"You got a scale there," Mama says.

"What?" the old lady says.

"Weigh it," Mama says.

"What?" the old lady says. "Are you telling me how to run my business?"

"Thanks very much for the food," Mama says.

"Just a minute," the old lady says.

"James," Mama says to me. I move toward the door.

"Just one minute, I said," the old lady says.

Me and Mama stop again and look at her. The old lady takes the meat out of the bag and unwraps it and cuts 'bout half of it off. Then she wraps it up again and juggs it back in the bag and gives the bag to Mama. Mama lays the quarter on the counter.

"Your kindness will never be forgotten," she says. "James," she says to me.

We go out, and the old lady comes to the door to look at us. After we go a little piece I look back, and she's still there watching us.

The sleet's coming down heavy, heavy now, and I turn up my coat collar to keep my neck warm. My mama tells me turn it right back down.

"You not a bum," she says. "You a man."

Fathers

and

Sons

Those Winter Sundays

ROBERT HAYDEN

Sundays too my father got up early
and put his clothes on in the blueblack cold,
then with cracked hands that ached
from labor in the weekday weather made
banked fires blaze. No one ever thanked him.

I'd wake and hear the cold splintering, breaking.
When the rooms were warm, he'd call,
and slowly I would rise and dress,
fearing the chronic angers of that house,

Speaking indifferently to him,
who had driven out the cold
and polished my good shoes as well.
What did I know, what did I know
of love's austere and lonely offices?

Forty in the Shade

JOHN MCCLUSKEY, JR.

The loves and lives of the daddies of daddies of daddies.
New blood in those extensions as they drive through their lives.
On his fortieth birthday, Roscoe Sr., had walked into the

kitchen, pushed his hat far back on his head, relit a stub of a
cigar, and spoken to his four sons gathered restlessly at the
kitchen table.

"Cut that playing out now." Then he had settled back in a
chair, stroking his belly upward. That was the signal. Roscoe
Jr., stopped cuffing his brothers on the sides of their heads. Irwin
snatched a wandering marble from under the table and straightened up.

"You boys young now. Or at least you pretend you young.
But I know you got sense. You lived in this house long enough
for you to have good sense. So believe me when I tell you that
you only as young as you feel. A lot of folks say that, but only
a few live by it. You can do anything you want if you decide
to. Anything, that is, except act too mannish and cross me and
your mama. Especially your mama. If you cross me, you'll get
stripes across your butts, just a whippin. But if you cross your
mama, you in for a stone beatin. You'll look worse than a zebra.
But I'm not here to scare you this day, just here to tell you that
I feel like a million dollars, and when y'all get to be forty years
old just remember what your old man was like on this day. And
that he announced that he would never die."

Looks were traded all around. Except that it was afternoon
and he was home with the family, he looked OK. There was
no madness burning brightly in the eyes, no nervous high-volt-
age wringing of the hands. These were the only cues the boys
knew, picked up from watching Mr. Otis Sparks whom everyone
called crazy. Sparks was a man who walked the back alleys at
night, crying, groaning, chanting to himself. Nutty as a fruitcake,
neighbors had whispered about him. But, no, there was nothing
like that about their father. And he said that he would live
forever!

They shrugged and watched him go tenderly among his gifts.
The can of cheap cigars was Emmanuel's idea. The shirts in
brilliant geometric designs were Irwin's. Irwin would be a whiz
with triangles and trigonometry. The checkered ties to balance
the shirts were Chris's gift, Irwin was just a kid after all. Roscoe

Sr., would wear those shirts and those ties, not together, however, but wear them just the same, for he would rather risk the teases of gin-drinking poker players than the disappointment of his sons.

And after the thank-yous and the bearhugs, the older boys would notice him slipping two fingers of bourbon into his tea. That afternoon, forty in the shade of his kitchen, he would sip from the cup, lean dangerously back in the chair, and tell them what they had heard only a few times before. About family and blood and time. About how the family was so tight and never took any mess from anything or anybody. He would lead them through the maze of family history, the broken line of steel mills, of stinking slaughterhouses, and the Ohio River, of Georgia pine forests. The end was the beginning, and a huge man and a town in Georgia—Georgia where the root ends were warmed at the fiery core. Of family of blood of time.

BUT, DADDY

And it was 1834, that end which was the beginning, and the lie of Major Riley. No one knew where the "major" part came from except, perhaps, that the old man was continually waiting around for a war to prove his courage. Such a war would never come, at least enough for him to recognize the daily struggles of men as war. The man died in 1859, mad, wrestling death in a shameful way, much like an old hound, its throat slashed, yet still closing in on a cornered raccoon.

But in 1834 his tall slave Caesar, the best blacksmith in south-central Georgia, bought his freedom. Was given a note from the courage-keeping major. "Return this boy to me." Caesar couldn't read, and thought the scribbling was sure enough freedom papers, a sign of mutual honor among men. He started north on a useless swaybacked horse that the major sold him. Only once did he bother to show that note. That one time was almost his undoing. He showed it to a kind-faced bank clerk who was riding out to a plantation to confirm some figures. The man greeted Caesar and summoned enough nerve to ask for the freedom paper. He read it, then rode down the road a piece with Caesar. When they came upon three paterollers, he turned Caesar over to them. Caesar was only five miles from Riley's plantation and somehow hoping that the North, the Ohio River, would be just over the next ridge. Tennessee as an acre, Kentucky as a backyard of his new life.

The three men led him back to the Major, the long-gone clerk done read them the note because they couldn't read either. They were grizzled men in tatters, "dirt-eaters" they used to call them. Well, they rode back a couple miles before Caesar took and slapped away the rifle of one of the men, slammed a right to the face of another man, crushing bone, and urged the broken-down horse toward the trees. A ball whizzed past his head. Another. He dug his heels into that horse's ribs. They got to the woods, crossed a stream, then headed for thicker cover. Whatever that horse was, he seemed to take to the forest, wasn't scared of the darkness and the trees, whatsoever. Caesar slapped that horse on, and they followed the stream away from Riley's plantation. Yells, curses, screams behind them. Were they a mile away from the paterollers? Were the men just at his ear? He didn't bother to look back, just pushing that horse on, knowing that it would fall out sooner or later from being so tired and from surprise that it could run so fast.

And away, away he rode, not knowing where except that it was away from the plantations. He rode for what seemed like hours until that horse slowed down and stopped. Caesar cursed and kicked that horse, then realized that it had done the best it could do. It needed rest. "Can you see him now, boys? Can you see him in those strange woods on foot?"

Roscoe Sr., had stood, his hat cocked well over one eye by then, fists raised. Then he removed his hat and ran his thumb across his forehead. From the front of the house came their mother's humming, the insistent hum that's never noticed until it stops. The boys didn't dare move, didn't dare speak.

"You must see him lead that horse out of the woods and look across a road to a big field of cotton. There must have been a dozen or so folk in the field, and every once in a while one of them would straighten up and half-scream, half-chant his way through a song. Like young Job who screamed like a woman and called that singing. Then down the road came a wagon. The driver was sitting up there with his head down, shoulders rocking slowly to the corner of his mouth, a large floppy hat draped low, shadowing his eyes. Caesar greeted the man, scaring him half to death. The driver looked around to see if the overseer was around.

"What do you want?" that driver must have asked.

"I want somebody to write a note for me." As he fanned flies, he explained all to the driver, trusting him. The man glanced again to the woods, to the broken-down horse nibbling brush at the wood's edge, to the big man standing in front of the wagon. Then he scratched his throat.

"Only person I know can write is back there about a mile. Name is Ola. But you better not try to see her. She in the house." He must have explained that the owner of the plantation was away, but that the head overseer was around. "You wait here off the road, back up in the piney woods. I'll take you to her."

"How long will that be?" Caesar asked. Any second now he expected the white trash to come busting out of those woods.

"I don't know. Just do like I say if you want me to help you."

Why should he trust that man he had never seen before? Just because they were the same color? He was never going back to Riley's plantation. Never. He faded into the trees, looking behind, around him, searching out sound, then watched the road. Again, the screamchant from the field.

And it seemed like hours before that wagon came back along the road, moving just as slow as it did before. Looking straight ahead as the wagon came up, the driver said, "Climb in back there and get under that blanket. And keep still if you don't want one hundred lashes."

"To hell with lashes," I can hear Caesar saying. "I take lashes off no man."

"Just hush up and get in back." Caesar could hear the man talking as that wagon started moving. He told Caesar about three men who stopped him three miles down the road. They asked him whether he had seen a big man on an ugly gray horse. The driver said that he had and pointed off in another direction. They lit out, not even bothering to thank him.

"Their horses looked a little tired. We don't have much time. They might come back trying to find me."

Yet Caesar still wondered at his faith. Suppose this man driving the wagon had told them otherwise? Suppose they were waiting up the road to take him in? They'd give the driver a new coat for his treason. You often trusted those you suffered with, but then only a few of those could be trusted with your life. The wagon slowed, picked up speed, slowed again. Either the man or the horse couldn't make up its mind. Why was it taking so long? Caesar kept an eye out, watched the brownish red road snake from under the wagon and away. The wagon pulled inside a gate, then stopped. He heard voices.

"Stay here and don't move, son. I'm bringing Ola for you."

The afternoon sun baked him under the scratchy cover. Flies discovered the smell of his sweat from the small opening he kept in order to breathe. Flies as traitors, the enemy that sun. And he waited, not moving, just the fingers still propping the cover to keep the air coming in, though it was as if a hand had been clapped over his nose and mouth. Then footsteps, a woman's voice shushed quiet.

"I got somebody here who can write. Tell her what you want. Just stay like you is."

Caesar could see only the gray cotton skirt draped over thin hips, an elbow with dry skin at the joint.

"Sho is hot, Cle," the voice said. Then she asked Caesar what he wanted her to write. He told her, watching her arm move. "Not so fast." She wrote on, the old man talking to himself about the weather, about fishing. Then several pieces of paper dropped past the opening. She pushed two pieces under the cover and picked up the others.

"Clumsy, ain't I?" she giggled.

"Thank you, girl. We'll see you later."

The gray dress moved away. Caesar heard the man climb in the wagon. They were moving again, turning in a circle.

"You going back to your horse and them piney woods now. Ola gave you two papers. You might lose one. You never know."

They moved on the bumpy road, and Caesar tried to make out the writing. He couldn't read, only judge script. But it was too dark to judge. He pushed the paper into the light.

"Put that paper back in! The woods got eyes, that cotton field got eyes. Them crows can spread secrets just as sure as I'm sitting here. Ain't you lived long enough to know that?"

Then soon the wagon stopped. "There's yo' hoss yonder. He should be good and rested by now. There's something for him in this here bucket. When you finish with the bucket leave it by the big bush over there. Walk back in the woods and wait until dark. Ain't too long now 'fore dark. Then y'all start north. Them po' trash will probably stop somewhere and get drunk come dark. You follow the north star, son. Just follow the star."

A HOME, WHERE?

Then Chris had shifted, Emmanuel shifted. The name, Daddy. Tell us about the name.

Sons, we here as testimony of Caesar's faith in the old man and his courage getting through woods at night. South Georgia was evil in them days, the devil's playground. If I could find you boys another word for it, I would tell it to you. But evil is the best I can do now 'cause your Mama in the next room half-listenin' and she don't want me introducin' y'all to cuss words . . .

His mind was on the North. On Canada and the snow. Somebody probably told him about cutting east to Savannah and catching a ship bound for Philadelphia or someplace like that. But Caesar was not excited about getting out on anybody's ocean, so he took his chances on land. Chance those paterollers, those mountains in Tennessee, past those caves in Kentucky that could hide a hundred bears, past those Indians in Ohio who caught and boiled runaway slaves for stew—that's what they used to tell them in those days, you know. He knew the dangers, though not the vastness of the land. Can you ride with him awhile?

Two days after he left the plantation with his new papers, he stopped just above a small town and rested under some big ol' pine trees. They probably smelled like turpentine. By now those things like slave catchers and Indians didn't bother him. Now it was his name that bothered him. He had told himself that he would take the Major's last name whenever he went free. That was before the Major tried to trick him back into slavery. No, he'd never call himself Riley.

He lay beneath that tree thinking, must have. It was nice there and he rested and the horse rested, and he knew that somewhere he would have to leave that horse and get another one. Gotta leave the best of your helpers sometimes. That town was quiet and peaceful, and somewhere he heard a bell ringing. He must have thought again about the North. If he had to stay in the woods, would there be plenty of fish in the creeks, plenty rabbits in the woods just like down there?

He decided just like that to take the name of that town because of that peaceful moment, nothing else. Somehow with the name he could always remember that moment of peace while struggling to get away. Americus was the name of the town. Americus was the name he took. Caesar Americus. (Years later somebody would tell him how the town got its name. It was named after the richest, powerfulest, and drunkest man around. The man used to claim that he was "a merry ole cuss" and so named his town after his ways. Some white folks got strange ways of makin' jokes, sons.)

He never told how he got from central Georgia. And to me that was always the part I wanted to hear about. Did he go west to the Mississippi and catch a boat going up past Memphis, St. Louis, and Cairo, Illinois? Did he get in with a free black family riding North in a wagon? We don't know, except three months later this warm-weather man done crossed the Ohio River and is working in Cincinnati. It was October and turning cold already. The first chill made him give up thinking about Canada for a while.

He worked on the river. After all, it wasn't the ocean and you could always see the other side. You could make a lot of money working the river. In those days, river rats was what they called the men working on the barges. And he soon became the heart of legends as something of an imitator. Could solo at the head of crews doing them Irish songs. Out-Irish the Irish, he could. Could do the same with the German language, too. Plus he could out-drink them red-faced Germans who came to Cincinnati with their beer recipes and would make whole fortunes on beer, then later on sausages and hams. And he stayed on in that town which on warm evenings grew to stink of river and a little further up among its hills to smell of slaughtered cows and pigs.

In 1842 Caesar opened a bar on the levee, a bar which became the prime target of threats and hisses from the local chapter of the Colored Women's Temperance Society. A window was once broken by an enraged woman screaming about the evils of drink. She called Caesar the devil's helper and a scoundrel who gave the race a bad name. She aimed a rock at the shingle with his name over the door, NORTH STAR CAFE, C. AMERICUS, ESQ., PROPRIETOR. Missed. Then the others joined in the screaming, looking around for rocks. Caesar pleaded with them. Told them they were taking food from the mouths of his young wife and baby sons. He promised a healthy donation to the society, to close at a decent hour, to allow no man to drink himself into a blind stupor. He told them he would even take the "bones" from the fists of the river rats. All this he told them, hating himself for having to say it. All this to save his North Star Café, a testimony to faith.

BUT, DADDY, WHERE IS HOME
IN THIS STRANGE LAND?

The bar would be passed down, battle-tried, standing squat there near the alley in Bucktown. From Caesar's oldest son Stewart to Stewart's oldest son Asbury to his second son Leo because Asbury's oldest, Theodore, my Daddy, had died in France in 1918. It stopped with Uncle Leo, who wasn't too interested in running a café. The family café died out until I come up here and opened up my little place over the B & O tracks. But it ain't good enough yet to call a real café in the way the family used to have. One of these days it will be.

But let me get back to Caesar. The business was his life, though he raised big strapping sons who worked the river. One went clear to Oberlin to hear the great Frederick Douglass and shake his hand. There were the two who fought for the Union, the same two who begged their father, fifty-year-old Caesar, to stay at the café and keep it open. Folks would need that kind of place to talk, lean back in their chairs, back into their lives. Although he could still floor a bull with one punch, they thought him too old to do anything else. He resigned himself to an uneasy peace of sheltering countless frightened families who crossed over from Kentucky, content to feed them hot meals and let the men sample his homemade whiskey.

He kept the bar open for blue-suited men who would limp in, their pants baggy, thinning in the seat and at the knees, and coats too tight. An army of men. They would sit long into the winter nights, and they would talk of battles along hills and rivers named after Indians. The men pointed to scars and said that they never wanted to see war again. When Caesar died, these same scarred men rode through the night to make one of the largest funerals ever held in Cincinnati.

Let me tell y'all right quick about the end of the North Star Café in that town. It was 1918, a little before the war ended. Leo, bless his soul, wasn't too good a manager. He thought the bar could run itself on its past history, I guess. So when he saw it was about to go under, he sold it to an Irishman named Gilligan. Didn't check with none of the family, just up and sold the place. Well, I was mad at him for that, stayed mad at him for that, stayed mad at him for years. I hung around town working in the stockyards and in a foundry for five or six years before I came up here. Heard that the steel and paper mills were hiring like crazy. When I got up here, I walked into the rolling mill office, and the man gave me a shovel and asked me if I could start that day. Worked long hours and made real good money, too. Then later on I fell in with a man named Herschel Evans, and old Herschel had him a truck. On weekends we'd drive down to the coal mines, right along the Ohio River below Portsmouth. We'd leave before the sun came up, get down there, and load that truck skyhigh with coal, buy some large jars of moonshine, and bring all that back here. We'd sell the coal and moonshine in one day, try to get some sleep, and then be back in the mill the next day. By and by I had enough money so that I could open me up an after-hours joint. Right where it is now at the B & O overpass. All these years I've wanted to buy another place, but it's never worked out that way. The depression came along and stopped everything. Settled over this town like a mean and suffocating fog.

It took until after the war for me to really recover. Started fish fries on Friday nights and chicken fries on Saturdays. Your mama did most of the cooking. They were fighting to get in here then, so many of them. I painted the windows black out of respect for the church folk and had to pay a little side-money to Officer Starkey to keep them quiet downtown at police head-quarters. There were four of y'all already. Bedrooms had to be added on and the kitchen needed new plumbing. Well, it got so we kept it open four nights a week.

AND DADDY WHAT MORE, EVEN NOW
FROM BEYOND DEATH, WHAT MORE?

And still what more of the birth, of work, of death of the fathers? The deaths were quick. Caesar died in the café, a loud laugh going to a rattling cough. He fell to the floor behind the bar. Stewart died just as suddenly, while breaking up an argument between two teamsters. Asbury died of pneumonia, the result of working in the rain while helping to put up a YMCA building. Dazed from gas, Theodore stepped on a mine in central France. But Roscoe Sr.'s death was the cruelest of all.

By his fiftieth birthday, Roscoe Sr., the Old Man, as the boys had begun to call him, could afford to drive a red Buick Dynaflow. He wore another dark hat, greying already along the brim, cocked to one side of his large head. There was always a half-smoked cigar in one corner of his mouth. On that fiftieth birthday he leaned back on a chair in the bright kitchen as he had done ten years before.

"Sons, gather close to you the ones you love and protect them if you can." That before the history.

Strange about the murderers of giants in this world—the thinness of their rage, their unforgivable isolation. It was snagga-toothed Jake Mays who did it. Few folks respected Mays and it wasn't just because of his weakness. A weak man can be tolerated and even loved by some. But Mays's weakness willed ugliness. He'd smack a woman or a child for show, but he never touched a man who insulted him.

It started, if it is ever clear when anything starts, when Mays lost his first ten fights as a child, when his father looked at him in pity, frowning at his fistless son. Or was it simply the day after the night Jake lost one hundred dollars in an American Legion crap game? That morning he was on his way to Robinson's Café for a cup of coffee. To tease the new big-legged waitress, maybe, and let any stray smile from her soothe his sense of hurt. Tyrone was playing touch football in the street with a gang of other boys. Quarterback for one of the teams, Tyrone faded back, as he had heard Otto Graham do, and fired a long pass to one of his men. The ball missed the outstretched arms of the receiver by a few yards and hit slow-moving Jake square in the face. The players leaned on fences, cars, on each other, snickering. Looked at Mays's hurt face and laughed some more. Tyrone ran to gather the ball and mumbled something about being sorry. But it was those grins and laughs that Mays saw and heard. He limped closer to Tyrone and smacked him hard. Once. No one moved. Then, as Mays moved away, Tyrone searched for a rock, a pop bottle, to throw. Whatever he found and threw missed. Mays turned around, stared at the boy, then walked on more quickly, looking back twice.

When Roscoe heard about it, he walked out of the house. He found Mays at Robinson's, hunched over coffee. He called Mays outside, and without a word he whipped Mays like a child. The few people in the café crowded in the door to watch, the slaps sounding like dull shots. Then Roscoe let him drop to the pavement, bleeding from a busted lip.

"Don't ever touch one of my boys again. Nobody touches my sons except me." Then he turned and walked away, wiping his hands as if he had touched something filthy.

But there is even a pride in cowardice, a desperate and nervous pride. Near dawn, with a knife and slipping up on the Old Man as he was closing up, Mays found a desperate strength to strike once, twice. Surprised at what he had done, he covered his opened mouth with both hands and ran. Another man, rushing to catch a hand in the last poker game, found Roscoe near the door trying to crawl inside. The knife lay only a few feet away. This man cried his way to a phone and called an ambulance. Then he called Roscoe's home. The sons beat the ambulance there. Beat the 6:30 freight train that rumbled past every morning, heading south, shaking the old blackeyed building.

By the time of the funeral it was decided between Roscoe and Emmanuel that they would have to catch Mays, that he would have to die. He already had a four-day headstart. The question was who. Roscoe Jr., was finishing his freshman year at Ohio State, and the boys argued that he should go back to school. When Earline overheard them, she tried to stop such talk. After all, there was a law, and to harm the worthless Mays would be two crimes committed. They told her that justice was a sometime thing if you didn't perform it yourself.

And Emmanuel packed a bag after talking with old Silas, a man who roomed in the same house with Mays. Silas, with the all-seeing eye, said Mays was in Chicago. Emmanuel left without saying good-bye to anyone, and by the next morning he was winding through Indiana, feeding a quart of oil to his old Ford every three hundred miles, a revolver resting beneath the front seat. No one heard from him for a month. And no one expected Emmanuel to return without Mays. Emmanuel, the quiet one who sang in the church choir and rarely had fights while growing up. But when he did fight he hurt others so badly. Didn't know where to stop, this Emmanuel, whose intensity silenced the agitators and forced them to look around for someone to stop these few fights.

Then the scribbled letters started coming and kept coming, one about every other month for the next three years. At first Earline would read the letters silently, then refold them. She hid them away, and all they knew were the names of the towns. "Your brother is in Battle Creek, Wyoming, now." After she died a letter mysteriously came to Baby Sister once a year. Baby Sister also found the earlier ones and shared them with Roscoe and any other brother who happened to visit her. All those tortured letters with no return addresses.

One letter said he had missed Mays by three days in St. Paul, Minnesota. When a letter came from Lincoln, Nebraska, the brothers figured Mays's time was up. In a place like that Mays should stick out like a rabbit against the snow. But then the letters came from Denver, Salt Lake City, Cheyenne. Denver again. Places Roscoe had never been, could barely imagine except as towns where cowboys shot up bars on Saturday nights.

Earline went to work in a container plant and raised her

children. She was too old to start factory work, but they needed the money. Factory work paid much better than domestic work. A sympathetic foreman understood and gave her the lightest job on the line. The boys helped her run the after-hours club on weekends. Baby Sister ran the house.

Earline had talked less and less about Emmanuel before she died, as she talked less and less about the law and justice. Her husband had died at the hands of a miserable and lonely man, and no matter how senseless and enraging the fact, nothing would ever bring the big man back home. Emmanuel would come back one day, and she had hoped to live to see that day. She hoped that when he did return he could still smile, that he could live again, that everything in his life had not been wasted.

OLD MAN, WHERE IS THE FAITH IN THE NOW OF OUR PASTS?

On the morning of his fortieth birthday, Roscoe Jr., stopped his car in front of the house where until two months ago he had lived. As if on cue, his two daughters rushed to the car, appearing as if they wanted to run, but were held in check by that shadow behind the front door. Roscoe waved to the shadow of his wife, then opened the door for his children.

"Give me a little of that good sugar," he begged them. "Thataway, thataway." Then he pulled them down and announced that he was taking them to the zoo. They clapped their hands, did mean shimmies in their gratitude. Real showboats, his girls. Real class. They presented him with a boldly striped silk tie, and he made a mighty fuss over it. Then he let them roll the window down partially, but not too much, he scolded, because once they would get on the expressway, the wind might just reach in and pull them out.

"Then we could fly?" asked Grace, the daughter with Roscoe's mouth and forehead.

Mayisha giggled. "The way you eat, Grace, you'd be too heavy to fly." Mayisha, with her mother's face, who would be very tall. Roscoe remembered the slouch of her shoulders as she walked to the car. Teach a tall woman to keep high her head and shoulders. Teach her to move like a natural queen. He would teach her not to deny nature's gift of elegant motions. Ever. It only made for stunted beauty.

The girls talked of approaching summer, of swimming lessons they looked forward to, of Bible school they wanted to avoid. Roscoe was relieved that they were still too young for boys. What would he do then? What will he do then? What will he do now? All that he knew for sure was that he was taking his two daughters out for a summer's day and nothing else—the bar, the insatiable Everjean, spiteful Charlotte—nothing else mattered.

Grace curled up next to him. "Daddy, when are we going to King's Point like you promised?"

"How come you're asking Daddy?" Mayisha asked. "You're scared of all the rides anyway."

"Well, let's just see how things turn out today, huh? Today is the zoo."

And the zoo was a hot round of cages with Roscoe coaxing the girls back to see the lions twice. Cotton candy, peanuts, and popcorn. He loved the zoo as much as they did. Zoos and circuses had always been weaknesses of his. Some people remembered cities by the weather or money made or lost there, by lovers. Roscoe remembered places by the food, the bars, and most important, the zoos. There were Washington and Cleveland and St. Louis and San Diego and the Bronx, good zoos in all those places. As he watched the lions for the second time, the girls fidgeted and hummed songs. He considered other places, other times.

Once into a time the air was much chillier, no leaves on the trees. For seven hours he held his wife's hands in the labor room of a hospital. Her lips dry, her eyes frequently opening in the stunned surprise of the cycle of pain. Roscoe held her hands and tried to think of the greatest pain he had known. The twisted knee in the Michigan game? The cracked rib much earlier in high school? None of the bumps, few of the smashes of bone against his muscle gave him pain great beyond the moment. Few caused hours of agony. As he looked at his wife he was a little embarrassed that there was a mystery about her pain that he could never know. Was it a ripple of pain moving wavelike across her belly? A sharp stab? Later in the waiting room after she had been wheeled into delivery, he studied the afternoon. Outside it was partly sunny with the temperature near freezing. He could hear the steady rhythm of a heavy wire against the flagpole in front of the hospital. The traffic flowed in the fitful movement of his luck. It would be a boy this time, he knew. A big healthy fat-cheeked baby boy to carry the family name. Then he thought again to the pain, though his wife would be numbed from her stomach down. Again, to the pain he could only guess at.

"Daddy, how come we can't do this every day?"

Grace. It was Grace talking through her mouthful of popcorn. Grace that afternoon, too.

"You'd like the zoo every day, Grace?" asked Roscoe, reaching to retie a ribbon around her hair.

"Well, not zoos all the time. Maybe parks, yeah, parks. Or swimming? Mama doesn't like to swim."

"Maybe your mama gets a little tired sometime working around the house. You have to understand that."

"I understand," she said, taking another fistful of popcorn. "But I still like the parks and swimming and stuff like that."

He and Charlotte had agreed not to get back at one another through the girls, not to use them as weapons. They would tell them that, even though they were separated, they still loved each other and the girls very very much. The children would nod helplessly and they wouldn't understand. They could not understand what their parents could not understand.

"Hey, girl, you almost finished with that popcorn? Let's go back to the bears."

Mayisha had been quietly watching the morning crowd, the

Cub Scout troops, the elderly folk with small bags of peanuts. Mayisha, the serene wise one. She'd be a painter, photographer, taking in all in the way she does. Roscoe knew that he'd screen the boys so roughly that only the most intelligent, the most aggressive would trouble themselves for her. After all, she wouldn't want to be bothered with idle chatter about clothes, cars, and dances. No, not his Mayisha.

With Roscoe holding his daughters' hands, they moved off through the bright afternoon. The times with his daughters were the best times. The lady days. Going home, he told them the funny animal stories his grandmother had once told him. One day he would tell them the family history.

Then in the speckled shade of an old maple tree in front of the house, Roscoe's ladies stepped grandly from the car. A finger lowered a slat in the front window venetian blinds. He was ready for the stare coming over it from the cool dark of the house he once called home. The stare of those last days, the last nights that he slept on the couch. The girls lingered at the curb. After the hugs and kisses, they stood there wanting more, expecting more, needing more. But there was only his smile.

"Will we see you tomorrow, daddy?"

"I can't promise tomorrow, but I can promise you Saturday. Where do you want to go?"

"Fun Park, can we Daddy, huh? I want to try the roller coaster this time."

Roscoe nodded and waved. "Take care of your pretty selves. And your mother."

He pulled off from the shadow of the old tree and down the quiet street into the gloom of memory. Stared into the mirror.

"Well, Old Man, what do you think now? Am I less of a man because I didn't go inside and hold the woman I've loved for seven of the last twelve years?"

Then he caught himself, as he noticed Mrs. Patterson pausing to watch him from among her daffodils. He smiled at the elderly woman who once brought them spice cakes. Waved, this man

Americus, this former husband, football and wrestling star—
waved and drove to the other side of town.

COMMENTARY ON
JOHN MCCLUSKEY, JR.

Forty in the Shade

Born in 1944 in Middletown, Ohio, John McCluskey received
a B.A. from Harvard and an M.A. in creative writing and English
from Stanford. He is a fiction writer, a critic, and professor of
African-American literature at the University of Indiana in
Bloomington. His short stories have appeared in *Best American
Short Stories, 1976; Stories of the Modern South; The Seattle Review* and
Callaloo. He has published two novels, *Look What They Done to
My Song* (1974) and *Mister America's Last Season Blues* (1983) from
which the story "Forty in the Shade" is taken. He is finishing a
new novel, *The River People,* and is coediting with Charles Johnson
a book of essays on black men in American society, entitled *The
Black Male and the 21st Century.*

"Forty in the Shade" focuses on Roscoe Jr. and his sense of
disappointment in his inability to live up to the legacy of the
line of patriarchs that reaches as far back as the runaway slave
Caesar Americus. There is a biblical quality to this list of patriarchal figures: Caesar begats Stewart who begats Asbury who
begats Theodore and Leo—down to Roscoe Sr. and his four
sons, Roscoe Jr., Irwin, Chris and Emmanuel. Each of the stories
of male family history told by Roscoe Sr. becomes significant
for Roscoe Jr. as he tries to understand why he is having such
a difficult time finding his place in that long, courageous line
of ancestors. This extended look at his past comes during the
breakup of Roscoe Jr.'s marriage, on his fortieth birthday when
he visits with his two daughters, Grace and Mayisha.

Roscoe's sensitivity to his two young daughters, his easy intimacy with them, his sharing in their births suggest that he has been empowered and encouraged through his relationships with the many fathers in his family history. His faith in that history is constructed out of fierce family loyalty, to a family "so tight [it] never took any mess from anything or anybody," and out of the great warmth and tenderness that the fathers have for their sons. Roscoe Sr., for example, wears the embarrassing clothes his sons give him on his birthday because he cannot bear to disappoint them.

The question the narrator asks, in the last section of this story, "*WHERE IS THE FAITH IN THE NOW OF OUR PASTS?*" reminds us of how heavily the past influences the present, the now. McCluskey may even be signifying on James Baldwin's "Sonny's Blues" (in both stories there is a daughter named Grace), since that story also interweaves past and present to show how our constantly shifting idea of family is created out of memory, out of shared history, out of stories that one generation preserves and passes down to the next.

But there is also a disturbing aspect to this story. Tracing his family line back only through his male ancestors and connecting his history to that most patriarchal text—the Bible—Roscoe Jr. renders invisible the experiences of the women in his family. These stories of the great warriors of the past—men of raw physical courage, grandiose deeds, legendary acts of power and endurance—construct a male version of culture in which women are not only repressed and silenced but necessarily become the opposite of men. Thus Roscoe Jr. wonders, as he watches his two daughters, about their gracefulness, their beauty and their power to attract men, qualities which suggest not the passion for living which drives the Americus men, but the passivity of objects whose value and status will be determined by the male gaze. That opposition between male and female is ultimately defeating, and Roscoe, Jr., a divorced father of daughters, worries that his failure to achieve patriarchal status makes him less of a man. A feminist reading of this text might well see Roscoe's questioning of these male stories and his desire to enter into female experience (his participation in the birth of his daughters and his relationship with them) not as failure but as a disruption of a male-dominated version of history and a challenge to the destructive images of manhood inherited from the fathers. Although women play only minor roles in the story, their presence continually undercuts that male history. Caesar's pass to freedom is written by a woman. Earline's hope that her lost son Emmanuel will be able to smile and live again is far more realistic than her sons' ineffectual desire to avenge their father's death. In the final scenes of this story Roscoe is surrounded by women. His ex-wife is peering at him through the window blinds as he hugs his daughters good-bye. And the gloomy memory of a disapproving father is displaced by the nurturing image of the elderly woman, standing among the daffodils, who once brought spice cakes to his family.

A Long Day in November

ERNEST J. GAINES

1: Somebody is shaking me but I don't want get up now, because I'm tired and I'm sleepy and I don't want get up now. It's warm under the cover here, but it's cold up there and I don't want get up now.

"Sonny?" I hear.

But I don't want get up, because it's cold up there. The cover is over my head and I'm under the sheet and the blanket and the quilt. It's warm under here and it's dark, because my eyes's shut. I keep my eyes shut because I don't want get up.

"Sonny?" I hear.

I don't know who's calling me, but it must be Mama because I'm home. I don't know who it is because I'm still asleep, but it must be Mama. She's shaking me by the foot. She's holding my ankle through the cover.

"Wake up, honey," she says.

But I don't want get up because it's cold up there and I don't want get cold. I try to go back to sleep, but she shakes my foot again.

"Hummm?" I say.

"Wake up, honey," I hear.

"Hummm?" I say.

"I want you get up and wee-wee," she says.

"I don't want wee-wee, Mama," I say.

"Come on," she says, shaking me. "Come on. Get up for Mama."

"It's cold up there," I say.

"Come on," she says. "Mama won't let her baby get cold."

I pull the sheet and blanket from under my head and push them back over my shoulder. I feel the cold and I try to cover up again, but Mama grabs the cover before I get it over me. Mama is standing 'side the bed and she's looking down at me, smiling. The room is dark. The lamp's on the mantelpiece, but it's kind of low. I see Mama's shadow on the wall over by Gran'mon's picture.

"I'm cold, Mama," I say.

"Mama go'n wrap his little coat round her baby," she says.

She goes over and get it off the chair where all my clothes's at, and I sit up in the bed. Mama brings the coat and put it on me, and she fastens some of the buttons.

"Now," she says. "See? You warm."

I gap' and look at Mama. She hugs me real hard and rubs her face against my face. My mama's face is warm and soft, and it feels good.

"I want my socks on," I say. "My feet go'n get cold on the floor."

Mama leans over and get my shoes from under the bed. She

takes out my socks and slip them on my feet. I gap' and look at Mama pulling my socks up.

"Now," she says.

I get up but I can still feel that cold floor. I get on my knees and look under the bed for my pot.

"See it?" Mama says.

"Hanh?"

"See it under there?"

"Hanh?"

"I bet you didn't bring it in," she says. "Any time you sound like that you done forgot it."

"I left it on the chicken coop," I say.

"Well, go to the back door," Mama says. "Hurry up before you get cold."

I get off my knees and go back there, but it's too dark and I can't see. I come back where Mama's sitting on my bed.

"It's dark back there, Mama," I say. "I might trip over something."

Mama takes a deep breath and gets the lamp off the mantelpiece, and me and her go back in the kitchen. She unlatches the door, and I crack it open and the cold air comes in.

"Hurry," Mama says.

"All right."

I can see the fence back of the house and I can see the little pecan tree over by the toilet. I can see the big pecan tree over by the other fence by Miss Viola Brown's house. Miss Viola Brown must be sleeping because it's late at night. I bet you nobody else in the quarter's up now. I bet you I'm the only little boy up. They got plenty stars in the air, but I can't see the moon. There must be ain't no moon tonight. That grass is shining—and it must be done rained. That pecan tree's shadow's all over the back yard.

I get my tee-tee and I wee-wee. I wee-wee hard, because I don't want get cold. Mama latches the door when I get through wee-wee-ing.

"I want some water, Mama," I say.

"Let it out and put it right back in, huh?" Mama says.

She dips up some water and pours it in my cup, and I drink. I don't drink too much at once, because the water makes my teeth cold. I let my teeth warm up, and I drink some more.

"I got enough," I say.

Mama drinks the rest and then me and her go back in the front room.

"Sonny?" she says.

"Hanh?"

"Tomorrow morning when you get up me and you leaving here, hear?"

"Where we going?" I ask.

"We going to Gran'mon," Mama says.

"We leaving us house?" I ask.

"Yes," she says.

"Daddy leaving too?"

"No," she says. "Just me and you."

"Daddy don't want leave?"

"I don't know what your daddy wants," Mama says. "But for sure he don't want me. We leaving, hear?"

"Uh-huh," I say.

"I'm tired of it," Mama says.

"Hanh?"

"You won't understand, honey," Mama says. "You too young still."

"I'm getting cold, Mama," I say.

"All right," she says. She goes and put the lamp up, and comes back and sit on the bed 'side me. "Let me take your socks off," she says.

"I can take them off," I say.

Mama takes my coat off and I take my socks off. I get back in bed and Mama pulls the cover up over me. She leans over and kiss me on the jaw, and then she goes back to her bed. Mama's bed is over by the window. My bed is by the fireplace. I hear Mama get in bed. I hear the spring, then I don't hear nothing because Mama's quiet. Then I hear Mama crying.

"Mama?" I call.

She don't answer me.

"Mama?" I call her.

"Go to sleep, baby," she says.

"You crying?" I ask.

"Go to sleep," Mama says.

"I don't want you to cry," I say.

"Mama's not crying," she says.

Then I don't hear nothing and I lay quiet, but I don't turn over because my spring'll make noise and I don't want make no noise because I want hear if my mama go'n cry again. I don't hear Mama no more and I feel warm in the bed and I pull the cover over my head and I feel good. I don't hear nothing no more and I feel myself going back to sleep.

Billy Joe Martin's got the tire and he's rolling it in the road, and I run to the gate to look at him. I want go out in the road, but Mama don't want me to play out there like Billy Joe Martin and the other children. . . . Lucy's playing 'side the house. She's jumping rope with—I don't know who that is. I go 'side the house and play with Lucy. Lucy beats me jumping rope. The rope keeps on hitting me on the leg. But it don't hit Lucy on the leg. Lucy jumps too high for it. . . . Me and Billy Joe Martin shoots marbles and I beat him shooting. . . . Mama's sweeping the gallery and knocking the dust out of the broom on the side of the house. Mama keeps on knocking the broom against the wall. Must be got plenty dust in the broom.

Somebody's beating on the door. Mama, somebody's beating on the door. Somebody's beating on the door, Mama.

"Amy, please let me in," I hear.

Somebody's beating on the door, Mama. Mama, somebody's beating on the door.

"Amy, honey; honey, please let me in."

I push the cover back and I listen. I hear Daddy beating on the door.

"Mama?" I say. "Mama, Daddy's knocking on the door. He want come in."

"Go back to sleep, Sonny," Mama says.

"Daddy's out there," I say. "He want come in."

"Go back to sleep, I told you," Mama says.

I lay back on my pillow and listen.

"Amy," Daddy says, "I know you woke. Open the door."

Mama don't answer him.

"Amy, honey," Daddy says. "My sweet dumpling, let me in. It's freezing out here."

Mama still won't answer Daddy.

"Mama?" I say.

"Go back to sleep, Sonny," she says.

"Mama, Daddy want come in," I say.

"Let him crawl through the key hole," Mama says.

It gets quiet after this, and it stays quiet a little while, and then Daddy says:

"Sonny?"

"Hanh?"

"Come open the door for your daddy."

"Mama go'n whip me if I get up," I say.

"I won't let her whip you," Daddy says. "Come and open the door like a good boy."

I push the cover back and I sit up in the bed and look over at Mama's bed. Mama's under the cover and she's quiet like she's asleep. I get on the floor and get my socks out of my shoes. I get back in the bed and slip them on, and then I go and unlatch the door for Daddy. Daddy comes in and rubs my head with his hand. His hand is hard and cold.

"Look what I brought you and your mama," he says.

"What?" I ask.

Daddy takes a paper bag out of his jumper pocket.

"Candy?" I say.

"Uh-huh."

Daddy opens the bag and I stick my hand in there and take a whole handful. Daddy wraps the bag up again and sticks it in his pocket.

"Get back in that bed, Sonny," Mama says.

"I'm eating candy," I say.

"Get back in that bed like I told you," Mama says.

"Daddy's up with me," I say.

"You heard me, boy?"

"You can take your candy with you," Daddy says. "Get back in the bed."

He follows me to the bed and tucks the cover under me. I lay in the bed and eat my candy. The candy is hard, and I sound just like Paul eating corn. I bet you little old Paul is some cold out there in that back yard. I hope he ain't laying in that water like he always do. I bet you he'll freeze in that water in all this cold. I'm sure glad I ain't a pig. They ain't got no mama and no daddy and no house.

I hear the spring when Daddy gets in the bed.

"Honey?" Daddy says.

Mama don't answer him.

"Honey?" he says.

Mama must be gone back to sleep, because she don't answer him.

"Honey?" Daddy says.

"Get your hands off me," Mama says.

"Honey, you know I can't keep my hands off you," Daddy says.

"Well, just do," Mama says.

"Honey, you don't mean that," Daddy says. "You know 'fore God you don't mean that. Come on, say you don't mean it. I can't shut these eyes till you say you don't mean it."

"Don't touch me," Mama says.

"Honey," Daddy says. Then he starts crying. "Honey, please."

Daddy cries a good little while, and then he stops. I don't chew on my candy while Daddy's crying, but when he stops I chew on another piece.

"Go to sleep, Sonny," he says.

"I want eat my candy," I say.

"Hurry then. You got to go to school tomorrow."

I put another piece in my mouth and chew on it.

"Honey?" I hear Daddy saying. "Honey, you go'n wake me up to go to work?"

"I do hope you stop bothering me," Mama says.

"Wake me up round four thirty, hear, honey?" Daddy says. "I can cut 'bout six tons tomorrow. Maybe seven."

Mama don't say nothing to Daddy, and I feel sleepy again. I finish chewing my last piece of candy and I turn on my side. I feel good because the bed is warm. But I still got my socks on.

"Daddy?" I call.

"Go to sleep," Daddy says.

"My socks still on," I say.

"Let them stay on tonight," Daddy says. "Go to sleep."

"My feet don't feel good in socks," I say.

"Please go to sleep, Sonny," Daddy says. "I got to get up at four thirty, and it's hitting close to two now."

I don't say nothing, but I don't like to sleep with my socks on. But I stay quiet. Daddy and Mama don't say nothing, either, and little bit later I hear Daddy snoring. I feel drowsy myself.

I run around the house in the mud because it done rained and I feel the mud between my toes. The mud is soft and I like to play in it. I try to get out the mud, but I can't get out. I'm not stuck in the mud, but I can't get out. Lucy can't come over and play in the mud because her mama don't want her to catch cold. . . . Billy Joe Martin shows me his dime and puts it back in his pocket. Mama bought me a pretty little red coat and I show it to Lucy. But I don't let Billy Joe Martin put his hand on it. Lucy can touch it all she wants, but I don't let Billy Joe Martin put his hand on it. . . . Me and Lucy get on the horse and ride up and down the road. The horse runs fast, and me and Lucy bounce on the horse and laugh. . . . Mama and Daddy and Uncle Al and Gran'mon's sitting by the fire talking. I'm outside shooting marbles, but I hear them. I don't know what they talking about, but I hear them. I hear them. I hear them. I hear them.

I don't want wake up, but I'm waking up. Mama and Daddy's talking. I want go back to sleep, but they talking too loud. I feel my foot in the sock. I don't like socks on when I'm in the bed. I want go back to sleep, but I can't. Mama and Daddy talking too much.

"Honey, you let me oversleep," Daddy says. "Look here, it's going on seven o'clock."

"You ought to been thought about that last night," Mama says.

"Honey, please," Daddy says. "Don't start a fuss right off this morning."

"Then don't open your mouth," Mama says.

"Honey, the car broke down," Daddy says. "What I was suppose to do, it broke down on me. I just couldn't walk away and not try to fix it."

Mama's quiet.

"Honey," Daddy says, "don't be mad with me. Come on, now."

"Don't touch me," Mama says.

"Honey, I got to go to work. Come on."

"I mean it," she says.

"Honey, how can I work without touching you? You know I can't do a day's work without touching you some."

"I told you not to put your hands on me," Mama says. I hear her slap Daddy on the hand. "I mean it," she says.

"Honey," Daddy says, "this is Eddie, your husband."

"Go back to your car," Mama says. "Go rub against it. You ought to be able to find a hole in it somewhere."

"Honey, you oughtn't talk like that in the house," Daddy says. "What if Sonny hear you?"

I stay quiet and I don't move because I don't want them to know I'm woke.

"Honey, listen to me," Daddy says. "From the bottom of my heart I'm sorry. Now, come on."

"I told you once," Mama says, "you not getting on me. Go get on your car."

"Honey, respect the child," Daddy says.

"How come you don't respect him?" Mama says. "How come you don't come home sometime and respect him? How come

you don't leave that car alone and come home and respect him?
How come you don't respect him? You the one need to respect
him."

"I told you it broke down," Daddy says. "I was coming home
when it broke down on me. I even had to leave it out on the
road. I made it here quick as I could."

"You can go back quick as you can, for all I care," Mama says.

"Honey, you don't mean that," Daddy says. "I know you don't
mean that. You just saying that because you mad."

"Just don't touch me," Mama says.

"Honey, I got to get out and make some bread for us," Daddy
says.

"Get out if you want," Mama says. "They got a jailhouse for
them who don't support their family."

"Honey, please don't talk about a jail," Daddy says. "It's too
cold. You don't know how cold it is in a jailhouse this time of
the year."

Mama's quiet.

"Honey?" Daddy says.

"I hope you let me go back to sleep," Mama says. "Please."

"Honey, don't go back to sleep on me," Daddy says.
"Honey—"

"I'm getting up," Mama says. "Damn all this."

I hear the springs mash down on the bed boards. My head's
under the cover, but I can just see Mama pushing the cover
down the bed. Then I hear her walking across the floor and
going back in the kitchen.

"Oh, Lord," Daddy says. "Oh, Lord. The suffering a man got
to go through in this world. Sonny?" he says.

"Don't wake that baby up," Mama says, from the door.

"I got to have somebody to talk to," Daddy says. "Sonny?"

"I told you not to wake him up," Mama says.

"You don't want talk to me," Daddy says. "I need somebody
to talk to. Sonny?" he says.

"Hanh?"

"See what you did?" Mama says. "You woke him up, and he
ain't going back to sleep."

Daddy comes across the floor and sits down on the side of the bed. He looks down at me and passes his hand over my face.

"You love your daddy, Sonny?" he says.

"Uh-huh."

"Please love me," Daddy says.

I look up at Daddy and he looks at me, and then he just falls down on me and starts crying.

"A man needs somebody to love him," he says.

"Get love from what you give love," Mama says, back in the kitchen. "You love your car. Go let it love you back."

Daddy shakes his face in the cover.

"The suffering a man got to go through in this world," he says. "Sonny, I hope you never have to go through all this."

Daddy lays there 'side me a long time. I can hear Mama back in the kitchen. I hear her putting some wood in the stove, and then I hear her lighting the fire. I hear her pouring water in the tea kettle, and I hear when she sets the kettle on the stove.

Daddy raises up and wipes his eyes. He looks at me and shakes his head, then he goes and puts his overalls on.

"It's a hard life," he says. "Hard, hard. One day, Sonny—you too young right now—but one day you'll know what I mean."

"Can I get up, Daddy?"

"Better ask your mama," Daddy says.

"Can I get up, Mama?" I call.

Mama don't answer me.

"Mama?" I call.

"Your paw standing in there," Mama says. "He the one woke you up."

"Can I get up, Daddy?"

"Sonny, I got enough troubles right now," Daddy say.

"I want get up and wee-wee," I say.

"Get up," Mama says. "You go'n worry me till I let you get up anyhow."

I crawl from under the cover and look at my feet. I got just one sock on and I look for the other one under the cover. I find it and slip it on and then I get on the floor. But that floor is still cold. I hurry up and put on my clothes, and I get my shoes and go and sit on the bed to put them on.

Daddy waits till I finish tying up my shoes, and me and him go back in the kitchen. I get in the corner 'side the stove and Daddy comes over and stands 'side me. The fire is warm and it feels good.

Mama is frying salt meat in the skillet. The skillet's over one hole and the tea kettle's over the other one. The water's boiling and the tea kettle is whistling. I look at the steam shooting up to the loft.

Mama goes outside and gets my pot. She holds my pot for me and I wee-wee in it. Then Mama carries my pot in the front room and puts it under my bed.

Daddy pours some water in the wash basin and washes his face, and then he washes my face. He dumps the water out the back door, and me and him sit at the table. Mama brings the food to the table. She stands over me till I get through saying my blessing, and then she goes back to the stove. Me and Daddy eat.

"You love your daddy?" he says.

"Uh-huh," I say.

"That's a good boy," he says. "Always love your daddy."

"I love Mama, too. I love her more than I love you."

"You got a good mama," Daddy says. "I love her, too. She the only thing keep me going—'cluding you, too."

I look at Mama standing 'side the stove, warming.

"Why don't you come to the table and eat with us," Daddy says.

"I'm not hungry," Mama says.

"I'm sorry, baby," Daddy says. "I mean it."

Mama just looks down at the stove and don't answer Daddy.

"You got a right to be mad," Daddy says. "I ain't nothing but a' old rotten dog."

Daddy eats his food and looks at me across the table. I pick up a piece of meat and chew on it. I like the skin because the skin is hard. I keep the skin a long time.

"Well, I better get going," Daddy says. "Maybe if I work hard I'll get me a couple tons."

Daddy gets up from the table and goes in the front room. He comes back with his jumper and his hat on. Daddy's hat is gray and it got a hole on the side.

"I'm leaving, honey," he tells Mama.

Mama don't answer Daddy.

"Honey, tell me ' 'Bye, old dog,' or something," Daddy says. "Just don't stand there."

Mama still don't answer him, and Daddy jerks his cane knife out the wall and goes on out. I chew on my meat skin. I like it because it's hard.

"Hurry up, honey," Mama says. "We going to Mama."

Mama goes in the front room and I stay at the table and eat. I finish eating and I go in the front room where Mama is. Mama's pulling a big bundle of clothes from under the bed.

"What's that, Mama?" I ask.

"Us clothes," she says.

"We go'n take us clothes down to Gran'mon?"

"I'm go'n try," Mama says. "Find your cap and put it on."

I see my cap hanging on the chair and I put it on and fasten the strap under my chin. Mama fixes my shirt in my pants, and then she goes and puts on her overcoat. Her overcoat is black and her hat is black. She puts on her hat and looks in the looking glass. I can see her face in the glass. Look like she want cry. She comes from the dresser and looks at the big bundle of clothes on the floor.

"Where's your pot?" she says. "Find it."

I get my pot from under the bed.

"Still got some wee-wee in it," I say.

"Go to the back door and dump it out," Mama says.

I go back in the kitchen and open the door. It's cold out there, and I can see the frost all over the grass. The grass is white with frost. I dump the wee-wee out and come back in the front.

"Come on," Mama says.

She drags the big bundle of clothes out on the gallery and I shut the door. Mama squats down and puts the bundle on her head, and then she stands up and me and her go down the steps. Soon's I get out in the road I can feel the wind. It's strong and it's blowing in my face. My face is cold and one of my hands is cold.

It's red over there back of the trees. Mr. Guerin's house is over there. I see Mr. Guerin's big old dog. He must be don't see me and Mama because he ain't barking at us.

"Don't linger back too far," Mama says.

I run and catch up with Mama. Me and Mama's the only two people walking in the road now.

I look up and I see the tree in Gran'mon's yard. We go little farther and I see the house. I run up ahead of Mama and hold the gate open for her. After she goes in I let the gate slam.

Spot starts barking soon's he sees me. He runs down the steps at me and I let him smell my pot. Spot follows me and Mama back to the house.

"Gran'mon?" I call.

"Who that out there?" Gran'mon asks.

"Me," I say.

"What you doing out there in all that cold for, boy?" Gran'mon says. I hear Gran'mon coming to the door fussing. She opens the door and looks at me and Mama.

"What you doing here with all that?" she asks.

"I'm leaving him, Mama," Mama says.

"Eddie?" Gran'mon says. "What he done you now?"

"I'm just tired of it," Mama says.

"Come in here out that cold," Gran'mon says. "Walking out there in all that weather . . ."

We go inside and Mama drops the big bundle of clothes on the floor. I go to the fire and warm my hands. Mama and Gran'mon come to the fire and Mama stands at the other end of the fireplace and warms her hands.

"Now what that no good nigger done done?" Gran'mon asks.

"Mama, I'm just tired of Eddie running up and down the road in that car," Mama says.

"He beat you?" Gran'mon asks.

"No, he didn't beat me," Mama says. "Mama, Eddie didn't get home till after two this morning. Messing around with that old car somewhere out on the road all night."

"I told you," Gran'mon says. "I told you when that nigger got that car that was go'n happen. I told you. No—you wouldn't listen. I told you. Put a fool in a car and he becomes a bigger fool. Where that yellow thing at now?"

"God telling," Mama says. "He left with his cane knife."

"I warned you 'bout that nigger," Gran'mon says. "Even 'fore you married him. I sung at you and sung at you. I said, 'Amy, that nigger ain't no good. A yellow nigger with a gap like that 'tween his front teeth ain't no good.' But you wouldn't listen."

"Can me and Sonny stay here?" Mama asks.

"Where else can y'all go?" Gran'mon says. "I'm your mon, ain't I? You think I can put you out in the cold like he did?"

"He didn't put me out, Mama, I left," Mama says.

"You finally getting some sense in your head," Gran'mon says. "You ought to been left that nigger years ago."

Uncle Al comes in the front room and looks at the bundle of clothes on the floor. Uncle Al's got on his overalls and got just one strap hooked. The other strap's hanging down his back.

"Fix that thing on you," Gran'mon says. "You not in a stable."

Uncle Al fixes his clothes and looks at me and Mama at the fire.

"Y'all had a round?" he asks Mama.

"Eddie and that car again," Mama says.

"That's all they want these days," Gran'mon says. "Cars. Why don't they marry them cars? No. When they got their troubles, they come running to the womenfolks. When they ain't got no troubles and when their pockets full of money they run jump in the car. I told you that when you was working to help him get that car."

Uncle Al stands 'side me at the fireplace, and I lean against him and look at the steam coming out a piece of wood. Lord knows I get tired of Gran'mon fussing all the time.

"Y'all moving in with us?" Uncle Al asks.

"For a few days," Mama says. "Then I'll try to find another place somewhere in the quarter."

"We got plenty room here," Uncle Al says. "This old man here can sleep with me."

Uncle Al gets a little stick out of the corner and hands it to me so I can light it for him. I hold it to the fire till it's lit, and I hand it back to Uncle Al. Uncle Al turns the pipe upside down in his mouth and holds the fire to it. When the pipe's good and lit, Uncle Al gives me the little stick and I throw it back in the fire.

"Y'all ate anything?" Gran'mon asks.

"Sonny ate," Mama says. "I'm not hungry."

"I reckon you go'n start looking for work now?" Gran'mon says.

"There's plenty cane to cut," Mama says. "I'll get me a cane knife and go out tomorrow morning."

"Out in all that cold?" Gran'mon says.

"They got plenty women cutting cane," Mama says. "I don't mind. I done it before."

"You used to be such a pretty little thing, Amy," Gran'mon says. "Long silky curls. Prettiest little face on this whole plantation. You could've married somebody worth something. But, no, you had to go throw yourself away to that yellow nigger who don't care for nobody, 'cluding himself."

"I loved Eddie," Mama says.

"Poot," Gran'mon says.

"He wasn't like this when we married," Mama says.

"Every nigger from Bayonne like this now, then, and forever," Gran'mon says.

"Not then," Mama says. "He was the sweetest person . . ."

"And you fell for him?" Gran'mon says.

"He changed after he got that car," Mama says. "He changed overnight."

"Well, you learned your lesson," Gran'mon says. "We all get teached something no matter how old we get. 'Live and learn,' what they say."

"Eddie's all right," Uncle Al says. "He—"

"You keep out of this, Albert," Gran'mon says. "It don't concern you."

Uncle Al don't say no more, and I can feel his hand on my shoulder. I like Uncle Al because he's good, and he never talk bad about Daddy. But Gran'mon's always talking bad about Daddy.

"Freddie's still there," Gran'mon says.

"Mama, please," Mama says.

"Why not?" Gran'mon says. "He always loved you."

"Not in front of him," Mama says.

Mama leaves the fireplace and goes to the bundle of clothes. I can hear her untying the bundle.

"Ain't it 'bout time you was leaving for school?" Uncle Al asks.

"I don't want go," I say. "It's too cold."

"It's never too cold for school," Mama says. "Warm up good and let Uncle Al button your coat for you."

I get closer to the fire and I feel the fire hot on my pants. I turn around and warm my back. I turn again, and Uncle Al leans over and buttons up my coat. Uncle Al's pipe almost gets in my face, and it don't smell good.

"Now," Uncle Al says. "You all ready to go. You want take a potato with you?"

"Uh-huh."

Uncle Al leans over and gets me a potato out of the ashes. He knocks all the ashes off and puts the potato in my pocket.

"Wait," Mama says. "Mama, don't you have a little paper bag?"

Gran'mon looks on the mantelpiece and gets a paper bag. There's something in the bag, and she takes it out and hands the bag to Mama. Mama puts the potato in the bag and puts it in my pocket. Then she goes and gets my book and tucks it under my arm.

"Now you ready," she says. "And remember, when you get out for dinner come back here. Don't you forget and go up home now. You hear, Sonny?"

"Uh-huh."

"Come on," Uncle Al says. "I'll open the gate for you."

" 'Bye, Mama," I say.

"Be a good boy," Mama says. "Eat your potato at recess. Don't eat it in class now."

Me and Uncle Al go out on the gallery. The sun is shining but it's still cold out there. Spot follows me and Uncle Al down the walk. Uncle Al opens the gate for me and I go out in the road. I hate to leave Uncle Al and Spot. And I hate to leave Mama—and I hate to leave the fire. But I got to, because they want me to learn.

"See you at twelve," Uncle Al says.

I go up the quarter and Uncle Al and Spot go back to the house. I see all the children going to school. But I don't see Lucy. When I get to her house I'm go'n stop at the gate and call her. She must be don't want go to school, cold as it is.

It still got some ice in the water. I better not walk in the water. I'll get my feet wet and Mama'll whip me.

When I get closer I look and I see Lucy and her mama on the gallery. Lucy's mama ties her bonnet for her, and Lucy comes down the steps. She runs down the walk toward the gate. Lucy's bonnet is red and her coat is red.

"Hi," I say.

"Hi," she says.

"It's some cold," I say.

"Unnn-hunnnn," Lucy says.

Me and Lucy walk side by side up the quarter. Lucy's got her book in her book sack.

"We moved," I say. "We staying with Gran'mon now."

"Y'all moved?" Lucy asks.

"Uh-huh."

"Y'all didn't move," Lucy says. "When y'all moved?"

"This morning."

"Who moved y'all?" Lucy asks.

"Me and Mama," I say. "I'm go'n sleep with Uncle Al."

"My legs getting cold," Lucy says.

"I got a potato," I say. "In my pocket."

"You go'n eat it and give me piece?" Lucy says.

"Uh-huh," I say. "At recess."

Me and Lucy walk up the quarter, and Lucy stops and touches the ice with her shoe.

"You go'n get your foot wet," I say.

"No, I'm not," Lucy says.

Lucy breaks the ice with her shoe and laughs. I laugh and I break a piece of ice with my shoe. Me and Lucy laugh and I see the smoke coming out of Lucy's mouth. I open my mouth and go, "Haaaa," and plenty smoke comes out of my mouth. Lucy laughs and points at the smoke.

Me and Lucy go on up the quarter to the schoolhouse. Billy Joe Martin and Ju-Ju and them's playing marbles right by the gate. Over 'side the schoolhouse Shirley and Dottie and Katie's jumping rope. On the other side of the schoolhouse some more children playing "Patty-cake, patty-cake, baker-man" to keep warm. Lucy goes where Shirley and them's jumping rope and asks them to play. I stop where Billy Joe Martin and them's at and watch them shoot marbles.

2: It's warm inside the schoolhouse. Bill made a big fire in the heater, and I can hear it roaring up the pipes. I look out the window and I can see the smoke flying across the yard. Bill sure knows how to make a good fire. Bill's the biggest boy in school, and he always makes the fire for us.

Everybody's studying their lesson, but I don't know mine. I wish I knowed it, but I don't. Mama didn't teach me any lesson last night, and she didn't teach it to me this morning, and I don't know it.

"Bob and Rex in the yard. Rex is barking at the cow." I don't know what all this other reading is. I see "Rex" again, and I see "cow" again—but I don't know what all the rest of it is.

Bill comes up to the heater and I look up and see him putting another piece of wood in the fire. He goes back to his seat and sits down 'side Juanita. Miss Hebert looks at Bill when he goes back to his seat. I look in my book at Bob and Rex. Bob's got on a white shirt and blue pants. Rex is a German police dog. He's white and brown. Mr. Bouie's got a dog just like Rex. He don't bite though. He's a good dog. But Mr. Guerin's old dog'll bite you for sure. I seen him this morning when me and Mama was going down to Gran'mon's house.

I ain't go'n eat dinner at us house because me and Mama don't stay there no more. I'm go'n eat at Gran'mon's house. I don't know where Daddy go'n eat dinner. He must be go'n cook his own dinner.

I can hear Bill and Juanita back of me. They whispering to each other, but I can hear them. Juanita's some pretty. I hope I was big so I could love her. But I better look at my lesson and don't think about other things.

"First grade," Miss Hebert says.

We go up to the front and sit down on the bench. Miss Hebert looks at us and make a mark in her roll book. She puts the roll book down and comes over to the bench where we at.

"Does everyone know his lesson today?" she asks.

"Yes, ma'am," Lucy says, louder than anybody else in the whole schoolhouse.

"Good," Miss Hebert says. "And I'll start with you today, Lucy. Hold your book in one hand and begin."

" 'Bob and Rex are in the yard,' " Lucy reads. " 'Rex is barking at the cow. The cow is watching Rex.' "

"Good," Miss Hebert says. "Point to barking."

Lucy points.

"Good. Now point to watching."

Lucy points again.

"Good," Miss Hebert says. "Shirley Ann, let's see how well you can read."

I look in the book at Bob and Rex. "Rex is barking at the cow. The cow is looking at Rex."

"William Joseph," Miss Hebert says.

I'm next, I'm scared. I don't know my lesson and Miss Hebert go'n whip me. Miss Hebert don't like you when you don't know your lesson. I can see her strap over there on the table. I can see the clock and the little bell, too. Bill split the end of the strap, and them little ends sting some. Soon's Billy Joe Martin finishes, then it's me. I don't know . . . Mama ought to been . . . "Bob and Rex" . . .

"Eddie," Miss Hebert says.

I don't know my lesson. I don't know my lesson. I don't know my lesson. I feel warm. I'm wet. I hear the wee-wee dripping on the floor. I'm crying. I'm crying because I wee-wee on myself. My clothes's wet. Lucy and them go'n laugh at me. Billy Joe Martin and them go'n tease me. I don't know my lesson. I don't know my lesson. I don't know my lesson.

"Oh, Eddie, look what you've done," I think I hear Miss Hebert saying. I don't know if she's saying this, but I think I hear her say it. My eye's shut and I'm crying. I don't want look at none of them, because I know they laughing at me.

"It's running under that bench there now," Billy Joe Martin says. "Look out for your feet back there, it's moving fast."

"William Joseph," Miss Hebert says. "Go over there and stand in that corner. Turn your face to the wall and stay there until I tell you to move."

I hear Billy Joe Martin leaving the bench, and then it's quiet. But I don't open my eyes.

"Eddie," Miss Hebert says, "go stand by the heater."

I don't move, because I'll see them, and I don't want see them.

"Eddie?" Miss Hebert says.

But I don't answer her, and I don't move.

"Bill?" Miss Hebert says.

I hear Bill coming up to the front and then I feel him taking me by the hand and leading me away. I walk with my eyes shut. Me and Bill stop at the heater, because I can feel the fire. Then Bill takes my book and leaves me standing there.

"Juanita," Miss Hebert says, "get a mop, will you, please."

I hear Juanita going to the back, and then I hear her coming back to the front. The fire pops in the heater, but I don't open my eyes. Nobody's saying anything, but I know they all watching me.

When Juanita gets through mopping up the wee-wee she carries the mop back to the closet, and I hear Miss Hebert going on with the lesson. When she gets through with the first graders, she calls the second graders up there.

Bill comes up to the heater and puts another piece of wood in the fire.

"Want turn around?" he asks me.

I don't answer him, but I got my eyes open now and I'm looking down at the floor. Bill turns me round so I can dry the back of my pants. He pats me on the shoulder and goes back to his seat.

After Miss Hebert gets through with the second graders, she tells the children they can go out for recess. I can hear them getting their coats and hats. When they all leave I raise my head. I still see Bill and Juanita and Veta sitting there. Bill smiles at me, but I don't smile back. My clothes's dry now, and I feel better. I know the rest of the children go'n tease me, though.

"Bill, why don't you and the rest of the seventh graders put your arithmetic problems on the board," Miss Hebert says. "We'll look at them after recess."

Bill and them stand up, and I watch them go to the blackboard in the back.

"Eddie?" Miss Hebert says.

I turn and I see her sitting behind her desk. And I see Billy Joe Martin standing in the corner with his face to the wall.

"Come up to the front," Miss Hebert says.

I go up there looking down at the floor, because I know she go'n whip me now.

"William Joseph, you may leave," Miss Hebert says.

Billy Joe Martin runs over and gets his coat, and then he runs outside to shoot marbles. I stand in front of Miss Hebert's desk with my head down.

"Look up," she says.

I raise my head and look at Miss Hebert. She's smiling, and she don't look mad.

"Now," she says. "Did you study your lesson last night?"

"Yes, ma'am," I say.

"I want the truth, now," she says. "Did you?"

It's a sin to story in the churchhouse, but I'm scared Miss Hebert go'n whip me.

"Yes, ma'am," I say.

"Did you study it this morning?" she asks.

"Yes, ma'am," I say.

"Then why didn't you know it?" she asks.

I feel a big knot coming up in my throat and I feel like I'm go'n cry again. I'm scared Miss Hebert go'n whip me, that's why I story to her.

"You didn't study your lesson, did you?" she says.

I shake my head. "No, ma'am."

"You didn't study it last night either, did you?"

"No, ma'am," I say. "Mama didn't have time to help me. Daddy wasn't home. Mama didn't have time to help me."

"Where is your father?" Miss Hebert asks.

"Cutting cane."

"Here on this place?"

"Yes, ma'am," I say.

Miss Hebert looks at me, and then she gets out a pencil and starts writing on a piece of paper. I look at her writing and I look at the clock and the strap. I can hear the clock. I can hear Billy Joe Martin and them shooting marbles outside. I can hear Lucy and them jumping rope, and some more children playing "Patty-cake."

"I want you to give this to your mother or your father when you get home," Miss Hebert says. "This is only a little note saying I would like to see them sometime when they aren't too busy."

"We don't live home no more," I say.

"Oh?" Miss Hebert says. "Did you move?"

"Me and Mama," I say. "But Daddy didn't."

that little bell in a little while. She getting ready to touch it
right now.

Soon 's Miss Hebert touches the bell all the children run go
get their hats and coats. I unhook my coat and drop it on the
bench till I put my cap on. Then I put my coat on, and I get
my book and leave.

I see Bill and Juanita going out the schoolyard, and I run and
catch up with them. Time I get there I hear Billy Joe Martin
and them coming up behind us.

"Look at that baby," Billy Joe Martin says.

"Piss on himself," Ju-Ju says.

"Y'all leave him alone," Bill says.

"Baby, baby, piss on himself," Billy Joe Martin sings.

"What did I say now?" Bill says.

"Piss on himself," Billy Joe Martin says.

"Wait," Bill says. "Let me take off my belt."

"Good-bye, piss pot," Billy Joe Martin says. Him and Ju-Ju
run down the road. They spank their hind parts with their hands
and run like horses.

"They just bad," Juanita says.

"Don't pay them no mind," Bill says. "They'll leave you alone."

We go on down the quarter and Bill and Juanita hold hands.
I go to Gran'mon's gate and open it. I look at Bill and Juanita
going down the quarter. They walking close together, and Juanita done put her head on Bill's shoulder. I like to see Bill and
Juanita like that. It makes me feel good. But I go in the yard
and I don't feel good any more. I know old Gran'mon go'n start
her fussing. Lord in Heaven knows I get tired of all this fussing,
day and night. Spot runs down the walk to meet me. I put my
hand on his head and me and him go back to the gallery. I
make him stay on the gallery, because Gran'mon don't want him
inside. I pull the door open and I see Gran'mon and Uncle Al
sitting by the fire. I look for my mama, but I don't see her.

"Where Mama?" I ask Uncle Al.

"In the kitchen," Gran'mon says. "But she talking to somebody."

I go back to the kitchen.

"Come back here," Gran'mon says.

"I want see my mama," I say.

"You'll see her when she come out," Gran'mon says.

"I want see my mama now," I say.

"Don't you hear me talking to you, boy?" Gran'mon hollers.

"What's the matter?" Mama asks. Mama comes out of the kitchen and Mr. Freddie Jackson comes out of there, too. I hate Mr. Freddie Jackson. I never did like him. He always want to be round my mama.

"That boy don't listen to nobody," Gran'mon says.

"Hi, Sonny," Mr. Freddie Jackson says.

I look at him standing there, but I don't speak to him. I take the note out of my pocket and hand it to my mama.

"What's this?" Mama says.

"Miss Hebert sent it."

Mama unfolds the note and take it to the fireplace to read it. I can see her mouth working. When she gets through reading, she folds the note up again.

"She want see me or Eddie sometime when we free," Mama says. "Sonny been doing pretty bad in his class."

"I can just see that nigger husband of yours in a schoolhouse," Gran'mon says. "I doubt if he ever went to one."

"Mama, please," Mama says.

Mama helps me off with my coat and I go to the fireplace and stand 'side Uncle Al. Uncle Al pulls me between his legs and he holds my hand out to the fire.

"Well?" I hear Gran'mon saying.

"You know how I feel 'bout her," Mr. Freddie Jackson says. "My house opened to her and Sonny any time she want come there."

"Well?" Gran'mon says.

"Mama, I'm still married to Eddie," Mama says.

"You mean you still love that yellow thing," Gran'mon says. "That's what you mean, ain't it?"

"I didn't say that," Mama says. "What would people say, out one house and in another one the same day?"

"Who care what people say?" Gran'mon says. "Let people say what they big enough to say. You looking out for yourself, not what people say."

"You understand, don't you, Freddie?" Mama says.

"I think I do," he says. "But like I say, Amy, any time—you know that."

"And there ain't no time like right now," Gran'mon says. "You can take that bundle of clothes down there for her."

"Let her make up her own mind, Rachel," Uncle Al says. "She can make up her own mind."

"If you know what's good for you you better keep out of this," Gran'mon says. "She my daughter and if she ain't got sense enough to look out for herself, I have. What you want to do, go out in that field cutting cane in the morning?"

"I don't mind it," Mama says.

"You done forgot how hard cutting cane is?" Gran'mon says. "You must be done forgot."

"I ain't forgot," Mama says. "But if the other women can do it, I suppose I can do it, too."

"Now you talking back," Gran'mon says.

"I'm not talking back, Mama," Mama says. "I just feel it ain't right to leave one house and go to another house the same day. That ain't right in nobody's book."

"Maybe she's right, Mrs. Rachel," Mr. Freddie Jackson says.

"Her trouble is she's still in love with that mariny," Gran'mon says. "That's what your trouble is. You ain't satisfied 'less he got you doing all the work while he rip and run up and down the road with his other nigger friends. No, you ain't satisfied."

Gran'mon goes back in the kitchen fussing. After she leaves the fire, everything gets quiet. Everything stays quiet a minute, and then Gran'mon starts singing back in the kitchen.

"Why did you bring your book home?" Mama says.

"Miss Hebert say I can stay home if I want," I say. "We had us lesson already."

"You sure she said that?" Mama says.

"Uh-huh."

"I'm go'n ask her, you know."

"She said it," I say.

Mama don't say no more, but I know she still looking at me, but I don't look at her. Then Spot starts barking outside and everybody look that way. But nobody don't move. Spot keeps on barking, and I go to the door to see what he's barking at. I see Daddy coming up the walk. I pull the door and go back to the fireplace.

"Daddy coming, Mama," I say.

"Wait," Gran'mon says, coming out the kitchen. "Let me talk to that nigger. I'll give him a piece of my mind."

Gran'mon goes to the door and pushes it open. She stands in the door and I hear Daddy talking to Spot. Then Daddy comes up to the gallery.

"Amy in there, Mama?" Daddy says.

"She is," Gran'mon says.

I hear Daddy coming up the steps.

"And where you think you going?" Gran'mon asks.

"I want speak to her," Daddy says.

"Well, she don't want speak to you," Gran'mon says. "So you might 's well go right on back down them steps and march right straight out of my yard."

"I want speak to my wife," Daddy says.

"She ain't your wife no more," Gran'mon says. "She left you."

"What you mean she left me?" Daddy says.

"She ain't up at your house no more, is she?" Gran'mon says. "That look like a good enough sign to me that she done left."

"Amy?" Daddy calls.

Mama don't answer him. She's looking down in the fire. I don't feel good when Mama's looking like that.

"Amy?" Daddy calls.

Mama still don't answer him.

"You satisfied?" Gran'mon says.

"You the one trying to make Amy leave me," Daddy says. "You ain't never like me—from the starting."

"That's right, I never did," Gran'mon says. "You yellow, you got a gap 'tween your teeth, and you ain't no good. You want me to say more?"

"You always wanted her to marry somebody else," Daddy says.

"You right again," Gran'mon says.

"Amy?" Daddy calls. "Can you hear me, honey?"

"She can hear you," Gran'mon says. "She's standing right there by that fireplace. She can hear you good 's I can hear you, and nigger, I can hear you too good for comfort."

"I'm going in there," Daddy says. "She got somebody in there and I'm going in there and see."

"You just take one more step toward my door," Gran'mon says, "and it'll take a' undertaker to get you out of here. So help me, God, I'll get that butcher knife out of that kitchen and chop on your tail till I can't see tail to chop on. You the kind of nigger like to rip and run up and down the road in your car long 's you got a dime, but when you get broke and your belly get empty you run to your wife and cry on her shoulder. You just take one more step toward this door, and I bet you somebody'll be crying at your funeral. If you know anybody who care that much for you, you old yellow dog."

Daddy is quiet a while, and then I hear him crying. I don't feel good, because I don't like to hear Daddy and Mama crying. I look at Mama, but she's looking down in the fire.

"You never liked me," Daddy says.

"You said that before," Gran'mon says. "And I repeat, no, I never liked you, don't like you, and never will like you. Now, get out my yard 'fore I put the dog on you."

"I want see my boy," Daddy says, "I got a right to see my boy."

"In the first place, you ain't got no right in my yard," Gran'mon says.

"I want see my boy," Daddy says. "You might be able to keep me from seeing my wife, but you and nobody else can keep me from seeing my son. Half of him is me and I want see my—I want see him."

"You ain't leaving?" Gran'mon asks Daddy.

"I want see my boy," Daddy says. "And I'm go'n see my boy."

"Wait," Gran'mon says. "Your head hard. Wait till I come back. You go'n see all kind of boys."

Gran'mon comes back inside and goes to Uncle Al's room. I look toward the wall and I can hear Daddy moving on the gallery. I hear Mama crying and I look at her. I don't want see my mama crying, and I lay my head on Uncle Al's knee and I want cry, too.

"Amy, honey," Daddy calls, "ain't you coming up home and cook me something to eat? It's lonely up there without you, honey. You don't know how lonely it is without you. I can't stay up there without you, honey. Please come home. . . ."

I hear Gran'mon coming out of Uncle Al's room and I look at her. Gran'mon's got Uncle Al's shotgun and she's putting a shell in it.

"Mama?" Mama screams.

"Don't worry," Gran'mon says. "I'm just go'n shoot over his head. I ain't go'n have them sending me to the pen for a good-for-nothing nigger like that."

"Mama, don't," Mama says. "He might hurt himself."

"Good," Gran'mon says. "Save me the trouble of doing it for him."

Mama runs to the wall. "Eddie, run," she screams. "Mama got the shotgun."

I hear Daddy going down the steps. I hear Spot running after him barking. Gran'mon knocks the door open with the gun barrel and shoot. I hear Daddy hollering.

"Mama, you didn't?" Mama says.

"I shot two miles over that nigger's head," Gran'mon says. "Long-legged coward."

We all run out on the gallery, and I see Daddy out in the road crying. I can see the people coming out on the galleries. They looking at us and they looking at Daddy. Daddy's standing out in the road crying.

"Boy, I would've like to seen old Eddie getting out of this yard," Uncle Al says.

Daddy's walking up and down the road in front of the house, and he's crying.

"Let's go back inside," Gran'mon says. "We won't be bothered with him for a while."

It's cold, and me and Uncle Al and Gran'mon go back inside. Mr. Freddie Jackson and Mama don't come back in right now, but after a little while they come in, too.

"Oh, Lord," Mama says.

Mama starts crying and Mr. Freddie Jackson takes her in his old arms. Mama lays her head on his old shoulder, but she just stays there a little while and then she moves.

"Can I go lay 'cross your bed, Uncle Al?" Mama asks.

"Sure," Uncle Al says.

I watch Mama going to Uncle Al's room.

"Well, I better be going," Mr. Freddie Jackson says.

"Freddie?" Gran'mon calls him, from the kitchen.

"Yes, ma'am?" he says.

"Come here a minute," Gran'mon says.

Mr. Freddie Jackson goes back in the kitchen where Gran'mon is. I get between Uncle Al's legs and look at the fire. Uncle Al rubs my head with his hand. Mr. Freddie Jackson comes out of the kitchen and goes in Uncle Al's room where Mama is. He must be sitting down on the bed because I can hear the springs.

"Gran'mon shot Daddy?" I ask.

Uncle Al rubs my head with his hand.

"She just scared him," he says. "You like your daddy?"

"Uh-huh."

"Your daddy's a good man," Uncle Al says. "A little foolish, but he's okay."

"I don't like Mr. Freddie Jackson," I say.

"How come?" Uncle Al says.

"I just don't like him," I say. "I just don't like him. I don't like him to hold my mama, neither. My daddy suppose to hold my mama. He ain't suppose to hold my mama."

"You want go back home?" Uncle Al asks.

"Uh-huh," I say. "But me and Mama go'n stay here now. I'm go'n sleep with you."

"But you rather go home and sleep in your own bed, huh?"

"Yes," I say. "I pull the cover 'way over my head. I like to sleep under the cover."

"You sleep like that all the time?" Uncle Al asks.

"Uh-huh."

"Even in the summertime, too?" Uncle Al says.

"Uh-huh," I say.

"Don't you ever get too warm?" Uncle Al says.

"Uh-uh," I say. "I feel good 'way under there."

Uncle Al rubs my head and I look down in the fire.

"Y'all come on in the kitchen and eat," Gran'mon calls.

Me and Uncle Al go back in the kitchen and sit down at the table. Gran'mon already got us food dished up. Uncle Al bows his head and I bow my head.

"Thank Thee, Father, for this food Thou has given us," Uncle Al says.

I raise my head and start eating. We having spaghetti for dinner. I pick up a string of spaghetti and suck it up in my mouth. I make it go *loo-loo-loo-loo-loo-loo-loop*. Uncle Al looks at me and laugh. I do it again, and Uncle Al laughs again.

"Don't play with my food," Gran'mon says. "Eat it right."

Gran'mon is standing 'side the stove looking at me. I don't like old Gran'mon. Shooting at my daddy—I don't like her.

"Taste good?" Uncle Al asks.

"Uh-huh," I say.

Uncle Al winks at me and wraps his spaghetti on his fork and sticks it in his mouth. I try to wrap mine on my fork, but it keeps falling off. I can just pick up one at a time.

Gran'mon starts singing her song again. She fools round the stove a little while, and then she goes in the front room. I get a string of spaghetti and suck it up in my mouth. When I hear her coming back I stop and eat right.

"Still out there," she says. "Sitting on that ditch bank crying like a baby. Let him cry. But he better not come back in this yard."

Gran'mon goes over to the stove and sticks a piece of wood in the fire. She starts singing again:

Oh, I'll be there,
I'll be there,
When the roll is called in Heaven, I'll be there.

Uncle Al finishes his dinner and waits for me. When I finish eating, me and him go in the front room and sit at the fire.

"I want go to the toilet, Uncle Al," I say.

I get my coat and cap and bring them to the fireplace, and Uncle Al helps me get in them. Uncle Al buttons up my coat for me, and I go out on the gallery. I look out in the road and I see Daddy sitting out on the ditch bank. I go round the house and go back to the toilet. The grass is dry like hay. There ain't no leaves on the trees. I see some birds in the tree. The wind's moving the birds's feathers. I bet you them little birds's some cold. I'm glad I'm not a bird. No daddy, no mama—I'm glad I'm not a bird.

I open the door and go in the toilet. I get up on the seat and pull down my pants. I squat over the hole—but I better not slip and fall in there. I'll get all that poo-poo on my feet, and Gran'mon'll kill me if I tramp all that poo-poo in her house.

I try hard and my poo-poo come. It's long. I like to poo-poo. Sometimes I poo-poo on my pot at night. Mama don't like for me to go back to the toilet when it's late. Scared a snake might bite me.

I finish poo-poo-ing and I jump down from the seat and pull up my pants. I look in the hole and I see my poo-poo. I look in the top of the toilet, but I don't see any spiders. We got spiders in us toilet. Gran'mon must be done killed all her spiders with some Flit.

I push the door open and I go back to the front of the house. I go round the gallery and I see Daddy standing at the gate looking in the yard. He sees me.

"Sonny?" he calls.

"Hanh?"

"Come here, baby," he says.

I look toward the door, but I don't see nobody and I go to

the gate where Daddy is. Daddy pushes the gate open and grabs me and hugs me to him.

"You still love your daddy, Sonny?" he asks.

"Uh-huh," I say.

Daddy hugs me and kisses me on the face.

"I love my baby," he says. "I love my baby. Where your mama?"

"Laying 'cross Uncle Al's bed in his room," I say. "And Mr. Freddie Jackson in there, too."

Daddy pushes me away real quickly and looks in my face.

"Who else in there?" he asks. "Who?"

"Just them," I say. "Uncle Al's in Gran'mon's room by the fire, and Gran'mon's in the kitchen."

Daddy looks toward the house.

"This is the last straw," he says. "I'm turning your Gran'mon in this minute. And you go'n be my witness. Come on."

"Where we going?" I ask.

"To that preacher's house," Daddy says. "And if he can't help me, I'm going back in the field to Madame Toussaint."

Daddy grabs my hand and me and him go up the quarter. I can see all the children going back to school.

". . . Lock her own daughter in a room with another man and got her little grandson there looking all the time," Daddy says. "She ain't so much Christian as she put out to be. Singing round that house every time you bat your eyes and doing something like that in broad daylight. Step it up, Sonny."

"I'm coming fast as I can," I say.

"I'll see about that," Daddy says. "I'll see about that."

When me and Daddy get to Reverend Simmons's house, we go up on the gallery and Daddy knocks on the door. Mrs. Carey comes to the door to see what we want.

"Mrs. Carey, is the Reverend in?" Daddy asks.

"Yes," Mrs. Carey says. "Come on in."

Me and Daddy go inside and I see Reverend Simmons sitting at the fireplace. Reverend Simmons got on his eyeglasses and he's reading the Bible. He turns and looks at us when we come in. He takes off his glasses like he can't see us too good with them on, and he looks at us again. Mrs. Carey goes back in the kitchen and me and Daddy go over to the fireplace.

"Good evening, Reverend," Daddy says.

"Good evening," Reverend Simmons says. "Hi, Sonny."

"Hi," I say.

"Reverend, I hate busting in on you like this, but I need your help," Daddy says. "Reverend, Amy done left me and her mama got her down at her house with another man and—"

"Now, calm down a second," Reverend Simmons says. He looks toward the kitchen. "Carey, bring Mr. Howard and Sonny a chair."

Mrs. Carey brings the chairs and goes right on back in the kitchen again. Daddy turns his chair so he can be facing Reverend Simmons.

"I come in pretty late last night 'cause my car broke down on me and I had to walk all the way—from the other side of Morgan up there," Daddy says. "When I get home me and Amy get in a little squabble. This morning we squabble again, but I don't think too much of it. You know a man and a woman go'n have their little squabbles every once in a while. I go to work in the field. Work like a dog. Cutting cane right and left—trying to make up lost time I spent at the house this morning. When I come home for dinner—hungry 's a dog—my wife, neither my boy is there. No dinner—and I'm hungry 's a dog. I go in the front room and all their clothes gone. Lord, I almost go crazy. I don't know what to do. I run out the house because I think she still mad at me and done gone down to her mama. I go down there and ask for her, and first thing I know here come Mama Rachel shooting at me with Uncle Al's shotgun."

"I can't believe that," Reverend Simmons says.

"If I'm telling a lie I hope to never rise from this chair," Daddy says. "And I reckon she would've got me if I wasn't moving fast."

"That don't sound like Sister Rachel," Reverend Simmons says.

"Sound like her or don't sound like her, she did it," Daddy says. "Sonny right over there. He seen every bit of it. Ask him."

Reverend Simmons looks at me but he don't ask me nothing. He just clicks his tongue and shakes his head.

"That don't sound like Sister Rachel," he says. "But if you say that's what she did, I'll go down there and talk to her."

"And that ain't all," Daddy says.

Reverend Simmons waits for Daddy to go on.

"She got Freddie Jackson locked up in a room with Amy," Daddy says.

Reverend Simmons looks at me and Daddy, then he goes over and gets his coat and hat from against the wall. Reverend Simmons's coat is long and black. His hat is big like a cowboy's hat.

"I'll be down the quarter, Carey," he tells Mrs. Simmons. "Be back quick as I can."

We go out of the house and Daddy holds my hand. Me and him and Reverend Simmons go out in the road and head on back down the quarter.

"Reverend Simmons, I want my wife back," Daddy says. "A man can't live by himself in this world. It too cold and cruel."

Reverend Simmons don't say nothing to Daddy. He starts humming a little song to himself. Reverend Simmons is big and he can walk fast. He takes big old long steps and me and Daddy got to walk fast to keep up with him. I got to run because Daddy's got my hand.

We get to Gran'mon's house and Reverend Simmons pushes the gate open and goes in the yard.

"Me and Sonny'll stay out here," Daddy says.

"I'm cold, Daddy," I say.

"I'll build a fire," Daddy says. "You want me build me and you a little fire?"

"Uh-huh."

"Help me get some sticks, then," Daddy says.

Me and Daddy get some grass and weeds and Daddy finds a big chunk of dry wood. We pile it all up and Daddy gets a match out his pocket and lights the fire.

"Feel better?" he says.

"Uh-huh."

"How come you not in school this evening?" Daddy asks.

"I wee-weed on myself," I say.

I tell Daddy because I know Daddy ain't go'n whip me.

"You peed on yourself at school?" Daddy asks. "Sonny, I thought you was a big boy. That's something little babies do."

"Miss Hebert want see you and Mama," I say.

"I don't have time to see nobody now," Daddy says. "I got my own troubles. I just hope that preacher in there can do something."

I look up at Daddy, but he's looking down in the fire.

"Sonny?" I hear Mama calling me.

I turn and I see Mama and all of them standing out there on the gallery.

"Hanh?" I answer.

"Come in here before you catch a death of cold," Mama says.

Daddy goes to the fence and looks across the pickets at Mama.

"Amy," he says, "please come home. I swear I ain't go'n do it no more."

"Sonny, you hear me talking to you?" Mama calls.

"I ain't go'n catch cold," I say. "We got a fire. I'm warm."

"Amy, please come home," Daddy says. "Please, honey. I forgive you. I forgive Mama. I forgive everybody. Just come home."

I look at Mama and Reverend Simmons talking on the gallery. The others ain't talking; they just standing there looking out in the road at me and Daddy. Reverend Simmons comes out the yard and over to the fire. Daddy comes to the fire where me and Reverend Simmons is. He looks at Reverend Simmons but Reverend Simmons won't look back at him.

"Well, Reverend?" Daddy says.

"She say she tired of you and that car," Reverend Simmons says.

Daddy falls down on the ground and cries.

"A man just can't live by himself in this cold, cruel world," he says. "He got to have a woman to stand by him. He just can't make it by himself. God, help me."

"Be strong, man," Reverend Simmons says.

"I can't be strong with my wife in there and me out here," Daddy says. "I need my wife."

"Well, you go'n have to straighten that out the best way you can," Reverend Simmons says. "And I talked to Sister Rachel. She said she didn't shoot to hurt you. She just shot to kind of scare you away."

"She didn't shoot to hurt me?" Daddy says. "And I reckon them things was jelly beans I heard zooming just three inches over my head?"

"She said she didn't shoot to hurt you," Reverend Simmons says. He holds his hands over the fire. "This fire's good, but I got to get on back up the quarter. Got to get my wood for tonight. I'll see you people later. And I hope everything comes out all right."

"Reverend, you sure you can't do nothing?" Daddy asks.

"I tried, son," Reverend Simmons says. "Now we'll leave it in God's hand."

"But I want my wife back now," Daddy says. "God take so long to—"

"Mr. Howard, that's blasphemous," Reverend Simmons says.

"I don't want blaspheme Him," Daddy says. "But I'm in a mess. I'm in a big mess. I want my wife."

"I'd suggest you kneel down sometime," Reverend Simmons says. "That always helps in a family."

Reverend Simmons looks at me like he's feeling sorry for me, then he goes on back up the quarter. I can see his coattail hitting him round the knees.

"You coming in this yard, Sonny?" Mama calls.

"I'm with Daddy," I say.

Mama goes back in the house and Gran'mon and them follow her.

"When you want one of them preachers to do something for you, they can't do a doggone thing," Daddy says. "Nothing but stand up in that churchhouse and preach 'bout Heaven. I hate to go to that old hoo-doo woman, but I reckon there ain't nothing else I can do. You want go back there with me, Sonny?"

"Uh-huh."

"Come on," Daddy says.

Daddy takes my hand and me and him leave the fire. When I get 'way down the quarter I look back and see the fire still burning. We cross the railroad tracks and I can see the people cutting cane. They got plenty cane all on the ground.

"Get me piece of cane, Daddy," I say.

"Sonny, please," Daddy says. "I'm thinking."

"I want piece of two-ninety," I say.

Daddy turns my hand loose and jumps over the ditch. He finds a piece of two-ninety and jumps back over. Daddy takes out a little pocketknife and peels the cane. He gives me a round and he cut him off a round and chew it. I like two ninety cane because it's soft and sweet and got plenty juice in it.

"I want another piece," I say.

Daddy cuts me off another round and hands it to me.

"I'll be glad when you big enough to peel your own cane," he says.

"I can peel my own cane now," I say.

Daddy breaks me off three joints and hands it to me. I peel the cane with my teeth. Two-ninety cane is soft and it's easy to peel.

Me and Daddy go round the bend, and then I can see Madame Toussaint's house. Madame Toussaint's got a' old house, and look like it want to fall down any minute. I'm scared of Madame Toussaint. Billy Joe Martin say Madame Toussaint's a witch, and he say one time he seen Madame Toussaint riding a broom.

Daddy pulls Madame Toussaint's little old broken-down gate open and we go in the yard. Me and Daddy go far as the steps, but we don't go up on the gallery. Madame Toussaint's got plenty trees round her house, little trees and big trees. And she got plenty moss hanging on every tree. I see a pecan over there on the ground but I'm scared to go and pick it up. Madame Toussaint'll put bad mark on me and I'll turn to a frog or something. I let Madame Toussaint's little old pecan stay right where it is. And I go up to Daddy and let him hold my hand.

"Madame Toussaint?" Daddy calls.

Madame Toussaint don't answer. Like she ain't there.

"Madame Toussaint?" Daddy calls again.

"Who that?" Madame Toussaint answers.

"Me," Daddy says. "Eddie Howard and his little boy Sonny."

"What you want, Eddie Howard?" Madame Toussaint calls from in her house.

"I want talk to you," Daddy says. "I need little advice on something."

I hear a dog bark three times in the house. He must be a big old dog because he's sure got a heavy voice. Madame Toussaint comes to the door and cracks it open.

"Can I come in?" Daddy says.

"Come in, Eddie Howard," Madame Toussaint says.

Me and Daddy go up the steps and Madame Toussaint opens the door for us. Madame Toussaint's a little bitty little old woman and her face is brown like cowhide. I look at Madame Toussaint and I walk close 'side Daddy. Me and Daddy go in the house and Madame Toussaint shuts the door and comes back to her fireplace. She sits down in her big old rocking chair and looks at me and Daddy. I look round Daddy's leg at Madame Toussaint, but I let Daddy hold my hand. Madame Toussaint's house don't smell good. It's too dark in here. It don't smell good at all. Madame Toussaint ought to have a window or something open in her house.

"I need some advice, Madame Toussaint," Daddy says.

"Your wife left you," Madame Toussaint says.

"How you know?" Daddy asks.

"That's all you men come back here for," Madame Toussaint says. "That's how I know."

Daddy nods his head. "Yes," he says. "She done left me and staying with another man."

"She left," Madame Toussaint says. "But she's not staying with another man."

"Yes, she is," Daddy says.

"She's not," Madame Toussaint says. "You trying to tell me my business?"

"No, ma'am," Daddy says.

"I should hope not," Madame Toussaint says.

Madame Toussaint ain't got but three old rotten teeth in her mouth. I bet you she can't peel no cane with them old rotten teeth. I bet you they'd break off in a hard piece of cane.

"I need advice, Madame Toussaint," Daddy says.

"You got money?" Madame Toussaint asks.

"I got some," Daddy says.

"How much?" she asks Daddy. She's looking up at Daddy like she don't believe him.

Daddy turns my hand loose and sticks his hand down in his pocket. He gets all his money out his pocket and leans over the fire to see how much he's got. I see some matches and piece of string and some nails in Daddy's hand. I reach for the piece of string and Daddy taps me on the hand with his other hand.

"I got about seventy-five cents," Daddy says. "Counting them pennies."

"My price is three dollars," Madame Toussaint says.

"I can cut you a load of wood," Daddy says. "Or make grocery for you. I'll do anything in the world if you can help me, Madame Toussaint."

"Three dollars," Madame Toussaint says. "I got all the wood I'll need this winter. Enough grocery to last me till summer."

"But this all I got," Daddy says.

"When you get more, come back," Madame Toussaint says.

"But I want my wife back now," Daddy says. "I can't wait till I get more money."

"Three dollars is my price," Madame Toussaint says. "No more, no less."

"But can't you give me just a little advice for seventy-five cents?" Daddy says. "Seventy-five cents worth? Maybe I can start from there and figure something out."

Madame Toussaint looks at me and looks at Daddy again.

"You say that's your boy?" she says.

"Yes, ma'am," Daddy says.

"Nice-looking boy," Madame Toussaint says.

"His name's Sonny," Daddy says.

"Hi, Sonny," Madame Toussaint says.

"Say 'Hi' to Madame Toussaint," Daddy says. "Go on."

"Hi," I say, sticking close to Daddy.

"Well, Madame Toussaint?" Daddy says.

"Give me the money," Madame Toussaint says. "Don't complain to me if you not satisfied."

"Don't worry," Daddy says. "I won't complain. Anything to get her back home."

Daddy leans over the fire again and picks the money out of his hand. Then he reaches it to Madame Toussaint.

"Give me that little piece of string," Madame Toussaint says. "It might come in handy sometime in the future. Wait," she says. "Run it 'cross the left side of the boy's face three times, then pass it to me behind your back."

"What's that for?" Daddy asks.

"Just do like I say," Madame Toussaint says.

"Yes, ma'am," Daddy says. Daddy turns to me. "Hold still, Sonny," he says. He rubs the little old dirty piece of cord over my face, and then he sticks his hand behind his back.

Madame Toussaint reaches in her pocket and takes out her pocketbook. She opens it and puts the money in. She opens another little compartment and stuffs the string down in it. Then she snaps the pocketbook and puts it back in her pocket. She picks up three little green sticks she got tied together and starts poking in the fire with them.

"What's the advice?" Daddy asks.

Madame Toussaint don't say nothing.

"Madame Toussaint?" Daddy says.

Madame Toussaint still don't answer him, she just looks down in the fire. Her face is red from the fire. I get scared of Madame Toussaint. She can ride all over the plantation on her broom. Billy Joe Martin say he seen her one night riding 'cross the houses. She was whipping her broom with three switches.

Madame Toussaint raises her head and looks at Daddy. Her eyes's big and white, and I get scared of her. I hide my face 'side Daddy's leg.

Miss Hebert looks at me, and then she writes some more on the note. She puts her pencil down and folds the note up.

"Be sure to give this to your mother," she says. "Put it in your pocket and don't lose it."

I take the note from Miss Hebert, but I don't leave the desk.

"Do you want to go outside?" she asks.

"Yes, ma'am."

"You may leave," she says.

I go over and get my coat and cap, and then I go out in the yard. I see Billy Joe Martin and Charles and them shooting marbles over by the gate. I don't go over there because they'll tease me. I go 'side the schoolhouse and look at Lucy and them jumping rope. Lucy ain't jumping right now.

"Hi, Lucy," I say.

Lucy looks over at Shirley and they laugh. They look at my pants and laugh.

"You want a piece of potato?" I ask Lucy.

"No," Lucy says. "And you not my boyfriend no more, either."

I look at Lucy and I go stand 'side the wall in the sun. I peel my potato and eat it. And look like soon's I get through, Miss Hebert comes to the front and says recess is over.

We go back inside, and I go to the back and take off my coat and cap. Bill comes back there and hang the things up for us. I go over to Miss Hebert's desk and Miss Hebert gives me my book. I go back to my seat and sit down 'side Lucy.

"Hi, Lucy," I say.

Lucy looks at Shirley and Shirley puts her hand over her mouth and laughs. I feel like getting up from there and socking Shirley in the mouth, but I know Miss Hebert'll whip me. Because I got no business socking people after I done wee-wee on myself. I open my book and look at my lesson so I don't have to look at none of them.

3: It's almost dinner time, and when I get home I ain't coming back here either, now. I'm go'n stay there. I'm go'n stay right there and sit by the fire. Lucy and them don't want play with me, and I ain't coming back up here. Miss Hebert go'n touch

"Give it up," I hear her say.

"Give what up?" Daddy says.

"Give it up," she says.

"What?" Daddy says.

"Give it up," she says.

"I don't even know what you talking 'bout," Daddy says. "How can I give up something and I don't even know what it is?"

"I said it three times," Madame Toussaint says. "No more, no less. Up to you now to follow it through from there."

"Follow what from where?" Daddy says. "You said three little old words: 'Give it up.' I don't know no more now than I knowed 'fore I got here."

"I told you you wasn't go'n be satisfied," Madame Toussaint says.

"Satisfied?" Daddy says. "Satisfied for what? You gived me just three little old words and you want me to be satisfied?"

"You can leave," Madame Toussaint says.

"Leave?" Daddy says. "You mean I give you seventy-five cents for three words? A quarter a word? And I'm leaving? No, Lord."

"Rollo?" Madame Toussaint says.

I see Madame Toussaint's big old black dog get up out of the corner and come where she is. Madame Toussaint pats the dog on the head with her hand.

"Two dollars and twenty-five cents more and you get all the advice you need," Madame Toussaint says.

"Can't I get you a load of wood and fix your house for you or something?" Daddy says.

"I don't want my house fixed and I don't need no more wood," Madame Toussaint says. "I got three loads of wood just three days ago from a man who didn't have money. Before I know it I'll have wood piled up all over my yard."

"Can't I do anything?" Daddy says.

"You can leave," Madame Toussaint says. "I ought to have somebody else dropping round pretty soon. Lately I've been having men dropping in three times a day. All of them just like you. What they can do to make their wives love them more. What they can do to keep their wives from running round with some other man. What they can do to make their wives give in. What they can do to make their wives scratch their backs. What they can do to make their wives look at them when they talking to her. Get out my house before I put the dog on you. You been here too long for seventy-five cents."

Madame Toussaint's big old jet-black dog gives three loud barks that makes my head hurt. Madame Toussaint pats him on the back to calm him down.

"Come on, Sonny," Daddy says.

I let Daddy take my hand and we go over to the door.

"I still don't feel like you helped me very much, though," Daddy says.

Madame Toussaint pats her big old jet-black dog on the head and she don't answer Daddy. Daddy pushes the door open and we go outside. It's some cold outside. Me and Daddy go down Madame Toussaint's old broken-down steps.

"What was them words?" Daddy asks me.

"Hanh?"

"What she said when she looked up out of that fire?" Daddy asks.

"I was scared," I say. "Her face was red and her eyes got big and white. I was scared. I had to hide my face."

"Didn't you hear what she told me?" Daddy asks.

"She told you three dollars," I say.

"I mean when she looked up," Daddy says.

"She say, 'Give it up,' " I say.

"Yes," Daddy says. " 'Give it up.' Give what up? I don't even know what she's talking 'bout. I hope she don't mean give you and Amy up. She ain't that crazy. I don't know nothing else she can be talking 'bout. You don't know, do you?"

"Uh-uh," I say.

" 'Give it up,' " Daddy says. "I don't even know what she's talking 'bout. I wonder who them other men was she was speaking of. Johnny and his wife had a fight the other week. It might be him. Frank Armstrong and his wife had a round couple weeks back. Could be him. I wish I knowed what she told them."

"I want another piece of cane," I say.

"No," Daddy says. "You'll be pee-ing in bed all night tonight."

"I'm go'n sleep with Uncle Al," I say. "Me and him go'n sleep in his bed."

"Please, be quiet, Sonny," Daddy says. "I got enough troubles on my mind. Don't add more to it."

Me and Daddy walk in the middle of the road. Daddy holds my hand. I can hear a tractor—I see it across the field. The people loading cane on the trailer back of the tractor.

"Come on," Daddy says. "We going over to Frank Armstrong."

Daddy totes me 'cross the ditch on his back. I ride on Daddy's back and I look at the stubbles where the people done cut the cane. Them rows some long. Plenty cane's laying on the ground. I can see cane all over the field. Me and Daddy go over where the people cutting cane.

"How come you ain't working this evening?" a man asks Daddy. The man's shucking a big armful of cane with his cane knife.

"Frank Armstrong round anywhere?" Daddy asks the man.

"Farther over," the man says. "Hi, youngster."

"Hi," I say.

Me and Daddy go 'cross the field. I look at the people cutting cane. That cane is some tall. I want another piece, but I might wee-wee in Uncle Al's bed.

Me and Daddy go over where Mr. Frank Armstrong and Mrs. Julie's cutting cane. Mrs. Julie got overalls on just like Mr. Frank got. She's even wearing one of Mr. Frank's old hats.

"How y'all?" Daddy says.

"So-so, and yourself?" Mrs. Julie says.

"I'm trying to make it," Daddy says. "Can I borrow your husband there a minute?"

"Sure," Mrs. Julie says. "But don't keep him too long. We trying to reach the end 'fore dark."

"It won't take long," Daddy says.

Mr. Frank and them got a little fire burning in one of the middles. Me and him and Daddy go over there. Daddy squats down and let me slide off his back.

"What's the trouble?" Mr. Frank asks Daddy.

"Amy left me, Frank," Daddy says.

Mr. Frank holds his hands over the fire.

"She left you?" he says.

"Yes," Daddy says. "And I want her back, Frank."

"What can I do?" Mr. Frank says. "She's no kin to me. I can't go and make her come back."

"I thought maybe you could tell me what you and Madame Toussaint talked about," Daddy says. "That's if you don't mind, Frank."

"What?" Mr. Frank says. "Who told you I talked with Madame Toussaint?"

"Nobody," Daddy says. "But I heard you and Julie had a fight, and I thought maybe you went back to her for advice."

"For what?" Mr. Frank says.

"So you and Julie could make up," Daddy says.

"Well, I'll be damned," Mr. Frank says. "I done heard everything. Excuse me, Sonny. But your daddy's enough to make anybody cuss."

I look up at Daddy, and I look back in the fire again.

"Please, Frank," Daddy says. "I'm desperate. I'm ready to try anything. I'll do anything to get her back in my house."

"Why don't you just go and get her?" Mr. Frank says. "That makes sense."

"I can't," Daddy says. "Mama won't let me come in the yard. She even took a shot at me once today."

"What?" Mr. Frank says. He looks at Daddy, and then he just bust out laughing. Daddy laughs little bit, too.

"What y'all talked about, Frank?" Daddy asks. "Maybe if I try the same thing, maybe I'll be able to get her back, too."

Mr. Frank laughs at Daddy, then he stops and just looks at Daddy.

"No," he says. "I'm afraid my advice won't help your case. You got to first get close to your wife. And your mother-in-law won't let you do that. No, mine won't help you."

"It might," Daddy says.

"No, it won't," Mr. Frank says.

"It might," Daddy says. "What was it?"

"All right," Mr. Frank says. "She told me I wasn't petting Julie enough."

"Petting her?" Daddy says.

"You think he know what we talking 'bout?" Mr. Frank asks Daddy.

"I'll get him piece of cane," Daddy says.

They got a big pile of cane right behind Daddy's back, and he crosses the row and gets me a stalk of two-ninety. He breaks off three joints and hands it to me. He throws the rest of the stalk back.

"So I start petting her," Mr. Frank says.

"What you mean 'petting her'?" Daddy says. "I don't even know what you mean now."

"Eddie, I swear," Mr. Frank says. "Stroking her. You know. Like you stroke a colt. A little horse."

"Oh," Daddy says. "Did it work?"

"What you think?" Mr. Frank says, grinning. "Every night, a little bit. Turn your head, Sonny."

"Hanh?"

"Look the other way," Daddy says.

I look down the row toward the other end. I don't see nothing but cane all over the ground.

"Stroke her a little back here," Mr. Frank says. I hear him hitting on his pants. "Works every time. Get along now like two peas in one pod. Every night when we get in the bed"—I hear him hitting again—"couple little strokes. Now everything's all right."

"You was right," Daddy says. "That won't help me none."

"My face getting cold," I say.

"You can turn round and warm," Daddy says.

I turn and look at Mr. Frank. I bite off piece of cane and chew it.

"I told you it wouldn't," Mr. Frank says. "Well, I got to get back to work. What you go'n do now?"

"I don't know," Daddy says. "If I had three dollars she'd give me some advice. But I don't have a red copper. You wouldn't have three dollars you could spare till payday, huh?"

"I don't have a dime," Mr. Frank says. "Since we made up, Julie keeps most of the money."

"You think she'd lend me three dollars till Saturday?" Daddy asks.

"I don't know if she got that much on her," Mr. Frank says. "I'll go over and ask her."

I watch Mr. Frank going 'cross the rows where Mrs. Julie's cutting cane. They start talking, and then I hear them laughing.

"You warm?" Daddy asks.

"Uh-huh."

I see Mr. Frank coming back to the fire.

"She don't have it on her but she got it at the house," Mr. Frank says. "If you can wait till we knock off."

"No," Daddy says. "I can't wait till night. I got to try to borrow it from somebody now."

"Why don't you go 'cross the field and try Johnny Green," Mr. Frank says. "He's always got some money. Maybe he'll lend it to you."

"I'll ask him," Daddy says. "Get on, Sonny."

Me and Daddy go back 'cross the field. I can hear Mr. Johnny Green singing, and Daddy turns that way and we go down where Mr. Johnny is. Mr. Johnny stops his singing when he sees me and Daddy. He chops the top off a' armful of cane and throws it 'cross the row. Mr. Johnny's cutting cane all by himself.

"Hi, Brother Howard," Mr. Johnny says.

"Hi," Daddy says. Daddy squats down and let me slide off.

"Hi there, little Brother Sonny," Mr. Johnny says.

"Hi," I say.

"How you?" Mr. Johnny asks.

"I'm all right," I say.

"That's good," Mr. Johnny says. "And how you this beautiful, God-sent day, Brother Howard?"

"I'm fine," Daddy says. "Johnny, I want know if you can spare me 'bout three dollars till Saturday?"

"Sure, Brother Howard," Mr. Johnny says. "You mind telling me just why you need it? I don't mind lending a good brother anything, long 's I know he ain't wasting it on women or drink."

"I want pay Madame Toussaint for some advice," Daddy says.

"Little trouble, Brother?" Mr. Johnny asks.

"Amy done left me, Johnny," Daddy says. "I need some advice. I just got to get her back."

"I know what you mean, Brother," Mr. Johnny says. "I had to visit Madame—you won't carry this no farther, huh?"

"No," Daddy says.

"Couple months ago I had to take a little trip back there to see her," Mr. Johnny says.

"What was wrong?" Daddy asks.

"Little misunderstanding between me and Sister Laura," Mr. Johnny says.

"She helped?" Daddy asks.

"Told me to stop spending so much time in church and little more time at home," Mr. Johnny says. "I couldn't see that. You know, far back as I can go in my family my people been good church members."

"I know that," Daddy says.

"My pappy was a deacon and my mammy didn't miss a Sunday long as I can remember," Mr. Johnny says. "And that's how I was raised. To fear God. I just couldn't see it when she first told me that. But I thought it over. I went for a long walk back in the field. I got down on my knees and looked up at the sky. I asked God to show me the way—to tell me what to do. And He did, He surely did. He told me to do just like Madame Toussaint said. Slack up going to church. Go twice a week, but spend the rest of the time with her. Just like that He told me. And I'm doing exactly what He said. Twice a week. And, Brother Howard, don't spread this round, but the way Sister Laura been acting here lately, there might be a little Johnny next summer sometime."

"No?" Daddy says.

"Uhnnnn-hunh," Mr. Johnny says.

"I'll be doggone," Daddy says. "I'm glad to hear that."

"I'll be the happiest man on this whole plantation," Mr. Johnny says.

"I know how you feel," Daddy says. "Yes, I know how you feel. But that three, can you lend it to me?"

"Sure, Brother," Mr. Johnny says. "Anything to bring a family back together. Nothing more important in this world than family love. Yes, indeed."

Mr. Johnny unbuttons his top overalls pocket and takes out a dollar.

"Only thing I got is five, Brother Howard," he says. "You wouldn't happen to have some change, would you?"

"I don't have a red copper," Daddy says. "But I'll be more than happy if you can let me have that five. I need some grocery in the house, too."

"Sure, Brother," Mr. Johnny says. He hands Daddy the dollar. "Nothing looks more beautiful than a family at a table eating something the little woman just cooked. But you did say Saturday didn't you, Brother?"

"Yes," Daddy says. "I'll pay you back soon 's I get paid. You can't ever guess how much this means to me, Johnny."

"Glad I can help, Brother," Mr. Johnny says. "Hope she can do likewise."

"I hope so too," Daddy says. "Anyhow, this a start."

"See you Saturday, Brother," Mr. Johnny says.

"Soon 's I get paid," Daddy says. "Hop on, Sonny, and hold tight. We going back."

4: Daddy walks up on Madame Toussaint's gallery and knocks on the door.

"Who that?" Madame Toussaint asks.

"Me. Eddie Howard," Daddy says. He squats down so I can slide off his back. I slide down and let Daddy hold my hand.

"What you want, Eddie Howard?" Madame Toussaint asks.

"I got three dollars," Daddy says. "I still want that advice."

Madame Toussaint's big old jet-black dog barks three times,

and then I hear Madame Toussaint coming to the door. She peeps through the keyhole at me and Daddy. She opens the door and let me and Daddy come in. We go to the fireplace and warm. Madame Toussaint comes to the fireplace and sits down in her big old rocking chair. She looks up at Daddy. I look for big old Rollo, but I don't see him. He must be under the bed or hiding somewhere in the corner.

"You got three dollars?" Madame Toussaint asks Daddy.

"Yes," Daddy says. He takes out the dollar and shows it to Madame Toussaint.

Madame Toussaint holds her hand up for it.

"This is five," Daddy says. "I want two back."

"You go'n get your two," Madame Toussaint says.

"Come to think of it," Daddy says, "I ought to just owe you two and a quarter, since I done already gived you seventy-five cents."

"You want advice?" Madame Toussaint asks Daddy. Madame Toussaint looks like she's getting mad with Daddy now.

"Sure," Daddy says. "But since—"

"Then shut up and hand me your money," Madame Toussaint says.

"But I done already—" Daddy says.

"Get out my house, nigger," Madame Toussaint says. "And don't come back till you learn how to act."

"All right," Daddy says, "I'll give you three more dollars."

He hands Madame Toussaint the dollar.

Madame Toussaint gets her pocketbook out her pocket. Then she leans close to the fire so she can look down in it. She sticks her hand in the pocketbook and gets two dollars. She looks at the two dollars a long time. She stands up and gets her eyeglasses off the mantelpiece and puts them on her eyes. She looks at the two dollars a long time, then she hands them to Daddy. She sticks the dollar bill Daddy gived her in the pocketbook, then she takes her eyeglasses off and puts them back on the mantelpiece. Madame Toussaint sits in her big old rocking chair and starts poking in the fire with the three sticks again. Her face gets red from the fire, her eyes get big and white. I turn my head and hide behind Daddy's leg.

"Go set fire to your car," Madame Toussaint says.

"What?" Daddy says.

"Go set fire to your car," Madame Toussaint says.

"You talking to me?" Daddy says.

"Go set fire to your car," Madame Toussaint says.

"Now, just a minute," Daddy says. "I didn't give you my hard-earned three dollars for that kind of foolishness. I dismiss that seventy-five cents you took from me, but not my three dollars that easy."

"You want your wife back?" Madame Toussaint asks Daddy.

"That's what I'm paying you for," Daddy says.

"Then go set fire to your car," Madame Toussaint says. "You can't have both."

"You must be fooling," Daddy says.

"I don't fool," Madame Toussaint says. "You paid for advice and I'm giving you advice."

"You mean that?" Daddy says. "You mean I got to go burn up my car for Amy to come back home?"

"If you want her back there," Madame Toussaint says. "Do you?"

"I wouldn't be standing here if I didn't," Daddy says.

"Then go and burn it up," Madame Toussaint says. "A gallon of coal oil and a penny box of match ought to do the trick. You got any gas in it?"

"A little bit—if nobody ain't drained it," Daddy says.

"Then you can use that," Madame Toussaint says. "But if you want her back there you got to burn it up. That's my advice to you. And if I was you I'd do it right away. You can never tell."

"Tell about what?" Daddy asks.

"She might be sleeping in another man's bed a week from now," Madame Toussaint says. "This man loves her and he's kind. And that's what a woman wants. That's what they need. You men don't know this, but you better learn it before it's too late."

"What's that other man's name?" Daddy asks. "Can it be Freddie Jackson?"

"It can," Madame Toussaint says. "But it don't have to be. Any man that'd give her love and kindness."

"I love her," Daddy says. "I give her kindness. I'm always giving her love and kindness."

"When you home, you mean," Madame Toussaint says. "How about when you running up and down the road in your car? How do you think she feels then?"

Daddy don't say nothing.

"You men better learn," Madame Toussaint says. "Now, if you want her, go and burn it. If you don't want her, go and get drunk off them two dollars and sleep in a cold bed tonight."

"You mean she'll come back tonight?" Daddy asks.

"She's ready to come back right now," Madame Toussaint says. "Poor little thing."

I look round Daddy's leg at Madame Toussaint. Madame Toussaint's looking in the fire. Her face ain't red no more; her eyes ain't big and white, either.

"She's not happy where she is," Madame Toussaint says.

"She's with her mama," Daddy says.

"You don't have to tell me my business," Madame Toussaint says. "I know where she is. And I still say she's not happy. She much rather be back in her own house. Women like to be in their own house. That's their world. You men done messed up the outside world so bad that they feel lost and out of place in it. Her house is her world. Only there she can do what she want. She can't do that in anybody else house—mama or nobody else. But you men don't know any of this. Y'all never know how a woman feels, because you never ask how she feels. Long 's she there when you get there you satisfied. Long 's you give her two or three dollars every weekend you think she ought to be satisfied. But keep on. One day all of you'll find out."

"Couldn't I sell the car or something?" Daddy asks.

"You got to burn it," Madame Toussaint says. "How come your head so hard?"

"But I paid good money for that car," Daddy says. "It wouldn't look right if I just jumped up and put fire to it."

"You, get out my house," Madame Toussaint says, pointing her finger at Daddy. "Go do what you want with your car. It's yours. But just don't come back here bothering me for no more advice."

"I don't know," Daddy says.

"I'm through talking," Madame Toussaint says. "Rollo? Come here, baby."

Big old jet-black Rollo comes up and puts his head in Madame Toussaint's lap. Madame Toussaint pats him on the head.

"That's what I got to do, hanh?" Daddy says.

Madame Toussaint don't answer Daddy. She starts singing a song to Rollo:

> *Mama's little baby,*
> *Mama's little baby.*

"He bad?" Daddy asks.

> *Mama's little baby,*
> *Mama's little baby.*

"Do he bite?" Daddy asks.

Madame Toussaint keeps on singing:

> *Mama's little baby,*
> *Mama's little baby.*

"Come on," Daddy says. "I reckon we better be going."

Daddy squats down and I climb up on his back. I look down at Madame Toussaint patting big old jet-black Rollo on his head.

Daddy pushes the door open and we go outside. It's cold outside. Daddy goes down Madame Toussaint's three old broken-down steps and we go out in the road.

"I don't know," Daddy says.

"Hanh?"

"I'm talking to myself," Daddy says. "I don't know about burning up my car."

"You go'n burn up your car?" I ask.

"That's what Madame Toussaint say to do," Daddy says.

"You ain't go'n have no more car?"

"I reckon not," Daddy says. "You want me and Mama to stay together?"

"Uh-huh."

"Then I reckon I got to burn it up," Daddy says. "But I sure hope there was another way out. I put better than three hundred dollars in that car."

Daddy walks fast and I bounce on his back.

"God, I wish there was another way out," Daddy says. "Don't look like that's right for a man to just jump up and set fire to something like that. What you think I ought to do?"

"Hanh?"

"Go back to sleep," Daddy says. "I don't know what I'm educating you for."

"I ain't sleeping," I say.

"I don't know," Daddy says. "That don't look right. All Frank Armstrong had to do was pop Julie on the butt little bit every night 'fore she went to sleep. All Johnny had to do was stop going to church so much. Neither one of them had to burn down anything. Johnny didn't have to burn down the church; Frank didn't have to burn down the bed—nothing. But me, I got to burn up my car. She charged all us the same thing—no, she even charged me seventy-five cents more, and I got to burn up a car I can still get some use out. Now, that don't sound right, do it?"

"Hanh?"

"I can't figure it," Daddy says. "Look like I ought to be able to sell it for little something. Get some of my money back. Burning it, I don't get a red copper. That just don't sound right to me. I wonder if she was fooling. No. She say she wasn't. But maybe that wasn't my advice she seen in that fireplace. Maybe that was somebody else advice. Maybe she gived me the wrong one. Maybe it belongs to the man coming back there after me. They go there three times a day, she can get them mixed up."

"I'm scared of Madame Toussaint, Daddy," I say.

"Must've been somebody else," Daddy says. "I bet it was. I bet you anything it was."

I bounce on Daddy's back and I close my eyes. I open them and I see me and Daddy going 'cross the railroad tracks. We go up the quarter to Gran'mon's house. Daddy squats down and I slide off his back.

"Run in the house to the fire," Daddy says. "Tell your mama come to the door."

Soon 's I come in the yard, Spot runs down the walk and starts barking. Mama and all of them come out on the gallery.

"My baby," Mama says. Mama comes down the steps and hugs me to her. "My baby," she says.

"Look at that old yellow thing standing out in that road," Gran'mon says. "What you ought to been done was got the sheriff on him for kidnap."

Me and Mama go back on the gallery.

"I been to Madame Toussaint's house," I say.

Mama looks at me and looks at Daddy out in the road. Daddy comes to the gate and looks at us on the gallery.

"Amy?" Daddy calls. "Can I speak to you a minute? Just one minute?"

"You don't get away from my gate, I'm go'n make that shotgun speak to you," Gran'mon says. "I didn't get you at twelve o'clock, but I won't miss you now."

"Amy, honey," Daddy calls. "Please."

"Come on, Sonny," Mama says.

"Where you going?" Gran'mon asks.

"Far as the gate," Mama says. "I'll talk to him. I reckon I owe him that much."

"You leave this house with that nigger, don't ever come back here again," Gran'mon says.

"You oughtn't talk like that, Rachel," Uncle Al says.

"I talk like I want," Gran'mon says. "She's my daughter; not yours, neither his."

Me and Mama go out to the gate where Daddy is. Daddy stands outside the gate and me and Mama stand inside.

"Lord, you look good, Amy," Daddy says. "Honey, didn't you miss me? Go on and say it. Go on and say how bad you missed me."

"That's all you want say to me?" Mama says.

"Honey, please," Daddy says. "Say you missed me. I been grieving all day like a dog."

"Come on, Sonny," Mama says. "Let's go back inside."

"Honey," Daddy says. "Please don't turn your back on me and go back to Freddie Jackson. Honey, I love you. I swear 'fore God I love you. Honey, you listening?"

"Come on, Sonny," Mama says.

"Honey," Daddy says, "if I burn the car like Madame Toussaint say, you'll come back home?"

"What?" Mama says.

"She say for Daddy—"

"Be still, Sonny," Mama says.

"She told me to set fire to it and you'll come back home," Daddy says. "You'll come back, honey?"

"She told you to burn up your car?" Mama says.

"If I want you to come back," Daddy says. "If I do it, you'll come back?"

"If you burn it up," Mama says. "If you burn it up, yes, I'll come back."

"Tonight?" Daddy says.

"Yes; tonight," Mama says.

"If I sold it?" Daddy says.

"Burn it," Mama says.

"I can get about fifty for it," Daddy says. "You could get couple dresses out of that."

"Burn it," Mama says. "You know what burn is?"

Daddy looks across the gate at Mama, and Mama looks right back at him. Daddy nods his head.

"I can't argue with you, honey," he says. "I'll go and burn it right now. You can come see if you want."

"No," Mama says, "I'll be here when you come back."

"Couldn't you go up home and start cooking some supper?" Daddy asks. "I'm just 's hungry as a dog."

"I'll cook when that car is burnt," Mama says. "Come on, Sonny."

"Can I go see Daddy burn his car, Mama?" I ask.

"No," Mama says. "You been in that cold long enough."

"I want see Daddy burn his car," I say. I start crying and stomping so Mama'll let me go.

"Let him go, honey," Daddy says. "I'll keep him warm."

"You can go," Mama says. "But don't come to me if you start that coughing tonight, you hear?"

"Uh-huh," I say.

Mama makes sure all my clothes's buttoned good, then she let me go. I run out in the road where Daddy is.

"I'll be back soon 's I can, honey," Daddy says. "And we'll straighten out everything, hear?"

"Just make sure you burn it," Mama says. "I'll find out."

"Honey, I'm go'n burn every bit of it," Daddy says.

"I'll be here when you come back," Mama says. "How you figuring on getting up there?"

"I'll go over and see if George Williams can't take me," Daddy says.

"I don't want Sonny in that cold too long," Mama says. "And you keep your hands in your pockets, Sonny."

"I ain't go'n take them out," I say.

Mama goes back up the walk toward the house. Daddy stands there just watching her.

"Lord, that's a sweet little woman," he says, shaking his head. "That's a sweet little woman you see going back to that house."

"Come on, Daddy," I say. "Let's go burn up the car."

Me and Daddy walk away from the fence.

"Let me get on your back and ride," I say.

"Can't you walk sometime," Daddy says. "What you think I'm educating you for—to treat me like a horse?"

5: Mr. George Williams drives his car to the side of the road, then we get out.

"Look like we got company," Mr. George Williams says.

Me and Daddy and Mr. George Williams go over where the people is. The people got a little fire burning, and some of them's sitting on the car fender. But most of them's standing round the little fire.

"Welcome," somebody says.

"Thanks," Daddy says. "Since this is my car you sitting on."

"Oh," the man says. He jumps up and the other two men jump up, too. They go over to the little fire and stand round it.

"We didn't mean no harm," one of them say.

Daddy goes over and peeps in the car. Then he opens the door and gets in. I go over to the car where he is.

"Go stand 'side the fire," Daddy says.

"I want get in with you," I say.

"Do what I tell you," Daddy says.

I go back to the fire, and I turn and look at Daddy in the car. Daddy passes his hand all over the car; then he just sit there quiet-like. All the people round the fire look at Daddy in the car. I can hear them talking real low.

After a little while, Daddy opens the door and gets out. He comes over to the fire.

"Well," he says, "I guess that's it. You got a rope?"

"In the trunk," Mr. George Williams says. "What you go'n do, drag it off the highway?"

"We can't burn it out here," Daddy says.

"He say he go'n burn it," somebody at the fire says.

"I'm go'n burn it," Daddy says. "It's mine, ain't it?"

"Easy, Eddie," Mr. George Williams says.

Daddy is mad but he don't say any more. Mr. George Williams looks at Daddy, then he goes over to his car and gets the rope.

"Ought to be strong enough," Mr. George Williams says.

He hands Daddy the rope, then he goes and turns his car around. Everybody at the fire looks at Mr. George Williams backing up his car.

"Good," Daddy says.

Daddy gets between the cars and ties them together. Some of the people come over and watch him.

"Y'all got a side road anywhere round here?" he asks.

"Right over there," the man says. "Leads off back in the field. You ain't go'n burn up that good car for real, is you?"

"Who field this is?" Daddy asks.

"Mr. Roger Medlow," the man says.

"Any colored people got fields round here anywhere?" Daddy asks.

"Old man Ned Johnson 'bout two miles farther down the road," another man says.

"Why don't we just take it on back to the plantation?" Mr. George Williams says. "I doubt if Mr. Claude'll mind if we burnt it there."

"All right," Daddy says. "Might as well."

Me and Daddy get in his car. Some of the people from the fire run up to Mr. George Williams's car. Mr. George Williams tells them something, and I see three of them jumping in. Mr. George Williams taps on the horn, then we get going. I sit 'way back in the seat and look at Daddy. Daddy's quiet. He's sorry because he got to burn up his car.

We go 'way down the road, then we turn and go down the quarter. Soon 's we get down there, I hear two of the men in Mr. George Williams's car calling to the people. I sit up in the seat and look out at them. They standing on the fenders, calling to the people.

"Come on," they saying. "Come on to the car-burning party. Free. Everybody welcome. Free."

We go farther down the quarter, and the two men keep on calling.

"Come on, everybody," one of them says.

"We having a car-burning party tonight," the other one says. "No charges."

The people start coming out on the galleries to see what all the racket is. I look back and I see some out in the yard, and some already out in the road. Mr. George Williams stops in front of Gran'mon's house.

"You go'n tell Amy?" he calls to Daddy. "Maybe she like to go, since you doing it all for her."

"Go tell your mama come on," Daddy says.

I jump out the car and run in the yard.

"Come on, everybody," one of the men says.

"We having a car-burning party tonight," the other one says. "Everybody invited. No charges."

I pull Gran'mon's door open and go in. Mama and Uncle Al and Gran'mon's sitting at the fireplace.

"Mama, Daddy say come on if you want see the burning," I say.

"See what burning?" Gran'mon asks. "Now don't tell me that crazy nigger going through with that."

"Come on, Mama," I say.

Mama and Uncle Al get up from the fireplace and go to the door.

"He sure got it out there," Uncle Al says.

"Come on, Mama," I say. "Come on, Uncle Al."

"Wait till I get my coat," Mama says. "Mama, you going?"

"I ain't missing this for the world," Gran'mon says. "I still think he's bluffing."

Gran'mon gets her coat and Uncle Al gets his coat; then we go on outside. Plenty people standing round Daddy's car now. I can see more people opening doors and coming out on the galleries.

"Get in," Daddy says. "Sorry I can't take but two. Mama, you want ride?"

"No, thanks," Gran'mon says. "You might just get it in your head to run off in that canal with me in there. Let your wife and child ride. I'll walk with the rest of the people."

"Get in, honey," Daddy says. "It's getting cold out there."

Mama takes my arm and helps me in; then she gets in and shuts the door.

"How far down you going?" Uncle Al asks.

"Near the sugar house," Daddy says. He taps on the horn and Mr. George Williams drives away.

"Come on, everybody," one of the men says.

"We having a car-burning party tonight," the other one says. "Everybody invited."

Mr. George Williams drives his car over the railroad tracks. I look back and I see plenty people following Daddy's car. I can't see Uncle Al and Gran'mon, but I know they back there, too.

We keep going. We get almost to the sugar house, then we turn down another road. The other road is bumpy and I have to bounce on the seat.

"Well, I reckon this's it," Daddy says.

Mama don't say nothing to Daddy.

"You know it ain't too late to change your mind," Daddy says. "All I got to do is stop George and untie the car."

"You brought matches?" Mama asks.

"All right," Daddy says. "All right. Don't start fussing."

We go a little farther and Daddy taps on the horn. Mr. George Williams stops his car. Daddy gets out his car and go and talk with Mr. George Williams. Little bit later I see Daddy coming back.

"Y'all better get out here," he says. "We go'n take it down the field a piece."

Me and Mama get out. I look down the headland and I see Uncle Al and Gran'mon and all the other people coming. Some of them even got flashlights because it's getting dark now. They come where me and Mama's standing. I look down the field and I see the cars going down the row. It's dark, but Mr. George Williams got bright lights on his car. The cars stop and Daddy get out his car and go and untie the rope. Mr. George Williams goes and turns around and come back to the headland where all the people standing. Then he turns his lights on Daddy's car so everybody can see the burning. I see Daddy getting some gas out the tank.

"Give me a hand down here," Daddy calls. But that don't even sound like Daddy's voice.

Plenty people run down the field to help Daddy. They get round the car and start shaking it. I see the car leaning; then it tips over.

"Well," Gran'mon says. "I never would've thought it."

I see Daddy going all round the car with the can, then I see him splashing some inside the car. All the other people back back to give him room. I see Daddy scratching a match and throwing it in the car. He scratches another one and throw that one in the car, too. I see little bit fire, then I see plenty.

"I just do declare," Gran'mon says. "I must be dreaming. He's a man after all."

Gran'mon the only person talking; everybody else is quiet. We stay there a long time and look at the fire. The fire burns down and Daddy and them go and look at the car again. Daddy picks up the can and pours some more gas on the fire. The fire gets big. We look at the fire some more.

"Never thought that was in Eddie," somebody says real low.

"You not the only one," somebody else says.

"He loved that car more than he loved anything."

"No, he must love her more," another person says.

The fire burns down again. Daddy and them go and look at the car. They stay there a good while, then they come out to the headland where we standing.

"What's that, George?" Mama asks.

"The pump," Mr. George Williams says. "Eddie gived it to me for driving him to get his car."

"Hand it here," Mama says.

Mr. George Williams looks at Daddy, but he hands the pump to Mama. Mama goes on down the field with the pump and throws it in the fire. I watch Mama coming back.

"When Eddie gets paid Saturday he'll pay you," Mama says. "You ready to go home, Eddie?"

Daddy nods his head.

"Sonny," Mama says.

I go where Mama is and Mama takes my hand. Daddy raises his head and looks at the people standing round looking at us.

"Thank y'all," he says.

Me and Mama go in Gran'mon's house and pull the big bundle out on the gallery. Daddy picks the bundle up and puts it on his head, then we go up the quarter to us house. Mama opens the gate and me and Daddy go in. We go inside and Mama lights the lamp.

"You hungry?" Mama asks Daddy.

"How can you ask that?" Daddy says. "I'm starving."

"You want eat now or after you whip me?" Mama says.

"Whip you?" Daddy asks. "What I'm go'n be whipping you for?"

Mama goes back in the kitchen. She don't find what she's looking for, and I hear her going outside.

"Where Mama going, Daddy?"

"Don't ask me," Daddy says. "I don't know no more than you."

Daddy gets some kindling out of the corner and puts it in the fireplace. Then he pours some coal oil on the kindling and lights a match to it. Me and Daddy squat down on the fireplace and watch the fire burning.

I hear the back door shut, then I see Mama coming in the front room. Mama's got a great big old switch.

"Here," she says.

"What's that for?" Daddy says.

"Here. Take it," Mama says.

"I ain't got nothing to beat you for, Amy," Daddy says.

"You whip me," Mama says, "or I turn right round and walk on out that door."

Daddy stands up and looks at Mama.

"You must be crazy," Daddy says. "Stop all that foolishness, Amy, and go cook me some food."

"Get your pot, Sonny," Mama says.

"Shucks," I say. "Now where we going? I'm getting tired walking in all that cold. 'Fore you know it I'm go'n have whooping cough."

"Get your pot and stop answering me back, boy," Mama says.

I go to my bed and pick up the pot again.

"Shucks," I say.

"You ain't leaving here," Daddy says.

"You better stop me," Mama says, going to the bundle.

"All right," Daddy says. "I'll beat you if that's what you want."
Daddy gets the switch off the floor and I start crying.

"Lord, have mercy," Daddy says. "Now what?"

"Whip me," Mama says.

"Amy, whip you for what?" Daddy says. "Amy, please, just go back there and cook me something to eat."

"Come on, Sonny," Mama says. "Let's get out of this house."

"All right," Daddy says. Daddy hits Mama two times on the legs. "That's enough," he says.

"Beat me," Mama says.

I cry some more. "Don't beat my mama," I say. "I don't want you to beat my mama."

"Sonny, please," Daddy says. "What y'all trying to do to me— run me crazy? I burnt up the car—ain't that enough?"

"I'm just go'n tell you one more time," Mama says.

"All right," Daddy says. "I'm go'n beat you if that's what you want."

Daddy starts beating Mama, and I cry some more; but Daddy don't stop beating her.

"Beat me harder," Mama says. "I mean it. I mean it."

"Honey, please," Daddy says.

"You better do it," Mama says. "I mean it."

Daddy keeps on beating Mama, and Mama cries and goes down on her knees.

"Leave my mama alone, you old yellow dog," I say. "You leave my mama alone." I throw the pot at him but I miss him, and the pot go bouncing 'cross the floor.

Daddy throws the switch away and runs to Mama and picks her up. He takes Mama to the bed and begs her to stop crying. I get on my own bed and cry in the cover.

I feel somebody shaking me, and I must've been sleeping.

"Wake up," I hear Daddy saying.

I'm tired and I don't feel like getting up. I feel like sleeping some more.

"You want some supper?" Daddy asks.

"Uh-huh."

"Get up then," Daddy says.

I get up. I got all my clothes on and my shoes on.

"It's morning?" I ask.

"No," Daddy says. "Still night. Come on back in the kitchen and eat supper."

I follow Daddy in the kitchen and me and him sit down at the table. Mama brings the food to the table and she sits down, too.

"Bless this food, Father, which we're about to receive, the nurse of our bodies, for Christ sake, amen," Mama says.

I raise my head and look at Mama. I can see where she's been crying. Her face is all swole. I look at Daddy and he's eating. Mama and Daddy don't talk, and I don't say nothing, either. I eat my food. We eating sweet potatoes and bread. I'm having a glass of clabber, too.

"What a day," Daddy says.

Mama don't say nothing. She's just picking over her food.

"Mad?" Daddy says.

"No," Mama says.

"Honey?" Daddy says.

Mama looks at him.

"I didn't beat you because you did us thing with Freddie Jackson, did I?" Daddy says.

"No," Mama says.

"Well, why then?" Daddy says.

"Because I don't want you to be the laughingstock of the plantation," Mama says.

"Who go'n laugh at me?" Daddy says.

"Everybody," Mama says. "Mama and all. Now they don't have nothing to laugh about."

"Honey, I don't mind if they laugh at me," Daddy says.

"I do mind," Mama says.

"Did I hurt you?"

"I'm all right," she says.

"You ain't mad no more?" Daddy says.

"No," Mama says. "I'm not mad."

Mama picks up a little bit of food and puts it in her mouth. "Finish eating your supper, Sonny," she says.

"I got enough," I say.

"Drink your clabber," Mama says.

I drink all my clabber and show Mama the glass.

"Go get your book," Mama says. "It's on the dresser."

I go in the front room to get my book.

"One of us got to go to school with him tomorrow," I hear Mama saying. I see her handing Daddy the note. Daddy waves it back. "Here," she says.

"Honey, you know I don't know how to act in no place like that," Daddy says.

"Time to learn," Mama says. She gives Daddy the note. "What page your lesson on, Sonny?"

I turn to the page, and I lean on Mama's leg and let her carry me over my lesson. Mama holds the book in her hand. She carries me over my lesson two times, then she makes me point to some words and spell some words.

"He knows it," Daddy says.

"I'll take you over it again tomorrow morning," Mama says. "Don't let me forget it now."

"Uh-uh."

"Your daddy'll carry you over it tomorrow night," Mama says. "One night me, one night you."

"With no car," Daddy says, "I reckon I'll be round plenty now. You think we'll ever get another one, honey?"

Daddy's picking in his teeth with a broom straw.

"When you learn how to act with one," Mama says. "I ain't got nothing against cars."

"I guess you right, honey," Daddy says. "I was going little too far."

"It's time for bed, Sonny," Mama says. "Go in the front room and say your prayers to your daddy."

Me and Daddy leave Mama back there in the kitchen. I put my book on the dresser and I go to the fireplace where Daddy is. Daddy puts another piece of wood on the fire and plenty sparks shoot up in the chimley. Daddy helps me to take off my clothes. I kneel down and lean against his leg.

"Start off," Daddy says. "I'll catch you if you miss something."

"Lay me down to sleep," I say. "I pray the Lord my soul to keep. If I should die before I wake, I pray the Lord my soul to take. God bless Mama and Daddy. God bless Gran'mon and Uncle Al. God bless the church. God bless Miss Hebert. God bless Bill and Juanita." I hear Daddy gaping. "God bless everybody else. Amen."

I jump up off my knees. Them bricks on the fireplace make my knees hurt.

"Did you tell God to bless Johnny Green and Madame Toussaint?" Daddy says.

"No," I say.

"Get down there and tell Him to bless them, too," Daddy says.

"Old Rollo, too?"

"That's up to you and Him for that," Daddy says. "Get back down there."

I get back on my knees. I don't get on the bricks because they make my knees hurt. I get on the floor and lean against the chair.

"And God bless Mr. Johnny Green and Madame Toussaint," I say.

"All right," Daddy says. "Warm up good."

Daddy goes over to my bed and pulls the cover back.

"Come on," he says. "Jump in."

I run and jump in the bed. Daddy pulls the cover up to my neck.

"Good night, Daddy."

"Good night," Daddy says.

"Good night, Mama."

"Good night, Sonny," Mama says.

I turn on my side and look at Daddy at the fireplace. Mama comes out of the kitchen and goes to the fireplace. Mama warms up good and goes to the bundle.

"Leave it alone," Daddy says. "We'll get up early tomorrow and get it."

"I'm going to bed," Mama says. "You coming now?"

"Uh-hunnnnn," Daddy says.

Mama comes to my bed and tucks the cover under me good. She leans over and kisses me and tucks the cover some more. She goes over to the bundle and gets her nightgown, then she goes in the kitchen and puts it on. She comes back and puts her clothes she took off on a chair 'side the wall. Mama kneels down and says her prayers, then she gets in the bed and covers up. Daddy stands up and takes off his clothes. I see Daddy in his big old long white BVD's. Daddy blows out the lamp, and I hear the spring when Daddy gets in the bed. Daddy never says his prayers.

"Sleepy?" Daddy says.

"Uh-uhnnn," Mama says.

I hear the spring. I hear Mama and Daddy talking low, but I don't know what they saying. I go to sleep some, but I open my eyes again. It's some dark in the room. I hear Mama and Daddy talking low. I like Mama and Daddy. I like Uncle Al, but I don't like old Gran'mon too much. Gran'mon's always talking bad about Daddy. I don't like old Mr. Freddie Jackson, either. Mama say she didn't do her and Daddy's thing with Mr. Freddie Jackson. I like Mr. George Williams. We went riding 'way up the road with Mr. George Williams. We got Daddy's car and brought it all the way back here. Daddy and them turned the car over and Daddy poured some gas on it and set it on fire. Daddy ain't got no more car now. . . . I know my lesson. I ain't go'n wee-wee on myself no more. Daddy's going to school with me tomorrow. I'm go'n show him I can beat Billy Joe Martin shooting marbles. I can shoot all over Billy Joe Martin. And I can beat him running, too. He thinks he can run fast. I'm go'n show Daddy I can beat him running. . . . I don't know why I had to say, "God bless Madame Toussaint." I don't like her. And I don't like old Rollo, either. Rollo can bark some loud. He made my head hurt with all that loud barking. Madame Toussaint's old house don't smell good. Us house smell good. I hear the spring on Mama and Daddy's bed. I get 'way under the cover. I go to sleep little bit, but I wake up. I go to sleep some more. I hear the spring on Mama and Daddy's bed. I hear it plenty now. It's some dark under here. It's warm. I feel good 'way under here.

Sisters

The House Slave

RITA DOVE

The first horn lifts its arm over the dew-lit grass
and in the slave quarters there is a rustling—
children are bundled into aprons, cornbread

and water gourds grabbed, a salt pork breakfast taken.
I watch them driven into the vague before-dawn
while their mistress sleeps like an ivory toothpick

and Massa dreams of asses, rum and slave-funk.
I cannot fall asleep again. At the second horn,
the whip curls across the backs of the laggards—

sometimes my sister's voice, unmistaken, among them.
"Oh! pray," she cries. "Oh! pray!" Those days
I lie on my cot, shivering in the early heat.

and as the fields unfold to whiteness,
and they spill like bees among the fat flowers,
I weep. It is not yet daylight.

Little Brother

JOHN EDGAR WIDEMAN

For Judy

Penny, don't laugh. Come on now, you know I love that little critter. And anyway, how you so sure it didn't work?

Tylenol?

Yep. Children's liquid Tylenol. The children's formula's not as strong and he was only a pup. Poured two teaspoons in his water dish. I swear it seemed to help.

Children's Tylenol.

With the baby face on it. You know. Lapped it up like he understood it was good for him. He's alive today, ain't he? His eye cleared up, too.

You never told me this story before.

Figured you'd think I was crazy.

His eye's torn up again.

You know Little Brother got to have his love life. Out tom-catting around again. Sticking his nose in where it don't belong. Bout once a month he disappears from here. Used to worry. Now I know he'll be slinking back in three or four days with his tail dragging. Limping around spraddle-legged. Sleeping all day cause his poor dickie's plumb wore out.

Geral.

It's true. Little Brother got it figured better than most people. Do it till you can't do it no more. Come home half dead and then you can mind your own business for a while.

Who you voting for?

None of them fools. Stopped paying them any mind long time ago.

I hear what you're saying, but this is special. It's for president.

One I would have voted for. One I would have danced for buck naked up on Homewood Avenue, is gone. My pretty preacher man's gone. Shame the way they pushed him right off the stage. The rest them all the same. Once they in they all dirty dogs. President's the one cut the program before I could get my weather stripping. Every time the kitchen window rattles and I see my heat money seeping out the cracks, I curse that mean old Howdy Doody turkey-neck clown.

How's Ernie?

Mr. White's fine.

Mama always called him Mr. White. And Ote said *Mr. White* till we shamed him out of it.

I called Ernie that too before we were married. When he needed teasing. Formal like Mama did. *Mr. White.* He was *Mr. White* to her till the day she died.

But Mama loved him.

Of course she did. Once she realized he wasn't trying to steal me away. Thing is she never had that to worry about. Not in a million years. I'd have never left Mama. Even when Ote was alive and staying here. She's been gone all these years but first thing I think every morning when I open my eyes is, You OK, Mama? I'm right here, Mama. Be there in a minute, to get you up. I still wake up hoping she's all right. That she didn't need me during the night. That I'll be able to help her through the day.

Sometimes I don't know how you did it.

Gwan, girl. If things had been different, if you didn't have a family of your own, if I'd had the children, you would have been the one to stay here and take care of Mama.

I guess you're right. Yes. I would.

No way one of us wouldn't have taken care of her. You. Ote. Sis or me. Made sense for me and Ote to do it. We stayed home. If you hadn't married, you'd have done it. And not begrudged her one moment of your time.

Ote would have been sixty in October.

I miss him. It's just Ernie and me and the dogs rattling around in this big house now. Some things I have on my mind I never get to say to anybody because I'm waiting to tell them to Ote.

He was a good man. I can still see Daddy pulling him around in that little wagon. The summer Ote had rheumatic fever and the doctor said he had to stay in bed and Daddy made him that wagon and propped him up with pillows and pulled him all over the neighborhood. Ote bumping along up and down Cassina Way with his thumb in his mouth half sleep and Daddy just as proud as a peacock. After three girls, finally had him a son to show off.

Ote just about ran me away from here when I said I was keeping Little Brother. Two dogs are enough, Geraldine. Why would you bring something looking like that in the house? Let that miserable creature go on off and find a decent place to die. You know how Ote could draw hisself up like John French. Let you know he was half a foot taller than you and carrying all that John French weight. Talked like him, too. *Geraldine*, looking down on me saying all the syllables of my name like Daddy used to when he was mad at me. *Geraldine*. Run that miserable thing away from here. When it sneaks up under the porch and dies, you won't be the one who has to get down on your hands and knees and crawl under there to drag it out.

But he was the one wallpapered Little Brother's box with insulation, wasn't he? The one who hung a flap of rug over the door to keep out the wind.

The one who cried like a baby when Pup-pup was hit.

Didn't he see it happen?

Almost. He was turning the corner of Finance. Heard the brakes screech. The bump. He was so mad. Carried Pup-pup and laid him on the porch. Fussing the whole time at Pup-pup. You stupid dog. You stupid dog. How many times have I told you not to run in the street. Like Pup-pup could hear him. Like Pup-pup could understand him if he'd been alive. Ote stomped in the house and up the stairs. Must have washed his hands fifteen minutes. Running water like we used to do when Mama said we better not get out of bed once we were in the bed so running and running that water till it made us pee one long last time before we went to sleep.

What are you girls doing up there wasting all that water? I'ma be up there in ten minutes and you best be under the covers.

Don't be the last one. Don't be on the toilet and just starting to pee good and bumpty-bump here she comes up the steps and means what she says. Uh ohh. It's Niagara Falls and you halfway over and ain't no stopping now. So you just sit there squeezing your knees together and work on that smile you don't hardly believe and she ain't buying one bit when she brams open the door and Why you sitting there grinning like a Chessy cat, girl. I thought I told youall ten minutes ago to get in bed.

Ote washed and washed and washed. I didn't see much blood. Pup-pup looked like Pup-pup laid out there on the porch. Skinny as he was you could always see his ribs moving when he slept. So it wasn't exactly Pup-pup because it was too still. But it wasn't torn up bloody or runned-over looking either.

Whatever Ote needed to wash off, he took his time. He was in the bathroom fifteen minutes, then he turned off the faucets and stepped over into his room and shut the door but you know how the walls and doors in this house don't stop nothing so I could hear him crying when I went out in the hall to call up and ask him if he was all right, ask him what he wanted to do with Pup-pup. I didn't say a word. Just stood there thinking about lots of things. The man crying on his bed was my baby brother. And I'd lived with him all my life in the same house. Now it was just the two of us. Me in the hall listening. Him on his bed, a grown man sobbing cause he's too mad to do anything else. You and Sis moved out first. Then Daddy gone. Then Mama. Just two of us left and two mutts in the house I've lived in all my life. Then it would be one of us left. Then the house empty. I thought some such sorrowful thoughts. And thought of poor Pup-pup. And that's when I decided to say yes to Ernie White after all those years of no.

Dan. If you want a slice of this sweet potato pie you better

don't understand it. He just fell apart, Penny. You've seen him. You remember how he once was. How many times have I called you and cried over the phone about Marky? Only so much any of us could do, then Ernie said it was too dangerous to have him in the house. Wouldn't leave me here alone with Marky. I about went out my mind then. Not safe in my own house with this child I'd taken in and raised. My husband's nephew who'd been like my own child, who I'd watched grow into a man. Not safe. Nothing to do but let him roam the streets.

None of the agencies or programs would help. What else could you do, Geral?

They said they couldn't take him till he did something wrong. What kind of sense does that make? They'll take him after the damage is done. After he freezes to death sleeping on a bench up in Homewood Park. Or's killed by the cops. Or stark raving foaming at the mouth. They'll take him then. Sorry, Mrs. White, our hands are tied.

Sorry, Mrs. White. Just like the receptionist at Dr. Franklin's. That skinny, pinched-nosed *sorry, Mrs. Whatever-your-name-is* cause they don't give a good goddamn they just doing their job and don't hardly want to be bothered, especially if it's you, and you're black and poor and can't do nothing for them but stand in line and wait your turn and as far as they're concerned you can wait forever.

Did I tell you what happened to me in Dr. Franklin's office, Penny? Five or six people in the waiting room. All of them white. Chattering about this and that. They don't know me and I sure don't know none of them but cause they see my hair ain't kinky and my skin's white as theirs they get on colored people and then it's niggers after they warm up awhile. Ain't niggers enough to make you throw up? Want everything and not willing to work a lick. Up in your face now like they think they own the world. Pushing past you in line at the A&P. Got so now you can't ride a bus without taking your life in your hands. This city's not what it used to be. Used to be a decent place to live till they started having all those nigger babies and now a white person's supposed to grin and bear it. It's three women talking mostly and the chief witch's fat and old as I am. And listen to this. She's afraid of being raped. She hears about white women attacked every day and she's fed up. Then she says, It's time somebody did something, don't you think? Killing's too good for those animals. Looking over at me with her head cocked and her little bit of nappy orange hair got the nerve to google at me like she's waiting for me to wag my head and cluck like the rest of those hens. Well I didn't say a word but the look I gave that heifer froze her mouth shut and kept it shut. Nobody uttered a word for the half hour till it was my turn to see Dr. Franklin. Like when we were bad and Mama'd sit us down and dare us to breathe till she said we could. They're lucky that's all I did. Who she think want to rape her? What self-respecting man, black, white, green or polka dot gon take his life in his hands scuffling with that mountain of blubber?

Geral.

Don't laugh. It wasn't funny. Rolling her Kewpie-doll eyes at me. Ain't niggers terrible? I was about to terrible her ass if I heard *nigger* one more time in her mouth.

Listen at you. Leave that poor woman alone. How old's Little Brother now?

We've had him nine years. A little older than that. Just a wee thing when he arrived on the porch. *Geraldine*. You don't intend bringing that scrawny rat into the house, do you?

And the funny thing is Little Brother must have heard Ote and been insulted. Cause Little Brother never set foot inside the front door. Not in the whole time he's lived here. Not a paw. First he just made a bed in the rags I set out by the front door. Then the cardboard box on the front porch. Then when he grew too big for that Ote built his apartment under the porch. I just sat and rocked the whole time Ote hammering and sawing and cussing when the boards wouldn't stay straight or wouldn't fit the way he wanted them too. Using Daddy's old rusty tools. Busy as a beaver all day long and I'm smiling to myself but I didn't say a mumbling word, girl. If I had let out so much as one signifying I-told-you-so peep, Ote woulda built another box and nailed me up inside. Little Brother went from rags to his own private apartment and in that entire time he's never been inside the house once. I coaxed him, Here, puppy, here, puppy, puppy, and put his food inside the hallway but that's one stubborn creature. Little Brother'd starve to death before he'd walk through the front door.

He about drove Pup-pup crazy. Pup-pup would sneak out and eat Little Brother's food. Drag his rags away and hide them. Snap and growl but Little Brother paid him no mind. Pup-pup thought Little Brother was nuts. Living outdoors in the cold. Not fighting back. Carrying a teddy bear around in his mouth. Peeing in his own food so Pup-pup wouldn't bother it. Pup-pup was so jealous. Went to his grave still believing he had to protect his territory. Pup-pup loved to roam the streets, but bless his heart, he became a regular stay-at-home. Figured he better hang around and wait for Little Brother to make his move. Sometimes I think that's why Pup forgot how to act in the street. In such a hurry to get out and get back, he got himself runned over.

That reminds me of Maria Indovina. Danny wanted me to walk around the neighborhood with him. He wanted to see the places we're always talking about. Mr. Conley's lot. Klein's store. Aunt Aida's. Hazel and Nettie's. Showed him the steps up to Nettie's and told him she never came down them for thirty years. He said, In youall's tales these sounded like the highest, steepest steps in creation. I said they were. Told him I'd follow you and Sis cause I was scared to go first. And no way in the world I'd be first coming back down. They didn't seem like much to him even when I reminded him we were just little girls and Aunt Hazel and Cousin Nettie like queens who lived in another world. Anyway, we were back behind Susquehanna where we used to play and there's a high fence back there on top of the stone wall. It's either a new fence or newly painted but the wall's the same old wall where the bread truck crushed poor Maria Indovina. I told him we played together in those days. Black kids and white kids. Mostly Italian then. Us and the Italians living on the same streets and families knowing each other by name. I told him and he said that's better than it is today. Tried to explain to him we lived on the same streets but didn't really mix. Kids playing together and Hello, how are you, Mr. So-and-so, Mrs. So-and-so, that and a little after-hours undercover mixing. Only time I ever heard Mama curse was when she called Tina Sabettelli a whorish bitch.

John French wasn't nobody's angel.

Well, I wasn't discussing none of that with Dan. I did tell him about the stain on the wall and how we were afraid to pass by it alone.

Speaking of white people how's your friend from up the street?

Oh, Vicki's fine. Her dresses are still too mini for my old fuddy-duddy taste. But no worse than what the other girls wearing. Her little girl Carolyn still comes by every afternoon for her piece of candy. She's a lovely child. My blue-eyed sweetheart. I worry about her. Auntie Gerry, I been a good girl today. You got me a sweet, Auntie Gerry? Yes, darling, I do. And I bring her whatever we have around the house. She'll stand in line with the twins from next door, and Becky and Rashad. They're my regulars but some the others liable to drop by, too. Hi, Aunt Gerry. Can I have a piece of candy, please? When they want something they're so nice and polite, best behaved lil devils in Homewood.

Yes, my friend Vicki's fine. Not easy being the only white person in the neighborhood. I told Fletcher and them to leave her alone. And told her she better respect herself a little more cause they sure won't if she don't. Those jitterbugs don't mean any harm, but boys will be boys. And she's not the smartest young lady in the world. These slicksters around here, you know how they are, hmmph. She better be careful is what I told her. She didn't like hearing what I said but I've noticed her carrying herself a little different when she walks by. Saw her dressed up real nice in Sears in East Liberty last week and she ducked me. I know why, but it still hurt me. Like it hurts me to think my little sugar Carolyn will be calling people niggers someday. If she don't already.

Did you love Ernie all those years you kept him waiting?

Love?

You know what I mean. Love.

Love love?

Love love love. You know what I'm asking you.

Penny. Did you love Billy?

Five children. Twenty-seven years off and on before he jumped up and left for good. I must have. Some of the time.

Real love? Hootchy-gootchy cooing and carrying on?

What did you say? Hootchy-koo? Is that what you said? To tell the truth I can't hardly remember. I must of had an operation when I was about eleven or twelve. Cut all that romance mess out. What's love got to do with anything, anyway.

You asked me first.

Wish I'd had the time. Can you picture Billy and Ernie dancing the huckle-buck, doing the hootchy-koo?

Whoa, girl. You gonna start me laughing.

Hootchy-gootchy-koo. Wish I'd had the time. Maybe it ain't too late. Here's a little hootchy-gootchy-koo for you.

Watch out. You're shaking the table. Whoa. Look at my drink.

Can't help it. I got the hootchy-goos. I'm in love.

Hand me one of those napkins.

Gootchy-gootchy-goo.

Behave now. The kids staring at us. Sitting here acting like two old fools.

So you think I ought to try Tylenol?

Two things for sure. Didn't kill Little Brother. And Princess is sick. Now the other sure thing is it might help Princess and it might not. Make sure it's the baby face. Kids' strength. Try that first.

I just might.

No you won't. You're still laughing at me.

No I'm not. I'm smiling thinking about Ote hammering and sawing an apartment for Little Brother and you rocking on the porch trying to keep your mouth shut.

Like to bust, girl.

But you didn't.

Held it in to this very day. Till I told you.

Hey, youall. Leave a piece of sweet potato pie for your cousin, Dan. It's his favorite.

COMMENTARY ON
JOHN EDGAR WIDEMAN

Little Brother

Born in 1941 in Washington, D.C., John Edgar Wideman spent his formative years in Pittsburgh, in the black neighborhood called Homewood, which is the setting for much of his fiction. Wideman lived in Homewood until his family moved to a predominantly white section of Pittsburgh where he completed high school and won a scholarship to the University of Pennsylvania. He was a basketball star and Phi Beta Kappa at Penn.

In 1963 he won a Rhodes scholarship and went to Oxford University where he worked on eighteenth-century studies and played on the Oxford basketball team. He has published four novels: *A Glance Away* (1967), published when he was twenty-six; *Hurry Home* (1969); *The Lynchers* (1973); *Hiding Place* (1981) and *Sent for You Yesterday* (1983), which won the prestigious P.E.N./Faulkner Award for the best volume of fiction in 1983. A book of short stories, *Damballah* (1981), focuses on Homewood and on family histories, which are the foundation of Homewood. His first book of nonfiction, *Brothers and Keepers* (1984), is a personal essay about Wideman and his brother, Robby, who was sentenced to life in prison for his part in an armed robbery. "Little Brother" is taken from Wideman's most recent collection of short stories, *Fever*, published in 1989.

The central character of "Little Brother" is Geraldine (called Geral), storyteller, observer, commentator and guardian of family history. She is talking to her sister Penny, first about mundane things like the care and feeding of the dog, Little Brother. As Penny and Geral, two women in their sixties, recite stories about their own personal histories, about their families, about the neighborhood, adding political and social commentary, inter-weaving the past and the present, they are engaging in the process Wideman considers crucial and sacred for storytelling:

> . . . the process for me that is going to knit up the culture, knit up the fabric of the family, the collective family—all of us—one crucial part of that is that we tell our own stories. That we learn to tell them and we tell them in our own words and that they embrace our values and that we keep on saying them, in spite of the madness, the chaos around us, and in spite of the pressure not to tell it. And so that storytelling activity is crucial to survival, individual survival, community survival.[1]

Geraldine and Penny's storytelling preserves the family, "knits up the fabric of the family," even though many of its members are gone: their brother Ote and their parents are dead, Penny's husband, Billy, has abandoned his family; Geraldine's husband's nephew has moved away from the home and into trouble. In a world where the neighborhood is becoming more threatening, where change means the loss of family members and the erosion of black political strength ("My pretty preacher man's gone. Shame the way they pushed him right off the stage"), what remains is the ability to reconstruct through story the strength and the values of that family. The fact that this story opens with a discussion of giving the dog, Little Brother, some children's liquid Tylenol is not accidental; these women have always been the caretakers in their family, taking care of their parents, their children, their husbands, and, finally, taking care of the stories themselves, the net in which all is saved.

As the main storyteller, Geraldine is engaged in a call-and-response with Penny. Wideman has indicated that this "call-and-response business" is necessary for the storyteller's voice to achieve its "fullest resonance" because the interrelationship between teller and listener shapes the tale. Although the ironic title seems to suggest an emphasis on males in the family, the sisterly relationship is the story's central concern.[2]

The ease and intimacy of the dialogue between Penny and Geraldine, their mutual respect and admiration, their shared history and, perhaps, most of all, their shared sense of humor mark their relationship as quite extraordinary. There is no third-person narrator in this story; it is told entirely through dialogue of these two women, another indication of the primacy of this sisterly relationship and Wideman's respect and affection for them. Husbands are, in fact, somewhat marginal in their lives, and romantic love is the occasion for laughter as Penny and Geraldine satirize the notion of love as it is typically portrayed in our culture.

Since so many stories about sisters in black literature focus on conflict, jealousy and rivalry, this depiction of sisters sharing the memories and the laughter which have enabled them to survive the madness and the chaos around them is a rare and unconventional one for this tradition.[3]

1. James W. Coleman, "Interview with John Edgar Wideman, August 12, 1988," *Blackness and Modernism: The Literary Career of John Edgar Wideman* (Jackson and London: University of Mississippi Press, 1989), p. 156.

2. Natalie S. Low, "The Sisterly Relationship: A Study of What It Means to Adult Women," *The Radcliffe Quarterly* (March 1990): 11–13. Low says that most studies of important adult relationships focus on marriage as the primary attachment in women's lives. Only the unmarried woman is assumed to maintain significant relationships with friends, sisters and parents even though current research has begun to show that the relationship between sisters is one of the major threads in a woman's life story whether she is married or single.

3. Although there are few stories in the black American tradition which focus on sisters, those few tend to emphasize conflict and rivalry. I include the four sisters in Dorothy West's novel *The Living Is Easy*, Dee and Maggie in Alice Walker's "Everyday Use," Selina and Ina in Paule Marshall's *Brown Girl, Brownstones*, Maud and Helen in Gwendolyn Brooks' *Maud Martha*. Celie and Nettie in Walker's *The Color Purple* and the sisters in Gloria Naylor's *Mama Day* are exceptions and perhaps indicate a new trend.

Adventures of the Dread Sisters

ALEXIS DE VEAUX

We crossing The Brooklyn Bridge. Traffic is slow going. Bumper to bumper. And cars everywhere. Taxis blowing horns. It's Saturday morning. Everybody making it to Manhattan. Us too. We got to get there soon. Before the snow. Threatening to cover the city. Any minute now. We going to the RALLY AGAINST GOVERNMENT TRUCKS HAULING NUCLEAR WASTE THROUGH HARLEM. Every day for a week they been saying on the radio

> *don't worry folks*
> *don't worry*
> *don't worry   it's safe*

I might be only 15 but even I know ain't nothing safe. Not on no city street. Anything could happen. So I don't believe nothing the government says. Personally, I'm through with the government. Too many people ain't got jobs. And whole families be living in the streets. I'm for get rid of the government, give life back to the people.

We stuck on this bridge. We got 25 minutes to get uptown.

Is that soot or snow I see
falling up ahead

Hope it ain't snow
The windshield wipers don't work
too tough
Nigeria says.

Nigeria and me, we call ourselves The Dread Sisters. We're not real sisters. She's not my real mother neither. But she raised me. So we are definite family. We even look alike. Both of us short and got big eyes. Both of us got dreadlocks. Just like the Africans in the pictures in Nigeria's books.

We got twenty minutes before the rally start. We slow dragging our wheels over the bridge's skin. Our blue Pinto crammed between two screaming-yellow taxis. The East River below us. The gray sky above. Manhattan coming slowly nearer. I stare at Nigeria out the corner of my eye. She sucking her teeth. Mashing on the brakes. She hate to be late. She catch me staring. Winks. Locks her eyes back on the road.

My sister Toni and me been living with Nigeria ever since we was little. She adopted us. Then moved us to a house on Adelphi Street. Got a backyard and a attic. Got my own room and so do Toni. Got a home. Nigeria be like our mother and father. And for my money, I wouldn't have it no other way. But Toni ain't like me and Nigeria. Toni be liking boys. She don't like books. She like to straighten her hair cause she in high school. Toni be the last person to get up before noon on a Saturday. Don't care whether it's a life and death thing like a rally or not. The whole planet could blow up it wouldn't wake Toni up.

Nigeria
What

I don't want to die in no nuclear war
Ain't gonna be no nuclear war pumpkin

she says in her Colored and Progressive Peoples' Campaign
office-voice

God won't allow it

People who make bombs
don't believe in God

I fires back at her. And she don't say nothing but roll down her
window. December hit us slap in the face.

Nigeria got a profile like a African sculpture. She be looking
carved outta black wood. Her lips be chiseled. And she got a
mole above her right cheek. Like somebody dotted her eyebrow.
Ain't nothing moving on this bridge.

It's what *you* believe that counts

she finally says

never play the game by the enemy's
rules fight back
Whether it's bullets or bombs
do the unexpected

then she pokes her head out the window. The red leather
Nefertiti-shaped crown holding her dreads falls to one side.
Three lanes of cars plug up the bridge. From one end to the
other. We move a little bit. Stop go. Stop. I open up my sketchbook. Flip through the drawings. Till I get to the ones I'm doing

on Afa Tu Twelve. Which is this made-up planet. Where all the females become Ebabas, the hooded blueblack women who fly.

Nigeria gave me my first sketchbook. And taught me how to draw. She's a painter. Used to work summers on the boardwalk in Atlantic City. Doing charcoal portraits. One for 3 dollars or two for 5. Me and Toni used to go with her. I remember one day a old Black lady came by Nigeria's stall. She was old but she was beautiful. All dressed in black. With a black hat and veil. Black summer gloves. Some medals pinned to the lapel of her dress. She walked with a military step. She had watched Nigeria draw all summer. And now she wanted her picture done. So Nigeria sat the old lady down and started drawing. It took nearly 3 hours. To do a job that usually takes 20 minutes. By the time she finished there was a crowd of people standing around *oooing* and *aaabing*. Everybody was saying how the old woman had jumped into Nigeria's eyes. Poured herself through Nigeria's fingers. Liquefied on the paper. The picture shimmered when it was finished. It made the old lady happy.

Daughter

she said to Nigeria

these is God's hands you got

and she kissed Nigeria's fingers and pressed a brand-new 20 dollar bill in Nigeria's hand. And walked away. Humming "Lift Every Voice and Sing." Nigeria still got that 20 dollar bill. Which she keep in a black silk handkerchief. Tied with a red string and a little piece of paper, "1967" written on it.

The year Langston Hughes
died

she's in the habit of reminding me because he was her favorite poet.

Anyway we caught in this no-moving traffic. Nigeria not mashing so hard on the brakes now. We stop and go some more. It is cold inside the car. She leans forward. Rolls up her window. Sits back. I ask before I think not to.

> *How come you never had no kids*
> *of your own Nigeria*
> *I didn't want any of my own*
> *I wanted some that belonged to the world*

Then she don't say no more. Look like she thinking. I'm thinking too. I wonder if there's gonna be a world.

Over our heads the sky is thick with the threat of snow. We stuck on the bridge. Nothing's moving. And it's 5-to-the-rally. Nigeria reaches into the back seat. Grabs a bunch of flyers. Gives me some.

> *If you can't get to the rally*
> *when it starts*
> *start the rally wherever you are*

she says. And jumps out the car. Her yellow wool coat whipped by the wind. And I'm right behind her. Snuggled up in my big jacket. My neck wrapped twice with cloth from Kenya. We leave Miss Pinto in a herd of cars. Nigeria take one lane. I take the other. We passing out flyers when sure enough here we are in another adventure cause here comes the snow.

THE END.

COMMENTARY ON
ALEXIS DE VEAUX

Adventures of the Dread Sisters

Born in 1948 in New York City, Alexis De Veaux is a playwright, a fiction writer, a poet and a political journalist. She has published four books, *Na-ni* (1973), a children's book; *Spirits in the Street* (1973); *Li Chen/Second Daughter First Son* (1975) and *Don't Explain: A Song of Billie Holiday* (1980). In the political essays she has written for *Essence* magazine she has attacked apartheid in South Africa and the treatment of Haitian refugees. Her feminist stance is quite clear in these essays, celebrating women guerrilla fighters in Zimbabwe and critiquing the subsequent social order that consigns them to inferior social and political positions. An activist herself, De Veaux has been involved in community work, teaching English in an Urban League program and at the Frederick Douglass Creative Arts Center in New York.

At the center of De Veaux's artistic world are poor and working-class black girls growing up in harsh urban environments in Harlem. They live in public housing enclosed by artificial parks and graffiti-covered walls. They are preyed on by men. In her earlier stories—"The Riddles of Egypt Brownstones" and "Remember Him a Outlaw"—there is little possibility of change for these girls.[1] In "Riddles," the young girl, Egypt, who is sexually abused by her mother's male friend, can only express her anger by bouncing and pounding a rubber ball. Later, when a female teacher she meets at City College asks Egypt to become a "kept woman," she is frightened but again offers no objection to being sexually exploited. In "Remember Him a Outlaw," the girl's father is a drug dealer and her beloved uncle is murdered trying to deliver drugs for him. She goes off to college knowing she is the only one who will escape a dead-end life. These stories document the harsh reality spoken by the narrator of *Spirits in the Street*: "the only (unreal) reason you be the one living in the cracks and holes is because you are the black one."

In "Adventures of the Dread Sisters," the spirit of collective action for political change signals a new plot for De Veaux. The setting is not Harlem but a bridge between Brooklyn and uptown New York, symbolizing her characters' movement from stasis to action. The central character is not an isolated teenager but a collective protagonist—the narrator and Nigeria—and the story offers resolutions that are dramatically different from De Veaux's earlier ones. The relationship between Nigeria and the narrator is empowering, not destructive. At the heart of that change is a self-created family rather than a given one. In what seems to be an informal arrangement, Nigeria has "adopted" the fifteen-year-old narrator and her sister, Toni; the young narrator asserts the power of that relationship—"we are definite family"—and she and Nigeria together proclaim themselves "The Dread Sisters." With African names, Rastafarian hair styles, their political activism, these characters signal a special political consciousness. Here family exists not just for itself but for a larger goal—the transformation of consciousness and society. While Toni (with the Hollywood name) likes boys, straightened hair and sleeping late on Saturday, Nigeria and the narrator have chosen African names, political work and the love of women, each choice suggesting opposition to the dominant social order.

I read this story as a critique of traditional plots for women. Nigeria has rejected the conventional female roles of wife and mother. Though she is both "mother and father" to the narrator, she treats her as a sister and an equal, allowing her to speak her mind and even to confront her. In an interesting reversal of the traditional grandmother figure, whose role is to nurture the next generation, the old black woman who comes to Nigeria to have her portrait painted becomes a shimmering object of art, one that has the crowd transfixed by her beauty—not a maternal figure.

The fictional world itself is challenged by historical and cultural allusions to the death of Langston Hughes and the Black National Anthem, which are inserted into the narrative as if to remind us of political meanings outside of the text. The narrator's own story about a planet of hooded blueblack women who fly also signals a search for a different kind of story, one which is not confined to realistic plots that limit women but which releases them into flight. Both Nigeria and the narrator look outward toward the world they wish to change. Their quest is to transform that world, not to be the object of male quest nor to be subsumed by the old plots which trap women into rage, passivity and silence.

Since the two women are stalled on the Brooklyn Bridge for the entire story, unable to go anywhere, the narrative calls attention to consciousness as the site of change. De Veaux is interested in exploring the change of consciousness which is possible when conventional ideas about women in narrative are overturned. As we observe the narrator thinking about her life with Nigeria, about their art, about self-defined sisterhood, and as she watches Nigeria think her way out of being immobilized, we become aware of the power of consciousness to effect change even when action seems impossible. In her book on narrative strategies of twentieth-century women writers, Rachel Blau Du Plessis says that new plots for women will envision radical challenges to existing ideologies of women. In these "narratives of future vision," we will see a number of significant changes: collective protagonists rather than individual ones; plots that displace accepted gender roles (i.e., detective stories, supernatural fiction, science fiction); narratives that visualize alternatives to dominant institutions like the nuclear family.[2] Incorporating many of these changes, "Adventures of the Dread Sisters" is pointing the way toward that new frontier in women's fiction.

1. Both of these stories are included in *Black-Eyed Susans/Midnight Birds: Stories By and About Black Women.* ed. Mary Helen Washington, New York: (Anchor Books, 1990).

2. Rachel Blau Du Plessis, " 'Kin With Each Other': Speculative Consciousness and Collective Protagonists," *Writing Beyond the Ending: Narrative Strategies of Twentieth-Century Women Writers* (Bloomington: Indiana University Press, 1985) pp. 178–97.

Brothers

come in here now and get it. It's leaving here fast. They're carting it away like sweet potato pie's going out of style.

It's his favorite.

That's why I bake one every time old Danny boy's home from school.

Did he tell you he saw Marky at Mellon Park?

No.

Dan was playing ball and Marky was in a bunch that hangs around on the sidelines. He said Marky recognized him. Mumbled hi. Not much more than that. He said Marky didn't look good. Not really with the others but sitting off to the side, on the ground, leaning back against the fence. Dan went over to him and Marky nodded or said hi, enough to let Danny know it really was Marky and not just somebody who looked like Marky, or Marky's ghost because Dan said it wasn't the Marky he remembered. It's the Marky who's been driving us all crazy.

At least he's off Homewood Avenue.

That's good I suppose.

Good and bad. Like everything else. He can move hisself off the Avenue and I'm grateful for that but it also means he can go and get hisself in worse trouble. A healthy young man with a good head on his shoulders and look at him. It's pitiful. Him and lots the other young men like zombies nodding on Homewood Avenue. Pitiful. But as long as he stays on Homewood the cops won't hassle him. What if he goes off and tries to rob somebody or break in somebody's house? Marky has no idea half the time who he is or what he's doing. He's like a baby. He couldn't get away with anything. Just hurt hisself or hurt somebody trying.

What can we do?

We kept him here as long as we could. Ernie talked and talked to him. Got him a job when he dropped out of school. Talked and talked and did everything he could. Marky just let hisself go. He stopped washing. Wore the same clothes night and day. And he was always such a neat kid. A dresser. Stood in front of the mirror for days arranging himself just so for the ladies. I

My Brother Is Homemade

SAM CORNISH

my brother is homemade
like he was the first real
black boy i ever knew

before Richard Wright
or James Baldwin found
black summers
he taught me how to drink at age
five and a half

& cleaned the streets
with bullies and stolen
bread and ice cream

he came into this
color thing lighter
than me
& to prove a point
grew darker than most

Sonny's Blues

JAMES BALDWIN

I read about it in the paper, in the subway, on my way to work. I read it, and I couldn't believe it, and I read it again. Then perhaps I just stared at it, at the newsprint spelling out his name, spelling out the story. I stared at it in the swinging lights of the subway car, and in the faces and bodies of the people, and in my own face, trapped in the darkness which roared outside.

It was not to be believed, and I kept telling myself that as I walked from the subway station to the high school. And at the same time I couldn't doubt it. I was scared, scared for Sonny. He became real to me again. A great block of ice got settled in my belly and kept melting there slowly all day long, while I taught my classes algebra. It was a special kind of ice. It kept melting, sending trickles of ice water all up and down my veins, but it never got less. Sometimes it hardened and seemed to expand until I felt my guts were going to come spilling out or that I was going to choke or scream. This would always be at a moment when I was remembering some specific thing Sonny had once said or done.

When he was about as old as the boys in my classes, his face had been bright and open, there was a lot of copper in it; and he'd had wonderfully direct brown eyes, and great gentleness and privacy. I wondered what he looked like now. He had been picked up, the evening before, in a raid on an apartment downtown, for peddling and using heroin.

I couldn't believe it: but what I mean by that is that I couldn't find any room for it anywhere inside me. I had kept it outside me for a long time. I hadn't wanted to know. I had had suspicions, but I didn't name them, I kept putting them away. I told myself that Sonny was wild, but he wasn't crazy. And he'd always been a good boy, he hadn't ever turned hard or evil or disrespectful, the way kids can, so quick, so quick, especially in Harlem. I didn't want to believe that I'd ever see my brother going down, coming to nothing, all that light in his face gone out, in the condition I'd already seen so many others. Yet it had happened and here I was, talking about algebra to a lot of boys who might, every one of them for all I knew, be popping off needles every time they went to the head. Maybe it did more for them than algebra could.

I was sure that the first time Sonny had ever had horse, he couldn't have been much older than these boys were now. These boys, now, were living as we'd been living then, they were growing up with a rush and their heads bumped abruptly against the low ceiling of their actual possibilities. They were filled with rage. All they really knew were two darknesses, the darkness of their lives, which was now closing in on them, and the darkness of the movies, which had blinded them to that other darkness, and in which they now, vindictively, dreamed, at once more together than they were at any other time, and more alone.

When the last bell rang, the last class ended, I let out my breath. It seemed I'd been holding it for all that time. My clothes were wet—I may have looked as though I'd been sitting in a steam bath, all dressed up, all afternoon. I sat alone in the classroom a long time. I listened to the boys outside, downstairs, shouting and cursing and laughing. Their laughter struck me for perhaps the first time. It was not the joyous laughter which— God knows why—one associates with children. It was mocking and insular, its intent was to denigrate. It was disenchanted, and in this, also, lay the authority of their curses. Perhaps I was listening to them because I was thinking about my brother and in them I heard my brother. And myself.

One boy was whistling a tune, at once very complicated and very simple, it seemed to be pouring out of him as though he were a bird, and it sounded very cool and moving through all that harsh, bright air, only just holding its own through all those other sounds.

I stood and walked over to the window and looked down into the courtyard. It was the beginning of the spring, and the sap was rising in the boys. A teacher passed through them every now and again, quickly, as though he or she couldn't wait to get out of that courtyard, to get those boys out of their sight and off their minds. I started collecting my stuff. I thought I'd better get home and talk to Isabel.

The courtyard was almost deserted by the time I got downstairs. I saw this boy standing in the shadow of a doorway, looking just like Sonny. I almost called his name. Then I saw that it wasn't Sonny, but somebody we used to know, a boy from around our block. He'd been Sonny's friend. He'd never been mine, having been too young for me, and, anyway, I'd never liked him. And now, even though he was a grown-up man, he still hung around that block, still spent hours on the street corner, was always high and raggy. I used to run into him from time to time, and he'd often work around to asking me for a quarter or fifty cents. He always had some real good excuse, too, and I always gave it to him, I don't know why.

But now, abruptly, I hated him. I couldn't stand the way he looked at me, partly like a dog, partly like a cunning child. I wanted to ask him what the hell he was doing in the school courtyard.

He sort of shuffled over to me, and he said, "I see you got the papers. So you already know about it."

"You mean about Sonny? Yes, I already know about it. How come they didn't get you?"

He grinned. It made him repulsive and it also brought to mind what he'd looked like as a kid. "I wasn't there. I stay away from them people."

"Good for you." I offered him a cigarette and I watched him through the smoke. "You come all the way down here just to tell me about Sonny?"

"That's right." He was sort of shaking his head and his eyes looked strange, as though they were about to cross. The bright sun deadened his damp dark brown skin and it made his eyes look yellow and showed up the dirt in his conked hair. He smelled funky. I moved a little away from him and I said, "Well, thanks. But I already know about it and I got to get home."

"I'll walk you a little ways," he said. We started walking. There were a couple of kids still loitering in the courtyard and one of them said good night to me and looked strangely at the boy beside me.

"What're you going to do?" he asked me. "I mean, about Sonny?"

"Look. I haven't seen Sonny for over a year, I'm not sure I'm going to do anything. Anyway, what the hell can I do?"

"That's right," he said quickly, "ain't nothing you can do. Can't much help old Sonny no more, I guess."

It was what I was thinking and so it seemed to me he had no right to say it.

"I'm surprised at Sonny, though," he went on—he had a funny way of talking, he looked straight ahead as though he were talking to himself—"I thought Sonny was a smart boy, I thought he was too smart to get hung."

"I guess he thought so, too," I said sharply, "and that's how he got hung. And how about you? You're pretty goddamn smart, I bet."

Then he looked directly at me, just for a minute. "I ain't smart," he said. "If I was smart, I'd have reached for a pistol a long time ago."

"Look. Don't tell *me* your sad story, if it was up to me, I'd give you one." Then I felt guilty—guilty probably, for never having supposed that the poor bastard *had* a story of his own, much less a sad one, and I asked, quickly, "What's going to happen to him now?"

He didn't answer this. He was off by himself someplace. "Funny thing," he said, and from his tone we might have been discussing the quickest way to get to Brooklyn, "when I saw the papers this morning, the first thing I asked myself was if I had anything to do with it. I felt sort of responsible."

I began to listen more carefully. The subway station was on the corner, just before us, and I stopped. He stopped, too. We were in front of a bar and he ducked slightly, peering in, but whoever he was looking for didn't seem to be there. The juke box was blasting away with something black and bouncy, and I half watched the barmaid as she danced her way from the juke box to her place behind the bar. And I watched her face as she laughingly responded to something someone said to her, still keeping time to the music. When she smiled one saw the little girl, one sensed the doomed, still-struggling woman beneath the battered face of the semi-whore.

"I never *give* Sonny nothing," the boy said finally, "but a long time ago I come to school high and Sonny asked me how it felt." He paused, I couldn't bear to watch him, I watched the barmaid, and I listened to the music which seemed to be causing the pavement to shake. "I told him it felt great." The music stopped, the barmaid paused and watched the juke box until the music began again. "It did."

All this was carrying me someplace I didn't want to go. I certainly didn't want to know how it felt. It filled everything, the people, the houses, the music, the dark, quicksilver barmaid, with menace; and this menace was their reality.

"What's going to happen to him now?" I asked again.

"They'll send him away someplace and they'll try to cure him." He shook his head. "Maybe he'll even think he's kicked the habit. Then they'll turn him loose"—He gestured, throwing his cigarette into the gutter. "That's all."

"What do you mean, that's *all?*"

But I knew what he meant.

"I *mean,* that's all." He turned his head and looked at me, pulling down the corners of his mouth. "Don't you know what I mean?" he asked softly.

"How the hell *would* I know what you mean?" I almost whispered it, I don't know why.

"That's right," he said to the air, "how would *he* know what I mean?" He turned toward me again, patient and calm, and yet I somehow felt him shaking, shaking as though he were going to fall apart. I felt that ice in my guts again, the dread I'd felt all afternoon; and again I watched the barmaid, moving about the bar, washing glasses, and singing. "Listen. They'll let him out and then it'll just start over again. That's what I mean."

"You mean—they'll let him out. And then he'll just start working his way back in again. You mean he'll never kick the habit. Is that what you mean?"

"That's right," he said, cheerfully. "*You* see what I mean."

"Tell me," I said at last, "why does he want to die? He must want to die, he's killing himself, why does he want to die?"

He looked at me in surprise. He licked his lips "He don't want to die. He wants to live. Don't nobody want to die, ever."

Then I wanted to ask him—too many things. He could not have answered, or if he had, I could not have borne the answers. I started walking. "Well, I guess it's none of my business."

"It's going to be rough on old Sonny," he said. We reached the subway station. "This is your station?" he asked. I nodded. I took one step down. "Damn!" he said, suddenly. I looked up at him. He grinned again. "Damn if I didn't leave all my money home. You ain't got a dollar on you, have you? Just for a couple of days, is all."

All at once something inside gave and threatened to come pouring out of me. I didn't hate him any more. I felt that in another moment I'd start crying like a child.

"Sure," I said. "Don't sweat." I looked in my wallet and didn't have a dollar, I only had a five. "Here," I said. "That hold you?"

He didn't look at it—he didn't want to look at it. A terrible, closed look came over his face, as though he were keeping the number on the bill a secret from him and me. "Thanks," he said, and now he was dying to see me go. "Don't worry about Sonny. Maybe I'll write him or something."

"Sure," I said. "You do that. So long."

"Be seeing you," he said. I went on down the steps.

And I didn't write Sonny or send him anything for a long time. When I finally did, it was just after my little girl died, he wrote me back a letter which made me feel like a bastard.

Here's what he said:

Dear brother,

You don't know how much I needed to hear from you. I wanted to write you many a time but I dug how much I must have hurt you and so I didn't write. But now I feel like a man who's been trying to climb up out of some deep, real deep and funky hole and just saw the sun up there, outside. I got to get outside.

I can't tell you much about how I got here. I mean I don't know how to tell you. I guess I was afraid of something or I was trying to escape from something and you know I have never been very strong in the head (smile). I'm glad Mama and Daddy are dead and can't see what's happened to their son and I swear if I'd known what I was doing I would never have hurt you so, you and a lot of other fine people who were nice to me and who believed in me.

I don't want you to think it had anything to do with me being a musician. It's more than that. Or maybe less than that. I can't get anything straight in my head down here and I try not to think about what's going to happen to me when I get outside again. Sometime I think I'm going to flip and *never* get outside and sometime I think I'll come straight back. I tell you one thing, though, I'd rather blow my brains out than go through this again. But that's what they all say, so they tell me. If I tell you when I'm coming to New York and if you could meet me, I sure would appreciate it. Give my love to Isabel and the kids and I was sure sorry to hear about little Gracie. I wish I could be like Mama and say the Lord's will be done, but I don't know it seems to me that trouble is the one thing that never does get stopped and I don't know what good it does to blame it on the Lord. But maybe it does some good if you believe it.

Your brother,
SONNY

Then I kept in constant touch with him and I sent him whatever I could and I went to meet him when he came back to New York. When I saw him, many things I thought I had forgotten came flooding back to me. This was because I had begun, finally, to wonder about Sonny, about the life that Sonny lived inside. This life, whatever it was, had made him older and thinner and it had deepened the distant stillness in which he had always moved. He looked very unlike my baby brother. Yet, when he smiled, when we shook hands, the baby brother I'd never known looked out from the depths of his private life, like an animal waiting to be coaxed into the light.

"How you been keeping?" he asked me.

"All right. And you?"

"Just fine." He was smiling all over his face. "It's good to see you again."

"It's good to see you."

The seven years' difference in our ages lay between us like a chasm: I wondered if these years would ever operate between us as a bridge. I was remembering, and it made it hard to catch my breath, that I had been there when he was born; and I had heard the first words he had ever spoken. When he started to walk, he walked from our mother straight to me. I caught him just before he fell when he took the first steps he ever took in this world.

"How's Isabel?"

"Just fine. She's dying to see you."

"And the boys?"

"They're fine, too. They're anxious to see their uncle."

"Oh, come on. You know they don't remember me."

"Are you kidding? Of course they remember you."

He grinned again. We got into a taxi. We had a lot to say to each other, far too much to know how to begin.

As the taxi began to move, I asked, "You still want to go to India?"

He laughed. "You still remember that. Hell, no. This place is Indian enough for me."

"It used to belong to them," I said.

And he laughed again. "They damn sure knew what they were doing when they got rid of it."

Years ago, when he was around fourteen, he'd been all hipped on the idea of going to India. He read books about people sitting on rocks, naked, in all kinds of weather, but mostly bad, naturally, and walking barefoot through hot coals and arriving at wisdom. I used to say that it sounded to me as though they were getting away from wisdom as fast as they could. I think he sort of looked down on me for that.

"Do you mind," he asked, "if we have the driver drive alongside the park? On the west side—I haven't seen the city in so long."

"Of course not," I said. I was afraid that I might sound as though I were humoring him, but I hoped he wouldn't take it that way.

So we drove along, between the green of the park and the stony, lifeless elegance of hotels and apartment buildings, toward the vivid, killing streets of our childhood. These streets hadn't changed, though housing projects jutted up out of them now like rocks in the middle of a boiling sea. Most of the houses in which we had grown up had vanished, as had the stores from which we had stolen, the basements in which we had first tried sex, the rooftops from which we had hurled tin cans and bricks. But houses exactly like the houses of our past yet dominated the landscape, boys exactly like the boys we once had been found themselves smothering in these houses, came down into the streets for light and air and found themselves encircled by disaster. Some escaped the trap, most didn't. Those who got out always left something of themselves behind, as some animals amputate a leg and leave it in the trap. It might be said, perhaps, that I had escaped, after all, I was a schoolteacher; or that Sonny had, he hadn't lived in Harlem for years. Yet, as the cab moved uptown through streets which seemed, with a rush, to darken with dark people, and as I covertly studied Sonny's face, it came to me that what we both were seeking through our separate cab windows was that part of ourselves which had been left behind.

It's always at the hour of trouble and confrontation that the missing member aches.

We hit 110th Street and started rolling up Lenox Avenue. And I'd known this avenue all my life, but it seemed to me again, as it had seemed on the day I'd first heard about Sonny's trouble, filled with a hidden menace which was its very breath of life.

"We almost there," said Sonny.

"Almost." We were both too nervous to say anything more.

We live in a housing project. It hasn't been up long. A few days after it was up it seemed uninhabitably new, now, of course, it's already rundown. It looked like a parody of the good, clean, faceless life—God knows the people who live in it do their best to make it a parody. The beat-looking grass lying around isn't enough to make their lives green, the hedges will never hold out the streets, and they know it. The big windows fool no one, they aren't big enough to make space out of no space. They don't bother with the windows, they watch the TV screen instead. The playground is most popular with the children who don't play at jacks, or skip rope, or roller skate, or swing, and they can be found in it after dark. We moved in partly because it's not too far from where I teach, and partly for the kids; but it's really just like the houses in which Sonny and I grew up. The same things happen, they'll have the same things to remember. The moment Sonny and I started into the house I had the feeling that I was simply bringing him back into the danger he had almost died trying to escape.

Sonny has never been talkative. So I don't know why I was sure he'd be dying to talk to me when supper was over the first night. Everything went fine, the oldest boy remembered him, and the youngest boy liked him, and Sonny had remembered to bring something for each of them; and Isabel, who is really much nicer than I am, more open and giving, had gone to a lot of trouble about dinner and was genuinely glad to see him. And she'd always been able to tease Sonny in a way that I haven't. It was nice to see her face so vivid again and to hear her laugh and watch her make Sonny laugh. She wasn't, or, anyway, she didn't seem to be, at all uneasy or embarrassed. She chatted as though there were no subject which had to be avoided and she got Sonny past his first, faint stiffness. And thank God she was there, for I was filled with that icy dread again. Everything I did seemed awkward to me, and everything I said sounded freighted with hidden meaning. I was trying to remember everything I'd heard about dope addiction and I couldn't help watching Sonny for signs. I wasn't doing it out of malice. I was trying to find out something about my brother. I was dying to hear him tell me he was safe.

"Safe!" my father grunted, whenever Mama suggested trying to move to a neighborhood which might be safer for children. "Safe, hell! Ain't no place safe for kids, nor nobody."

He always went on like this, but he wasn't, ever, really as bad as he sounded, not even on weekends, when he got drunk. As a matter of fact, he was always on the lookout for "something a little better," but he died before he found it. He died suddenly, during a drunken weekend in the middle of the war, when Sonny was fifteen. He and Sonny hadn't ever got on too well. And this was partly because Sonny was the apple of his father's eye. It was because he loved Sonny so much and was frightened for him, that he was always fighting with him. It doesn't do any good to fight with Sonny. Sonny just moves back, inside himself, where he can't be reached. But the principal reason that they never hit it off is that they were so much alike. Daddy was big and rough and loud-talking, just the opposite of Sonny, but they both had—that same privacy.

Mama tried to tell me something about this, just after Daddy died. I was home on leave from the army.

This was the last time I ever saw my mother alive. Just the same, this picture gets all mixed up in my mind with pictures I had of her when she was younger. The way I always see her is the way she used to be on a Sunday afternoon, say, when the old folks were talking after the big Sunday dinner. I always see her wearing pale blue. She'd be sitting on the sofa. And my father would be sitting in the easy chair, not far from her. And the living room would be full of church folks and relatives. There they sit, in chairs all around the living room, and the night is creeping up outside, but nobody knows it yet. You can see the darkness growing against the windowpanes and you hear the street noises every now and again, or maybe the jangling beat of a tambourine from one of the churches close by, but it's real quiet in the room. For a moment nobody's talking, but every face looks darkening, like the sky outside. And my mother rocks a little from the waist, and my father's eyes are closed. Everyone is looking at something a child can't see. For a minute they've forgotten the children. Maybe a kid is lying on the rug, half asleep. Maybe somebody's got a kid in his lap and is absent-mindedly stroking the kid's head. Maybe there's a kid, quiet and big-eyed, curled up in a big chair in the corner. The silence, the darkness coming, and the darkness in the faces frighten the child obscurely. He hopes that the hand which strokes his forehead will never stop—will never die. He hopes that there will never come a time when the old folks won't be sitting around the living room, talking about where they've come from, and what they've seen, and what's happened to them and their kinfolk.

But something deep and watchful in the child knows that this is bound to end, is already ending. In a moment someone will get up and turn on the light. Then the old folks will remember the children and they won't talk any more that day. And when light fills the room, the child is filled with darkness. He knows that every time this happens he's moved just a little closer to that darkness outside. The darkness outside is what the old folks have been talking about. It's what they've come from. It's what they endure. The child knows that they won't talk any more because if he knows too much about what's happened to *them*, he'll know too much too soon, about what's going to happen to *him*.

The last time I talked to my mother, I remember I was restless. I wanted to get out and see Isabel. We weren't married then and we had a lot to straighten out between us.

There Mama sat, in black, by the window. She was humming an old church song, *Lord, you brought me from a long ways off.* Sonny was out somewhere. Mama kept watching the streets.

"I don't know," she said, "if I'll ever see you again, after you go off from here. But I hope you'll remember the things I tried to teach you."

"Don't talk like that," I said, and smiled. "You'll be here a long time yet."

She smiled, too, but she said nothing. She was quiet for a long time. And I said, "Mama, don't you worry about nothing. I'll be writing all the time, and you be getting the checks. . . ."

"I want to talk to you about your brother," she said, suddenly. "If anything happens to me, he ain't going to have nobody to look out for him."

"Mama," I said, "ain't nothing going to happen to you *or* Sonny. Sonny's all right. He's a good boy and he's got good sense."

"It ain't a question of his being a good boy," Mama said, "nor of his having good sense. It ain't only the bad ones, nor yet the dumb ones that gets sucked under." She stopped, looking at me. "Your Daddy once had a brother," she said, and smiled in a way that made me feel she was in pain. "You didn't never know that, did you?"

"No," I said. "I never knew that," and I watched her face.

"Oh, yes," she said, "your Daddy had a brother." She looked out of the window again. "I know you never saw your Daddy cry. But *I* did—many a time, through all these years."

I asked her, "What happened to his brother? How come nobody's ever talked about him?"

This was the first time I ever saw my mother look old.

"His brother got killed," she said, "when he was just a little younger than you are now. I knew him. He was a fine boy. He was maybe a little full of the devil, but he didn't mean nobody no harm."

Then she stopped, and the room was silent, exactly as it had sometimes been on those Sunday afternoons. Mama kept looking out into the streets.

"He used to have a job in the mill," she said, "and, like all young folks, he just liked to perform on Saturday nights. Saturday nights, him and your father would drift around to different places, go to dances and things like that, or just sit around with people they knew, and your father's brother would sing, he had a fine voice, and play along with himself on his guitar. Well, this particular Saturday night, him and your father was coming home from some place, and they were both a little drunk and there was a moon that night, it was bright like day. Your father's brother was feeling kind of good, and he was whistling to himself, and he had his guitar slung over his shoulder. They was coming down a hill, and beneath them was a road that turned off from the highway. Well, your father's brother, being always kind of frisky, decided to run down this hill, and he did, with that guitar banging and clanging behind him, and he ran across the road, and he was making water behind a tree. And your father was sort of amused at him and he was still coming down the hill, kind of slow. Then he heard a car motor and that same minute his brother stepped from behind the tree, into the road, in the moonlight. And he started to cross the road. And your father started to run down the hill, he says he don't know why. This car was full of white men. They was all drunk, and when they seen your father's brother they let out a great whoop and holler and they aimed the car straight at him. They was having fun, they just wanted to scare him, the way they do sometimes, you know. But they was drunk. And I guess the boy, being drunk, too, and scared, kind of lost his head. By the time he jumped it was too late. Your father says he heard his brother scream when the car rolled over him, and he heard the wood of that guitar when it give, and he heard them strings go flying, and he heard them white men shouting, and the car kept on a-going and it ain't stopped till this day. And, time your father got down the hill, his brother weren't nothing but blood and pulp."

Tears were gleaming on my mother's face. There wasn't anything I could say.

"He never mentioned it," she said, "because I never let him mention it before you children. Your Daddy was like a crazy man that night and for many a night thereafter. He says he never in his life seen anything as dark as that road after the lights of that car had gone away. Weren't nothing, weren't nobody on that road, just your Daddy and his brother and that busted guitar. Oh, yes. Your Daddy never did really get right again. Till the day he died he weren't sure but that every white man he saw was the man that killed his brother."

She stopped and took out her handkerchief and dried her eyes and looked at me.

"I ain't telling you all this," she said, "to make you scared or bitter or to make you hate nobody. I'm telling you this because you got a brother. And the world ain't changed."

I guess I didn't want to believe this. I guess she saw this in my face. She turned away from me, toward the window again, searching those streets.

"But I praise my Redeemer," she said at last, "that he called your Daddy home before me. I ain't saying it to throw no flowers at myself, but, I declare, it keeps me from feeling too cast down to know I helped your father get safely through this world. Your father always acted like he was the roughest, strongest man on earth. And everybody took him to be like that. But if he hadn't had *me* there—to see his tears!"

She was crying again. Still, I couldn't move. I said, "Lord, Lord, Mama, I didn't know it was like that."

"Oh, honey," she said, "there's a lot that you don't know. But you are going to find it out." She stood up from the window and came over to me. "You got to hold on to your brother," she said, "and don't let him fall, no matter what it looks like is happening to him and no matter how evil you gets with him. You going to be evil with him many a time. But don't you forget what I told you, you hear?"

"I won't forget," I said. "Don't you worry, I won't forget. I won't let nothing happen to Sonny."

My mother smiled as though she were amused at something

she saw in my face. Then, "You may not be able to stop nothing from happening. But you got to let him know you's *there*."

Two days later I was married, and then I was gone. And I had a lot of things on my mind and I pretty well forgot my promise to Mama until I got shipped home on a special furlough for her funeral.

And, after the funeral, with just Sonny and me alone in the empty kitchen, I tried to find out something about him.

"What do you want to do?" I asked him.

"I'm going to be a musician," he said.

For he had graduated, in the time I had been away, from dancing to the juke box to finding out who was playing what, and what they were doing with it, and he had bought himself a set of drums.

"You mean, you want to be a drummer?" I somehow had the feeling that being a drummer might be all right for other people but not for my brother Sonny.

"I don't think," he said, looking at me very gravely, "that I'll ever be a good drummer. But I think I can play a piano."

I frowned. I'd never played the role of the older brother quite so seriously before, had scarcely ever, in fact, *asked* Sonny a damn thing. I sensed myself in the presence of something I didn't really know how to handle, didn't understand. So I made my frown a little deeper as I asked: "What kind of musician do you want to be?"

He grinned. "How many kinds do you think there are?"

"Be *serious*," I said.

He laughed, throwing his head back, and then looked at me. "I *am* serious."

"Well, then, for Christ's sake, stop kidding around and answer a serious question. I mean, do you want to be a concert pianist, you want to play classical music and all that, or—or, what?" Long before I finished he was laughing again. "For Christ's *sake*, Sonny!"

He sobered, but with difficulty. "I'm sorry. But you sound so—*scared!*" And he was off again.

"Well, you may think it's funny now, baby, but it's not going to be so funny when you have to make your living at it, let me tell you *that*." I was furious because I knew he was laughing at me and I didn't know why.

"No," he said, very sober now, and afraid, perhaps, that he'd hurt me, "I don't want to be a classical pianist. That isn't what interests me. I mean"—he paused, looking hard at me, as though his eyes would help me to understand, and then gestured helplessly, as though perhaps his hand would help—"I mean, I'll have a lot of studying to do, and I'll have to study *everything*, but, I mean, I want to play *with*—jazz musicians." He stopped. "I want to play jazz," he said.

Well, the word had never before sounded as heavy, as real, as it sounded that afternoon in Sonny's mouth. I just looked at him and I was probably frowning a real frown by this time. I simply couldn't see why on earth he'd want to spend his time hanging around night clubs, clowning around on bandstands, while people pushed each other around a dance floor. It seemed—beneath him, somehow. I had never thought about it before, had never been forced to, but I suppose I had always put jazz musicians in a class with what Daddy called "good-time people."

"Are you *serious*?"

"Hell, *yes*, I'm serious."

He looked more helpless than ever, and annoyed, and deeply hurt.

I suggested, helpfully: "You mean—like Louis Armstrong?"

His face closed as though I'd struck him. "No. I'm not talking about none of that old-time, down home crap."

"Well, look, Sonny, I'm sorry, don't get mad. I just don't altogether get it, that's all. Name somebody—you know, a jazz musician you admire."

"Bird."

"Who?"

"Bird! Charlie Parker! Don't they teach you nothing in the goddamn army?"

I lit a cigarette. I was surprised and then a little amused to discover that I was trembling. "I've been out of touch," I said. "You'll have to be patient with me. Now. Who's this Parker character?"

"He's just one of the greatest jazz musicians alive," said Sonny, sullenly, his hands in his pockets, his back to me. "Maybe *the* greatest," he added bitterly, "that's probably why *you* never heard of him."

"All right," I said, "I'm ignorant. I'm sorry. I'll go out and buy all the cat's records right away, all right?"

"It don't," said Sonny, with dignity, "make any difference to me. I don't care what you listen to. Don't do me no favors."

I was beginning to realize that I'd never seen him so upset before. With another part of my mind I was thinking that this would probably turn out to be one of those things kids go through and that I shouldn't make it seem important by pushing it too hard. Still, I didn't think it would do any harm to ask: "Doesn't all this take a lot of time? Can you make a living at it?"

He turned back to me and half leaned, half sat, on the kitchen table. "Everything takes time," he said, "and—well, yes, sure, I can make a living at it. But what I don't seem to be able to make you understand is that it's the only thing I want to do."

"Well, Sonny," I said gently, "you know people can't always do exactly what they want to do—"

"*No*, I don't know that," said Sonny, surprising me. "I think people *ought* to do what they want to do, what else are they alive for?"

"You getting to be a big boy," I said desperately, "it's time you started thinking about your future."

"I'm thinking about my future," said Sonny, grimly. "I think about it all the time."

I gave up. I decided, if he didn't change his mind, that we could always talk about it later. "In the meantime," I said, "you got to finish school." We had already decided that he'd have to move in with Isabel and her folks. I knew this wasn't the ideal arrangement because Isabel's folks are inclined to be dicty and they hadn't especially wanted Isabel to marry me. But I didn't know what else to do. "And we have to get you fixed up at Isabel's."

There was a long silence. He moved from the kitchen table to the window. "That's a terrible idea. You know it yourself."

"Do you have a *better* idea?"

He just walked up and down the kitchen for a minute. He was as tall as I was. He had started to shave. I suddenly had the feeling that I didn't know him at all.

He stopped at the kitchen table and picked up my cigarettes. Looking at me with a kind of mocking, amused defiance, he put one between his lips. "You mind?"

"You smoking already?"

He lit the cigarette and nodded, watching me through the smoke. "I just wanted to see if I'd have the courage to smoke in front of you." He grinned and blew a great cloud of smoke to the ceiling. "It was easy." He looked at my face. "Come on, now. I bet you was smoking at my age, tell the truth."

I didn't say anything but the truth was on my face, and he laughed. But now there was something very strained in his laugh. "Sure. And I bet that ain't all you was doing."

He was frightening me a little. "Cut the crap," I said. "We already decided that you was going to go and live at Isabel's. Now what's got into you all of a sudden?"

"*You* decided it," he pointed out. "*I* didn't decide nothing." He stopped in front of me, leaning against the stove, arms loosely folded. "Look, brother. I don't want to stay in Harlem no more, I really don't." He was very earnest. He looked at me, then over toward the kitchen window. There was something in his eyes I'd never seen before, some thoughtfulness, some worry all his own. He rubbed the muscle of one arm. "It's time I was getting out of here."

"Where do you want to *go*, Sonny?"

"I want to join the army. Or the navy, I don't care. If I say I'm old enough, they'll believe me."

Then I got mad. It was because I was so scared. "You must be crazy. You goddamn fool, what the hell do you want to go and join the *army* for?"

"I just told you. To get out of Harlem."

"Sonny, you haven't even finished *school*. And if you really want to be a musician, how do you expect to study if you're in the *army*?"

He looked at me, trapped, and in anguish. "There's ways. I might be able to work out some kind of deal. Anyway, I'll have the G.I. Bill when I come out."

"*If* you come out." We stared at each other. "Sonny, please. Be reasonable. I know the setup is far from perfect. But we got to do the best we can."

"I ain't learning nothing in school," he said. "Even when I go." He turned away from me and opened the window and threw his cigarette out into the narrow alley. I watched his back. "At least, I ain't learning nothing you'd want me to learn." He slammed the window so hard I thought the glass would fly out, and turned back to me. "And I'm sick of the stink of these garbage cans!"

"Sonny," I said, "I know how you feel. But if you don't finish school now, you're going to be sorry later that you didn't." I grabbed him by the shoulders. "And you only got another year. It ain't so bad. And I'll come back and I swear I'll help you do *whatever* you want to do. Just try to put up with it till I come back. Will you please do that? For me?"

He didn't answer and he wouldn't look at me.

"Sonny. You hear me?"

He pulled away. "I hear you. But you never hear anything *I* say."

I didn't know what to say to that. He looked out of the window and then back at me. "OK," he said, and sighed. "I'll try."

Then I said, trying to cheer him up a little, "They got a piano at Isabel's. You can practice on it."

And as a matter of fact, it did cheer him up for a minute. "That's right," he said to himself. "I forgot that." His face relaxed a little. But the worry, the thoughtfulness, played on it still, the way shadows play on a face which is staring into the fire.

But I thought I'd never hear the end of that piano. At first, Isabel would write me, saying how nice it was that Sonny was so serious about his music and how, as soon as he came in from school, or wherever he had been when he was supposed to be at school, he went straight to that piano and stayed there until suppertime. And, after supper, he went back to that piano and stayed there until everybody went to bed. He was at that piano all day Saturday and all day Sunday. Then he bought a record player and started playing records. He'd play one record over and over again, all day long sometimes, and he'd improvise along with it on the piano. Or he'd play one section of the record, one chord, one change, one progression, then he'd do it on the piano. Then back to the record. Then back to the piano.

Well, I really don't know how they stood it. Isabel finally confessed that it wasn't like living with a person at all, it was like living with sound. And the sound didn't make any sense to her, didn't make any sense to any of them—naturally. They began, in a way, to be afflicted by this presence that was living in their home. It was as though Sonny were some sort of god, or monster. He moved in an atmosphere which wasn't like theirs at all. They fed him and he ate, he washed himself, he walked in and out of their door; he certainly wasn't nasty or unpleasant or rude, Sonny isn't any of those things; but it was as though he were all wrapped up in some cloud, some fire, some vision all his own; and there wasn't any way to reach him.

At the same time, he wasn't really a man yet, he was still a child, and they had to watch out for him in all kinds of ways. They certainly couldn't throw him out. Neither did they dare to make a great scene about that piano because even they dimly sensed, as I sensed, from so many thousands of miles away, that Sonny was at that piano playing for his life.

But he hadn't been going to school. One day a letter came from the school board, and Isabel's mother got it—there had, apparently, been other letters but Sonny had torn them up. This day, when Sonny came in, Isabel's mother showed him the letter and asked where he'd been spending his time. And she finally got it out of him that he'd been down in Greenwich Village, with musicians and other characters, in a white girl's apartment. And this scared her and she started to scream at him, and what came up, once she began—though she denies it to this day— was what sacrifices they were making to give Sonny a decent home and how little he appreciated it.

Sonny didn't play the piano that day. By evening, Isabel's mother had calmed down but then there was the old man to deal with, and Isabel herself. Isabel says she did her best to be calm but she broke down and started crying. She says she just watched Sonny's face. She could tell, by watching him, what was happening with him. And what was happening was that they penetrated his cloud, they had reached him. Even if their fingers had been a thousand times more gentle than human fingers ever are, he could hardly help feeling that they had stripped him naked and were spitting on that nakedness. For he also had to see that his presence, that music, which was life or death to him, had been torture for them and that they had endured it, not at all for his sake, but only for mine. And Sonny couldn't take that. He can take it a little better today than he could then but he's still not very good at it and, frankly, I don't know anybody who is.

The silence of the next few days must have been louder than the sound of all the music ever played since time began. One morning, before she went to work, Isabel was in his room for something and she suddenly realized that all of his records were gone. And she knew for certain that he was gone. And he was. He went as far as the navy would carry him. He finally sent me a postcard from someplace in Greece, and that was the first I knew that Sonny was still alive. I didn't see him any more until we were both back in New York and the war had long been over.

He was a man by then, of course, but I wasn't willing to see

it. He came by the house from time to time, but we fought
almost every time we met. I didn't like the way he carried himself,
loose and dreamlike all the time, and I didn't like his friends,
and his music seemed to be merely an excuse for the life he led.
It sounded just that weird and disordered.

Then we had a fight, a pretty awful fight, and I didn't see
him for months. By and by I looked him up, where he was living,
in a furnished room in the Village, and I tried to make it up.
But there were lots of other people in the room, and Sonny just
lay on his bed, and he wouldn't come downstairs with me, and
he treated these other people as though they were his family
and I weren't. So I got mad and then he got mad, and then I
told him that he might just as well be dead as live the way he
was living. Then he stood up and he told me not to worry about
him any more in life, that he *was* dead as far as I was concerned.
Then he pushed me to the door, and the other people looked
on as though nothing were happening, and he slammed the door
behind me. I stood in the hallway, staring at the door. I heard
somebody laugh in the room and then the tears came to my
eyes. I started down the steps, whistling to keep from crying, I
kept whistling to myself, *You going to need me, baby, one of these
cold, rainy days.*

I read about Sonny's trouble in the spring. Little Grace died
in the fall. She was a beautiful little girl. But she only lived a
little over two years. She died of polio and she suffered. She
had a slight fever for a couple of days, but it didn't seem like
anything and we just kept her in bed. And we would certainly
have called the doctor, but the fever dropped, she seemed to
be all right. So we thought it had just been a cold. Then, one
day, she was up, playing, Isabel was in the kitchen fixing lunch
for the two boys when they'd come in from school, and she
heard Grace fall down in the living room. When you have a lot
of children you don't always start running when one of them
falls, unless they start screaming or something. And, this time,
Grace was quiet. Yet, Isabel says that when she heard that *thump*

and then that silence, something happened in her to make her afraid. And she ran to the living room and there was little Grace on the floor, all twisted up, and the reason she hadn't screamed was that she couldn't get her breath. And when she did scream, it was the worst sound, Isabel says, that she'd ever heard in all her life, and she still hears it sometimes in her dreams. Isabel will sometimes wake me up with a low, moaning, strangled sound, and I have to be quick to awaken her and hold her to me and where Isabel is weeping against me seems a mortal wound.

I think I may have written Sonny the very day that little Grace was buried. I was sitting in the living room in the dark, by myself, and I suddenly thought of Sonny. My trouble made his real.

One Saturday afternoon, when Sonny had been living with us, or, anyway, been in our house, for nearly two weeks, I found myself wandering aimlessly about the living room, drinking from a can of beer, and trying to work up the courage to search Sonny's room. He was out, he was usually out whenever I was home, and Isabel had taken the children to see their grandparents. Suddenly I was standing still in front of the living-room window, watching Seventh Avenue. The idea of searching Sonny's room made me still. I scarcely dared to admit to myself what I'd be searching for. I didn't know what I'd do if I found it. Or if I didn't.

On the sidewalk across from me, near the entrance to a barbecue joint, some people were holding an old-fashioned revival meeting. The barbecue cook, wearing a dirty white apron, his conked hair reddish and metallic in the pale sun, and a cigarette between his lips, stood in the doorway, watching them. Kids and older people paused in their errands and stood there, along with some older men and a couple of very tough-looking women who watched everything that happened on the avenue, as though they owned it, or were maybe owned by it. Well, they were watching this, too. The revival was being carried on by three sisters in black, and a brother. All they had were their voices and their Bibles and a tambourine. The brother was testifying and while he testified two of the sisters stood together, seeming to say, Amen, and the third sister walked around with the tambourine outstretched and a couple of people dropped coins into it. Then the brother's testimony ended, and the sister who had been taking up the collection dumped the coins into her palm and transferred them to the pocket of her long black robe. Then she raised both hands, striking the tambourine against the air, and then against one hand, and she started to sing. And the two other sisters and the brother joined in.

It was strange, suddenly, to watch, though I had been seeing these street meetings all my life. So, of course, had everybody else down there. Yet, they paused and watched and listened and I stood still at the window. " 'Tis the old ship of Zion," they sang, and the sister with the tambourine kept a steady, jangling beat, "it has rescued many a thousand!" Not a soul under the sound of their voices was hearing this song for the first time, not one of them had been rescued. Nor had they seen much in the way of rescue work being done around them. Neither did they especially believe in the holiness of the three sisters and the brother, they knew too much about them, knew where they lived, and how. The woman with the tambourine, whose voice dominated the air, whose face was bright with joy, was divided by very little from the woman who stood watching her, a cigarette between her heavy, chapped lips, her hair a cuckoo's nest, her face scarred and swollen from many beatings, and her black eyes glittering like coal. Perhaps they both knew this, which was why, when, as rarely, they addressed each other, they addressed each other as Sister. As the singing filled the air, the watching, listening faces underwent a change, the eyes focusing on something within; the music seemed to soothe a poison out of them; and time seemed, nearly, to fall away from the sullen, belligerent, battered faces, as though they were fleeing back to their first condition, while dreaming of their last. The barbecue cook half shook his head and smiled, and dropped his cigarette and disappeared into his joint. A man fumbled in his pockets for change and stood holding it in his hand impatiently, as though he had just remembered a pressing appointment further up the avenue. He looked furious. Then I saw Sonny, standing on the edge of the crowd. He was carrying a wide, flat notebook with a green cover, and it made him look, from where I was standing, almost like a schoolboy. The coppery sun brought out the copper in his skin, he was very faintly smiling, standing very still. Then the singing stopped, the tambourine turned into a collection plate again. The furious man dropped in his coins and vanished, so did a couple of the women, and Sonny dropped some change in the plate, looking directly at the woman with a little smile. He started across the avenue, toward the house. He has a slow, loping walk, something like the way Harlem hipsters walk, only he's imposed on this his own half-beat. I had never really noticed it before.

I stayed at the window, both relieved and apprehensive. As Sonny disappeared from my sight, they began singing again. And they were still singing when his key turned in the lock.

"Hey," he said.

"Hey, yourself. You want some beer?"

"No. Well, maybe." But he came up to the window and stood beside me, looking out. "What a warm voice," he said.

They were singing *If I could only hear my mother pray again!*

"Yes," I said, "and she can sure beat that tambourine."

"But what a terrible song," he said, and laughed. He dropped his notebook on the sofa and disappeared into the kitchen. "Where's Isabel and the kids?"

"I think they went to see their grandparents. You hungry?"

"No." He came back into the living room with his can of beer. "You want to come someplace with me tonight?"

I sensed, I don't know how, that I couldn't possibly say no. "Sure. Where?"

He sat down on the sofa and picked up his notebook and started leafing through it. "I'm going to sit in with some fellows in a joint in the Village."

"You mean, you're going to play, tonight?"

"That's right." He took a swallow of his beer and moved back to the window. He gave me a sidelong look. "If you can stand it."

"I'll try," I said.

He smiled to himself, and we both watched as the meeting across the way broke up. The three sisters and the brother, heads bowed, were singing *God be with you till we meet again*. The faces around them were very quiet. Then the song ended. The small crowd dispersed. We watched the three women and the lone man walk slowly up the avenue.

"When she was singing before," said Sonny, abruptly, "her voice reminded me for a minute of what heroin feels like some-times—when it's in your veins. It makes you feel sort of warm and cool at the same time. And distant. And—and sure." He sipped his beer, very deliberately not looking at me. I watched his face. "It makes you feel—in control. Sometimes you've got to have that feeling."

"Do you?" I sat down slowly in the easy chair.

"Sometimes." He went to the sofa and picked up his notebook again. "Some people do."

"In order," I asked, "to play?" And my voice was very ugly, full of contempt and anger.

"Well"—he looked at me with great, troubled eyes, as though, in fact, he hoped his eyes would tell me things he could never otherwise say—"they *think* so. And *if* they think so—!"

"And what do *you* think?" I asked.

He sat on the sofa and put his can of beer on the floor. "I don't know," he said, and I couldn't be sure if he were answering my question or pursuing his thoughts. His face didn't tell me. "It's not so much to *play*. It's to *stand* it, to be able to make it at all. On any level." He frowned and smiled: "In order to keep from shaking to pieces."

"But these friends of yours," I said, "they seem to shake them-selves to pieces pretty goddamn fast."

"Maybe." He played with the notebook. And something told me that I should curb my tongue, that Sonny was doing his best to talk, that I should listen. "But of course you only know the ones that've gone to pieces. Some don't—or at least they haven't *yet* and that's just about all *any* of us can say." He paused. "And then there are some who just live, really, in hell, and they know it and they see what's happening and they go right on. I don't know." He sighed, dropped the notebook, folded his arms. "Some guys, you can tell from the way they play, they on something *all* the time. And you can see that, well, it makes something real for them. But of course," he picked up his beer from the floor and sipped it and put the can down again, "they *want* to, too, you've got to see that. Even some of them that say they don't— *some,* not all."

"And what about you?" I asked—I couldn't help it. "What about you? Do *you* want to?"

He stood up and walked to the window and remained silent for a long time. Then he sighed. "Me," he said. Then: "While I was downstairs before, on my way here, listening to that woman sing, it struck me all of a sudden how much suffering she must have had to go through—to sing like that. It's *repulsive* to think you have to suffer that much."

I said: "But there's no way not to suffer—is there, Sonny?"

"I believe not," he said, and smiled, "but that's never stopped anyone from trying." He looked at me. "Has it?" I realized, with this mocking look, that there stood between us, forever, beyond the power of time or forgiveness, the fact that I had held silence—so long!—when he had needed human speech to help him. He turned back to the window. "No, there's no way not to suffer. But you try all kinds of ways to keep from drowning in it, to keep on top of it, and to make it seem—well, like *you.* Like you did something, all right, and now you're suffering for it. You know?" I said nothing. "Well you know," he said, impatiently, "why *do* people suffer? Maybe it's better to do something to give it a reason, *any* reason."

"But we just agreed," I said, "that there's no way not to suffer. Isn't it better, then, just to—take it?"

"But nobody just takes it," Sonny cried, "that's what I'm telling you! *Everybody* tries not to. You're just hung up on the *way* some people try—it's not *your* way!"

The hair on my face began to itch, my face felt wet. "That's not true," I said, "that's not true. I don't give a damn what other people do, I don't even care how they suffer. I just care how *you* suffer." And he looked at me. "Please believe me," I said, "I don't want to see you—die—trying not to suffer."

"I won't," he said, flatly, "die trying not to suffer. At least, not any faster than anybody else."

"But there's no need," I said, trying to laugh, "is there, in killing yourself?"

I wanted to say more, but I couldn't. I wanted to talk about will power and how life could be—well, beautiful. I wanted to say that it was all within; but was it? Or, rather, wasn't that exactly the trouble? And I wanted to promise that I would never fail him again. But it would all have sounded—empty words and lies.

So I made the promise to myself and prayed that I would keep it.

"It's terrible sometimes, inside," he said, "that's what's the trouble. You walk these streets, black and funky and cold, and there's not really a living ass to talk to, and there's nothing shaking, and there's no way of getting it out—that storm inside. You can't talk it and you can't make love with it, and when you finally try to get with it and play it, you realize *nobody's* listening. So *you've* got to listen. You got to find a way to listen."

And then he walked away from the window and sat on the sofa again, as though all the wind had suddenly been knocked out of him. "Sometimes you'll do *anything* to play, even cut your mother's throat." He laughed and looked at me. "Or your brother's." Then he sobered. "Or your own." Then: "Don't worry. I'm all right now and I think I'll *be* all right. But I can't forget—where I've been. I don't mean just the physical place I've been, I mean where I've *been*. And *what* I've been."

"What have you been, Sonny?" I asked.

He smiled—but sat sideways on the sofa, his elbow resting

on the back, his fingers playing with his mouth and chin, not looking at me. "I've been something I didn't recognize, didn't know I could be. Didn't know anybody could be." He stopped, looking inward, looking helplessly young, looking old. "I'm not talking about it now because I feel *guilty* or anything like that— maybe it would be better if I did, I don't know. Anyway, I can't really talk about it. Not to you, not to anybody." And now he turned and faced me. "Sometimes, you know, and it was actually when I was most out of the world, I felt that I was in it, that I was *with* it, really, and I could play or I didn't really have to *play*, it just came out of me, it was there. And I don't know how I played, thinking about it now, but I know I did awful things, those times, sometimes, to people. Or it wasn't that I *did* anything to them—it was that they weren't real." He picked up the beer can; it was empty; he rolled it between his palms: "And other times—well, I needed a fix, I needed to find a place to lean, I needed to clear a space to *listen*—and I couldn't find it, and I— went crazy, I did terrible things to *me*, I was terrible *for* me." He began pressing the beer can between his hands, I watched the metal begin to give. It glittered, as he played with it, like a knife, and I was afraid he would cut himself, but I said nothing. "Oh well. I can never tell you. I was all by myself at the bottom of something, stinking and sweating and crying and shaking, and I smelled it, you know? *My* stink, and I thought I'd die if I couldn't get away from it and yet, all the same, I knew that everything I was doing was just locking me in with it. And I didn't know," he paused, still flattening the beer can. "I didn't know, I still *don't* know, something kept telling me that maybe it was good to smell your own stink, but I didn't think that *that* was what I'd been trying to do—and—who can stand it?" And he abruptly dropped the ruined beer can, looking at me with a small, still smile, and then rose, walking to the window as though it were the lodestone rock. I watched his face, he watched the avenue. "I couldn't tell you when Mama died—but the reason I wanted to leave Harlem so bad was to get away from drugs. And then, when I ran away, that's what I was running from—

really. When I came back, nothing had changed, *I* hadn't changed, I was just—older." And he stopped, drumming with his fingers on the windowpane. The sun had vanished, soon darkness would fall. I watched his face. "It can come again," he said, almost as though speaking to himself. Then he turned to me. "It can come again," he repeated. "I just want you to know that."

"All right," I said at last. "So it can come again. All right."

He smiled, but the smile was sorrowful. "I had to try to tell you," he said.

"Yes," I said. "I understand that."

"You're my brother," he said, looking straight at me, and not smiling at all.

"Yes," I repeated, "yes. I understand that."

He turned back to the window looking out. "All that hatred down there," he said, "all that hatred and misery and love. It's a wonder it doesn't blow the avenue apart."

We went to the only night club on a short, dark street, downtown. We squeezed through the narrow, chattering, jam-packed bar to the entrance of the big room, where the bandstand was. And we stood there for a moment, for the lights were very dim in this room and we couldn't see. Then, "Hello, boy," said a voice, and an enormous black man, much older than Sonny or myself, erupted out of all that atmospheric lighting and put an arm around Sonny's shoulder. "I been sitting right here," he said, "waiting for you."

He had a big voice, too, and heads in the darkness turned toward us.

Sonny grinned and pulled a little away, and said, "Creole, this is my brother. I told you about him."

Creole shook my hand. "I'm glad to meet you, son," he said, and it was clear that he was glad to meet me *there*, for Sonny's sake. And he smiled. "You got a real musician in *your* family," and he took his arm from Sonny's shoulder and slapped him, lightly, affectionately, with the back of his hand.

"Well. Now I've heard it all," said a voice behind us. This was another musician, and a friend of Sonny's, a coal-black, cheerful-looking man, built close to the ground. He immediately began confiding to me, at the top of his lungs, the most terrible things about Sonny, his teeth gleaming like a lighthouse and his laugh coming up out of him like the beginning of an earthquake. And it turned out that everyone at the bar knew Sonny, or almost everyone; some were musicians, working there, or nearby, or not working, some were simply hangers-on, and some were there to hear Sonny play. I was introduced to all of them and they were all very polite to me. Yet, it was clear that, for them, I was only Sonny's brother. Here, I was in Sonny's world. Or, rather: his kingdom. Here, it was not even a question that his veins bore royal blood.

They were going to play soon, and Creole installed me, by myself, at a table in a dark corner. Then I watched them, Creole, and the little black man, and Sonny, and the others, while they horsed around, standing just below the bandstand. The light from the bandstand spilled just a little short of them and, watching them laughing and gesturing and moving about, I had the feeling that they, nevertheless, were being most careful not to step into that circle of light too suddenly: that if they moved into the light too suddenly, without thinking, they would perish in flame. Then, while I watched, one of them, the small, black man, moved into the light and crossed the bandstand and started fooling around with his drums. Then—being funny and being, also, extremely ceremonious—Creole took Sonny by the arm and led him to the piano. A woman's voice called Sonny's name, and a few hands started clapping. And Sonny, also being funny and being ceremonious, and so touched, I think, that he could have cried, but neither hiding it nor showing it, riding it like a man, grinned, and put both hands to his heart and bowed from the waist.

Creole then went to the bass fiddle and a lean, very bright-skinned brown man jumped up on the bandstand and picked up his horn. So there they were, and the atmosphere on the bandstand and in the room began to change and tighten. Someone stepped up to the microphone and announced them. Then there were all kinds of murmurs. Some people at the bar shushed others. The waitress ran around, frantically getting in the last orders, guys and chicks got closer to each other, and the lights on the bandstand, on the quartet, turned to a kind of indigo. Then they all looked different there. Creole looked about him for the last time, as though he were making certain that all his chickens were in the coop, and then he—jumped and struck the fiddle. And there they were.

All I know about music is that not many people ever really hear it. And even then, on the rare occasions when something opens within, and the music enters, what we mainly hear, or hear corroborated, are personal, private, vanishing evocations. But the man who creates the music is hearing something else, is dealing with the roar rising from the void and imposing order on it as it hits the air. What is evoked in him, then, is of another order, more terrible because it has no words, and triumphant, too, for that same reason. And his triumph, when he triumphs, is ours. I just watched Sonny's face. His face was troubled, he was working hard, but he wasn't with it. And I had the feeling that, in a way, everyone on the bandstand was waiting for him, both waiting for him and pushing him along. But as I began to watch Creole, I realized that it was Creole who held them all back. He had them on a short rein. Up there, keeping the beat with his whole body, wailing on the fiddle, with his eyes half closed, he was listening to everything, but he was listening to Sonny. He was having a dialogue with Sonny. He wanted Sonny to leave the shore line and strike out for the deep water. He was Sonny's witness that deep water and drowning were not the same thing—he had been there, and he knew. And he wanted Sonny to know. He was waiting for Sonny to do the things on the keys which would let Creole know that Sonny was in the water.

And, while Creole listened, Sonny moved, deep within, exactly like someone in torment. I had never before thought of how awful the relationship must be between the musician and his instrument. He has to fill it, this instrument, with the breath of life, his own. He has to make it do what he wants it to do. And a piano is just a piano. It's made out of so much wood and wires and little hammers and big ones, and ivory. While there's only so much you can do with it, the only way to find this out is to try to try and make it do everything.

And Sonny hadn't been near a piano for over a year. And he wasn't on much better terms with his life, not the life that stretched before him now. He and the piano stammered, started one way, got scared, stopped; started another way, panicked, marked time, started again; then seemed to have found a direction, panicked again, got stuck. And the face I saw on Sonny I'd never seen before. Everything had been burned out of it, and, at the same time, things usually hidden were being burned in, by the fire and fury of the battle which was occurring in him up there.

Yet, watching Creole's face as they neared the end of the first set, I had the feeling that something had happened, something I hadn't heard. Then they finished, there was scattered applause, and then, without an instant's warning, Creole started into something else, it was almost sardonic, it was *Am I Blue*. And, as though he commanded, Sonny began to play. Something began to happen. And Creole let out the reins. The dry, low, black man said something awful on the drums, Creole answered, and the drums talked back. Then the horn insisted, sweet and high, slightly detached perhaps, and Creole listened, commenting now and then, dry, and driving, beautiful and calm and old. Then they all came together again, and Sonny was part of the family again. I could tell this from his face. He seemed to have found, right there beneath his fingers, a damn brand-new piano. It seemed that he couldn't get over it. Then, for a while, just being happy with Sonny, they seemed to be agreeing with him that brand-new pianos certainly were a gas.

Then Creole stepped forward to remind them that what they were playing was the blues. He hit something in all of them, he hit something in me, myself, and the music tightened and deepened, apprehension began to beat the air. Creole began to tell us what the blues were all about. They were not about anything very new. He and his boys up there were keeping it new, at the risk of ruin, destruction, madness, and death, in order to find new ways to make us listen. For, while the tale of how we suffer, and how we are delighted, and how we may triumph is never new, it always must be heard. There isn't any other tale to tell, it's the only light we've got in all this darkness.

And this tale, according to that face, that body, those strong hands on those strings, has another aspect in every country, and a new depth in every generation. Listen, Creole seemed to be saying, listen. Now these are Sonny's blues. He made the little black man on the drums know it, and the bright, brown man on the horn. Creole wasn't trying any longer to get Sonny in the water. He was wishing him Godspeed. Then he stepped back, very slowly, filling the air with the immense suggestion that Sonny speak for himself.

Then they all gathered around Sonny, and Sonny played. Every now and again one of them seemed to say, Amen. Sonny's fingers filled the air with life, his life. But that life contained so many others. And Sonny went all the way back, he really began with the spare, flat statement of the opening phrase of the song. Then he began to make it his. It was very beautiful because it wasn't hurried and it was no longer a lament. I seemed to hear with what burning he had made it his, with what burning we had yet to make it ours, how we could cease lamenting. Freedom lurked around us and I understood, at last, that he could help us to be free if we would listen, that he would never be free until we did. Yet, there was no battle in his face now. I heard what he had gone through, and would continue to go through until he came to rest in earth. He had made it his: that long line, of which we knew only Mama and Daddy. And he was giving it back, as everything must be given back, so that, passing through death, it can live forever. I saw my mother's face again, and felt, for the first time, how the stones of the road she had walked on must have bruised her feet. I saw the moonlit road where my father's brother died. And it brought something else back to me, and carried me past it. I saw my little girl again and felt Isabel's tears again, and I felt my own tears begin to rise. And I was yet aware that this was only a moment, that the world waited outside, as hungry as a tiger, and that trouble stretched above us, longer than the sky.

Then it was over. Creole and Sonny let out their breath, both soaking wet, and grinning. There was a lot of applause and some of it was real. In the dark, the girl came by and I asked her to take drinks to the bandstand. There was a long pause, while they talked up there in the indigo light and after a while I saw the girl put a Scotch and milk on top of the piano for Sonny. He didn't seem to notice it, but just before they started playing again, he sipped from it and looked toward me, and nodded. Then he put it back on top of the piano. For me, then, as they began to play again, it glowed and shook above my brother's head like the very cup of trembling.

COMMENTARY ON
JAMES BALDWIN

Sonny's Blues

James Baldwin's writing has always been permeated with a sense of religious intensity. A member of the Mount Cavalry of the Pentecostal Faith Church, Baldwin was a junior minister in that church, preaching at the age of fourteen, and he has always remained the preacher. Steeped in themes and symbols from both Old and New Testament, "Sonny's Blues" reads like an ancient biblical parable of brothers, fathers and sons. As in the story of Cain and Abel, the narrator of this story demands, out of his own guilt, "Am I my brother's keeper?" The story also echoes the parable of the Prodigal Son, in which two brothers are alienated from each other because the older brother is unable to forgive his younger brother's failings or to understand the meaning of the father's love for his erring younger son. None of the male characters in the story is named; even "Sonny" is a generic nickname pointing to his place as a member in the family. The uncle is always referred to as "your father's brother," and the only two characters who are named in the story (and both names are symbolic) are Isabel and Grace. Thus the story's emphasis is on men defining their relationships in the family.

As the narrator-brother tries to understand how he has come to be so alienated from his brother, he reaches back into family history as if to uncover some secret (some story) that will provide the answer. As he moves further and further into the past, his sense of the family gradually enlarges as though he were turning the pages of a family album. But, like the older brother in the Prodigal Son parable, the narrator is unable to interpret the meaning of these family stories. When his mother tells him the story of his father's brother killed by white men in the South, he refuses to hear her message, reassuring her glibly that nothing will happen to either her or Sonny. Had he understood his mother's story, he would recognize that he is just as powerless as was his father to protect his brother from disaster, and that, like his father, he will remain angry with his brother until he is able to break through the ice of his own frozen emotional life.

The narrator's emotional distance from himself, from others in his family and from his community is depicted in several ways, most often in his physical separation from other people. When he describes the students from his classroom as they leave school, he is standing at an upstairs window, looking down at the courtyard where the boys are playing, and, though he sees something of himself in their struggle and gestures, his sarcastic comment that for all he knows they might all be strung out on drugs indicates how little he knows of their actual lives. The image of the narrator standing outside and above the community is repeated when he sees a revival meeting outside his apartment building. As he stands in the window looking down at the gathering, he sees Sonny standing on the edge of the group—

smiling, listening and looking directly at the revivalists. Sonny tries to remind the narrator that what is important is the meaning of the words of the songs they are singing, but the narrator dismisses the entire experience with the unfeeling and superficial response: "she can sure beat that tambourine."

The narrator's distance from community is replicated in his alienation from his own emotional life. His own feelings of vulnerability, grief and fear are nearly always projected onto the women in his life. He describes his baby daughter's illness and death as though he himself were a spectator at an event involving only his wife and daughter. It is Gracie who screams and falls, and Isabel who wakes at night and weeps. And earlier, when his mother tells the story of his murdered uncle, it is she who has tears gleaming on her face. When she tries to warn him about Sonny, the narrator's characteristic response is that everything will be all right because he will be sending her checks and "writing all the time." For the narrator, words are a shield against feeling. As long as he can write and talk, he can maintain the pose that protects him from the terror of his own feelings. The opening lines of the narration have already prepared us for the narrator's use of words as a defense against his sense of helplessness. Of his brother's incarceration, he tells us, "I read about it in the paper."

Although Baldwin does not deal explicitly with the themes of homosexuality in "Sonny's Blues," that theme is present indirectly in the critique the story makes of the narrator's macho behavior. His inability to cry or express grief, his isolation from others, his authoritarian treatment of his younger brother and his willingness to let his wife and his mother assume the emotional weight in the family are all signs of conventionally acceptable male attitudes. What the blues requires of him is empathy, vulnerability, a willingness to experience suffering, not to control the power of his own words but to be moved by the power of an art form that can speak without words. There is only the tiniest indication of change as the narrator, listening to Sonny's blues, allows his own tears to rise.

Baldwin is playing with several definitions of family in "Sonny's Blues." The revivalists are a kind of family. Their rituals represent a shared history and a place of refuge, but they seem especially like family because of their knowledge and acceptance of one another and because of their willingness to live with both the terrible and the good in their lives. Their addressing one another as brother and sister becomes a critical commentary on the lack of brotherliness in the narrator's life.

The group of musicians Sonny plays with at the club is another portrait of a family. The narrator immediately recognizes the familial quality of the group: "Sonny was part of the family again." Even the narrator is included in this family; Creole calls the narrator "son" and begins to tell him "terrible" stories about Sonny which the narrator obviously doesn't know. Sonny's drug addiction does not exclude him from this family, for there is no attempt among these musicians to disguise or avoid pain, suffering, or failure. Like the revivalist family, it achieves its status as family by its openness to both the terrible and the good; and it is among this "family" that the narrator is able to reenter his own painful memories and to begin to be healed.

The most compelling images of family are found in the narrator's memories of his own family and in the family memories that his mother passes on to him. When the narrator remembers the old folks gathered around in the living room after church on a Sunday afternoon, enclosing the children in a kind of spiritual embrace, he understands the paradox of family life— that the family provides a temporary refuge, but it cannot provide safety. The narrator's reference to "the darkness outside" specifically comments on the black family because the "darkness" which puts these children in such jeopardy is related to the violence of racism and poverty. The story the mother tells of the murder of the father's brother is a further example of the necessity of memory in constructing the family. Not until the narrator hears this story and learns to interpret it can he begin to salvage his relationship with his own brother. As in all of Baldwin's stories, memories of kin—stories handed down from one generation to the next—unlock the hidden mysteries of the self.

Aunts
and
Uncles

The House on Norwood

TOI DERRICOTTE

That brick bungalow
rose out of the storm
of racism like an ark.
We found a way—the post office workers,
the teachers, principals—we found
a nest, a mile of wilderness,
and farmed the bones of our children
out of it. Suburban, up
from the South, our boys
not shot, our girls not pregnant
with belly after belly
of welfare children.
No matter how I hated and feared
the rages, the silences,
we did grow
iron bones.

I'd wake on cold dark mornings
earlier than the packing of the factory lunchpails,
my father breathing
like an engine, my mother next to him, almost
invisible,
my leg over the crib rail, quietly,
slowly,
down the stairs in my wet cold pants,

padding through the living room, the dining room, the hall,
to where she lay,
my Aunt Lenora,
warm, still sleeping, who
hid me when my father came—
"Is Toi in there?" She'd lie.
I'd crawl under the sheet,
sneak her nightdress up around
her thighs and peek.
She'd snore, limp, trusting.

Aunt Carrie

RITA DOVE

The train! The train station with its iron and glass! Still invisible but roaring it came, and the roar grew louder. It roared, it rumbled, it growled like some wild thing. I thought it must be something much more terrible than anything I had ever experienced before. And as it roared out of the dark direction of Pittsburgh I knew that I had always thought of Pittsburgh as something dark and roaring though I had never been there.

I was in my first train station. I couldn't understand why Aunt Carrie was there. Aunt Carrie, Mom said, had come along for the ride. What I understood even less was why Mom did not speak to Aunt Carrie. Aunt Carrie of the dark and wrinkled countenance. Aunt Carrie who no one believed was only six years older than my mother. Aunt Carrie: watery eyes, the smile with a missing tooth, the slight leer Mom said came from sticking her mouth where it didn't belong. She's always smelling her own upper lip, Mom said. I felt sorry for Aunt Carrie. She wore lots of lipstick to make herself look pretty but she wasn't, her face sagged.

How come Aunt Carrie hadn't recognized my drawing? My father had a moustache ever since I could remember. It was thin and curved, like two rat-tails. Maybe my lines were a little shaky and his mouth was a little crooked, but it was him, no mistake about it, and I had drawn it from memory.

"Your father doesn't have a moustache," she said. Of course he had! What kind of aunt was she?

A garbled announcement came over the loudspeaker. The train was rolling into the station. And that train carried my daddy.

"It's time to go," said Mom in a weird voice.

We descended to the platform. There the cool stale air swept upwards like the breath of the underworld. Funny that it was cool.

Aunt Carrie had taken out a hanky and was twisting it—that looked funny. We waited on the platform for the train to come and stop. And it came and stopped and it was not like the long and awful sound that had come before it. It was like the movies when the light shines cheerily from its one eye and the squeal of the brakes is exciting, and the people pour off and into other people's arms.

I fell into my father's arms. "What did you bring me, what did you bring me?" I screamed, because he himself seemed too terribly still, too far from me to kiss. I needed some souvenir, some proof that he had actually come from Pittsburgh. He'd brought me his name tag. "Ernest Price, Goodrich" it said. His shoulder smelled of pipe smoke whiskey cologne and hair pomade and very faintly, the train.

"Your lovely sister's here, too," Mom said, and I thought she sounded even stranger than before, her back arched in the last stages of pregnancy, her belly pushed out tight against her white blouse. Aunt Carrie stood a little to the side, her coat still buttoned. I could barely see her.

"I happened to read an interesting letter she wrote you a while ago, Ernest," Mom kept on saying in the strange voice. "I thought it only proper that she come, too."

Daddy tightened and then pushed me away, gently, but it

was still a push. They were going to have an argument again, except this time it looked like Daddy was going to cry, and I couldn't stand that. No one moved. They stood still so long I got fidgety and wanted to run, but I didn't know who to run to, they all looked so strange. Aunt Carrie was pulling on that hankie for all it was worth and then I could see that she was crying. It wasn't nice for Mom to call her lovely when she wasn't. That must be what they're going to argue about. I had a pain in my stomach. I wanted to go home.

"What do you take in your tea, Aunt Carrie?"

"The same as you, dear. I don't take much to tea usually—never had occasion to, I guess."

"Would you like something else then?"

"No, thank you, dear." She chuckled. "You must have learned this in the Big World."

"Learned what?"

"Having tea in the middle of the day."

"Listen, Aunt Carrie, I want to apologize for not getting in touch with you sooner, I mean, right when I got into town. I've been so busy—"

"Don't go apologizing to me. I'm not one for apologies, makes me blush. You young people got all that life ahead of you, it's no wonder you're busy. We know how it is. We may talk a lot about you not coming to see us and all, but we know how it is." She took a handkerchief from her purse—small and white with a pink rose in one corner. She dabbed at her eyelids. "I remember when I used to babysit you you liked to draw a lot. You drew up every piece of paper you could get your hands on. Your dad had to lock his desk."

I watched her hands. They wrapped one corner of the hankie around the right index finger, pulled it straight, started again with the left index.

"I meant to ask you a question, Aunt Carrie," I said.

"What, dear?"

"Why my parents moved to Florida when I was nine, right

before my little sister was born. I never figured it out, really."

"Your father got an offer—"

"I know that story." I watched her hands. Sometimes the rose could be seen among the twisted ends of the cotton, a delicate blemish. "But I also remember a summer day in Fort Myers when I was playing in the flower bed under the kitchen window. I wasn't supposed to be there, which is why I didn't stand up at first when I heard my parents' voices inside. They were arguing. Dad yelled that he had settled for less and had left his home town just because of her, and now she still couldn't—and then he walked over to shut the window and saw me kneeling there. He didn't say anything, just stared. Then he shut the window. They didn't talk much for months."

I poured myself another cup of tea. "I thought over that scene often, but I never dared to ask anyone about it. Neither him nor, heaven help me, Mom. Do you know what was going on? You were with us at the train station when it all started. . . ."

Aunt Carrie stopped twisting her hanky abruptly. She became so still that I knew I was very close to the secret—if I only persisted. I looked into Aunt Carrie's eyes.

"I need your help," I said quietly.

The stilled figure in the corner of the sofa became a little more erect, and a sigh, barely audible, issued from her lips and hung like dry scent in the air.

"It's hard," she whispered. She straightened her back a little more, placed her hands in her lap and like a schoolgirl reciting her lesson began to speak, her voice trembly at first but gaining strength:

"I thought about it a lot. Not when it happened. When it happened, I didn't think about nothing at all. No one did. But afterwards, I thought about it. If you remembered the night at the train station. If you could make sense out of it at all. If your mother ever mentioned me to you. It was so hard not to be able to talk to anyone about it. It happened so long ago. I didn't mean your mother any harm. I couldn't have." She took a deep breath. "I thought a lot about how I would tell my side if anyone asked. I knew I couldn't cry or get indignant. It's nobody's fault. Long ago I decided that if anyone asked me, I would tell everything as I felt and saw it from the beginning.

"My daddy—your grandfather—ran off at the beginning of the Depression. I was thirteen, your father was nine. Mama began taking in washing, cleaning up white folks' houses—anything to bring in a few dollars. My older brothers and sisters were married off or sent to find work as soon as they were old enough to walk without wetting their pants it seemed. I had seven brothers and sisters older than me and I never saw them much, except on holidays. Mama let me stay home and take care of Ernie— your dad. He was the smart one in the family and we all loved him the best. Ernie was our shining star, and we did everything to protect him from things. So I stayed home and took care of him while Mama went to work. I cooked him breakfast and sent him out to school, and tried to help him with his homework. Ernie never heard a harsh word about his daddy—in those days men left their women for all sorts of reasons . . . and nobody blamed them much, because times were hard. But when Ernie finally learned that Daddy had left us holding the bills and the babies, he went furious and never spoke his name again.

"I was the runt of the family and the homeliest. I knew it— no one had to tell me. I could see it in the mirror and in the eyes of people when they came to visit. So when your father got to be grown enough to fix his own breakfast, there was the problem of Carrie. What can she do? Not smart enough for business, not pretty enough for marriage. But they found me someone to marry, finally. A widower, forty-two years old, who ran a barber shop. Numbers racket on the side. I was seventeen.

"Folks said Sam Rogers was a good soul. He'd lost his wife of twenty years to an accident and was helpless without her. He needed a woman to clean and cook and to give him a little comfort in the declining years of his life. I was perfect, folks said. In a way, moving into his little house was so much like living at home that I barely had to adjust. He come home at night and I'd have a good dinner waiting for him—Dixie butter peas from the garden and baked yams, chitterlings on weekends.

I washed his clothes and kept the house clean. He barely noticed me. It was like taking care of my baby brother.

"Everyone thought I was coping so well. The older ladies would wink and ask me how I liked having a man in the house, and I'd smile. I didn't let on that Sam hadn't touched me. Not that I minded. Sam Rogers was big and sweaty, and when he sat down at the dinner table I sometimes thought of a big slimy frog. He had bugged-out eyes that were bloodshot—not from drink but because the air and dust could get to them so easy—and he grunted when he walked, almost like sounds would help him along. But he was kind, and I got used to him. Little by little he began to come out of his grieving. After a few months he began talking about his wife's cooking. 'Could you fry me some green tomatoes for tomorrow?' he'd ask. 'Edna used to make them.' I asked around to find out how to fry green tomatoes, and they'd be on his plate next morning. 'You cook nearly as good as Edna,' he'd say, and it pleased me to know I was doing a good job.

"Then one summer evening after dinner he was sitting in his chair and I was on the sofa, crocheting a doily for the armrest, when he turned to me and said, 'I want to tell you about Edna.' I put down my handwork, and he was hunched down in that chair so that his head nearly touched his knees, almost as if he was in pain. He talked about Edna when he first saw her, at fifteen, and their wedding, and the baby that died because she hadn't known what to do and couldn't get into town to a midwife. He talked about how she lost all her shyness when the lights were out. I sat there and listened to him, a great big piece of a man humped over in that chair like a child with a stomach ache, talking about what ailed him. He must have talked for hours. It began to get dark. Do you know how twilight makes the air look like it's full of feathers? Everything seems to come apart and float around, and heavy things like tables and chairs take on a grainy look, like old sugar. I listened and watched Sam melt too, just like the furniture. He seemed so delicate all of a sudden.

"When he finished he looked at me without sitting up—just

turned his head and looked at me from his knees. He smiled. Then he laughed. Then he reached out his hand and I went to him.

"I got to tell you all this because you've got to see what it was like. I mean, I'd been taught for so long to be thankful for whatever I got that I didn't think to ask for more out of life. I took whatever came to me and was satisfied. I didn't know what I was missing. Which was why, a couple years later, I about went crazy when he up and died. Lord knows I didn't have the world, but the little piece of it I had I didn't want to give up and have to start all over again. But there I was—a teenage widow with little money.

"So I went back home. I kept house and helped Mama with her washing sometimes, and I babysat the children in the neighborhood. Everyone started calling me Aunt Carrie. Aunt Carrie was there to do whatever needed to be done. Ernie was fifteen by then and was growing in his sleep it seemed like. He was near to six feet already—and handsome, slim and tough with straight black eyebrows and broad shoulders. But he was too serious for his own good. Every spare moment his head was in a book. He studied so much that it got so he looked a little cramped, like some twisted-up fungus that grows in the dark. He looked pale under his color—ashy. For all his book learning, though, he didn't know beans. Never went out with girls . . . never even looked at them. People'd say, 'That boy's going to make something out of himself,' but I'd worry."

She paused, and for a moment the sound of laughter came from outside. Boys in the street, their feet slapping the pavement, small thudding sounds clustered together, a shout. . . .

"Anyway," Aunt Carrie continued, "spring came—not spring exactly, just the first blowsy days. I'd been washing sheets and had hung them out on the clothesline. But like I said, the weather was unpredictable that time of year—clothes will dry in a couple hours if a rain don't come up and drench them, or if a storm don't appear out of nowhere and dash them all into the mud. That afternoon about three o'clock, it suddenly looked like it might rain. I ran outside and began taking down the sheets, when I happened to look up and see the most beautiful man in the world walking down the street. He had on a white shirt, and his head rose out of that white shirt like a statue. I felt myself go weak, and then I realized that I wasn't dead yet. I bent over the laundry basket, then peeked another look. He raised his free hand and waved.

"I was so confused and ashamed that for a moment I couldn't lift my head. I stayed bent over the basket, playing with the clothespins. I was ashamed, but the feeling wouldn't go away. I could have stayed right there, kneeling in the mud, and cried. But there was this feeling, this strength inside the weakness, which made me stand up and reach for the next sheet. Soon I sensed him next to me. He was playing around, joking—like he'd take down two pins at once and hold the sheet above the dirt with his hands and teeth. But then he reached around me to get my end of a sheet, and I felt the heat from his chest rising up against my back, and something went inside of me and I held onto that clothesline like I was drowning. He thought I was playing and tugged at the sheet. I wouldn't let go . . . if I had I would've fallen down. I stood there listening to the wind slap that sheet against my face, and I could feel the bottom of the sheet flicking my shins. It was like being caught in a sail, and flying, flying over everything. He gave up and let go, and I finally got it all folded and ready. He carried the basket inside for me. I must have walked funny, because he asked me if I felt well. I said I was a little dizzy and might lay down for a spell. He said he'd help me make the bed.

"So he took the basket into the bedroom and I went to the bathroom to try to pull myself together. But I didn't know what I was doing. I went in to splash water on my face and found myself undressing down to my slip. I could still feel that sheet beating against me, like a bird gone wild. When I walked into the bedroom, he was kneeling on the bed, trying to tuck the bottom sheet into the headboard. He whistled and plopped over on his back. 'I don't see how you women do this sort of stuff,' he said. I didn't answer. I was in a trance. 'There's nothing smells better than freshly washed sheets,' he said then, turning his head to the side and sniffing. He didn't suspect a thing. And without really expecting that I'd really go through with it, I bent over and touched his cheek. His face turned and looked into mine. That was the first moment he knew anything. I remember seeing the pulse start up under his Adam's apple. And you know what he felt like to touch? Like onion skins. Soft and dry."

For a moment we sat without speaking. *What he felt like to touch,* I thought. *Soft and dry.*

Aunt Carrie's tone became brisker: "But that's what was important for me. What's important for you is what comes afterwards. We were together most of that spring and summer. I think he never really thought much about it. It was pleasant, and when it was over, he forgot about it. I'm sure of that. I stopped it because I realized it was crazy. I don't know if anyone suspected us. Mama was away so much of the time, and the neighbors thought Ernie was inside studying." She paused. "After a long while I got it out of my head, too, and when he married your mother there couldn't have been anyone happier than the two of them. When your mother asked me to babysit you and your brother, I didn't think about it at all. I don't know if I'm explaining it right. It was like it happened to somebody else— not to another me, but that he had been someone else."

My thoughts went in many different places. Was I shocked? But there were last questions—questions of routine, map-outs of procedure.

"How did my mother find out?"

"The time he went to Pittsburgh was the first time he'd been away from Belle since they were married. She was pregnant with your little sister, and she must have been lonely—I remember how clean the house was that week. When she got to shining up this picture of Mama, somehow she got it in her head to surprise him by getting a new gold-plated frame for it. That's when she found the note."

"Note?"

"To Ernie . . . a note I wrote him after the first time. Afterwards I was so confused, I ran out and didn't come back till right around dinnertime. When I got my senses back, I knew that whatever happened I had to make sure he didn't feel bad or that he'd been a failure . . . whatever goes on in a boy's head. So I wrote him a note telling how nice it had been—that he was a man now and should always hold up his head. I slipped it under his pillow. He must have thought about hiding it from Mama, so he put it where he was sure she wouldn't look—behind the frame of her own picture. It stood on his dresser for years and it went with him when he got married. I didn't know he had kept it. I don't know what he thought. But I know nobody would have known if it hadn't been for that note behind the picture frame." Aunt Carrie took a deep breath. "That night at the station your mother gave it back to me."

She sat very still in an attitude of waitful repose, her eyes straight ahead.

"I always wondered if you remembered that night." She spoke with her gaze focused on air, like a statue come to life. "Your mother couldn't be reasoned with. And your father loved her— he loved her more than anything in the world. He did everything to hold his family together—took the job in Florida, cut himself off from his kinfolk—I never saw him again."

I kept silent; I felt suddenly very relaxed.

"What did your mother have to say about me when you children were growing up in Florida? I know it's silly to care after all these years, but I'd like to know."

"She never said a word. We—" I had started to say *We forgot all about you.*

Carrie was nodding slowly. "That would have been the best way." A deep and irrevocable sadness. "Well, I'm your crazy old aunt." She paused. "Mrs. Evans always said you didn't know nothing."

"Grandma Evans?"

"Yes. She's the one who told me how her daughter found the note. She was there. When Belle called me up to ask if I wanted to go to the station, Mrs. Evans tried to stop her. 'Let lying dogs lie,' she told her, but Belle wouldn't listen.'"

Aunt Carrie laughed.

She laughed so hard tears rolled down her cheeks, and for a moment I was afraid she was going to be hysterical. Then she stopped, as suddenly as she had begun.

"I've been thinking about telling it all these years, and when it gets round to doing it I tell it all wrong." Her face turned to marble again. "After your mother handed me my own note back, she never spoke to me directly again. I didn't know how she had got hold of it, and I was too sick to ask. That night was the last time I saw Ernie, too, so I couldn't ask him. I don't know if I would've asked him if I could've. It didn't seem so important then. But later, after you all had moved and I had plenty of time to think back, I wondered. I didn't think I'd ever find out. Then your Granddaddy Evans died, and Mrs. Evans moved into Saferstein Towers. One day she called me on the phone. 'I'm lonely,' she said, 'why don't you come up for a visit?' I thought it was a little funny, but I went.

"She told me what she knew. She didn't want to hear my story. 'Old bones, dead and buried,' she said. So we became friends."

"Aunt Carrie—"

"Don't say nothing. I ain't expecting nothing."

I reached across the table, took her hand.

The old woman looked over at me slowly. "Honey—I have to be going."

This hand, soft and cold and dry. I squeezed it, gently. "I'd like to see you again, Aunt Carrie," I said. "I'll call you."

COMMENTARY ON
RITA DOVE

Aunt Carrie

Born in Akron, Ohio, in 1952, Rita Dove is best known as a poet. She is the author of three books of poetry: *The Yellow House on the Corner* (1980), *Museum* (1983) and *Thomas and Beulah*, a narrative based on the lives of her grandparents, for which she won the Pulitzer Prize for poetry in 1987. *Fifth Sunday*, from which "Aunt Carrie" is taken, is her first collection of short stories.

Though aunts are often significant people in extended families—especially in black families—they tend to be represented in literature as childless, marginal figures. By definition they enter narratives in relation to someone else's child or children and are therefore not seen as having full, autonomous lives of their own. Uncles rarely appear at all, but there are a number of aunts in black American literature who play an important role in the lives of nieces and/or nephews. Most are not married, but even if they have been married at some point in their lives, they appear in these narratives as childless and without husbands—either through desertion, death, separation or divorce. The three aunts in Ernest Gaines' collection *Bloodline*—Aunt Fe and Aunt Lou in "Just Like a Tree" and Auntie in "The Sky Is Gray"—all unmarried, are extremely important women to the young male narrators of these stories, filling in where a maternal presence is lacking. We have, however, no sense of their lives outside of that maternal role. The three aunts in Dorothy West's novel *The Living Is Easy* (1948)—Lily, Charity and Serena—are sisters of the main character, Cleo, and are manipulated by Cleo into leaving their husbands to come and take care of her; in effect they become (un)married in order to enter the narrative. By the time John Grimes, the main character in James Baldwin's *Go Tell It on the Mountain* (1953), knows his Aunt Florence, she has been deserted by her husband, and when we encounter Florence in the novel she is a "barren" older woman, dying of cancer, bitter, angry and lonely. Her major purpose in the novel is to protect her nephew John from his stepfather, Gabriel, who is her brother. Aunt Sophronia in Ann Petry's "Miss Muriel" is an unmarried woman living with the narrator's family, with very little life of her own; and, even though she is a professionally trained pharmacist, it is her spinster status rather than her work which becomes the focus of the story.

Rita Dove's Aunt Carrie is married when she is a young girl, but for the purposes of the narrative, she too is both unmarried (i.e., widowed) and childless. Marginal to the main family of this story, her feelings of homeliness and inferiority make her seem pathetic. She values herself only as a caretaker, first for her brother, Ernie, then for her much older husband, Sam, then as a baby-sitter for her niece. As she acknowledges in her own words when she is no longer able to play these roles: "there was the problem of Carrie." Conditioned to passivity, she is unable to see herself as agent even in her own story. She tells the story of her love affair with her brother as if she were directed by some external force: "But I didn't know what I was doing. I went in to splash water on my face and found myself undressing down to my slip." Finally she dismisses the end of her narrative in order to focus on what is important to the niece: "But that's what was important to me. What's important for you is what comes afterwards." Her life's story is shaped by the needs of someone else as though even her narrative is part of her caretaking role.

In spite of her marginality, Aunt Carrie manages to exert tremendous influence on her niece's family—first by the incestuous relationship with her brother, then by the note she leaves behind. Even her choice to tell this story to her niece is a way of inserting herself into a story in which she is considered the outsider, an outsider, however, who is profoundly threatening. And what does her story threaten? Certainly it threatens the marriage bonds and all its conventions. Even the way the niece's mother discovers Carrie's note suggests Carrie's threatening role. The mother is in a frenzy of housecleaning, trying to assuage the loneliness of marriage and pregnancy when she finds the note hidden in a framed portrait of Ernie and Carrie's mother. In order to reestablish her value as wife and mother, she forces her family to move and to cut off all relations with the forbidden Aunt Carrie.

There is considerable ambivalence in this portrait of Aunt Carrie as I think there is in many stories about aunts. Since aunts in narrative remain unmarried or get divorced or work outside the home they are often fairly unconventional women. They come into the story when there is a gap the parents cannot fill, but they represent both a help and a threat, fulfilling a need but suggesting a life larger than the life of the mother. Carrie's story may protest against the conventional story of love and marriage by being outside of it, but the narrative also undermines that protest by reducing Carrie to such a pathetic state.

Toi Derricotte's poem "The House on Norwood" suggests, as "Aunt Carrie" does, that the relationship between niece and aunt relieves the intensity of the parent-child relationship. In extended families, the additional protection from aunts and uncles enabled children to survive intact, not to get shot or get pregnant, to grow what Derricotte calls "iron bones." Nonetheless, like the mother's story, which is most often told from the daughter's point of view, the aunt's story nearly always gets told from the point of view of the niece of nephew, leaving us to wonder—again—about the rich, unexplored female life outside of that narrow range.

Gorilla, My Love

TONI CADE BAMBARA

That was the year Hunca Bubba changed his name. Not a change up, but a change back, since Jefferson Winston Vale was the name in the first place. Which was news to me cause he'd been my Hunca Bubba my whole lifetime, since I couldn't manage Uncle to save my life. So far as I was concerned it was a change completely to somethin soundin very geographical weatherlike to me, like somethin you'd find in a almanac. Or somethin you'd run across when you sittin in the navigator seat with a wet thumb on the map crinkly in your lap, watchin the roads and signs so when Granddaddy Vale say "Which way, Scout," you got sense enough to say take the next exit or take a left or whatever it is. Not that Scout's my name. Just the name Granddaddy call whoever sittin in the navigator seat. Which is usually me cause I don't feature sittin in the back with the pecans. Now, you figure pecans all right to be sittin with. If you thinks so, that's your business. But they dusty sometime and make you cough. And they got a way of slidin around and dippin down sudden, like maybe a rat in the buckets. So if you scary like me, you sleep with the lights on and blame it on Baby Jason and, so as not to waste good electric, you study the maps. And that's how come I'm in the navigator seat most times and get to be called Scout.

So Hunca Bubba in the back with the pecans and Baby Jason, and he in love. And we got to hear all this stuff about this woman he in love with and all. Which really ain't enough to keep the mind alive, though Baby Jason got no better sense than to give his undivided attention and keep grabbin at the photograph which is just a picture of some skinny woman in a countrified dress with her hand shot up to her face like she shame fore cameras. But there's a movie house in the background which I ax about. Cause I am a movie freak from way back, even though it do get me in trouble sometime.

Like when me and Big Brood and Baby Jason was on our own last Easter and couldn't go to the Dorset cause we'd seen all the Three Stooges they was. And the RKO Hamilton was closed readying up for the Easter Pageant that night. And the West End, the Regun and the Sunset was too far, less we had grownups with us which we didn't. So we walk up Amsterdam Avenue to the Washington and *Gorilla, My Love* playin, they say, which suit me just fine, though the "my love" part kinda drag Big Brood some. As for Baby Jason, shoot, like Granddaddy say, he'd follow me into the fiery furnace if I say come on. So we go in and get three bags of Havmore potato chips which not only are the best potato chips but the best bags for blowin up and bustin real loud so the matron come trottin down the aisle with her chunky self, flashin that flashlight dead in your eye so you can give her some lip, and if she answer back and you already finish seein the show anyway, why then you just turn the place out. Which I love to do, no lie. With Baby Jason kickin at the seat in front, egging me on, and Big Brood mumblin bout what fiercesome things we goin do. Which means me. Like when the big boys come up on us talkin bout Lemme a nickel. It's me that hide the money. Or when the bad boys in the park take Big Brood's Spaudeen way from him. It's me that jump on they back and fight awhile. And it's me that turns out the show if the matron get too salty.

So the movie come on and right away it's this churchy music and clearly not about no gorilla. Bout Jesus. And I am ready to kill, not cause I got anything gainst Jesus. Just that when you fixed to watch a gorilla picture you don't wanna get messed around with Sunday School stuff. So I am mad. Besides, we see this raggedy old brown film *King of Kings* every year and enough's enough. Grownups figure they can treat you just anyhow. Which burns me up. There I am, my feet up and my Havmore potato chips really salty and crispy and two jawbreakers in my lap and the money safe in my shoe from the big boys, and here comes this Jesus stuff. So we all go wild. Yellin, booin, stompin and carryin on. Really to wake the man in the booth up there who musta went to sleep and put on the wrong reels. But no, cause he holler down to shut up and then he turn the sound up so we really gotta holler like crazy to even hear ourselves good. And the matron ropes off the children section and flashes her light all over the place and we yell some more and some kids slip under the rope and run up and down the aisle just to show it take more than some dusty ole velvet rope to tie us down. And

I'm flingin the kid in front of me's popcorn. And Baby Jason kickin seats. And it's really somethin. Then here come the big and bad matron, the one they let out in case of emergency. And she totin that flashlight like she gonna use it on somebody. This here the colored matron Brandy and her friends call Thunderbuns. She do not play. She do not smile. So we shut up and watch the simple ass picture.

Which is not so simple as it is stupid. Cause I realize that just about anybody in my family is better than this god they always talkin about. My daddy wouldn't stand for nobody treatin any of us that way. My mama specially. And I can just see it now, Big Brood up there on the cross talkin bout Forgive them Daddy cause they don't know what they doin. And my Mama say Get on down from there you big fool, whatcha think this is, playtime? And my Daddy yellin to Granddaddy to get him a ladder cause Big Brood actin the fool, his mother side of the family showin up. And my mama and her sister Daisy jumpin on them Romans beatin them with they pocketbooks. And Hunca Bubba tellin them folks on they knees they better get out the way and go get some help or they goin to get trampled on. And Granddaddy Vale sayin Leave the boy alone, if that's what he wants to do with his life we ain't got nothin to say about it. Then Aunt Daisy givin him a taste of that pocketbook, fussin bout what a damn fool old man Granddaddy is. Then everybody jumpin in his chest like the time Uncle Clayton went in the army and come back with only one leg and Granddaddy say somethin stupid about that's life. And by this time Big Brood off the cross and in the park playin handball or skully or somethin. And the family in the kitchen throwin dishes at each other, screamin bout if you hadn't done this I wouldn't had to do that. And me in the parlor trying to do my arithmetic yellin Shut it off.

Which is what I was yellin all by myself which make me a sittin target for Thunderbuns. But when I yell We want our money back, that gets everybody in chorus. And the movie windin up with this heavenly cloud music and the smart-ass up

there in his hole in the wall turns up the sound again to drown
us out. Then there comes Bugs Bunny which we already seen
so we know we been had. No gorilla my nuthin. And Big Brood
say Awwww sheeet, we goin to see the manager and get our
money back. And I know from this we business. So I brush the
potato chips out of my hair which is where Baby Jason like to
put em, and I march myself up the aisle to deal with the manager
who is a crook in the first place for lyin out there sayin _Gorilla,
My Love_ playin. And I never did like the man cause he oily and
pasty at the same time like the bad guy in the serial, the one
that got a hideout behind a push-button bookcase and play
"Moonlight Sonata" with gloves on. I knock on the door and
I am furious. And I am alone, too. Cause Big Brood suddenly
got to go so bad even though my mama told us bout goin in
them nasty bathrooms. And I hear him sigh like he disgusted
when he get to the door and see only a little kid there. And
now I'm really furious cause I get so tired grownups messin
over kids just cause they little and can't take em to court. What
is it, he say to me like I lost my mittens or wet on myself or
am somebody's retarded child. When in reality I am the smartest kid P.S. 186 ever had in its whole lifetime and you can
ax anybody. Even them teachers that don't like me cause I won't
sing them Southern songs or back off when they tell me my
questions are out of order. And cause my Mama come up
there in a minute when them teachers start playin the dozens
behind colored folks. She stalk in with her hat pulled down
bad and that Persian lamb coat draped back over one hip
on account of she got her fist planted there so she can talk
that talk which gets us all hypnotized, and teacher be comin
undone cause she know this could be her job and her behind
cause Mama got pull with the Board and bad by her own self
anyhow.

So I kick the door open wider and just walk right by him
and sit down and tell the man about himself and that I want my
money back and that goes for Baby Jason and Big Brood too.
And he still trying to shuffle me out the door even though I'm

sittin which shows him for the fool he is. Just like them teachers do fore they realize Mama like a stone on that spot and ain't backin up. So he ain't gettin up off the money. So I was forced to leave, takin the matches from under his ashtray, and set a fire under the candy stand, which closed the raggedy ole Washington down for a week. My Daddy had the suspect it was me cause Big Brood got a big mouth. But I explained right quick what the whole thing was about and I figured it was even-steven. Cause if you say Gorilla, My Love, you suppose to mean it. Just like when you say you goin to give me a party on my birthday, you gotta mean it. And if you say me and Baby Jason can go South pecan haulin with Granddaddy Vale, you better not be comin up with no stuff about the weather look uncertain or did you mop the bathroom or any other trickified business. I mean even gangsters in the movies say My word is my bond. So don't nobody get away with nothin far as I'm concerned. So Daddy put his belt back on. Cause that's the way I was raised. Like my Mama say in one of them situations when I won't back down, Okay Badbird, you right. Your point is well-taken. Not that Badbird my name, just what she say when she tired arguin and know I'm right. And Aunt Jo, who is the hardest head in the family and worse even than Aunt Daisy, she say, You absolutely right Miss Muffin, which also ain't my real name but the name she gave me one time when I got some medicine shot in my behind and wouldn't get up off her pillows for nothin. And even Granddaddy Vale—who got no memory to speak of, so sometime you can just plain lie to him, if you want to be like that— he say, Well if that's what I said, then that's it. But this name business was different they said. It wasn't like Hunca Bubba had gone back on his word or anything. Just that he was thinkin bout gettin married and was usin his real name now. Which ain't the way I saw it at all.

So there I am in the navigator seat. And I turn to him and just plain ole ax him. I mean I come right on out with it. No sense goin all around that barn the old folks talk about. And like my mama say, Hazel—which is my real name and what she remembers to call me when she bein serious—when you got somethin on your mind, speak up and let the chips fall where they may. And if anybody don't like it, tell em to come see your mama. And Daddy look up from the paper and say, You hear your mama good, Hazel. And tell em to come see me first. Like that. That's how I was raised.

So I turn clear round in the navigator seat and say, "Look here, Hunca Bubba or Jefferson Windsong Vale or whatever your name is, you gonna marry this girl?"

"Sure am," he say, all grins.

And I say, "Member that time you was baby-sittin me when we lived at four-o-nine and there was this big snow and Mama and Daddy got held up in the country so you had to stay for two days?"

And he say, "Sure do."

"Well. You remember how you told me I was the cutest thing that ever walked the earth?"

"Oh, you were real cute when you were little," he say, which is suppose to be funny. I am not laughin.

"Well. You remember what you said?"

And Grandaddy Vale squintin over the wheel and axin Which way, Scout. But Scout is busy and don't care if we all get lost for days.

"Watcha mean, Peaches?"

"My name is Hazel. And what I mean is you said you were going to marry *me* when I grew up. You were going to wait. That's what I mean, my dear Uncle Jefferson." And he don't say nuthin. Just look at me real strange like he never saw me before in life. Like he lost in some weird town in the middle of night and lookin for directions and there's no one to ask. Like it was me that messed up the maps and turned the road posts round. "Well, you said it, didn't you?" And Baby Jason lookin back and forth like we playin ping-pong. Only I ain't playin. I'm hurtin and I can hear that I am screamin. And Grandaddy Vale mumblin how we never gonna get to where we goin if I don't turn around and take my navigator job serious.

"Well, for cryin out loud, Hazel, you just a little girl. And I was just teasin."

" 'And I was just teasin,' " I say back just how he said it so he can hear what a terrible thing it is. Then I don't say nuthin. And he don't say nuthin. And Baby Jason don't say nuthin nohow. Then Granddaddy Vale speak up. "Look here, Precious, it was Hunca Bubba what told you them things. This here, Jefferson Winston Vale." And Hunca Bubba say, "That's right. That was somebody else. I'm a new somebody."

"You a lyin dawg," I say, when I meant to say treacherous dog, but just couldn't get hold of the word. It slipped away from me. And I'm crying and crumplin down in the seat and just don't care. And Granddaddy say to hush and steps on the gas. And I'm losin my bearins and don't even know where to look on the map cause I can't see for cryin. And Baby Jason cryin too. Cause he is my blood brother and understands that we must stick together or be forever lost, what with grownups playin change-up and turnin you round every which way so bad. And don't even say they sorry.

COMMENTARY ON
TONI CADE BAMBARA
Gorilla, My Love

Toni Cade Bambara was born in New York City in 1939. She added Bambara to her original name when she discovered that name as a signature on a sketchbook in her grandmother's trunk. While still a student at Queen's College, majoring in Theater Arts and English, Bambara began writing fiction, publishing her first story, "Sweet Town," in *Vendome* magazine in 1959. After receiving a Master's degree, she taught at City College of New York from 1965 to 1969 and in black studies programs at Rutgers and Duke universities and has been writer-in-residence at Spelman College in Atlanta. Her anthology, *The Black Woman* (1970), was the first of its kind, a collection of essays, stories and poems dealing with issues of black feminism. She has published two collections of her own short stories, *Gorilla, My Love* (1972) and *The Sea Birds Are Still Alive* (1977), and a novel, *The Salt Eaters* (1980).

The main characters of Bambara's stories in *Gorilla, My Love* are young black girls from working-class urban areas (generally New York City). They speak a hip, contemporary black English, have a facility with words and are intelligent, honest observers of their worlds. Despite their tough, self-confident exteriors, which reflect the comfort they feel in their communities, they are also extremely vulnerable in the world of adults. The title story, which is included in this collection, is narrated by Hazel (full name: Hazel Elizabeth Deborah Parker, a.k.a. Peaches) who is coming to terms with growing up and with the disillusionment and loss which are part of that process: "I ain't playin. I'm hurtin and I can hear that I am screamin" she says of her confrontation with her uncle, when he is unable to explain why he has reneged on his promise to marry her when she grows up. She is truly hurt when her grandfather and her uncle try to justify his behavior by pretending that his name change accounts for his change of heart. The real betrayal in the story is not the uncle's failure to keep his word to marry her but his emotional duplicity and his failure to respond to her feelings of rejection and shame.

There is a long digression in this story, nearly five pages of subplot in which Hazel and her brother go to the movies and discover another form of adult betrayal. The marquee advertises an exciting feature film, *Gorilla, My Love*, but the manager shows instead an insipid and sentimental version of the life of Christ. Because this is a children's feature, the adults think the children have no right to retaliate for the false advertisement: "Grownups figure they can treat you just anyhow," Hazel laments. Within this digression, Bambara manages to tell us a great deal about Hazel, her family and her community. We see that her toughness of spirit is a family trait passed down to her and encouraged by

her parents, her aunts and her grandfather. The significance of
names and name-changing is another theme in Hazel's life. She
is called by several different names: Scout, Badbird, Miss Muffin,
Hazel and Peaches; the only name she rejects is "Peaches" because she recognizes that her uncle's dishonesty has made that
name meaningless. Her other names have integrity because they
reflect accurately and truthfully something essential about her.

Hazel's infatuation with her uncle is an experience typical of
young children, but in this story Hazel's relationship with the
man she affectionately names "Hunca Bubba" is a sign of intense
familial ties, Hazel is so deeply involved with her family that
family values prevail over the other lessons the culture seeks to
impose. When the school tries to squelch her spirit, her mother
intervenes, teaching Hazel how to resist its attempts to dominate
her. Her rejection of the simplistic, religious messages of the
film is also conditioned by the family's philosophy of resistance.
The power of these family relationships is what allows Hazel
to trust her own interpretation of reality. Even the disillusionment with her uncle is a part of the complex interactions between
Hazel and her extended family. That she has "fallen in love"
with her Hunca Bubba is a sign of how significant he has been
in her life.

Grandparents

My Grandfather Walks in the Woods

MARILYN WANIEK

Somewhere
in the light above the womb,
black trees
and white trees
populate a world.

It is a March landscape,
the only birds around are small
and black.
What do they eat,
sitting in the birches
like warnings?

The branches of the trees
are black and white.
Their race is winter.
They thrive in cold.

There is my grandfather
walking among the trees.
He does not notice
his fingers are cold.
His black felt hat
covers his eyes.

He is knocking on each tree,
listening to their voices
as they answer slowly
deep, deep from their roots.
I am John, he says,
are you my father?

They answer
with voices like wind
blowing away from him.

The Weakness

TOI DERRICOTTE

That time my grandmother dragged me
through the perfume aisles at Saks, she held me up
by my arm, hissing, "Stand up,"
through clenched teeth, her eyes
bright as a dog's
cornered in the light.
She said it over and over,
as if she were Jesus,
and I were dead. She had been
solid as a tree,
a fur around her neck, a
light-skinned matron whose car was parked, who walked on swirling
marble and passed through
brass openings—in 1945.
There was not even a black
elevator operator at Saks.
The saleswoman had brought velvet
leggings to lace me in, and cooed,

as if in the service of all grandmothers.
My grandmother had smiled, but not
hungrily, not like my mother
who hated them, but wanted to please,
and they had smiled back, as if
they were wearing wooden collars.
When my legs gave out, my grandmother
dragged me up and held me like God
holds saints by the
roots of the hair. I begged her
to believe I couldn't help it. Stumbling,
her face white
with sweat, she pushed me through the crowd, rushing
away from those eyes
that saw through
her clothes, under
her skin, all the way down
to the transparent
genes confessing.

To Da-duh,
In Memoriam

PAULE MARSHALL

". . . Oh Nana! all of you is not involved in this evil business
Death,
Nor all of us in life."
—From "At My Grandmother's Grave," by Lebert Bethune

I did not see her at first I remember. For not only was it
dark inside the crowded disembarkation shed in spite of the

daylight flooding in from outside, but standing there waiting for her with my mother and sister I was still somewhat blinded from the sheen of tropical sunlight on the water of the bay which we had just crossed in the landing boat, leaving behind us the ship that had brought us from New York lying in the offing. Besides, being only nine years of age at the time and knowing nothing of islands I was busy attending to the alien sights and sounds of Barbados, the unfamiliar smells.

I did not see her, but I was alerted to her approach by my mother's hand which suddenly tightened around mine, and looking up I traced her gaze through the gloom in the shed until I finally made out the small, purposeful, painfully erect figure of the old woman headed our way.

Her face was drowned in the shadow of an ugly rolled-brim brown felt hat, but the details of her slight body and of the struggle taking place within it were clear enough—an intense, unrelenting struggle between her back which was beginning to bend ever so slightly under the weight of her eighty-odd years and the rest of her which sought to deny those years and hold that back straight, keep it in line. Moving swiftly toward us (so swiftly it seemed she did not intend stopping when she reached us but would sweep past us out the doorway which opened onto the sea and like Christ walk upon the water!), she was caught between the sunlight at her end of the building and the darkness inside—and for a moment she appeared to contain them both: the light in the long severe old-fashioned white dress she wore which brought the sense of a past that was still alive into our bustling present and in the snatch of white at her eye; the darkness in her black high-top shoes and in her face which was visible now that she was closer.

It was as stark and fleshless as a death mask, that face. The maggots might have already done their work, leaving only the framework of bone beneath the ruined skin and deep wells at the temple and jaw. But her eyes were alive, unnervingly so for one so old, with a sharp light that flicked out of the dim clouded depths like a lizard's tongue to snap up all in her view. Those eyes betrayed a child's curiosity about the world, and I wondered vaguely seeing them, and seeing the way the bodice of her ancient dress had collapsed in on her flat chest (what had happened to her breasts?), whether she might not be some kind of child at the same time that she was a woman, with fourteen children, my mother included, to prove it. Perhaps she was both, both child and woman, darkness and light, past and present, life and death—all the opposites contained and reconciled in her.

"My Da-duh," my mother said formally and stepped forward. The name sounded like thunder fading softly in the distance.

"Child," Da-duh said, and her tone, her quick scrutiny of my mother, the brief embrace in which they appeared to shy from each other rather than touch, wiped out the fifteen years my mother had been away and restored the old relationship. My mother, who was such a formidable figure in my eyes, had suddenly with a word been reduced to my status.

"Yes, God is good," Da-duh said with a nod that was like a tic. "He has spared me to see my child again."

We were led forward then, apologetically because not only did Da-duh prefer boys but she also liked her grandchildren to be "white," that is, fair-skinned; and we had, I was to discover, a number of cousins, the outside children of white estate managers and the like, who qualified. We, though, were as black as she.

My sister being the oldest was presented first. "This one takes after the father," my mother said and waited to be reproved.

Frowning, Da-duh tilted my sister's face toward the light. But her frown soon gave way to a grudging smile, for my sister with her large mild eyes and little broad winged nose, with our father's high-cheeked Barbadian cast to her face, was pretty.

"She's goin' be lucky," Da-duh said and patted her once on the cheek. "Any girl child that takes after the father does be lucky."

She turned then to me. But oddly enough she did not touch me. Instead leaning close, she peered hard at me, and then quickly drew back. I thought I saw her hand start up as though to shield her eyes. It was almost as if she saw not only me, a thin truculent child who it was said took after no one but myself, but something in me which for some reason she found disturbing, even threatening. We looked silently at each other for a long time there in the noisy shed, our gaze locked. She was the first to look away.

"But Adry," she said to my mother and her laugh was cracked, thin, apprehensive. "Where did you get this one here with this fierce look?"

"We don't know where she came out of, my Da-duh," my mother said, laughing also. Even I smiled to myself. After all I had won the encounter. Da-duh had recognized my small strength—and this was all I ever asked of the adults in my life then.

"Come, soul," Da-duh said and took my hand. "You must be one of those New York terrors you hear so much about."

She led us, me at her side and my sister and mother behind, out of the shed into the sunlight that was like a bright driving summer rain and over to a group of people clustered beside a decrepit lorry. They were our relatives, most of them from St. Andrews although Da-duh herself lived in St. Thomas, the women wearing bright print dresses, the colors vivid against their darkness, the men rusty black suits that encased them like straitjackets. Da-duh, holding fast to my hand, became my anchor as they circled round us like a nervous sea, exclaiming, touching us with their calloused hands, embracing us shyly. They laughed in awed bursts: "But look Adry got big-big children!" / "And see the nice things they wearing, wrist watch and all!" / "I tell you, Adry has done all right for sheself in New York. . . ."

Da-duh, ashamed at their wonder, embarrassed for them, admonished them the while. "But oh Christ," she said, "why you all got to get on like you never saw people from 'Away' before? You would think New York is the only place in the world to hear wunna. That's why I don't like to go anyplace with you St. Andrews people, you know. You all ain't been colonized."

We were in the back of the lorry finally, packed in among

the barrels of ham, flour, cornmeal and rice and the trunks of clothes that my mother had brought as gifts. We made our way slowly through Bridgetown's clogged streets, part of a funereal procession of cars and open-sided buses, bicycles and donkey carts. The dim little limestone shops and offices along the way marched with us, at the same mournful pace, toward the same grave ceremony—as did the people, the women balancing huge baskets on top their heads as if they were no more than hats they wore to shade them from the sun. Looking over the edge of the lorry I watched as their feet slurred the dust. I listened, and their voices, raw and loud and dissonant in the heat, seemed to be grappling with each other high overhead.

Da-duh sat on a trunk in our midst, a monarch amid her court. She still held my hand, but it was different now. I had suddenly become her anchor, for I felt her fear of the lorry with its asthmatic motor (a fear and distrust, I later learned, she held of all machines) beating like a pulse in her rough palm.

As soon as we left Bridgetown behind though, she relaxed, and while the others around us talked she gazed at the canes standing tall on either side of the winding marl road. "C'dear," she said softly to herself after a time. "The canes this side are pretty enough."

They were too much for me. I thought of them as giant weeds that had overrun the island, leaving scarcely any room for the small tottering houses of sunbleached pine we passed or the people, dark streaks as our lorry hurtled by. I suddenly feared that we were journeying, unaware that we were, toward some dangerous place where the canes, grown as high and thick as a forest, would close in on us and run us through with their stiletto blades. I longed then for the familiar: for the street in Brooklyn where I lived, for my father who had refused to accompany us ("Blowing out good money on foolishness," he had said of the trip), for a game of tag with my friends under the chestnut tree outside our aging brownstone house.

"Yes, but wait till you see St. Thomas canes," Da-duh was saying to me. "They's canes father, bo," she gave a proud arrogant nod. "Tomorrow, God willing, I goin' take you out in the ground and show them to you."

True to her word Da-duh took me with her the following day out into the ground. It was a fairly large plot adjoining her weathered board and shingle house and consisting of a small orchard, a good-sized canepiece and behind the canes, where the land sloped abruptly down, a gully. She had purchased it with Panama money sent her by her eldest son, my uncle Joseph, who had died working on the canal. We entered the ground along a trail no wider than her body and as devious and complex as her reasons for showing me her land. Da-duh strode briskly ahead, her slight form filled out this morning by the layers of sacking petticoats she wore under her working dress to protect her against the damp. A fresh white cloth, elaborately arranged around her head, added to her height, and lent her a vain, almost roguish air.

Her pace slowed once we reached the orchard, and glancing back at me occasionally over her shoulder, she pointed out the various trees.

"This here is a breadfruit," she said. "That one yonder is a papaw. Here's a guava. This is a mango. I know you don't have anything like these in New York. Here's a sugar apple." (The fruit looked more like artichokes than apples to me.) "This one bears limes. . . ." She went on for some time, intoning the names of the trees as though they were those of her gods. Finally, turning to me, she said, "I know you don't have anything this nice where you come from." Then, as I hesitated: "I said I know you don't have anything this nice where you come from. . . ."

"No," I said and my world did seem suddenly lacking.

Da-duh nodded and passed on. The orchard ended and we were on the narrow cart road that led through the canepiece, the canes clashing like swords above my cowering head. Again she turned and her thin muscular arms spread wide, her dim gaze embracing the small field of canes, she said—and her voice almost broke under the weight of her pride, "Tell me, have you got anything like these in that place where you were born?"

"No."

"I din' think so. I bet you don't even know that these canes here and the sugar you eat is one and the same thing. That they does throw the canes into some damn machine at the factory and squeeze out all the little life in them to make sugar for you all so in New York to eat. I bet you don't know that."

"I've got two cavities and I'm not allowed to eat a lot of sugar."

But Da-duh didn't hear me. She had turned with an inexplicably angry motion and was making her way rapidly out of the canes and down the slope at the edge of the field which led to the gully below. Following her apprehensively down the incline amid a stand of banana plants whose leaves flapped like elephants ears in the wind, I found myself in the middle of a small tropical wood—a place dense and damp and gloomy and tremulous with the fitful play of light and shadow as the leaves high above moved against the sun that was almost hidden from view. It was a violent place, the tangled foliage fighting each other for a chance at the sunlight, the branches of the trees locked in what seemed an immemorial struggle, one both necessary and inevitable. But despite the violence, it was pleasant, almost peaceful in the gully, and beneath the thick undergrowth the earth smelled like spring.

This time Da-duh didn't even bother to ask her usual question, but simply turned and waited for me to speak.

"No," I said, my head bowed. "We don't have anything like this in New York."

"Ah," she cried, her triumph complete. "I din' think so. Why, I've heard that's a place where you can walk till you near drop and never see a tree."

"We've got a chestnut tree in front of our house," I said.

"Does it bear?" She waited. "I ask you, does it bear?"

"Not anymore," I muttered. "It used to, but not anymore."

She gave the nod that was like a nervous twitch. "You see," she said. "Nothing can bear there." Then, secure behind her scorn, she added, "But tell me, what's this snow like that you hear so much about?"

Looking up, I studied her closely, sensing my chance, and then I told her, describing at length and with as much drama as I could summon not only what snow in the city was like, but what it would be like here, in her perennial summer kingdom.

". . . And you see all these trees you got here," I said. "Well, they'd be bare. No leaves, no fruit, nothing. They'd be covered in snow. You see your canes. They'd be buried under tons of snow. The snow would be higher than your head, higher than your house, and you wouldn't be able to come down into this here gully because it would be snowed under. . . ."

She searched my face for the lie, still scornful but intrigued. "What a thing, huh?" she said finally, whispering it softly to herself.

"And when it snows you couldn't dress like you are now," I said. "Oh no, you'd freeze to death. You'd have to wear a hat and gloves and galoshes and ear muffs so your ears wouldn't freeze and drop off, and a heavy coat. I've got a Shirley Temple coat with fur on the collar. I can dance. You wanna see?"

Before she could answer I began, with a dance called the Truck which was popular back then in the 1930's. My right forefinger waving, I trucked around the nearby trees and around Da-duh's awed and rigid form. After the Truck I did the Suzy-Q, my lean hips swishing, my sneakers sidling zigzag over the ground. "I can sing," I said and did so, starting with "I'm Gonna Sit Right Down and Write Myself a Letter," then without pausing, "Tea for Two," and ending with "I Found a Million Dollar Baby in a Five and Ten Cent Store."

For long moments afterwards Da-duh stared at me as if I were a creature from Mars, an emissary from some world she did not know but which intrigued her and whose power she both felt and feared. Yet something about my performance must have pleased her, because bending down she slowly lifted her long skirt and then, one by one, the layers of petticoats until she came to a drawstring purse dangling at the end of a long strip of cloth tied round her waist. Opening the purse she handed me a penny. "Here," she said half-smiling against her will. "Take this to buy yourself a sweet at the shop up the road. There's nothing to be done with you, soul."

From then on, whenever I wasn't taken to visit relatives, I accompanied Da-duh out into the ground, and alone with her amid the canes or down in the gully I told her about New York. It always began with some slighting remark on her part: "I know they don't have anything this nice where you come from," or "Tell me, I hear those foolish people in New York does do such and such. . . ." But as I answered, recreating my towering world of steel and concrete and machines for her, building the city out of words, I would feel her give way. I came to know the signs of her surrender: the total stillness that would come over her little hard dry form, the probing gaze that like a surgeon's knife sought to cut through my skull to get at the images there, to see if I were lying; above all, her fear, a fear nameless and profound, the same one I had felt beating in the palm of her hand that day in the lorry.

Over the weeks I told her about refrigerators, radios, gas stoves, elevators, trolley cars, wringer washing machines, movies, airplanes, the cyclone at Coney Island, subways, toasters, electric lights: "At night, see, all you have to do is flip this little switch on the wall and all the lights in the house go on. Just like that. Like magic. It's like turning on the sun at night."

"But tell me," she said to me once with a faint mocking smile, "do the white people have all these things too or it's only the people looking like us?"

I laughed. "What d'ya mean," I said. "The white people have even better." Then: "I beat up a white girl in my class last term."

"Beating up white people!" Her tone was incredulous.

"How you mean!" I said, using an expression of hers. "She called me a name."

For some reason Da-duh could not quite get over this and repeated in the same hushed, shocked voice, "Beating up white people now! Oh, the lord, the world's changing up so I can scarce recognize it anymore."

One morning toward the end of our stay, Da-duh led me into

a part of the gully that we had never visited before, an area darker and more thickly overgrown than the rest, almost impenetrable. There in a small clearing amid the dense bush, she stopped before an incredibly tall royal palm which rose cleanly out of the ground, and drawing the eye up with it, soared high above the trees around it into the sky. It appeared to be touching the blue dome of sky, to be flaunting its dark crown of fronds right in the blinding white face of the late morning sun.

Da-duh watched me a long time before she spoke, and then she said very quietly, "All right, now, tell me if you've got anything this tall in that place you're from."

I almost wished, seeing her face, that I could have said no. "Yes," I said. "We've got buildings hundreds of times this tall in New York. There's one called the Empire State Building that's the tallest in the world. My class visited it last year and I went all the way to the top. It's got over a hundred floors. I can't describe how tall it is. Wait a minute. What's the name of that hill I went to visit the other day, where they have the police station?"

"You mean Bissex?"

"Yes, Bissex. Well, the Empire State Building is way taller than that."

"You're lying now!" she shouted, trembling with rage. Her hand lifted to strike me.

"No, I'm not," I said. "It really is, if you don't believe me I'll send you a picture postcard of it soon as I get back home so you can see for yourself. But it's way taller than Bissex."

All the fight went out of her at that. The hand poised to strike me fell limp to her side, and as she stared at me, seeing not me but the building that was taller than the highest hill she knew, the small stubborn light in her eyes (it was the same amber as the flame in the kerosene lamp she lit at dusk) began to fail. Finally, with a vague gesture that even in the midst of her defeat still tried to dismiss me and my world, she turned and started back through the gully, walking slowly, her steps groping and uncertain, as if she were suddenly no longer sure of the way, while I followed triumphant yet strangely saddened behind.

The next morning I found her dressed for our morning walk but stretched out on the Berbice chair in the tiny drawing room where she sometimes napped during the afternoon heat, her face turned to the window beside her. She appeared thinner and suddenly indescribably old.

"My Da-duh," I said.

"Yes, nuh," she said. Her voice was listless and the face she slowly turned my way was, now that I think back on it, like a Benin mask, the features drawn and almost distorted by an ancient abstract sorrow.

"Don't you feel well?" I asked.

"Girl, I don't know."

"My Da-duh, I goin' boil you some bush tea," my aunt, Da-duh's youngest child, who lived with her, called from the shed roof kitchen.

"Who tell you I need bush tea?" she cried, her voice assuming for a moment its old authority. "You can't even rest nowadays without some malicious person looking for you to be dead. Come girl," she motioned me to a place beside her on the old-fashioned lounge chair, "give us a tune."

I sang for her until breakfast at eleven, all my brash irreverent Tin Pan Alley songs, and then just before noon we went out into the ground. But it was a short, dispirited walk. Da-duh didn't even notice that the mangoes were beginning to ripen and would have to be picked before the village boys got to them. And when she paused occasionally and looked out across the canes or up at her trees it wasn't as if she were seeing them but something else. Some huge, monolithic shape had imposed itself, it seemed, between her and the land, obstructing her vision. Returning to the house she slept the entire afternoon on the Berbice chair.

She remained like this until we left, languishing away the mornings on the chair at the window gazing out at the land as if it were already doomed; then, at noon, taking the brief stroll with me through the ground during which she seldom spoke, and afterwards returning home to sleep till almost dusk sometimes.

On the day of our departure she put on the austere, ankle-length white dress, the black shoes and brown felt hat (her town clothes she called them), but she did not go with us to town. She saw us off on the road outside her house and in the midst of my mother's tearful protracted farewell, she leaned down and whispered in my ear, "Girl, you're not to forget now to, send me the picture of that building, you hear."

By the time I mailed her the large colored picture postcard of the Empire State Building she was dead. She died during the famous '37 strike which began shortly after we left. On the day of her death England sent planes flying low over the island in a show of force—so low, according to my aunt's letter, that the downdraft from them shook the ripened mangoes from the trees in Da-duh's orchard. Frightened, everyone in the village fled into the canes. Except Da-duh. She remained in the house at the window so my aunt said, watching as the planes came swooping and screaming like monstrous birds down over the village, over her house, rattling her trees and flattening the young canes in her field. It must have seemed to her lying there that they did not intend pulling out of their dive, but like the hardback beetles which hurled themselves with suicidal force against the walls of the house at night, those menacing silver shapes would hurl themselves in an ecstasy of self-immolation onto the land, destroying it utterly.

When the planes finally left and the villagers returned they found her dead on the Berbice chair at the window.

She died and I lived, but always, to this day even, within the shadow of her death. For a brief period after I was grown I went to live alone, like one doing penance, in a loft above a noisy factory in downtown New York and there painted seas of sugarcane and huge swirling Van Gogh suns and palm trees striding like brightly-plumed Tutsi warriors across a tropical landscape, while the thunderous tread of the machines downstairs jarred the floor beneath my easel, mocking my efforts.

COMMENTARY ON
PAULE MARSHALL

To Da-duh, In Memoriam

Paule Marshall's parents emigrated from Barbados to the United States in the 1920s. A second-generation Barbadian-American, Marshall grew up in Brooklyn where she attended Brooklyn College, graduating Phi Beta Kappa in 1953. She worked for a while as a journalist for the magazine *Our World*, and began to write fiction. Her first novel, *Brown Girl, Brownstones*, was published in 1959, followed by *The Chosen Place, The Timeless People* in 1969, a book of short stories, *Soul Clap Hands and Sing*, in 1961 and a third novel, *Praisesong for the Widow*, in 1984. Marshall lives in Richmond, Virginia, where she teaches at Virginia Commonwealth University and is completing her fourth novel.

Like *Brown Girl, Brownstones* and much of Marshall's other fiction, "To Da-duh, In Memoriam" deals with West Indians who have left their homeland, fleeing from a colonial system that made them outsiders in their own country. Disenfranchised, deprived of advanced schooling, their culture considered inferior to that of the British colonizers, they came to America whenever they had an opportunity.[1] Especially in New York, the place they called "The City of the Almighty Dollar," they felt that any smart hardworking "Bajan" could "study the dollar" and "buy house." And some, like Silla, the mother in *Brown Girl, Brownstones*, did just that; but in order to attain that dream, they had to choose a passion for money and status over a passion for life, for land, for communal values, for a past in Barbados where, as one character says, "people does take a drink while the sun hot-hot and yuh wun know whether it was the sun or the rum or both that had yuh feeling so sweet."

That loss of passion and the need to recover it is the underlying theme of all of Marshall's fiction, and thus the journey home becomes a primary task for her characters. At the end of *Brown Girl*, Selina plans to return to Barbados, the birthplace of her parents, in order to understand what went wrong for her parents in America. In *The Chosen Place*, Merle Kinbona returns to the mythical West Indian island of Bournehills. Avey Johnson, in *Praisesong for the Widow*, finds herself, almost against her will, going to the Grenadian island of Carriacou where she encounters her ancestral past. Finally the nine-year-old narrator of "Da-duh" makes her first journey to the homeland to experience for the first time the uniqueness and complexity of her cultural heritage.

But the journey back is fraught with ambivalence and pain. Marshall's protagonists (except for Merle Kinbona) are very much a part of the machine age, and Marshall respects the power of those Barbadians who learned to "master" the machine just as Da-duh has a grudging admiration for the New York ways of her granddaughter. In *Brown Girl*, it is the father, with his love of colors, gaiety and the sun, who is identified with Barbados, and it is he who loses an arm to the machine in the factory. The mother, Silla, is tough and skillful enough to prevail over the machine, to turn it to profit, to "buy house" and give her daughters what she thinks is a better life. With its tall canes, grown as high and thick as a forest, Barbados is at first frightening to Da-duh's grandchild. She is used to a world of steel and concrete, and there is a need in her to be on the side of power. In her naïveté, she boasts of the Empire State Building; of Shirley Temple, whose blue eyes and blond hair defined whiteness as the ideal for little girls; of all the inventions of a technological age that are the antithesis of the fertile life-giving culture of her ancestors. Marshall's little narrator, like Marshall herself, is caught between two cultures, grieving for a lost past, trying to re-create in art what has been lost in life.

The grandmother appears often in black literature as a major figure in the rearing of grandchildren, sometimes even taking the place of a parent. In Maya Angelou's autobiography, *I Know Why the Caged Bird Sings*, there are two grandmothers, one in rural Arkansas and the other in St. Louis, both of whom take their grandchildren into their homes for extended periods of time. As Angelou notes, there were many black children who took that journey back to the South to live with grandparents when their parents met with economic hard times.[2] The grandmothers in the slave narratives of Frederick Douglass and Harriet Jacobs are a major economic and psychological support in families deprived of fathers by the system of slavery. Richard Wright lives for part of his youth with a tyrannical grandmother who enabled the family to survive the desertion of his father. Perhaps the most famous grandmother in black literature is Nanny in Zora Neale Hurston's *Their Eyes Were Watching God*, who, although she is later rejected by her granddaughter, Janie, provides both the economic and philosophical underpinnings for Janie's quest for identity. In Toni Morrison's *Sula*, Sula's grandmother, Eva, remains the head of her clan, providing bed and board for her two children, Plum and Hannah, even after they are grown. Economic necessity, then, seems to be a part of the reason for the significant role the grandmother plays in black families. But she also has another important function. Sometimes she stands between parent and child (I am thinking especially of mother and daughter) to help the grandchild define herself apart from the parent. In *Sula*, Helene's daughter Nel goes with her mother to New Orleans to the funeral of her great-grandmother Cecile; and there in the South Nel meets her grandmother Rochelle for the first time. She is immediately taken with this beautiful woman dressed in yellow, smelling like gardenias and speaking softly in Creole, who is so different from the austere and puritanical Helene. It is after this trip that Nel finds the courage to define herself in opposition to her mother and takes up a friendship with the wildly unconventional Sula.

Da-duh also grants her granddaughter a kind of power that is related to the mother's loss of power. In their first encounter with Da-duh, the granddaughter is aware that her grandmother's presence immediately alters the mother's stature—the mother is the child—and she "who was such a formidable figure in my eyes, had suddenly with a word been reduced to my status." The grandmother takes her granddaughter on as an equal, listening to the girl's stories of New York, watching her dance and sing, recognizing her as a serious and worthy rival. For the narrator of "Da-duh," the relationship with her grandmother (the most vivid representative of her lost culture) allows her to experience herself as powerful, and the power of that relationship inspires and enables her art.

1. Mary Helen Washington, "Afterword" to Paule Marshall, *Brown Girl, Brownstones* (New York: Feminist Press, 1981), p. 311.
2. Mildred A. Hill-Lubin, "The Grandmother in African and African-American Literature: A Survivor of the African Extended Family," *Ngambeka: Studies of Women in African Literature*, ed. Carole Boyce Davies and Anne Adams Graves (Trenton: African World Press, Inc., 1986), pp. 257–70.

Miss Cynthie

RUDOLPH FISHER

For the first time in her life somebody had called her "madam." She had been standing, bewildered but unafraid, while innumerable Red Caps appropriated piece after piece of the baggage arrayed on the platform. Neither her brief seventy years' journey through life nor her long two days' travel northward had dimmed the live brightness of her eyes, which, for all their bewilderment, had accurately selected her own treasures out of the row of luggage and guarded them vigilantly. "These yours, madam?"

The biggest Red Cap of all was smiling at her. He looked for all the world like Doc Crinshaw's oldest son back home. Her little brown face relaxed; she smiled back at him.

"They got to be. You all done took all the others."

He laughed aloud. Then—"Carry 'em for you?"

She contemplated his bulk. "Reckon you can manage it—puny little feller like you?"

Thereupon they were friends. Still grinning broadly, he surrounded himself with her impedimenta, the enormous brown extension-case on one shoulder, the big straw suitcase in the opposite hand, the carpetbag under one arm. She herself held fast to the umbrella. "Always like to have sump'm in my hand when I walk. Can't never tell when you'll run across a snake."

"There aren't any snakes in the city."

"There's snakes everywhere, chile."

They began the tedious hike up the interminable platform. She was small and quick. Her carriage was surprisingly erect, her gait astonishingly spry. She said:

"You liked to took my breath back yonder, boy, callin' me 'madam.' Back home everybody call me 'Miss Cynthie.' Even their chillun. Black folks, white folks too. 'Miss Cynthie.' Well when you come up with that 'madam' o' yourn, I say to myself, 'Now, I wonder who that chile's a-grinnin' at? "Madam" stands for mist'ess o' the house, and I sho' ain' mist'ess o' nothin' in this hyeh New York.'"

"Well, you see, we call everybody 'madam.'"

"Everybody?—Hm." The bright eyes twinkled. "Seem like that'd worry me some—if I was a man."

He acknowledged his slip and observed, "I see this isn't your first trip to New York."

"First trip any place, son. First time I been over fifty miles from Waxhaw. Only travelin' I've done is in my head. Ain' seen many places, but I's seen a passel o' people. Reckon places is pretty much alike after people been in 'em awhile."

"Yes, ma'am. I guess that's right."

"You ain' no reg'lar bag-toter, is you?"

"Ma'am?"

"You talk too good."

"Well, I only do this in vacation-time. I'm still in school."

"You is. What you aimin' to be?"

"I'm studying medicine."

"You is?" She beamed. "Aimin' to be a doctor, huh? Thank the Lord for that. That's what I always wanted my David to be. My grandchile hyeh in New York. He's to meet me hyeh now."

"I bet you'll have a great time."

"Mussn't bet, chile. That's sinful. I tole him 'for' he left home, I say, 'Son, you the only one o' the chillun what's got a chance to amount to sump'm. Don't th'ow it away. Be a preacher or a doctor. Work yo' way up and don' stop short. If the Lord don' see fit for you to doctor the soul, then doctor the body. If you don't get to be a reg'lar doctor, be a tooth doctor. If you jes' can't make that, be a foot doctor. And if you don't get that fur, be a undertaker. That's the least you must be. That ain' so bad. Keep you acquainted with the house of the Lord. Always mind the house o' the Lord—whatever you do, do like a church steeple: aim high and go straight.' "

"Did he get to be a doctor?"

"Don' b'lieve he did. Too late startin', I reckon. But he's done succeeded at sump'm. Mus' be at least a undertaker, 'cause he started sendin' the home folks money, and he come home las' year dressed like Judge Pettiford's boy what went off to school in Virginia. Wouldn't tell none of us 'zackly what he was doin', but he said he wouldn' never be happy till I come and see for myself. So hyeh I is." Something softened her voice. "His mammy died befo' he knowed her. But he was always sech a good chile—" The something was apprehension. "Hope he is a undertaker."

They were mounting a flight of steep stairs leading to an exit gate, about which clustered a few people still hoping to catch sight of arriving friends. Among these a tall young brown-skinned man in a light gray suit suddenly waved his panama and yelled, "Hey, Miss Cynthie!"

Miss Cynthie stopped, looked up, and waved back with a delighted umbrella. The Red Cap's eyes lifted too. His lower jaw sagged.

"Is that your grandson?"

"It sho' is," she said and distanced him for the rest of the

climb. The grandson, with an abandonment that superbly ignored onlookers, folded the little woman in an exultant, smothering embrace. As soon as she could, she pushed him off with
breathless mock impatience.

"Go 'way, you fool you. Aimin' to squeeze my soul out my
body befo' I can get a look at this place?" She shook herself into
the semblance of composure. "Well. You don't look hungry,
anyhow."

"Ho-ho! Miss Cynthie in New York! Can y' imagine this?
Come on. I'm parked on Eighth Avenue."

The Red Cap delivered the outlandish luggage into a robin's-
egg-blue open Packard with scarlet wheels, accepted the grandson's dollar and smile, and stood watching the car roar away up
Eighth Avenue.

Another Red Cap came up. "Got a break, hey, boy?"

"Dave Tappen himself—can you beat that?"

"The old lady hasn't seen the station yet—starin' at him."

"That's not the half of it, bozo. That's Dave Tappen's grandmother. And what do you s'pose she hopes?"

"What?"

"She hopes that Dave has turned out to be a successful
undertaker!"

"Undertaker? Undertaker!"

They stared at each other a gaping moment, then doubled
up with laughter.

"Look—through there—that's the Chrysler Building. Oh, hel-
lelujah! I meant to bring you up Broadway—"

"David—"

"Ma'am?"

"This hyeh wagon yourn?"

"Nobody else's. Sweet buggy, ain't it?"

"David—you ain't turned out to be one of them moonshiners,
is you?"

"Moonshiners—? Moon—Ho! No indeed, Miss Cynthie. I
got a better racket 'n that."

"Better which?"

"Game. Business. Pick-up."

"Tell me, David. What is yo' racket?"

"Can't spill it yet, Miss Cynthie. Rather show you. Tomorrow night you'll know the worst. Can you make out till tomorrow night?"

"David, you know I always wanted you to be a doctor, even if 'twasn' nothin' but a foot doctor. The very leas' I wanted you to be was a undertaker."

"Undertaker! Oh, Miss Cynthie!—with my sunny disposition?"

"Then you ain' even a undertaker?"

"Listen, Miss Cynthie. Just forget 'bout what I am for awhile. Must till tomorrow night. I want you to see for yourself. Tellin' you will spoil it. Now stop askin', you hear?—because I'm not answerin'—I'm surprisin' you. And don't expect anybody you meet to tell you. It'll mess up the whole works. Understand? Now give the big city a break. There's the elevated train going up Columbus Avenue. Ain't that hot stuff?"

Miss Cynthie looked. "Humph!" she said. "'Tain' half high as that trestle two mile from Waxhaw."

She thoroughly enjoyed the ride up Central Park West. The stagger lights, the extent of the park, the high, close, kingly buildings, remarkable because their stoves cooled them in summer as well as heated them in winter, all drew nods of mild interest. But what gave her special delight was not these: it was that David's car so effortlessly sped past the headlong drove of vehicles racing northward.

They stopped for a red light; when they started again their machine leaped forward with a triumphant eagerness that drew from her an unsuppressed "Hot you, David! That's it!"

He grinned appreciatively. "Why, you're a regular New Yorker already."

"New York nothin'! I done the same thing fifty years ago— befo' I knowed they was a New York."

"What!"

" 'Deed so. Didn' I use to tell you 'bout my young mare, Betty?

Chile, I'd hitch Betty up to yo' grandpa's buggy and pass anything on the road. Betty never knowed what another horse's dust smelt like. No 'ndeedy. Shuh, boy, this ain' nothin' new to me. Why that broke-down Fo'd yo uncle Jake's got ain' nothin'—nothin' but a sorry mess. Done got so slow I jes' won' ride in it—I declare I'd rather walk. But this hyeh thing, now, this is right nice." She settled back in complete, complacent comfort, and they sped on, swift and silent.

Suddenly she sat erect with abrupt discovery.

"David—well—bless my soul!"

"What's the matter, Miss Cynthie?"

Then he saw what had caught her attention. They were traveling up Seventh Avenue now, and something was miraculously different. Not the road; that was as broad as ever, wide, white gleaming in the sun. Not the houses; they were lofty still, lordly, disdainful, supercilious. Not the cars; they continued to race impatiently onward, innumerable, precipitate, tumultuous. Something else, something at once obvious and subtle, insistent, pervasive, compelling.

"David—this mus' be Harlem!"

"Good Lord, Miss Cynthie—!"

"Don' use the name of the Lord in vain, David."

"But I mean—gee!—you're no fun at all. You get everything before a guy can tell you."

"You got plenty to tell me, David. But don' nobody need to tell me this. Look a yonder."

Not just a change of complexion. A completely dissimilar atmosphere. Sidewalks teeming with leisurely strollers, at once strangely dark and bright. Boys in white trousers, berets, and green shirts, with slickened black heads and proud swagger. Bareheaded girls in crisp organdie dresses, purple, canary, gay scarlet. And laughter, abandoned strong Negro laughter, some falling full on the ear, some not heard at all, yet sensed—the warm life-breath of the tireless carnival to which Harlem's heart quickens in summer.

"This is it," admitted David. "Get a good eyeful. Here's 125th

Street—regular little Broadway. And here's the Alhambra, and up ahead we'll pass the Lafayette."

"What's them?"

"Theaters."

"Theaters? Theaters. Humph! Look, David—is that a colored folks church?" They were passing a fine gray-stone edifice.

"That? Oh. Sure it is. So's this one on this side."

"No! Well, ain' that fine? Splendid big church like that for colored folks."

Taking his cue from this, her first tribute to the city, he said, "You ain't seen nothing yet. Wait a minute."

They swung left through a side street and turned right on a boulevard. "What do you think o' that?" And he pointed to the quarter-million-dollar St. Mark's.

"That a colored church, too?"

" 'Tain' no white one. And they built it themselves, you know. Nobody's hand-me-down gift."

She heaved a great happy sigh. "Oh, yes, it was a gift, David. It was a gift from on high." Then, "Look a hyeh—which a one you belong to?"

"Me? Why, I don't belong to any—that is, none o' these. Mine's over in another section. Y'see, mine's Baptist. These are all Methodist. See?"

"M—m. Uh-huh. I see."

They circled a square and slipped into a quiet narrow street overlooking a park, stopping before the tallest of the apartment houses in the single commanding row.

Alighting, Miss Cynthie gave this imposing structure one sidewise, upward glance, and said, "Y'all live like bees in a hive, don't y'?—I boun' the women does all the work, too." A moment later, "So this is a elevator? Feel like I'm glory-bound sho' nuff."

Along a tiled corridor and into David's apartment. Rooms leading into rooms. Luxurious couches, easy chairs, a brown-walnut grand piano, gay-shaded floor lamps, paneled walls, deep rugs, treacherous glass-wood floors—and a smiling golden-

skinned girl in a gingham housedress, approaching with outstretched hands.

"This is Ruth, Miss Cynthie."

"Miss Cynthie!" said Ruth.

They clasped hands. "Been wantin' to see David's girl ever
since he first wrote us 'bout her."

"Come—here's your room this way. Here's the bath. Get out
of your things and get comfy. You must be worn out with the
trip."

"Worn out? Worn out? Shuh. How you gon' get worn out
on a train. Now if 'twas a horse, maybe, or Jake's no-count
Fo'd—but a train—didn' but one thing bother me on that
train."

"What?"

"When the man made them beds down, I jes' couldn' manage to undress same as home. Why, s'posin' sump'm bus' the
train open—where'd you be? Naked as a jaybird in a dewberry
time."

David took in her things and left her to get comfortable. He
returned, and Ruth, despite his reassuring embrace, whispered:

"Dave, you can't fool old folks—why don't you go ahead and
tell her about yourself? Think of the shock she's going to get—
at her age."

David shook his head. "She'll get over the shock if she's there
looking on. If we just told her, she'd never understand. We've
got to railroad her into it. Then she'll be happy."

"She's nice. But she's got the same ideas as all old folks—"

"Yea—but with her you can change 'em. Specially if everything is really all right. I know her. She's for church and all, but
she believes in good times too, if they're right. Why, when I
was a kid—" He broke off. "Listen!"

Miss Cynthie's voice came quite distinctly to them, singing
a jaunty little rhyme:

> *Oh I danced with the gal with the hole in her stockin'*
> *And her toe kep' a-kickin' and her heel kep' a-knockin'—*

Come up, Jesse, and get a drink o' gin,
'Cause you near to heaven as you'll ever get ag'in'.

"She taught me that when I wasn't knee-high to a cricket,"
David said.

Miss Cynthie still sang softly and merrily:

Then I danced with the gal with the dimple in her cheek,
And if she'd 'a' kep' a-smilin', I'd 'a' danced for a week—

"God forgive me," prayed Miss Cynthie as she discovered
David's purpose the following night. She let him and Ruth lead
her, like an early Christian martyr, into the Lafayette Theatre.
The blinding glare of the lobby produced a merciful self-anes-
thesia, and she entered the sudden dimness of the interior as
involuntarily as in a dream. . . .

Attendants outdid each other for Mr. Dave Tappen. She heard
him tell them, "Fix us up till we go on," and found herself sitting
between Ruth and David in the front row of a lower box. A
miraculous device of the devil, a motion picture that talked, was
just ending. At her feet the orchestra was assembling. The motion picture faded out amid a scattered round of applause. Lights
blazed and the orchestra burst into an ungodly rumpus.

She looked out over the seated multitude, scanning row upon
row of illumined faces, black faces, white faces, yellow, tan,
brown: bald heads, bobbed heads, kinky and straight heads; and
upon every countenance, expectancy—scowling expectancy in
this case, smiling in that, complacent here, amused there, com-
mentative elsewhere, but everywhere suspense, abeyance, antic-
ipation.

Half a dozen people were ushered down the nearer aisle to
reserved seats in the second row. Some of them caught sight of
David and Ruth and waved to them. The chairs immediately
behind them in the box were being shifted. "Hello, Tap!" Miss
Cynthie saw David turn, rise, and shake hands with two men.
One of them was large, bald and pink, emanating good cheer;

the other short, thin, sallow with thick black hair and a sour mien. Ruth also acknowledged their greeting. "This is my grand-mother," David said proudly. "Miss Cynthie, meet my managers, Lou and Lee Goldman." "Pleased to meet you," managed Miss Cynthie. "Great lad, this boy of yours," said Lou Goldman. "Great little partner he's got, too," added Lee. They also settled back expectantly.

"Here we go!"

The curtain rose to reveal a cotton field at dawn. Pickers in blue denim overalls, bandannas, and wide-brimmed straws, or in gingham aprons and sunbonnets, were singing as they worked. Their voices, from clearest soprano to richest bass, blended in low concordances, first simply humming a series of harmonies, until, gradually, came words, like figures forming in mist. As the sound grew, the mist cleared, the words came round and full, and the sun rose bringing light as if in answer to the song. The chorus swelled, the radiance grew, the two, as if emanating from a single source, fused their crescendos, till at last they achieved a joint transcendence of tonal and visual brightness.

"Swell opener," said Lee Goldman.

"Ripe," agreed Lou.

David and Ruth arose. "Stay here and enjoy the show, Miss Cynthie. You'll see us again in a minute."

"Go to it, kids," said Lou Goldman

"Yea—burn 'em up," said Lee.

Miss Cynthie hardly noted that she had been left, so absorbed was she in the spectacle. To her, the theater had always been the antithesis of church. As the one was the refuge of righ-teousness, so the other was the stronghold of transgression. But this first scene awakened memories, captured and held her at-tention by offering a blend of truth and novelty. Having thus baited her interest, the show now proceeded to play it like the trout through swift-flowing waters of wickedness. Resist as it might, her mind was caught and drawn into the impious subsequences.

The very music that had just rounded out so majestically now distorted itself into ragtime. The singers came forward and turned to dancers; boys, a crazy, swaying background, threw up their arms and kicked out their legs in a rhythmic jamboree; girls, an agile, brazen foreground, caught their skirts up to their hips and displayed their copper calves, knees, thighs, in shameless, incredible steps. Miss Cynthie turned dismayed eyes upon the audience, to discover that mob of sinners devouring it all with fond satisfaction. Then the dancers separated and with final abandon flung themselves off the stage in both directions.

Lee Goldman commented through the applause, "They work easy, them babies."

"Yea," said Lou. "Savin' the hot stuff for later."

Two black-faced cotton pickers appropriated the scene, indulging in dialogue that their hearers found uproarious.

"Ah'm tired."

"Ah'm hongry."

"Dis job jes' wears me out."

"Starves me to death."

"Ah'm so tired—you know what Ah'd like to do?"

"What?"

"Ah'd like to go to sleep and dream I was sleepin'."

"What good dat do?"

"Den I could wake up and still be 'sleep."

"Well y'know what Ah'd like to do?"

"No. What?"

"Ah'd like to swaller me a hog and a hen."

"What good dat do?"

"Den Ah'd always be full o' ham and eggs."

"Ham? Shuh. Don't you know a hog has to be smoked 'fo' he's a ham?"

"Well, if I swaller him, he'll have a smoke all around him, won' he?"

Presently Miss Cynthie was smiling like everyone else, but her smile soon fled. For the comics departed, and the dancing girls returned, this time in scant travesties on their earlier voluminous costumes—tiny sunbonnets perched jauntily on one side of their glistening bobs, bandannas reduced to scarlet neck ribbons, waists mere brassieres, skirts mere gingham sashes.

And now Miss Cynthie's whole body stiffened with a new and surpassing shock; her bright eyes first widened with unbelief, then slowly grew dull with misery. In the midst of a sudden great volley of applause her grandson had broken through that bevy of agile wantons and begun to sing.

He too was dressed as a cotton picker, but a Beau Brummel among cotton pickers; his hat bore a pleated green band, his bandanna was silk, his overalls blue satin, his shoes black patent leather. His eyes flashed, his teeth gleamed, his body swayed, his arms waved, his words came fast and clear. As he sang, his companions danced a concerted tap, uniformly wild, ecstatic. When he stopped singing, he himself began to dance, and without sacrificing crispness of execution, seemed to absorb into himself every measure of the energy which the girls, now merely standing off and swaying, had relinquished.

"Look at that boy go," said Lee Goldman.

"He ain't started yet," said Lou.

But surrounding comment, Dave's virtuosity, the eager enthusiasm of the audience, were all alike lost on Miss Cynthie. She sat with stricken eyes watching this boy whom she'd raised from a babe, taught right from wrong, brought up in the church, and endowed with her prayers, this child whom she had dreamed of seeing a preacher, a regular doctor, a tooth doctor, a foot doctor, at the very least an undertaker—sat watching him disport himself for the benefit of a sinsick, flesh-hungry mob of lost souls, not one of whom knew or cared to know the loving kindness of God; sat watching a David she'd never foreseen, turned tool of the devil, disciple of lust, unholy prince among sinners.

For a long time she sat there watching with wretched eyes, saw portrayed on the stage David's arrival in Harlem, his escape from "old friends" who tried to dupe him; saw him working as a trap drummer in a nightclub, where he fell in love with Ruth, a dancer; not the gentle Ruth Miss Cynthie knew, but a wild and shameless young savage who danced like seven devils—in only a girdle and breastplates; saw the two of them join in a song-and-dance act that eventually made them Broadway head-liners, an act presented *in toto* as the pre-finale of this show. And not any of the melodies, not any of the sketches, not all the comic philosophy of the tired-and-hungry duo, gave her figure a moment's relaxation or brightened the dull defeat in her staring eyes. She sat apart, alone in the box, the symbol, the epitome of supreme failure. Let the rest of the theater be riotous, clam-oring for more and more of Dave Tappen, "Tap," the greatest tapster of all time, idol of uptown and downtown New York. For her, they were lauding simply an exhibition of sin which centered about her David.

"This'll run a year on Broadway," said Lee Goldman.

"Then we'll take it to Paris."

Encores and curtains with Ruth, and at last David came out on the stage alone. The clamor dwindled. And now he did something quite unfamiliar to even the most consistent of his followers. Softly, delicately, he began to tap a routine designed to fit a particular song. When he had established the rhythm, he began to sing the song:

> *Oh I danced with the gal with the hole in her stockin'*
> *And her toe kep' a-kickin' and her heel kep' a-knockin'—*

> *Come up, Jesse, and get a drink o' gin,*
> *'Cause you near to the heaven as you'll ever get ag'in'—*

As he danced and sang this song, frequently smiling across at Miss Cynthie, a visible change transformed her. She leaned forward incredulously, listened intently, then settled back in limp wonder. Her bewildered eyes turned on the crowd, on those serried rows of shriftless sinners. And she found in their faces now an overwhelming curious thing: a grin, a universal grin, a gleeful and sinless grin such as not the nakedest chorus in the performance had produced. In a few seconds, with her own song,

David had dwarfed into unimportance, wiped off their faces, swept out of their minds every trace of what had seemed to be sin; had reduced it all to mere trivial detail and revealed these revelers as a crowd of children, enjoying the guileless antics of another child. And Miss Cynthie whispered:

"Bless my soul! They didn' mean nothin' . . . They jes' didn' see no harm in it—"

> Then I danced with the gal with the dimple in her cheek,
> And if she'd 'a' kep' a-smilin', I'd 'a' danced for a week—

"Come up, Jesse—"

The crowd laughed, clapped their hands, whistled. Someone threw David a bright yellow flower. "From Broadway!"

He caught the flower. A hush fell. He said:

"I'm really happy tonight, folks. Y'see this flower? Means success, don't it? Well, listen. The one who is really responsible for my success is here tonight with me. Now what do you think o' that?"

The hush deepened.

"Y'know folks, I'm sump'm like Adam—I never had no mother. But I've got a grandmother. Down home everybody calls her Miss Cynthie. And everybody loves her. Take that song I just did for you. Miss Cynthie taught me that when I wasn't knee-high to a cricket. But that wasn't all she taught me. Far back as I can remember, she used to always say one thing: Son, do like a church steeple—aim high and go straight. And for doin' it"—he grinned, contemplating the flower—"I get this."

He strode across to the edge of the stage that touched Miss Cynthie's box. He held up the flower.

"So y'see, folks, this isn't mine. It's really Miss Cynthie's." He leaned over to hand it to her. Miss Cynthie's last trace of doubt was swept away. She drew a deep breath of revelation; her bewilderment vanished, her redoubtable composure returned,

her eyes lighted up; and no one but David, still holding the
flower toward her, heard her sharply whispered reprimand:

"Keep it, you fool. Where's yo' manners—givin' 'way what
somebody give you?"

David grinned:

"Take it, tyro. What you tryin' to do—crab my act?"

Thereupon, Miss Cynthie, smiling at him with bright, mean-
ingful eyes, leaned over without rising from her chair, jerked a
tiny twig off the stem of the flower, then sat decisively back,
resolutely folding her arms, with only a leaf in her hand.

"This'll do me," she said.

The finale didn't matter. People filed out of the theater. Miss
Cynthie sat awaiting her children, her foot absently patting time
to the orchestra's jazz recessional. Perhaps she was thinking,
"God moves in a mysterious way," but her lips were unques-
tionably forming the words:

> —*danced with the gal—hole in her stockin'*—
> —*toe kep' a-kickin'—heel kep' a-knockin'.*

COMMENTARY ON
RUDOLPH FISHER

Miss Cynthie

Born in 1897 in Washington, D.C., Rudolph Fisher was one of
the literary lights of the Harlem Renaissance. The son of middle-
class parents—his father was a Baptist minister—he was Phi Beta
Kappa at Brown University and a graduate of the Harvard University Medical School. Though a medical specialist doing sci-
entific research, he was also a writer and a musician. He once
toured as accompanist and arranger with Paul Robeson. While
interning at Freedman's Hospital in Washington, D.C., Fisher
was also working on his short stories, one of which won the

Spingarn prize for fiction in 1926. His biographer John Mc-Cluskey marvels at his ability to carry through work on ultra-violet rays, musical sketches and short fiction simultaneously.[1] Fisher was always trying to integrate the many facets of his cultural and personal history. As a child of the black bourgeoisie and a brilliant medical student, he found himself drawn to the lives of ordinary blacks and to the cabarets and speakeasies of Harlem, where he moved to start his medical practice. The need for that integration is the subject of most of his fiction. The theme of cultural synthesis, central to all of Fisher's stories, is most successfully carried out in his 1933 short story "Miss Cynthie." Miss Cynthie represents the traditional values, the southern communal life, the forms and expressions of folk culture, which are the source of her grandson's art. While she doesn't realize it at first, the musical revue created and performed by her grandson, Dave Tappen, seemingly so alien to her and her values, owes its aesthetic integrity, its "blend of truth and novelty" to the very folk culture that she embodies. The song she taught him as a child has the same "comic philosophy," the same ragtime spirit and blues sensibility as the Broadway show her grandson has created. In this story, Fisher is obviously working out one of the major issues of Harlem Renaissance writers: how to reconcile formal art with the expressive forms of the African-American folk; in critic John McCluskey's words, how to stretch literary forms to achieve a "truer synthesis with black culture."

I think of Miss Cynthie and the revelation that allows her to accept her grandson's art as Fisher's challenge to critics like W. E. B. DuBois who wanted more portraits of "better-class Negroes." In spite of the constraints of her religious beliefs Miss Cynthie recognizes immediately the distinctiveness and vibrancy of Harlem that Harlem Renaissance writers were trying to claim for their art. Her symbolic function in this story as an authenticator of black art, approving and validating her grandson's appropriation of the folk culture, partially accounts for her idealized portrayal. She remains throughout the story the archetypal black grandmother figure, full of folk wisdom, erect, spry, intellectually vigorous, sufficiently indulgent of her grandson to set aside her own ways in order to support him. The grandmother in Paule Marshall's story, "To Da-duh, In Memoriam," serves the same symbolic function as Miss Cynthie; however, the complex ambivalent portrait of Da-duh in Marshall's story calls into question the more sentimentalized Miss Cynthie and the neat orderly resolution of Fisher's story, which obscures more troublesome issues underlying the appropriation of folk material. After her visit with Da-duh, the granddaughter, like Dave Tappen, tries to recapture black folk life in her art, but her efforts to paint are thwarted by the jarring noises from the factory below, suggesting that reconciliation with a distant cultural past is not so easily achieved.

1. John McCluskey, Jr., ed., *The City of Refuge: The Collected Stories of Rudolph Fisher* (Columbia: University of Missouri Press, 1987), p. xv.

Mary Helen Washington is originally from Cleveland, Ohio. A member of the faculty of English at the University of Massachusetts–Boston, she is currently a visiting professor at the University of Maryland at College Park. She has received research fellowships from Harvard University and Wellesley College. She is also the author of *Invented Lives: Narratives of Black Women 1860–1960* (Anchor Books, 1987) and the editor of *Black-Eyed Susans/Midnight Birds* (Anchor Books, 1990).